PROCEEDINGS

OF THE

SOCIETY OF ANTIQUARIES
OF LONDON.

28th NOVEMBER, 1901, TO 18th JUNE, 1903.

SECOND SERIES, VOL. XIX.

LONDON:

PRINTED BY J. B. NICHOLS AND SONS, FOR

THE SOCIETY OF ANTIQUARIES,

BURLINGTON HOUSE.

LIST OF ILLUSTRATIONS.

* The Society is indebted to Mr. C. E. Keyser, M.A., F S.A , for the loan of
these illustrations.

iv

* The Society is indebted to Sir John Evans, K.C.B., V.P., for part of the
cost of this illustration.

† The Society is indebted to Messrs. Archibald Constable & Co. for the loan
of this illustration.

PROCEEDINGS

OF THE

SOCIETY OF ANTIQUARIES

OF LONDON.

SESSION 1901—1902.

Thursday, 28th November, 1901.

Viscount DILLON, President, in the Chair.

The following gifts were announced, and thanks for the same ordered to be returned to the donors:

From the Earl of Crawford, K T , F.S A. —Bibliotheca Lindesiana First revision hand-list of Proclamations. Vol III —Victoria, 1837-1901 Fol Aberdeen, 1901.

From the Author —Five East Riding Churches. By A.D.H. Leadman, F S A 8vo. Leeds, 1901.

From the Author .—The Services of the Barons of the Cinque Ports at the Coronation of the Kings and Queens of England, and the Precedency of Hastings Port. By Charles Dawson, F.S A 8vo Lewes, 1901

From the Author .

    1. Medals of the Ulster Volunteers. By Robert Day, F.S A. 8vo. Belfast, 1901.

    2. Note on a bronze spearhead found at Lough Erne. 8vo n.p. n d

From the Trustees of the British Museum :

    1. Guide to the Alfred the Great Millenary Exhibition. 8vo. 1901

    2. Guide to the Exhibition in the King's Library illustrating the history of Printing, Music-printing, and Bookbinding 8vo. 1901

From the Author .—The Signs of the Old Houses in the Strand in the Seventeenth and Eighteenth Centuries. By F. G. Hilton Price 8vo. London. n d

From the Author :—Excavations on the Site of the Romano-British Civitas at Wilderspool, years 1899-1900. By Thomas May. 8vo. Liverpool, 1901.

From the Author :—The Architecture of "Coriolanus" at the Lyceum Theatre, 1901. By R. P. Spiers. 8vo. London, 1901.

From the Author :—Mediæval Colchester—Town, Castle, and Abbey—from MSS. in the British Museum. By Rev. H. J. D. Astley. 8vo. n.p. 1901.

From the Author :—Geological Notes on the New Reservoirs in the Valley of the Lea, near Walthamstow, Essex. By T. V. Holmes. 8vo. n.p. 1901.

From Robert Steele, Esq., F.S.A. :—The oldest type-printed book in existence : a Disquisition on the Relative Antiquity of the Pfister and Mazarin Bibles : prefaced by a Brief History of the Invention of Printing. By G. W. Moon. Privately printed. 4to. London, 1901.

From W. Bruce Bannerman, Esq., F.S.A. :—Calendar of the Laing Charters, A.D. 854-1837, belonging to the University of Edinburgh. Edited by Rev. John Anderson. 8vo. Edinburgh, 1899.

From the Editor :—The Epistles of Erasmus from his earliest letters to his 51st Year arranged in order of time. Edited by F. M. Nichols, F.S.A. 8vo. London, 1901.

From the Author :—The Ornaments of the Rubric (Alcuin Club Tracts, 1). Third Edition. By J. T. Micklethwaite, F.S.A. 8vo. London, 1901.

From the Author :—Bristol Archæological Notes for 1900. By J. E. Pritchard, F.S.A. 8vo. Bristol. n.d.

From the Author :—Bath, Mercian and West Saxon. By Rev. C. S. Taylor. 8vo. Bristol. n.d.

From the Society of Arts :—Report of the Committee on Leather for Bookbinding. 8vo. London, 1901.

From the Author :—The Church Bells of Worcestershire. Part I. The Mediæval Period. By H. B. Walters, M A., F.S.A. 8vo. n.p.

From the Author :—The Stone Crosses of the County of Northampton. By C. A. Markham, F.S.A. 8vo. London, 1901.

From the Author :—Painted Wall-Cloths in Sweden. By Frances Murray. 8vo. Glasgow, 1900.

From M. Léon Morel, Hon. F.S.A. :

1. La Champagne Souterraine, text and album of plates. 8vo and oblong folio. Reims, 1898.

2. Description de la Collection Léon Morel. 8vo. Reims, 1893.

3. Description de deux sépultures importantes du cimetière Franc de Breban. 8vo. Vitry-le-François, 1892.

4. Notes sur differentes découvertes archéologiques. 8vo. Reims, 1895.

5. Rareté des bijoux d'or dans les Necropoles de la Marne. Notes sur quelques Torques décorés de figures. 8vo. Paris, 1898.

6. Discours d'ouverture prononcé à la Séance publique de l'Académie Nationale de Reims, 20 juillet, 1899. 8vo. Reims. n.d.

7. Denier Rémois attribué a Hugues de Vermandois. 8vo. Reims, 1900.

From the Board of Education, South Kensington :—

  1. Classified Catalogue of Printed Books in National Art Library on Heraldry. 8vo London, 1901.

  2. Classified List of Photographs of Works of Decorative Art in the Victoria and Albert Museum and other Collections Part III Textile Fabrics and Lace. 8vo. London, 1901.

From the Author —Some resemblances between the religions and magical ideas of modern savage peoples and those of the Prehistoric non-Celtic Races of Europe. By Rev. H. J D. Astley. 8vo. London, 1901.

From R D. Darbishire, Esq , F S.A. ·

  1. Romisches Denkmal zu Igel Folio. Lützemburg. n.d.

  2. Roemische Mosiaken aus Trier und dessen Umgegend, von Domkapi tular J. N. von Wilmowsky. Folio. Trier, 1888

  3. Die Römische Villa zu Nennig, von Domkapitular, von Wilmowsky Folio. Trier, 1868.

  4 Die Römische Villa zu Nennig und ihr Mosaik, von Domkapitular von Wilmowsky. Folio Bonn, 1865

  5 Geschichte des Trierischen Landes und Volkes, von Johann Leonardy. 8vo. Trier, 1874

  6. Geschichte der Stadt Köln von Dr. L. Ennen. 8vo. Dusseldorf, 1880.

  7. Die Bundes-Briefe der alten Eidgenossen 1291-1513, von J. J. von Ah. 8vo. Einsiedeln, 1891

  8. Die Romischen Steindenkmaler des Provinzialmuseums zu Trier, von Prof. Dr. Felix Hettner. 8vo. Trier, 1893.

  9. Essais historiques sur la ville de Valence, par Jules Ollivier. 8vo Valence, 1885

  10 Die Pfalz und die Pfalzer, von August Becker. 12mo. Leipzig, 1858.

  11. Panorama von Trier und dessen Umgebungen, von Johann Leonardy. 12mo Trier, 1868.

  12 Description de quelques églises Romanes des arrondissements de Clermont et de Riom. 12mo. Clermont-Ferrand, 1863

  13. Willkuren der Brockmanner eines freyen friesischen Volkes, von Dr. T. D. Wiarda 8vo. Berlin, 1820.

  14. Bibliothèque d'art ancien Ravenne. Étude d'archéologie byzantine, par Charles Diehl. Small 4to. Paris, 1886.

  15. Om Throndhjems Domkirke, af O Krefting 8vo. Throndhjem, 1885.

  16 Description historique de l eglise de l'ancienne abbaye royale de Saint-Riquier en Ponthieu, par A. P M. Gilbert. 8vo Amiens, 1836.

  Also six volumes of pamphlets on Roman and other antiquities at Treves, etc.

From the Corporation of the City of London —A medal struck to commemorate the raising and equipment of the City of London Imperial Volunteers, October, 1900.

A special vote of thanks was accorded to R. D. Darbishire, Esq , F S A., for his gifts to the Library.

The Rev. William Gilchrist Clark-Maxwell, M.A., was admitted Fellow.

The Right Hon. GODFREY CHARLES, BARON TREDEGAR, was proposed as a Fellow, and his election being thereupon proceeded with in accordance with the Statutes, ch. i. § 5, he was duly elected Fellow of the Society.

A list of Local Secretaries, nominated by the Council, having been laid upon the table, the following Resolution was carried unanimously:

> " That the list of Local Secretaries recommended by
> the Council and this day laid before the Society,
> be approved and adopted, and that the gentlemen
> named therein be appointed for a period of four
> years, commencing from the last anniversary,
> 23rd April, 1901; such appointments, however, to
> be subject to the Statutes, ch. xvii."

In accordance with the Statutes, ch. xii. § 3, notice was given that at the next Meeting the Society would be asked to sanction :

(i.) An expenditure of £200 on the purchase of an extensive collection of architectural and other drawings relating to Lincoln and Lincolnshire, made by the late Mr. Edward James Willson, F.S.A.

(ii.) An estimated expenditure of £223 10s. on additional bookcases in the Council Room and Inner Hall.

In accordance with the statutory notice which had been sent to all the Fellows, the Meeting was made Special at 8.45 p.m., for the purpose of determining what action, if any, should be taken by the Society with regard to the legal proceedings instituted on behalf of the Treasury against the Trustees of the British Museum to obtain possession of the Irish gold ornaments.

The SECRETARY made a concise statement with regard to the circumstances connected with the subject of the Meeting, founded upon the summary account printed by the Treasury as an official paper.

A discussion followed in which Messrs. W. A. Littledale, A. Prevost, H. L. T Lyon, W Gowland, G. H. Blakesley, G L Gomme, R. Steele, and others took part.

Finally the following Resolution, which had previously received the approval of the Council, was proposed by Mr. Gowland and seconded by the Treasurer:

> "That the Fellows of the Society of Antiquaries of London, in Special Meeting assembled, desire most earnestly to protest against the action of the Lords Commissioners of the Treasury in raising a claim on behalf of the Crown which would deprive the British Museum of valuable antiquities in the national collection under the allegation that they are treasure-trove.
>
> That this Resolution be communicated to the Lords Commissioners of the Treasury, and be humbly laid before His Majesty the King, the august Patron of the Society."

After further discussion the Resolution was by leave of the Meeting withdrawn, and it was resolved to reaffirm the following Resolution, which had been unanimously adopted at the Meeting of the Society on 21st June, 1900:

> "That the Society of Antiquaries of London, which takes a keen interest in all matters connected with the Archæology of these islands, views with marked dissatisfaction the proposal to remove from the British Museum certain gold ornaments lately acquired from Ireland.
>
> The Society is of opinion that the cause of Archæology will be best served by the retention of these interesting objects in the central Museum of the Empire, where they are accessible to a greater number of students than would be the case elsewhere; while, as remains of the art of the Ancient Britons, and having only an accidental connection with Ireland, these relics could be placed nowhere more appropriately than in the British Museum."

It was also Resolved:

> "That this Resolution be communicated to the Lords Commissioners of the Treasury, and be humbly laid before His Majesty The King, the august Patron of the Society."

The Resolution was carried with only four dissentients.

The Ordinary Meeting of the Society was then resumed.

Sir JOHN EVANS, K.C.B., V.P., read the following note on a mould for Samian bowls found at Lezoux, Puy-de-Dôme:

"I beg to exhibit a terra-cotta mould for Samian bowls which I purchased in 1898 at Clermont-Ferrand in the Auvergne, and which in all probability was found at Lezoux within the Department of the Puy-de-Dôme.

The mould has been broken and a small portion of it lost, but is otherwise well preserved. It is cup-shaped, $8\frac{1}{2}$ inches in diameter and $3\frac{7}{8}$ inches high. It stands on a moulded base 4 inches in diameter, and the upper $1\frac{1}{4}$ inch of the cup has nearly vertical sides springing from a bold angular moulding, nearly horizontal on the lower side.

A plaster bowl has been produced from the mould by the skilful hands of Mr. W. Talbot Ready, which exactly shows the character of the Samian bowls that the potter had on sale in ancient times. This bowl is 8 inches in diameter, and stands $3\frac{1}{4}$ inches high, on a moulded base 4 inches in diameter, which, however, is an addition to the bowl as moulded. Around the upper part of the bowl runs a concave moulding, below which is a frieze, with a kind of degenerate egg and arrow ornament. Below this is a beaded line in relief, making the whole frieze to occupy the depth of an inch. Below it the whole body of the bowl is ornamented in relief; the upper part of the decoration consisting of the four-fold repetition of a hunting scene. In each is a large bear running at full speed towards a retreating horseman who turns his face towards the bear, and in his right hand holds a short sword in readiness to strike. The head of the horse, which is considerably smaller than the bear, is also turned backwards. Below the bear is a small hound running in the opposite direction. In the lower part of the decoration another hunting scene is shown, but only in duplicate, and not four times over. The central figure in this case is a stag running to the left at full speed from a large long-tailed hound in pursuit, but meeting another hound that is running in the opposite direction. Among the animals are some spirally coiled objects like hanks of wool, and four curved objects like staves or branches The name of the potter appears once only in large letters in relief occupying a length of $1\frac{3}{4}$ inch. It is ƎⅠⱮƧ⅂Ɑ or PATERNI retrograde. Possibly the final five marks stand for M or

Manu. Paternus is the name of a well-known potter whose works occur both on the continent and in Britain. In the Roach Smith Collection[*] his name appears as PATERNI, PATIIR NV and PATERNI OF. In the British Museum are other examples, one with PATERNI M.[†] Reading from right to left it has been found at Headington, near Oxford [‡] ΡΑΤΕЯИ/ИΛ It has likewise occurred in a form almost identical with that now before us in London, York, and Kirkby Thore, Westmoreland.[§] Examples from Geneva, Toulouse, and other places in South-east Gaul [||] have also been described.

A specimen in the Museum at Annecy is described as having hunting scenes upon it, and I in consequence wrote to the Curator, M. Marc Le Roux, to inquire what is its character. He informs me that it is a large red cup with the signature PATERNVS reversed and with a bear-hunt above and a stag-hunt below. He does not enter into details, as from my description he seems satisfied that the bowl proceeded from the mould now exhibited In the *Revue Archéologique*[¶] are described two pieces of pottery from Hermes, near Beauvais, in the collection of the Abbé G Hamard One of them bears the name of Paternus in relief and reversed, twice over. The other is less perfect From sketches that the Abbé has been so good as to send me, there seems no room to doubt that these fragments were formed in the mould now exhibited.

In the Pitt-Rivers Museum at Oxford are some pseudo-Samian bowls labelled as having been found at Lezoux, but they are not works of Paternus. The labels speak of Lezoux as the ancient Liusannum, but on what authority this name is given, I am unable to ascertain.

Inasmuch as an example of the pottery of Paternus was found, as already mentioned, at Headington, near Oxford, his mould will I think find a proper resting-place in the Ashmolean Museum."

Sir JOHN EVANS, K.C.B, V.P, also read the following account of the opening of a barrow near Hoddesdon, Herts.

"I have to report on the opening of another barrow in Hertfordshire, about 4 miles south and by west of that at Easneye, on which I reported in the year 1899 [**]

[*] *Catal. Lond. Ant.*, p 45, *Roman London*, p 105
[†] Cf. *Corp Insc. Lat*, vol. vii. 1336, 799 *et seqq*
[‡] *Arch. Assoc Jour*, vi (1851), p 66.
[§] *C.I.L.*, vol vii. 1337, 56.
[||] *C.I L*, vol. xii 5686, 677.
[¶] Sept, Oct, 1901, 3rd S., xxxix. p. 254.
[**] *Proc Soc. Ant*, xviii 8

It lies on the property of Horace J. Smith-Bosanquet, Esquire, of Broxbornebury, who undertook the exploration, and who kindly invited me to come and stay with him so as to superintend the work. The barrow is situated in a small wood or plantation adjoining Broxbornebury Park and immediately opposite the farm buildings of Hoddesdon Bury, from which it is separated by a lane running east and west, known as Cock Lane. The Roman road, the Ermine Street, running nearly north and south, is distant a little more than half a mile to the west.

The barrow itself is about 70 feet in diameter, and is surrounded by a ditch, the level of which is about 6 feet below that of the neighbouring land. The height of the central part of the tumulus is about 9 feet above that of the ditch which surrounds it. At the northern side the mound seems at some time to have had soil removed from it, and the same appears to have been the case with the outer side of the ditch. As a consequence there was some difficulty in ascertaining what was the exact centre of the mound. Not improbably the removal of the soil was connected with the formation of the road already mentioned as Cock Lane. A considerable number of trees grew upon the mound, but none of great age, and what seemed to be the centre was fairly free.

The examination of the tumulus was conducted in the following manner. A trench with vertical sides was carried in from south to north, its bottom being approximately on a level with the bottom of the surrounding ditch, and its width about 5 feet. It was soon evident that the lower part of the trench was carried through virgin soil to a depth of about 3 feet, but this was deliberately carried on with the view that if there were any grave or original excavation in the ground it should be exposed in the trench. Nothing of the kind was, however, laid bare. This virgin soil was a fairly heavy grey clay of glacial origin, having in it a considerable number of blocks of flint and some quartz and quartzite pebbles. In the upper part of the clay and near the centre of the mound a flat block of black lava from 7 to $8\frac{1}{2}$ inches in length, from $3\frac{1}{2}$ to $4\frac{1}{2}$ inches in breadth, and from 1 to $1\frac{1}{4}$ inch in thickness, was found. At first sight this had the appearance of being part of a quern formed of Andernach lava, but in order to settle the question of its date and origin a part of it was submitted to Mr. F. W. Rudler, of the Museum of Practical Geology, who reports upon it as follows: ' It seemed to me on merely examining your Hoddesdon specimen with the naked eye that you were correct in identifying it with the

mill-stone lava of Niedermendig, near Andernach. But to
fortify my opinion I submitted the rock to Mr. Teall, who has
had a microscopic section cut, and also a section cut from a
piece of the Rhenish mill-stone lava in our Museum. He tells
me that his examination shows that they are practically
identical. Moreover, with his wide knowledge of British
petrography, he does not know any similar rock in this
country. It seems, therefore, that you will be quite safe in
referring the Hoddesdon specimen to a Rhenish origin ; and
I suppose such a material is not likely to have been imported
in pre-Roman times.'

The importance of the discovery of this portion of a mill-
stone formed of Niedermendig lava will become apparent when
the date of the barrow has to be discussed

The trench was carried on at the low level until it had
passed the centre of the barrow, and was then continued at
the level of the original surface of the soil until it attained
the length of 40 feet. At the approximate centre of the
mound trenches about 6 feet in width were cut east and west
to a distance of about 4 feet, but without revealing anything
of the nature of a deposit.

The material of which the mound consisted is a loam more
yellow in colour and more sandy in character than the virgin
soil at the bottom of the trench. It seems, however, to have
been mainly derived from digging the ditch surrounding the
tumulus, and it is a characteristic of the glacial deposits of the
district that they vary in character within very limited
distances.

The remarkable feature of the barrow was this, that when
the trench had been cut to a distance of about 25 feet from
the margin a layer of ashes and charcoal was encountered,
extending across the whole trench   Excavation was carefully
made, but little more than charred vegetable remains were
found, though eventually the sides of the vertical trench
exposed a section of a wide saucer-like depression in the
original soil about 15 feet to 15 feet 6 inches in diameter,
with a depth of 1 foot 6 inches in the centre, on either side of
which a depth of 1 foot 10 inches had been reached, showing
that the bottom of the saucer had had a rounded elevation in
the middle rising 4 inches above its lowest parts. The whole
surface was well marked by charcoal and ashes. Some fragments which have been examined by Mr. V. H. Blackman, of
the Botanical Department of the British Museum, appear to be
undoubtedly of oak.

There was also a fragment of what seemed to be charred
bone

The general result of the examination seems to show that before the mound was thrown up a saucer-like depression was made in the surface of the ground, in which a large fire was kindled, in all probability a funeral pyre, and that subsequently, without disturbing the ashes, earth was heaped upon the spot to form a monumental mound. If it were a funeral pyre the ashes of the deceased have either been buried in some other part of the mound than that which has been examined, or have been dissolved and carried away by natural agencies or possibly have been removed for interment elsewhere.

From a section made through the ditch it appeared that it had originally a flat bottom about 6 feet in width. The method of deriving the soil for the formation of a burial-mound, or a great part of it, from sinking a ditch around it, is so simple and saves so much labour that it can hardly be regarded as indicative of any particular period.

In the Broxbornebury barrow no flint or bronze implements were found, nor indeed, with three exceptions, anything suggestive of the handiwork of man beyond the coating of ashes in the saucer-like depression.

Of these exceptions two are fragments of what is apparently Roman pottery found near the margin of the tumulus before my arrival on the spot. Both are of grey ware, one a portion of the mouth of an urn formed on the potter's wheel, and the other a fragment of the body of an urn. I am assured that they were lying about two feet within the body of the mound, and if this be true they afford good grounds for regarding the barrow as being either of Roman or post-Roman date. The absence of any deposit in the centre of the mound is against it being Roman, and in form it differs from the Roman barrows of the district, such as that at Youngs-bury,* opened in 1889.

But the third exception is conclusive. It is the fragment of a small quern or hand mill-stone, formed of the lava from Niedermendig, near Andernach, on the Rhine, a material in constant use by the Romans for their querns, and perhaps even more widely in use for this purpose than the Hertfordshire lower tertiary conglomerate or pudding-stone. This fragment cannot I think be accepted as being of earlier than Roman date, and as it lay beneath the charred lining of the saucer-shaped depression, and as the characteristics of the barrow are not such as to indicate a Roman date, we are driven to the conclusion that the barrow must be regarded as belonging to post-Roman times.

* *Archaeologia*, lii. 286.

Such being the case, we must now consider whether there is any ancient foundation for what has now grown into a kind of popular tradition, that the name of Hoddesdon, the hamlet or market-town in which this barrow is situated, derives its name from the tumulus, which was the burial-place of a certain Danish chief named Oddo.

Chauncy—the earliest to write a detailed history of Hertfordshire, for we may leave Camden, Norden, and Cox on one side so far as this question is concerned—writing in the year, 1700, speaks of 'Hodesdon' as follows * 'A fair Hamlet, shews itself upon a small hill, which gives the name to it situated about two miles distant from St. Margaret's towards the west, in the Parishes of Amwell and Brokesborne.'

Salmon, in his history of Hertfordshire, 1728, is far more diffuse †: 'It might be named from *Oddo* or *Otto*, some Danish commander, whose *Tumulus* was here. This was a Name of great Repute amongst that People, as appears from the writings of *Saxo Grammaticus*. It might be from *Woods-Down*, the rising Ground lying near the great Woods belonging to this Manor, as *Woodcot* we often find for a house near a Wood. Or from Wodens-Done, where the *Saxons* had a place of worship. For the Word will not undergo more Change this Way than it does in Wiltshire, where *Wansdish* the Border of Mercia is allowed to come from *Wodens-Ditch* These Guesses every Reader is desired to accept, reject, or improve as he finds Reason.'

These remarks of Salmon seem to be an expansion of Chauncey's 'small hill,' and the first of his etymological vagaries is evidently baseless and not founded upon any local tradition, or he would not have sought for Oddo in *Saxo Grammaticus* instead of in the *Saxon Chronicle*. Nevertheless his speculation as to the name of the place being derived from that of the barrow, and as to this latter being derived from the name of a Danish chief has taken root and almost become a popular tradition. In Lewis's *Topographical Dictionary* (1835), we find under Hoddesdon · 'The name of this place is supposed to have been derived from its having been the residence of Hodo or Oddo, a Danish chief, or from a tumulus or barrow raised here to his memory.'

Apart from all these speculations we must bear in mind that some few years before the Lady of Mercia, Aethelflaed, and King Edward the Elder constructed the northern and southern burhs at Hertford, the whole of the district border-

* P. 286.
† P 21

ing on the Lea was in the power of the Danes, who probably used that river as their highway. The Lea at Hoddesdon is but little over a mile distant from the barrow, and assuming that the fragments of Roman pottery and the Andernach millstone prove this to be post-Roman in date, we may after all, though discarding Oddo, have here a tumulus thrown up during the Danish occupation It is at all events within the bounds of possibility, and if we give full play to our imagination, we may go so far as to assume that the barrow was the site of the cremation of some Danish chief, and not his burial place, his ashes having been collected and carried away by his adherents for honourable interment in his native land"

Thanks were ordered to be returned for these communications

———

Thursday, 5th December, 1901.

Viscount DILLON, President, in the Chair.

The following gifts were announced, and thanks for the same ordered to be returned to the donors :

From the Author ·—English Coronation Records, by Leopold G. Wickham Legg, B A. 8vo. London, 1901

From the Library Committee of the Carlton Club —Catalogue of the Library of the Carlton Club. 8vo London, 1901

From the Right Hon the Earl of Crawford, K T , F.S A .—Bibliotheca· Lindesiana. First revision hand-list of proclamations Supplement. (Privately printed) 8vo 1901.

From the Author.—On some pardons or indulgences preserved in Yorkshire, 1412-1527 By Rev. Chr. Wordsworth 8vo n p, n.d.

From W. Bruce Bannerman, Esq , F S A. —Mayle-Jempson-Brooker Manuscript entries in a Black-letter Bible, 1502 Single sheet, 8vo. n p, n.d.

From the Author :—Some local reforms of the Divine Service attempted on the Continent in the 16th century By J Wickham Legg, F.S.A 4to. London, 1901.

From the Author —Address to the Annual Meeting of the Egypt Exploration Fund, November, 1901. By Sir John Evans, K C.B , V.P S.A. 8vo. London, 1901.

From the Author —The ancient model of boat and warrior crew from Roos Carrs, near Withernsea By Thomas Sheppard. 8vo. n p. 1901

From F. C Penrose, Esq., F,R.S., F S A :—An attempt to ascertain the date
of the Original Construction of Stonehenge from its Orientation. By Sir
Norman Lockyer, K C.B , F.R.S., and F C. Penrose, F.R.S   8vo. London,
1901

From the Author :—The Sacred Beetle , A Popular Treatise on Egyptian
Scarabs in Art and History. By John Ward, F.S A. 8vo. London, 1902.

From Charles H. Read, Esq , Secretary —Two Lantern Slides of a Russian
Ikon of the Virgin of Kazan

Alfred Cooper Fryer, Esq. Ph.D , M.A., was admitted
Fellow.

In accordance with the Statutes, chap. xii. § 2, a proposal
on the part of the Council to expend :

> (a) A sum of £200 on the purchase of a collection
> of architectural and other drawings relating to
> Lincoln and Lincolnshire, made by the late Mr.
> Edward James Willson, F S.A.; and

> (b) An estimated sum of £223 10s. on additional book-
> cases in the Council Room and Inner Hall

was laid before the Society and approved.

The Rev. WILLIAM GREENWELL, D.C.L., F R S., F.S A ,
communicated a Paper on some rare forms of Bronze Weapons
and Implements, which will be printed in *Archaeologia*

C. H. READ, Esq., Secretary, read the following notes on

> (a) A hoard of bronze implements found at Guils-
> field, Montgomeryshire, exhibited by the Right
> Hon. the Earl of Powis;

> (b) A hoard of like implements from Bromley-by-
> Bow ; and

> (c) A hoard of bronze implements found at Broadward,
> Herefordshire.

" The bronze hoard exhibited by Lord Powis is only part
of the objects discovered, the rest being in the Museums at
Shrewsbury and Ludlow. I find that portions of them have
been exhibited before the Society on previous occasions , first,
in the year 1863; and, later, at the Bronze Age Exhibition,
which was one of the last acts of the Society before leaving
Somerset House. They are published in *Proceedings* *

The sword chape shown in the figure is of an unusual form,
hitherto unpublished The transverse section is of a narrow
lozenge or fusil shape. The ornamentation consists of three

* 2nd Series, 11. 249, and v. 422.

groups of vertical lines on back and front, and on the right-hand side of the middle group on each face is a hole, such as is commonly found in such chapes. It doubtless served to receive the rivet which made fast the wooden sheath to the chape. The upper corners of the chape are slightly curved inwards.

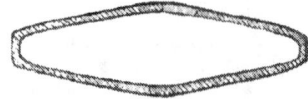

BRONZE SWORD CHAPE FOUND AT GUILSFIELD, MONTGOMERYSHIRE. (¼).

The hoard that I beg to exhibit from Bromley-by-Bow, has but few unusual features, but I consider that it is desirable to bring all such hoards to the notice of the Society in order that they may be recorded.

These objects were found in September last, 4 feet 6 inches deep, between Devon's Road and Brickfield Road. They consist of :

> Seven socketed celts of the plainer sort, ranging from 4½ to 3 inches long, some with a single or double band round the neck ;
>
> Ten fragments of similar celts, two of them, however, being of much larger dimensions, the cutting edge of one being 2⅕ inches in width. One of these fragments, which has a peculiar colour, upon being filed shows an unusually white metal, and one may assume that it has been found defective owing to an excess of tin ;

A spear-head 4¾ inches long, with the point broken.

This may be compared with one in the British Museum from Nettleham, Lincolnshire, figured in Evans, No. 382;

Part of a sword, just below the grip, 3 inches long. A plain example of the ordinary leaf shape;

Handle and part of the blade of a socketed dagger or knife, with two rivet holes through the socket, present length 2¾ inches It resembles one from Reach Fen, Cambridge, Evans, No. 241;

An oblong knife, formed of a stout blade of bronze with an edge all round, and a hole through the middle, length 2⅘ inches. This is the only unusual specimen in the hoard, and is unlike any known to me, although it may be thought to resemble one in the British Museum from Cottle, Berks, Evans, No. 262. I would suggest that this tool has been used by inserting a loop through the hole so that the blade could revolve freely, and that any of the four edges could be used as desired.

In addition to the above-mentioned specimens there were, as usual, fragments of copper cakes, which I do not think present any unusual features.

The third hoard that I have the honour to exhibit was found as long ago as 1867, but I am not aware that it has been shown before the Society. For many years past a portion of this hoard has been in the British Museum, and a good account of it was published by the Rev. E. L. Barnwell in *Archæologia Cambrensis,** with figures of some of the specimens now before the Meeting. The peculiar character of the spearheads has been fully discussed by Mr. Barnwell, and also by Sir John Evans, and others. But there is a point in connection with them that has not been cleared up, and that is in what way they became covered with such a thick oxide as in some cases to make their shapes very uncertain. From the fact that most, if not all, of the spears had the remains of the wooden shafts still in the sockets, it seems unlikely that these objects were part of a founder's hoard. More probably they were perhaps buried together, and at first sight it seems likely that they have been subjected to fire either accidentally, or with some purpose.

Mr. Gowland has been good enough to examine the material in the sockets of the spears, and confirms the statement that

* 4th Series, iii. 388.

it is carbonized wood, while other specimens still retain the
cores used in casting. This latter fact would seem to be
in favour of the founder's hoard. He has also specially
examined the contents of the curious implement combining a
loop and a tube (Evans, fig. 495), the use of which has always
been an enigma. He finds that part of the contents of the
straight tube is a fragment of carbonized wood of which the
grain runs parallel to the tube, from which it might be inferred that a rod ran through the tube. I think this has
been found to be the case with other examples"

H. SWAINSON COWPER, Esq , F S.A., exhibited three bronze
figures recently acquired by him on the coast of Asia Minor,
on which he has communicated the following notes:

"The most interesting, archæologically, is a very archaic
female statuette from Samos, 4½ inches high, wearing a
remarkable wig-like headdress, and with both arms raised.
The costume is a long robe, and the body almost without any
modelling to indicate the contours of the human form. The
figure stands bolt upright, with the feet side by side There
are bronze figures, both from the Islands and Etruria, somewhat similar, but more ornate, and no doubt later, but the
little Samos figure seems to stand very near in type to the
well-known statue found in Delos, but dedicated to Artemis
by one Nicandra of Naxos This statue is generally quoted
as the most archaic example of Greek statuary. The statue
now in the Louvre from the Haræum at Samos is a little
more advanced, but like Nicandra's figure, seems, from the
post- or tree-like shape of the body, to have been designed on
the model of an early cult effigy. The Samos figure may be
of a date betwixt the two, possibly about 560 B C This is
the more interesting as this date is, as nearly as possible, that
of the Samian sculptors, Rhœcus, Theodorus, and Telekles,
the last two of whom studied art in Egypt (probably under
Amasis) and according to the tradition invented bronze
casting for statuary. Probably the truth is that by some
masterpiece of the art they gave it a new stimulus. But it is
interesting to find this little bronze from Samos seemingly
just of their period. The wig-like headdress shows probably
Egyptian influence
The figure was probably votive, like the larger stone
figures in similar attitudes.
With this figure was bought a fine bronze sword or spear-
head (for the use of the type is not quite certain) which was
said to have been found with it. Canon Greenwell, to whom

I sent a drawing, writes me that he has never seen anything exactly like it, and is of opinion that it is an early form. I hope to exhibit this at a later date.

The prettiest of the three bronzes is a figure of Artemis the huntress, 5⅞ inches high This is from Ephesus. It is the true huntress dashing forwards, with short flying chiton, girdle, knotted hair, and sandals. The left hand has held the bow, and the right possibly a torch or a dead gazelle. This little figure is exceedingly graceful, and the treatment and modelling good. Probably it is of Hellenistic time.

The third figure is a curiously grotesque trumpeter said to be from Mylasa in Caria It is 2¹¹⁄₁₆ inches high and has a huge and disproportionate head, with a strange cap with a peak falling backwards. The trumpet has a wide or bell end, and it seems possible that the strongly-marked moustache and collar on the neck (apparently the only costume) are really a barbarous translation of the cheek band of a Greek flute-player. This is a mere suggestion, since nothing like the figure seems known, and what the art is and what is the period, are *sub judice*."

Thanks were ordered to be returned for these communications and exhibitions

------

Thursday, 12th December, 1901.

J. T. MICKLETHWAITE, Esq., Vice-President, in the Chair.

The following gifts were announced, and thanks for the same ordered to be returned to the donors:

From the New Spalding Club —The Family of Burnett of Leys, with collateral branches. From the MSS of the late George Burnett, edited by Colonel James Allardyce 4to Aberdeen, 1901.

From J. P. Rylands, Esq , F S.A. :—A Memoir of Thomas Glazebrook Rylands of Highfields, Thelwall, Cheshire Compiled by R. D. Radcliffe Privately printed 8vo. Exeter, 1901

From E. W. Brabrook, Esq., C B., F S.A.:

    1 The First Fifty Years of the Cocked Hat Club, 1852-1901. Privately printed. 12mo. London, 1901

    2 Provident Societies and Industrial Welfare. By E W. Brabrook, C B 8vo. London, 1898

Also two Rubbings of Matrices of Monumental Brasses from Hawton, Notts, from T. M Blagg, Esq

Notice was given of a Ballot for the election of Fellows on Thursday, 9th January, 1902, and a list of candidates to be balloted for was read.

Colonel J. G. WILLIAMS, by permission of the Mayor and Corporation, exhibited the State swords of the City of Lincoln, on which he also read the following paper :

"Of the three state swords which the city of Lincoln possesses, the chief interest centres in that which is known as the King Richard the Second Sword, of which tradition says that it was presented to the city in 1386 by that king, together with the privilege of having it carried before the mayor and his successors.

The right to have a sword carried before the chief officer of a municipality exists either by prescription or by royal grant confirmed by charter or letters patent. The right to this privilege in the case of the city of Lincoln, as also in that of the city of London, is prescriptive, no reference thereto being contained in any of our earlier charters or in the patent rolls.

Not only are our charters silent with reference to this sword, but the corporation possesses no other documentary evidence of the gift, as our earlier records which might have contained some reference to it have unfortunately been destroyed.

In our existing records there are references to one sword as 'the best' and 'the great' sword, and it is believed that they refer to this of King Richard, but his name is never associated in writing with it.

There are, however, fortunately, ancient documents still in existence, though not in the possession of the Corporation, which support the tradition of the gift of this sword by Richard II. They consist of two lists of mayors, bailiffs, and sheriffs of the city, of which one is in the registry of the Bishop of Lincoln, and the other in the possession of the Dean and Chapter. That in the Bishop's Registry is the more important, and probably the older of these lists, and is contained in a roll which was found amongst documents relating to the episcopate of Henry of Lexington (1254-1258). The roll commences with a list of the Kings of England from the earliest times until Charles I., and is followed by the list of mayors, etc. The latter is not continuous or complete, but in three sections, the first extending from 1313 to 1357, the second from 1359 to 1564, and the third from 1587 to 1599 inclusive. The first section commences, without any introductory heading, with the following entry :

'Civitas ⎱
Lincolñ ⎰ Anno vij^{mo} Edwardi secundi Henricus Bere maior.'

Edward II. ascended the throne 8th July, 1307, so that his seventh year would be 1313-1314 The mayor of Lincoln was in those days elected on the day of the Exaltation of the Holy Cross (14th September), and entered into his office on the following Old Michaelmas day, and the date of his mayoralty has for many years past been fixed by the year of its commencement. In such case the date of Henry Bere's mayoralty would, according to the above entry, be 1313, but the list of mayois in the Chapter Muniment Room, which also commences with Henry Bere, gives his date as 1314, whilst our published lists give the name as 'Best,' with the same date.

This section of the Bishop's Roll is in different handwriting from the others, and appears to have been] written *temp.* Elizabeth. It contains the names of mayors only, and ends with the year 1356

The second section commences 34 Edward III. (1359) with the following heading: 'Ista Rotula pertinet michi Thome Towrnay Generoso qui scribi fecit. Memorandum. Hic sunt nomina maiorum Civitatis Lincolñ ac suorum ballivorum ac vicecomitum. Anno regni Regis Edwardi tercii tricesimo Quarto.'

The first entry is as follows:

xxx°iiij° Petrus Balassis Maior   Johannes Welton ⎱ ballivi.
                                    Adam Blome   ⎰

This section of the list contains occasionally, beneath the name of the mayor, a note in red ink of any important event which may have occurred in his year of office. Amongst the entries relating to the mayors who served during the reign of Richard II. we find the following:

A.°X.° Johannes Sutton Maior

Hic predictus rex Lincolñ   Johannes Notyngham ⎱
et concessit maiori Gladi-   Radulphus Scromby   ⎬ ballivi.
um portandum coram eo   Robertus Lawende   ⎰
in futurum.

The note may be rendered: 'This aforesaid King (visited) Lincoln and granted to the mayor (the privilege) of having a sword carried before him in futuie.'

The date when this section of the list was compiled is not given, the handwriting, however, changes after the entry

23 Henry VIII. (1531-2), and if, from that fact, we may infer that the first part of the section was written at that time, then we may conclude also that the tradition as to the sword was then in existence, and has been current for at least five hundred years.

The next authority is a list in the handwriting of Dean Honywood (1660-80), in the possession of the Dean and Chapter of Lincoln, containing the names of mayors, bailiffs, and sheriffs of the city. It is written on paper, and commences as follows :

Anno Regni		Anno Domini.
7 Ed. 2	Henricus Bere	1314

and ends 1 Henry VIII. (1509-10).

The entry relating to the mayoralty of John Sutton is as follows :

10 Joan Sutton Hoc anno Potestas gladium portandi concessa.	{ Joan Nottingham Radulphus Scromby Robert Lawende }	1386

The Chapter also possess another list on parchment, which, however, commences 1 Henry VI., and concludes with the name of Edward Grantham, who was mayor in 1505, 21 Henry VII. It gives no dates, and is by no means identical with Dean Honywood's list, variations being frequent, not in the spelling only (which might be expected), but in the individual names. It appears to have been written in the time of Henry VII.

There is also in the Topographical Collection in the Lincoln Stock Library, a comparatively modern manuscript list of the mayors, etc. of Lincoln, extending from 1314 to 1783, which is said to have been compiled by Mr. James Bunch, a local antiquary, who died about 1840. His list, however, is most inaccurate and unreliable. It contains the following reference to the Richard Sword, which is significant, in connection with the doubt hereinafter discussed, as to the date of the King's visit to Lincoln. The reference is attached to the mayoralty of John Norman, 1385, and is as follows:—' This year King Richard 2 came to Lincoln, and granted John Norman, the Mayor, the sword, to be carried before him and his successors.' But just below, under the entry relating to the mayoralty of John Sutton, 1386, the scribe has written ' or this,' as if in doubt as to the mayoralty in which the above event occurred.

These are the only authorities that I have met with which refer to the Richard Sword, and it will be observed that it is not stated in any of them that the sword itself was presented by the king. But the grant of a dignity was usually accompanied with the gift of its appropriate symbol. Thus the grant of an earldom was confirmed by the gift of a sword and of a cap of maintenance, and when it is remembered that the title of earl sprang from that of ealdorman, and that our civic rulers were called ealdormen before they received the title of mayor, it seems appropriate that a royal recognition of our chief civic officer should take the form of similar gifts. Lincoln possesses this civic sword and a cap of maintenance. There is no record as to the date of origin of the latter, but I claim for Lincoln that she was the first city to receive the honourable distinction of the gift of a sword, and probably also of a cap of maintenance, from the hands of a sovereign. Similar honours were conferred upon York by Richard II. in 1388, and his charter, dated 1396, which confirms the grant of the sword, refers to it as ' per nos datum.' Chester also claims to have received a sword in 1394 from the same king, Coventry in 1387, and Newcastle in 1391.

It must not be forgotten that at this period of our history Lincoln was one of the most ancient cities in England, having been a Roman colony. It possessed many special privileges: was a staple town and an important trade centre with a merchant guild, and ranked third amongst the principal towns of the kingdom. It was a walled town, and the castle of Lincoln, erected by William the Conqueror, with the Bail of Liberty attached to it, formed parcel of the royal demesnes. It had been held for the Plantagenet kings by the Earls of Lincoln, loyally supported by the citizens, in the war between King John and the barons, and after his death the city resisted a siege by the disloyal barons of Henry III. King Richard in March, 1378, soon after his accession, had confirmed all the city charters, and the celebrated John of Gaunt, the king's uncle, held the castle for him as Earl of Lincoln at the time of his visit. The commencement of his reign had been disturbed by the Peasant Rebellion under Wat Tyler, which though most violent in Kent and Essex, is said to have extended to Lincolnshire, but to have found no support from the citizens of Lincoln.

The then mayor, John Sutton, was a member of an influential family in the city. His father had been mayor and also member of Parliament. His brother Robert had also been mayor, and was at the time of the king's visit to Lincoln, its member, and, off and on, continued to represent it up to

1401. The borough members in Parliament were beginning
to make their influence felt, and the king may have been
advised to seek the friendship of the burgers by conferring
honours upon their mayors.

The city therefore, had some claims to the king's favour,
and if he bestowed swords upon York and Chester we may, I
think, fairly assume that the tradition that he gave one to
Lincoln is well founded.

But perhaps the best evidence that the sword was a royal
gift is supplied by the fact that it was a royal sword. It was
customary, when the shape of the pommel permitted, to
place upon it the shield of arms of the owner. The pommel
of this sword bears the shield of Edward III., the king's
grandfather, the same which the king, in the early part of
his reign, also adopted, before he appropriated the cross and
martlets of Edward the Confessor as part of his armorial
ensigns. This shield seems to prove that the sword had
belonged either to the king or one of his ancestors, and that
it is contemporary with them is also proved by the opinion
of experts, who agree in assigning it to the fourteenth century.

The occasion on which the sword was presented is said to
have been a visit by the king, who was then only 20 years
old, to his uncle, John of Gaunt. The exact date cannot be
fixed; it will be observed, however, that in both the Bishop's
and Chapter's List of Mayors it is stated to have been in the
10th year of the king's reign and during the mayoralty of
John Sutton; and the Chapter List gives as the date, 1386.
Now Richard ascended the throne 22nd June, 1377, so that
the 10th year commenced 22nd June, 1386. Sutton's mayoralty commenced 29th September, 1386, so that the visit, if
the lists are correct, must have taken place after that date.
It was about this time, however, that John of Gaunt was
asserting his claim to the throne of Castile, and eventually
left the country with an army to enforce it, remaining abroad
until 1389.

Camden says, under date 1386, that about Easter, John,
Duke of Lancaster *prepared for* Spain. Hollinshed, however, says that 'in the 9th year of King Richard (though by
other writers it should seem to be rather in the year following) the Duke of Lancaster *went into* Spain,' and he
subsequently mentions the month of March as the time of his
departure from England. If Camden and the 'other
writers' be correct, which is probably the case, as Hollinshed
is not always to be relied upon, the duke departed about
Easter, 1387, in which case the king visited him at Lincoln
sometime between Michaelmas, 1386, and that date.

When, in 1900, I had the honour of being mayor of Lincoln,

I undertook to deliver a lecture on our Civic Insignia, for which purpose I had occasion to inquire particularly into the history of our municipal swords, with the result that I formed the opinion that two of them, of which the Richard II. Sword was one, must have been tampered with by the removal of their original blades.

The following is a description of the Richard Sword as I found it:

The sword has a total length of 3 feet 8½ inches, and its hilt is about 11 inches in length   The cross guard of the hilt is straight with the ends of the quillons slightly deflected. It bears traces of gilt ornamentation, and the face towards the blade is inscribed : JHESUS EST AMOR = = = MEUS. A DEO ET REGE.*

The pommel is a hollow iron disc 2 inches in thickness, weighing 1 lb. 13 oz. 8 dr., and covered with silver gilt. It is of wheel pattern, flat and circular, with a circular raised centre on each side, supported by a hollow groove engraved with pointed rays. On each of the central discs the arms of Richard II are engraved, encircled by ostrich plumes, adopted by him as one of his badges, and the broad rim of the wheel is decorated with fleurs de lys and roses alternately. The pommel is so affixed to the hilt that the shield upon it is reversed when the sword is sheathed. The grip is 8 inches in length and closely bound by thin silver wire   The coronals are said by Captain Hutton to be certainly of the sixteenth century.

The blade is 2 feet 9½ inches in length, 1⅝ inch in width at the base and 1¼ inch at four inches from the point. It is two-edged and has a shallow central groove on one side, within which, reading from hilt to point, is inscribed : INVΛIINIIΛ. On one side, beyond the groove, is a well-defined running Wolf mark, and on the other side the Orb and Cross mark. The sides of the grooves are defined by lines terminating in a design composed of six points .·. in a pyramidal form.

The entire sword weighs 4 lbs 7 oz. 10½ dr, the blade and tang detached 1 lb. 4 oz. 6½ dr, and the hilt, i.e., quillons, grip and pommel, 3 lbs. 3 oz. 4 dr

Desiring to ascertain whether from the markings on the blade, the name of the armourer, or the place of its manufacture could be ascertained, I sent a photograph of it to Captain

* Mr W H. St John Hope has since pointed out to me that the inscription on the quillons, which is in Roman capitals, and all the engraving on the pommel are of late sixteenth century date.   This work was probably done in 1595, when it was agreed that "the greatest and the least swordes be newele repareid in scabottes hiltes pumbles handells and cheapes wth such coste and fashone as shalbe thought good by Mr. Maior."

Alfred Hutton, who also subsequently inspected it on a visit to Lincoln. Captain Hutton expressed the decided opinion that the blade was not of the same date as the hilt, that whilst the latter was of the assigned date, viz: fourteenth century, the blade was either late sixteenth or early seventeenth century Captain Hutton's startling announcement as to the different dates of the hilt of the sword and its blade at once raised doubts as to the authenticity of the tradition that the sword had been presented by Richard II Anxious therefore, to ascertain whether there were any signs confirming his opinion, I proceeded to examine the parts of the sword more closely, with the result that I found evidence that the blade did not originally belong to the hilt I observed that the blade does not fit the aperture in the cross guard into which its base is inserted. The upper aperture is $2\frac{3}{8}$ inches, and the base $1\frac{1}{8}$ inch long, whereas the blade is only $1\frac{3}{8}$ inch wide at its junction with the guard. The aperture is also wider than required by the thickness of the blade.

On handling the sword one could not help being struck with the disproportion of the hilt, which is apparently that of a two-handed sword, with the weight of the blade, and also with the balance of the sword, the hilt being far heavier than the blade.

Again, remembering that when the city only possessed two swords, viz , this Richard Sword and one known as the Second or Lent Sword, the city records, when referring to them, designated this the "Great" Sword, I measured them, and found that it is at least $\frac{1}{4}$ inch shorter than the Second Sword.

All these circumstances combined to prove that the original blade had been removed from its hilt, and a sixteenth century one substituted; but as the Richard Sword, after it came into the possession of the city in 1386, would only be used on state occasions, it seemed improbable that its original blade could have been broken or destroyed, and I proceeded therefore to inquire whether it might not be still in existence, and with this object to investigate the history of the other swords.

One of these is called the Second or Lent or Mourning Sword, because in olden times it was carried before the mayor in the lenten season and at funerals. It is said to be a complete ancient fighting sword of the fifteenth century. Its total length is 3 feet $8\frac{3}{4}$ inches, the blade 2 feet $11\frac{1}{4}$ inches in length, and $2\frac{1}{4}$ inches in width at the base, tapering to $\frac{3}{4}$ inch at four inches from the point. Its weight is 4 lbs. 9 oz. 12 dr It is two-edged and perfectly plain, having neither grooves, nor armourer's, nor other distinctive marks. The hilt is 9 inches in length and terminates with a pear-shaped pommel, originally gilded, having eight faces covered with a foliated design, of which the greater part has been obscured by a covering of black varnish.

The quillons of the crossguard are curved with rounded and deflected terminations and damascened with a gilded scroll pattern which has also been defaced with black varnish, no doubt in conformity with the user ot the sword.

The first mention of this sword in our civic records is under date 25th November, 1544, when an order was made for a new scabbard, and an inquiry respecting ' certeyn grey- hounds lyons & diagons of sylver and guylt which ar lost & gone of the Second Swerde.'   These decorations were badges peculiar to Henry VII, who twice visited Lincoln, viz., in 1486, on the commencement of his reign, and again in June, 1487, immediately after his victory at Stoke over the Earl of Lincoln , and I think it is not improbable that this second sword was presented to the city by this king together with a new cap of maintenance, of which the city became possessed about the same time.

This second sword then appears to be an original and perfect weapon, and bears no signs of having been tampered with

In the course of my inquiries into the history of our swords, I found an entry in our City Register for 1676 respecting certain ' Ensignes of Authority' which were delivered to the then mayor. They are enumerated, and include ' *three* swords,' etc.   The entry is repeated annually in different forms until 1699, after which it ceases alto- gether

The existing records are silent as to when and under what circumstances this third sword came into possession of the Corporation, neither do they contain any description of it

The other two swords in existence in 1676 were the Richard Sword and the Mourning Sword which are said to be still in our possession

We have now also a third sword, but its date is said to be 1734, and therefore cannot be the third sword of 1676.

The 1676 sword appears to have been lost sometime after 1699, but there is no record as to when or how it was so lost, and I doubt whether it has altogether disappeared for reasons which will be explained hereafter.

The second sword, presenting therefore no appearance of having been altered, I next examined our present third or State Sword.

The total length of this sword is 4 feet 6¼ inches. Its blade is large, being 3 feet 5⅜ inches in length, $2\frac{7}{16}$ inches in width at its base, and $\frac{13}{16}$ inch at four inches from the point. The weight of the blade and tang is 2 lbs. 7 oz. 11 dr. avoir. It is double-edged, and appears to possess a smooth surface, but on close examination there can be discerned near the hilt slight traces of two grooves.

On one side the blade bears the mark of an encircled Greek

Cross with four crescents and on the other a

peculiar mark which, when reversed, bears some resemblance to the forepart of a galloping animal, and may possibly have been intended for the forepart of the Wolf mark.

On each side of the blade, a little beyond these principal marks and nearer the point, is another smaller mark composed of small indentations which form a figure resembling a badly-formed R, thus: All the marks on this blade retain traces of having originally been inlaid with gold.

Turning now to the hilt of the State Sword we perceive at once that it is of recent date. It is of silver gilt, and the quillons bear the London hall-mark for 1734-5, and the maker's mark N.Y. with a pellet over. The pommel is a large oval, and is engraved on one side, thus:

THE CITY OF LINCOLN

JOHN KENT, MAYOR

1734.

So that both by inscription and hall-mark the year 1734 is fixed as the date of origin of the hilt.

John Kent was again mayor in 1777, which fact he was also careful to record by another inscription on the other side of the pommel.

The crossguard presents some peculiar features. It has a square central body, 1⅞ inch in width, through which the tang of the blade passes. The blade at its base is 2½ inches in width, and is not set in the body of the crossguard but in a beaded rim which serves to hide the rough base and is only connected with it by the tang. The edges of the blade project on both sides of the body of the crossguard.

Another remarkable feature of the crossguard is that it bears on the front the motto: JESUS EST AMOR MEUS, and on the back, A DEO ET REGE; that is to say, the identical mottoes inscribed on the crossguard of the Richard II. hilt, differing only in the spelling of the word JESUS. Why was this modern hilt so inscribed ? The mottoes are not those of the city, but seem to belong exclusively to the Richard Sword.

Now it is significant that in the mayoralty of this same John Kent in 1734, the Common Council ordered the great mace to be new gilt, a new scabbard to be had for the sword, and a new hat for the swordbearer. The hat is still in existence, and likewise bears the name of John Kent, mayor. The scabbard is not, so far as we know, in existence, the present one having been obtained in 1818 It will be observed that the order says nothing about providing a *new* sword, or even a *new hilt* for the sword, yet we find on examining the audited accounts of the receipts and payments of John Kent in connection with his 1734 mayoralty, which have fortunately been preserved, the following items:

'Paid for a new Hatt, *a new Sword*, and Mace Gilding, £59 4 0.
'Paid for mending the mourning Sword, 6d '

Now we have seen that it is probable that at the time this order was made the corporation possessed three swords, so that, if an entirely new sword was provided by Mayor Kent, there should be four in existence. We possess, however, now only three swords, so that, either one has been since lost, or the so-called 'New Sword' was only one of the three presented in a new guise.

Considering these facts, the conclusion seemed irresistible that Mayor Kent, brought by order of his council into contact with the insignia, and having possibly in his travels seen some gorgeous new civic sword, conceived the design, and seized this opportunity of providing them with a grand up-to-date state sword, with which his memory should ever after be connected.

In furtherance of this design, I suggest that this large ornamental pageant hilt of silver gilt was alone obtained, and that the large blade of the Richard Sword was removed from its own hilt and transferred to it, the combination forming indeed a great State Sword.

To preserve, however, the Richard hilt, and to provide it with a blade, I further suggest that the original third, or 1676 sword, was broken up, its blade transferred to the Richard hilt, and its own hilt destroyed or otherwise disposed of, thus accounting for the presence of a sixteenth or early seventeenth century blade in the Richard hilt.

At the same time, I suggest further that at the same time, and probably, with the idea of preserving the identity of the Richard blade in its new position, the Richard mottoes were transcribed on the crossguard of the State Sword But, alas! in vain! Blades may be broken and require replacement, and the nationality and date of a sword is therefore taken from the fashion of its hilt. Through the obvious claims of the hilt of the Richard Sword to antiquity, its present blade has been admired and spoken of as of even date with it, whilst on the other hand, persons, claiming to be experts, misled by the obvious modernity of the hilt of the State Sword, have scornfully pushed it aside, and refused even to look at its blade!

Turning once more to the Richard hilt for confirmation of my suspicion that the blade of the State Sword really belonged to it, I found that the width of the base of the blade corresponded with the width of the upper aperture in the crossguard, and the width of the tang, with the width of the under aperture, and that, if replaced, the length of the restored sword would be 4 feet 5 inches, and its weight 5 lbs 10 oz 15 dr, fully entitling it to the name of the 'Great' Sword by which the Richard Sword is described in our records

My theory of the tampering with the Richard Sword appearing to be confirmed, I have sought the opinion of gentlemen, experts in the matter of swords, as to its correctness.

Captain Hutton has inspected the swords, and is of opinion that the blade of the Richard Sword is of the sixteenth or seventeenth century, and not of even date with the hilt into which it has been inserted at a later date. He is also of opinion that the inscription is intended to convey the impression that the blade was of Spanish make, and was manufactured by I. N. of Valencia

Viscount Dillon, to whom I submitted photographs of the swords, is of opinion that the Richard Sword has been tampered with, and points out that it is not well mounted, the blade edge being not equidistant from the axis of the grip He considers the present blade a Solingen one, either of the sixteenth or seventeenth century, with one of those undecypherable inscriptions so often found on swords, and presumed to be bad imitations of some famous name or inscription. On this point the new catalogue of the Museum of Artillery at Paris, vol. iii., 1901, warns collectors thus:—
' It must be noted that a great number of German imitations

of Spanish blades exist   Proper names mutilated, bad execution of capital letters denouncing these frauds'

Mr. Parker Brewis, of Newcastle, has taken great interest in the swords, and has examined them closely twice. He points out that the pommel of the Richard Sword is reversed, the shield upon a wheel pommel invariably being placed with its base towards the quillons. This change indicates that at some time it has been removed and replaced by an ignorant workman, which may have happened in 1681, inasmuch as I find it recorded, that amongst the articles then delivered to the mayor was 'One peece of Silver wch came of on a sword pumill,' and which Mr. Parker Brewis thinks would probably be the terminal of the pommel, or rivetting button, which was common to wheel pommels.

Mr. Brewis, on closely examining the blade at present in the state hilt, observed that it bears traces of two grooves, and also some distance up the blade on one side, some small detached indentations, forming a diamond, nearer one edge than the other. Also, a little further on, one similar complete diamond-shaped indentation still retaining traces of gold. He also pointed out on this blade, and about $14\frac{1}{2}$ inches from its base, the slight but distinct indentation of the 'Bishop's Staff' mark, similar to those on swords in the Dresden Collection He is of opinion that this blade, which is now almost smooth, has at some time or other been ground and repolished over the whole of its surface, probably to make it look new Also, that it once bore an inscription running up each side, which was removed by this polishing, the marks still remaining having survived, through having been more deeply struck. Mr. Brewis thinks that these remaining marks were originally portion of an ornamentation in the nature of the Genoa 'Sickle' mark, which so frequently divides inscriptions on sword blades. He was also struck by the balance of the present Richard Sword, and observed that the centre of percussion was so near the hilt, as to make it no fighting sword. Noticing also the difference in the length of the grips of the two swords, that of the Richard Sword being shorter than that of the State Sword, Mr. Brewis suggested that an examination of the tangs of the swords would materially assist in the solution of the question, whether the blade of the State Sword belonged to the Richard hilt, as in such case, its tang must bear signs of having been lengthened. Accordingly, with the permission of the Corporation, I had the hilts of the swords carefully removed and the tangs examined. That of the present blade of the

Richard Sword showed no signs of .having been altered, but that of the blade of the State Sword had unmistakeably been lengthened as anticipated by Mr. Brewis, its present length being 12⅞ inches

I have not yet been able to obtain any satisfactory explanation of the markings of the swords Mr Brewis kindly forwarded photographs to Herr von Ehrenthal, director of the Royal Historical Museum, Dresden, and he described the peculiar head-shaped mark as a ·half knot,' a somewhat similar mark being found on one of the swords No. 16, A.D. 1340-1400, in the Dresden Museum.

The Greek Cross with crescents mark occurs on the blade of a sword in the Museum of Artillery, Paris, J. 86, where it is catalogued as 'a mark borrowed from the Saracens.' It also occurs on blades in the Armouries at Madrid and at Dresden. It is described in Demmin's *Weapons of War* (p. 580) as having had a symbolical meaning in the secret tribunals of the free judges (Vehmgerichte), but Herr von Ehrenthal does not think that in this instance it has any connection with the Vehmgerichte, because the tapering form of the blade is not that of a Sword of Justice.

Herr von Ehrenthal is of opinion that the State Sword blade dates about 1400 and the present Richard blade about 1600, and that the latter is probably of Solingen make.

In Jewitt and Hope's *Corporation Plate and Insignia of Office of the Cities and Towns of England and Wales*, Mr. St. John Hope has described the Lincoln swords.* Of the oldest sword he says that it 'has a Solingen blade with the armourer's mark, a wolf and the orb and cross.   The hilt, grip, and pommel are all original.'

The second or mourning sword he says 'is another fine ancient example, of fifteenth century date, and complete with its original blade, which is seemingly of English manufacture.'

Of the state sword he says that it is 'of eighteenth century date; the blade, however, appears to be an old one of Solingen make, with the mark of the wolf and the orb and cross.'

P.S.—So far, the result of the inquiries which I had made had been to confirm my theory as to the transfer of the Richard blade, but before I ventured to ask my Corporation to restore it to its proper hilt I solicited the opinion of the Society of Antiquaries. I had the honour of reading the above paper upon the subject, and to receive a unanimous expression of opinion that my views were correct. The

* Vol. ii. 73.

C. F. Keil & Son, Photo-Print.

STATE SWORD OF THE CITY OF LINCOLN.

Corporation of Lincoln have accordingly authorised the restoration of the Richard Sword and the manufacture of a suitable scabbard decorated with the emblems of the king."

W. NIVEN, Esq., F.S.A., communicated a paper on the Garden House at Beckett, near Shrivenham.

Mr. Niven's paper will be printed in *Archaeologia*.

Professor A. H. CHURCH, M.A., D.Sc., F.R.S., F.S.A., by

ROUNDEL WITH THE ARMS OF VANPAGE OR VAMPAGE, CO. WORCESTER, FOUND AT CIRENCESTER. (½).

permission of Mr. T. B. Bravender, exhibited the following antiquities, which were found lately at Cirencester, during drainage operations:

1. A small round bronze seal with moulded trefoil handle, having for device two interlaced triangles with a rose in the centre, and the legend:

✻ PVR LA ROSE SV IEO FET

2. A bronze roundel, 3 inches in diameter, with hole for suspension, bearing a shield of arms, *an eagle within a flory tressure.* Some existing traces of dark blue enamel give the colour of the field, but there is nothing to show whether the

charges were gilded or silvered. The arms appear to those of the Worcestershire family of Vanpage or Vampage. The roundel is of the fifteenth century, and has some remains of lead or solder on the back, as if it had once been affixed to something.

Sir J. CHARLES ROBINSON, F.S.A., exhibited the silver terminals of a strap or belt with suspendor for a purse or some such object. The terminals are $2\frac{1}{2}$ inches long, and enclosed a flattened strap about $\frac{1}{4}$ inch wide and $\frac{1}{8}$ inch thick. The upper surfaces are decorated with filigree scrollwork and the sides with sexfoil studs. At the lower end of each terminal is a beaded oval loop, which pass through smaller loops on the sides of a small roundel with an enamelled shield of the arms of France on a red ground. From the roundel is suspended from a third loop by an ornamental ring, a second roundel with a shield, also enamelled, of the arms of Castile on a blue ground. The roundel hangs from the ring by a beaded loop and has another below from which to suspend something.

Nothing is known of the history of the object, which appears to be of late thirteenth or early fourteenth century date.

Mr. Hope pointed out that Ferdinand la Cerda, prince of Castile, who died *vita pâtris* in 1275, married in 1269 Blanche, daughter of Louis IX. of France, who died in 1320; but he was not able to say what arms Ferdinand bore as prince of Castile.

Thanks were ordered to be returned for these communications and exhibitions.

Thursday, 19th December, 1901.

Viscount DILLON, President, in the Chair.

The following gifts were announced, and thanks for the same ordered to be returned to the donors:

From the East Riding Antiquarian Society :—Transactions, vols. iv.-viii. 8vo. Hull, 1896-1900.

From the Author :—A complete memoir of Richard Haines. By C. R. Haines. 8vo. n.p. 1899.

From the Executors of the late Samuel Barfield, Esq. :—Thatcham, Berks, and its Manors. By the late Samuel Barfield, 2 vols 4to Oxford and London, 1901.

Notice was again given of a Ballot for the election of Fellows on Thursday, 9th January, 1902, and a list of candidates to be balloted for was read.

W. GOWLAND, Esq., F.S.A., read a paper descriptive of the results of excavations carried out under his supervision at Stonehenge during the month of September, with a view of securing the leaning stone of the great trilithon. He also exhibited in illustration a large number of stone implements and other objects found during the operations.

Mr. Gowland's paper will be printed in *Archaeologia*.

Thanks were ordered to be returned for this communication.

Thursday, 9th January, 1902.

J. T. MICKLETHWAITE, Esq., Vice-President, in the Chair.

The following gifts were announced, and thanks for the same ordered to be returned to the donors .

From the Author:—On the "Implements from the Chalk Plateau," in Kent, their character and importance. By R D. Darbishire, F S A 8vo. Manchester, 1901

From W A. Lindsay, Esq., K C, F S A —Publications of the Clan Lindsay Society. No. 1 8vo. Edinburgh, 1901.

Special votes of thanks were accorded to the editors of *The Athenæum*, *The Builder*, and *Notes and Queries*, for the gift of their publications during the past year.

The following letters were read :

> "Marlborough House,
> Pall Mall, S.W.
> 23rd December, 1901

SIR,

I have had the honour of submitting your letter and the copy of a Resolution which accompanied it, in respect of

certain Celtic Gold Ornaments, now in the British Museum, to
The King.

His Majesty is glad to hear the views of the Society on this
important subject.

I am, Sir,

Your obedient servant,

FRANCIS KNOLLYS

The Secretary,
   The Society of Antiquaries."

" Treasury Chambers.
13 December 1901.

My LORD,

I am directed by the Lords Commissioners of His Majesty's
Treasury to acknowledge the receipt of your Secretary's letter
of the 2nd instant transmitting a copy of a Resolution with
regard to certain Celtic gold ornaments now in the British
Museum, passed at a Special Meeting of the Society of
Antiquaries of London held at Burlington House on the 28th
of November last.

I am, my Lord,

Your obedient servant,

FRANCIS MOWATT.

The President,
   Society of Antiquaries of London,
      Burlington House, Piccadilly, W."

This being an evening appointed for the election of Fellows
no papers were read.

W. GOWLAND, Esq., F.S.A., again exhibited the stone
implements, etc. found by him at Stonehenge in September,
1901.

PHILIP NORMAN, Esq., Treasurer, exhibited a miniature
painting of the seventeenth century, representing the martyr-
dom of a female saint.

Thanks were ordered to be returned for these exhibitions.

A suggestion was made by Mr. E. W. BRABROOK, C B, that
as a means of conducing to the greater fitness of candidates
for election into the Society, the Council should be asked to
append to the certificate now in use some such direction as

" This Form is issued to Fellows only, and should not
be filled up by the Candidate.

It is considered irregular for a Candidate to ask Fellows to sign it "

Mr. Brabrook's suggestion was favourably received by the Meeting.

The Ballot opened at 8.45 p m. and closed at 9.30 p.m., when the following gentlemen were declared duly elected Fellows of the Society :

Robert Alexander Stewart MacAlister, Esq , M.A.
Frederick William Cock, Esq , M D.
Francis Frederick Fox, Esq.
Rev. Morgan Thomas Peaiman, M A.
Rev. Charles William Shickle, M.A.
Walter Jonathan Andrew, Esq.
Rev. George Herbert Engleheart, M.A.
Rev. Charles Samuel Taylor, M.A.

Thursday, 16th, January 1902.

Viscount DILLON, President, in the Chair.

The following gift was announced, and thanks for the same ordered to be returned to the donor:

From Walter Money, Esq , F.S.A —A Perfect Booke of all the landes within the Hundreds of Evenger, Chutlye, Kingsclere, Pastroe, and Overton, in 1575. Printed from an original manuscript in the Wood Library, Whit-church, Hants. 8vo. Newbury, 1901

The Rev. Charles Samuel Taylor, M A., was admitted Fellow.

THOMAS ASHBY, junr , Esq., F.S.A., and A. T. MARTIN, Esq., M.A , F.S A., submitted an account of excavations on the site ·of the Roman town at Caerwent in 1901, which will be printed in *Archaeologia.*

HERBERT SOUTHAM, Esq , F.S.A., exhibited (1) a brass candlestick, perhaps of the seventeenth century, found at Shrewsbury; (2) an example of a horn-book, and (3) a wooden cup, apparently of yew, 6¾ inches high, engraved with simple arcading, probably of early seventeenth-century work.

Thanks were ordered to be returned for this communication and exhibition.

Thursday, 23rd January, 1902.

Viscount DILLON, President, in the Chair.

The following gifts were announced, and thanks for the same ordered to be returned to the donors:

From Rev J B Wilson, M A , F S.A —The parish book of St Helen's Church in Worcester, containing the parish registers from 1538 to 1812. 2 vols 8vo. London, 1900.

From the Trustees of the British Museum :—Reproductions of prints in the British Museum New Series, Part X. Additional specimens of line-engraving by the earliest masters working in England (about 1580-1630). Folio. London, 1901.

From the Author ·—Hertfordshire maps · a descriptive catalogue of the maps of the county, 1579-1900. By H. G. Fordham. Part I. 8vo. n p. n.d.

The following gentlemen were admitted Fellows:

Rev. Charles William Shickle, M.A.
Francis Frederick Fox, Esq.
The Right Hon. Sir Herbert Eustace Maxwell, bt., M P., President of the Society of Antiquaries of Scotland.

J. H. ROUND, Esq., M.A., read a paper on the Castles of the Conquest, which will be printed in *Archaeologia.*

Thanks were ordered to be returned for this communication.

Thursday, 30th January, 1902.

J. T. MICKLETHWAITE, Esq., Vice-President, in the Chair.

The following gifts were announced, and thanks for the same ordered to be returned to the donors :

From the Author ·—On the Needle and Thread at Langford Budville   By F. T. Elworthy, F S A. 8vo. 1901.

From the Author —Huntingdon Shaw and the Hampton Court Ironwork. By R Garraway Rice, F S A. 8vo London, 1902.

From the Author:—On an Incrustation from the Stone Gallery of St Paul's Cathedral. By E G. Clayton, F I.C. 8vo. London, 1901.

From Viscount Dillon, President —The Defensive Armour and the Weapons and Engines of War of Mediæval Times, and of the "Renaissance." By R. C. Clephan. 8vo. London, 1900.

The Rev. George Herbert Engleheart, M.A., was admitted Fellow.

The Rev. H. D. RAWNSLEY, M.A., Hon. Canon of Carlisle, through the Secretary, exhibited a number of stone implements lately found at Portinscale, near Derwentwater, on which he submitted the following notes:

"The four stone celts which are exhibited unpolished are of various sizes as follows:

	Length.	Greatest Girth
No. 1.	$10\frac{3}{4}$	$7\frac{1}{8}$
„ 2	9	$7\frac{1}{2}$
„ 3.	$7\frac{7}{8}$	$6\frac{1}{4}$
„ 4.	$7\frac{1}{2}$	$4\frac{3}{4}$

They were discovered at the end of November last by a workman named Downey, who was employed by the contractor, Thomas Birkett, to remove the peat and dig out the peaty bottom to form a fish pond for Mr. Tindal Harris of Moss Garth, at a place called the Moss, which lies a quarter of a mile from Portinscale on the right hand of the road to Newlands, just at the gates of Derwent Bank. The ground rises between the Moss and Derwentwater, and it is very little likely that it was ever submerged by the waters of the lake.

It is possible that in old days there was a backwater from the plain and meadows of Ullock which would more or less render the Moss a marsh The workmen who were digging threw out three other celts at a point about 50 yards to the eastward. They did not recognise them, and buried them again. It is hoped they may yet be recovered. These four celts were discovered laid along by the side of the trunk of a small oak tree about 12 inches in diameter which was lying on the blue clay about 22 inches beneath the surface of the Moss. The tree in question was one of many similar ones which were laid about in various directions, but there was nothing in the lie of these tree-remains to indicate that they had been used for stockades or lake dwellings. The tree in question by which they were found was much disintegrated, and my theory is that whoever worked them was surprised by some sudden attack, or had to go on a journey elsewhere and leave them hidden by the tree trunk. Death may have overtaken him; he never returned to claim them. Of course if the celts were originally laid on the surface of the moss and simply sank by gravitation to the blue clay level this suggestion probably was not the case. One would hardly expect that the celts and the tree would sink together.

The celts themselves may have been worked out of the fine volcanic lava boulders that were lying all about at this spot. One of these boulders was curiously cleft, and looked almost as if it had been cut off a large boulder, but there were no flakes or chippings that I could discover, though the men said they had seen such. Nor was I able after much search to find any stones that had been used and bruised in the process of chipping flints, as have been found at other finds of stone axes made on the spot.

The boulders have all white patina upon them similar to the patina upon the celts. In the St. John's valley seven years ago two stone axes made of the same material were discovered, and both of these are finely polished. In the Ehenside-Tarn find, now in the British Museum, there are two axes of the same type, one polished and one unpolished.

It is fair to remember that the high camp, or seat of Sweyn the Viking, which we call Swinside to-day, rises on the southern side of the same moss   Whether these stone axes were likely to be still in use in Viking times I cannot say. Dr. Greenwell tells me that in the Neolithic age it is pretty clear that both the polished and unpolished axes were used contemporaneously.

The little boulder stone I showed you, of which I have sent photographs to Mr. Collingwood, was found within 100 yards of the place where the 'celts' were discovered, and on what I think may have been the Roman Finkle *Street*, or if not this a *pilgrims' way* from Nichol ending on the lake and island in Derwentwater, wherein was after 1374 a famous pilgrim's shrine. I think you thought the stone might be late fourteenth century.

Addendum:

On Monday, January 27, 1902, at a place about 30 yards from the former find of stone axes, and about 2 yards from a spring, there was dug out of the blue clay that underlaid the peat a half-polished celt (length 8 inches, greatest girth 7 inches). It was about 2 feet 6 inches beneath the surface of the ground, and was so imbedded in the clay that it was not seen by the man who filled the barrow. By good luck Mr. Tindall Harris, the owner of Moss Earth, was close by when the barrow was tilted for the making of a garden terrace, and he noticed it partly uncovered by the process of tipping.

On the following day I picked up an oblong stone of quartzite from near the place of the original find, which so resembles in size those I have seen as flakers in other finds, that I cannot help thinking it may have been meant for a tool by the axe-makers.

On the same day one of Birkett's men found sticking in a crevice, between two boulders of volcanic ash, a flake of flint which looks as if it had been half worked for a rough spear- or arrow-head, the only piece of flint discovered so far

Birkett also, in moving a small boulder of volcanic lava (length 13 inches, depth 8 inches) noticed what appeared to be bore holes on each side of it. One of them was filled with what seemed to be lime packing. They were both bored slantwise, not vertically, and were oval in shape, as though worked by the thin end of an axehead or pick of some sort. One of them was apparently packed with lime. He split the stone and found the bore holes had been made on what is locally termed the 'ridd' of the stone, that is the cleavage, and he carefully preserved the bit of core which fell out. He tells me that people in Barrowdale still split the native stone by boring a hole, filling it with lime, inserting a pricker and 'stemming' the lime, that is ramming it down round the pricker, then, withdrawing the pricker, they pour water into the space left by it, and hammer a bit of wood on to the top. The water and lime expand inside their prison-house and split the stone. If our surmise is correct, we have here an example of a custom which has been preserved since Neolithic times.

I asked Birkett why he split this boulder, and he said he could see by the bore holes that 't'old fellers had been at the stean, and he would gaily weal hav liket to try his hand at making a stone axe.'

Close by the boulder he found a piece of what he considers is the same kind of lime, caked hard, which was used by the said 'old fellows.'

I have sent this piece of lime and a bit of the core also for your examination.

Another stone which may be of interest has been dis- covered. I have forwarded it to London along with the half- polished celt.

It looks as it were the polishing stone, and certainly fits the hand wonderfully

One other stone which may be of interest is also sent. It is grooved in the sort of way which a stone might be grooved which was used for grinding axeheads.

I am sorry to say this last was broken by the men who dug it up, and I cannot find the missing part "

J G. WALLER, Esq., F.S.A., read the following notes on part of a *tabella* found at Blythburgh, Suffolk, and exhibited by Seymour Lucas, Esq., R.A., F.S.A.

"The object exhibited by our friend and Fellow, Mr. Seymour Lucas, and which I class amongst the *tabellæ* or table-books, was found on some land at Blythburgh, Suffolk, now his property, but formerly belonging to the Priory of Black Canons, a cell to the Abbey of St. Osith, Essex, founded in the reign of Henry I. The table-books in use by both Greeks and Romans seem to have been made usually of wood, and one was preserved in the collection of my old friend C. R Smith, F.S.A , and is now in the British Museum In his *Roman London* he has given an interesting account of the use of such *tabellæ*, from which I extend my remarks. At page 137 are representations of *tabellæ* showing an excavated surface on one side, with a rim all round to preserve the wax, when melted and poured into it. Upon this surface an instrument called a stile (*stilus* or *graphium*) was used, having a sharp point for writing on the soft substance and a blunt end for effacing it, when required. Three of these instruments were found with the leaf of the *tabellæ* represented On one side of the rim are two small holes for the cord to pass through and bind the parts together when in use. Thus Plautus in his *Bacchides*,* when one is about to write:

' Effer cito stilum, ceram, et tabellas, et linum.'

Examples of the stiles are common in our museums, but the *tabellæ* are rarely found.

But Mr. Smith has recorded that in Transylvania an example was found complete not only with the waxen surface but with the writing upon it quite legible.†

The practice of using the *tabella* for epistolary correspondence or the making of notes passed from Roman times into that of the Middle Ages, as Du Cange, quoting an anonymous

* *Bacchides,* iv. 4, 6. etc.
† C R. Smith, *Catalogue of Museum of London Antiquities,* 77.

writer of the fourteenth century, speaks of tables of wax for
writing:

'Les uns se prennent à écrire
De greffes en tables de cire.'

The example before you is smaller than those alluded to,
being only $3\frac{3}{4}$ inches in length and $2\frac{1}{2}$ inches wide, and is
made of bone, but of what animal I must leave to the osteo-
logical authority. I have pointed out the small holes for the
cord in the Roman examples; here they are very large, as if
for a thong of leather, and evidently were made before the
excavation for receiving the wax as a small ridge is made
around them to prevent the melted wax flowing through.
This seems to me an obvious proof of the intended use of wax,
else it would have been unnecessary.

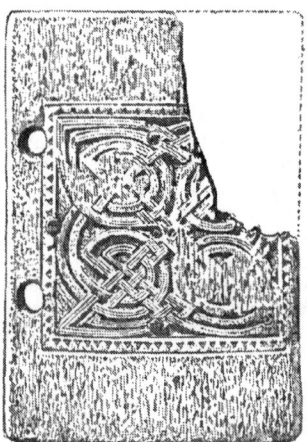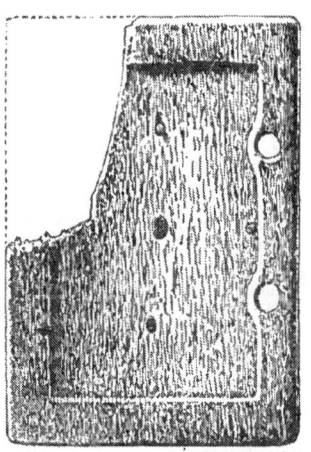

PART OF A "TABELLA" FOUND AT BLYTHBURGH, SUFFOLK.   OBVERSE
AND REVERSE.   ($\frac{3}{4}$ linear.)

I must now have a few words on the reticulated ornament
on the outward side, which proves it to have been the cover.
This interlacing had its origin in late Roman work, but was
afterwards taken up and elaborated into intricate combinations
on this side of the Alps, and numerous manuscripts from the
ninth to the eleventh century have examples which closely
illustrate the object before us. The celebrated Bible of St.
Paul at Rome, of the ninth century, has several remarkable

instances of this complicated interweaving; but similar ones are found down to the close of the eleventh century, when it seems to have died out, probably owing to the new development that was now at hand. The beaded border it is as well to notice, as it is so frequently associated with the same, and it adds to the interest. It is hazardous to attempt to fix a precise date, but I do not think it can be put later than the twelfth century.

There is yet another point to be noted. The cover has been perforated through the ornamental quadrangle by seven brass pins, portions of which remain, with some symmetry in arrangement, one in the centre, with four others equidistant, and two at each end, at what would be the junction of other leaves, two now lost by the fracture. This could never have formed part of the original arrangement, as it injures the design and would have interfered with the covering of wax and its use. I can only imagine that it represents a means by which a harder material was substituted in the place of wax, and a disuse of the ordinary stile.

I do not pursue the history of the use of table-books, which Shakespeare twice alludes to, as in some form they were used even to our own times, in small ivory tablets marked with days of the week, and chiefly used by ladies to enter their engagements or for other notes."

Mr. Read reminded the meeting of the elaborate paper in *Archaeologia* (vol. lv. 257) on the subject of writing tablets, with special reference to those of mediæval date. With regard to the specimen now shown, he expressed his opinion that the material was whale's bone, and pointed out the identity of the interlaced design with that found on the borders of the Book of Kells (Westwood, *Facsimiles* . . . . *of Anglo-Saxon and Irish MSS.*). He had the satisfaction of announcing that Mr. Seymour Lucas intended to present this interesting object to the British Museum.

Robert Blair, Esq., F.S.A., communicated the following report as Local Secretary for Northumberland :

"When visiting Mr. Spencer Percival at Longwitton, in Northumberland, a month or two ago, he showed me a Roman inscribed stone which he found there when he went to reside at the place. I have searched the *Lapidarium Septentrionale*, and it does not appear to have been published. It is of the usual centurial kind, an oblong with ansated ends, the face of the stone being 15 inches long by 7½ inches wide, and the inscription reads :

LEG II AVGVS | FE////

Whence it came my friend knows not.   .

For several years objects have been discovered on the beach
at South Shields after heavy easterly storms followed by strong
west winds, the former washing up the articles with the sand,
the latter blowing back the sand and leaving them exposed
The discovery of so many things is evidence of the wreck,
about the time of Edward III., on the Herdsand of some
vessel, as numberless coins of him and of Edward I. and II.,
and of contemporary Scottish kings, have turned up   These
coins consist chiefly of pennies of Edward I.-III. and of
Alexander, the Roberts, and the Davids of Scotland, and of
groats of Edward III., and of both the Edinburgh and Perth
mints of David and Robert.

In addition to these coins, an early silver spoon with acorn
handle and a large number of pewter plates of various sizes
have been picked up   One of the smallest of the plates is
now before you, and is interesting from the fact that it bears
incised on the rim a crosier, and two keys in saltire, the date
of which is of about the fourteenth century. It bears also
a stamped maker's mark, apparently a crown encircling a
sceptre

I may say that the mouth of the Tyne has on the north
side the bold promontory, projecting well into the sea, on
which stand the village, castle, and ruins of the priory of
Tynemouth, while the Herdsand, which is now always covered
with water, though formerly dry at low tide, projects to an
equal distance on the south side. On this sand, as on the
rocks on the opposite side of the river, hundreds of ships have
been lost with their crews.

Objects of earlier date than those mentioned have occasionally been cast up ; for instance, the fine bronze *patera*, wanting
its handle, in my possession, bearing round the central boss a
dedicatory inscription to Apollo Anextiomarus. This, I think,
has been exhibited to the Society.

Not far off were also found the fine inscribed oblong shield
boss formerly belonging to the Rev. W. Greenwell, and now
in the British Museum, and the cheek-piece of a Roman
helmet on which is the punctured device of a horseman
standing by the side of his horse."

The Rev. A. E. SORBY, M.A., exhibited and presented photographs of an alabaster tomb and effigies of a knight and lady
in Darfield church, Yorks.

The effigy of the knight belongs to the last quarter of the
fourteenth century, and probably represents John, the son of
Sir Roger Bosvile, who married Isabel, sister and co-heir of
Sir William Dronsfield. The lady's effigy is somewhat later

than the knight's, and is also shorter; it may therefore have belonged to another tomb.

C. H. READ, Esq., Secretary, exhibited one-half of a side of a carved ivory mirror case of the fourteenth century. (*See* illustration.)

It consists of rather more than half of one side of the mirror case, carved in relief with military subjects. The design is in three zones, of which the uppermost one shows a knight in armour riding, holding a heart-shaped shield, and with his vizor up; his horse wears housings, and he is accompanied by two other cavaliers and others, seven figures in all. The middle zone shows eight knights standing fully armed, wearing full suits of mail, covered by a surcoat to the knees, and each carrying a heater-shaped shield. It is noticeable that there are four types of helmets worn, a helmet with vizor, both raised and closed, a pointed iron cap with nasal, a similar cap with a turned-out rim and no nasal, and a plain bowl-shaped cap placed on the top of the mail cap. Some of the figures, but not all, have a plate defence for the lower leg and wear a prick spur. The lowest zone shows a single knight, in similar attire, seated, and asleep with his head resting on his knee beside his shield; behind him stands his helm; and it is thus clear that the plain bowl-shaped cap, which he also wears, was worn beneath the helm. There is a narrow encircling border of roses, and the remains of two lions show that these animals have formed the corners. Compare a similar mirror case, showing the diversions of knights in peace, in *Archaeologia*, vol. xvi. pl. xlix. This is of the same size and design as the piece now in question.

MONTAGU BROWNE, Esq., Local Secretary for Leicestershire, exhibited a number of miscellaneous antiquities found in or near Leicester.

Thanks were ordered to be returned for these communications and exhibitions.

CARVED IVORY MIRROR CASE OF THE 14TH CENTURY.

Thursday, 6th February, 1902.

Viscount DILLON, President, in the Chair.

The following gifts were announced, and thanks for the same ordered to be returned to the donors:

From the Author :—Tribal Custom in Anglo-Saxon Law. By Frederic Seebohm, LL D , F.S.A 8vo. London, 1902

From J. Horace Round, Esq , M A. :—A Series of ten Lantern Slides illustrative of his Paper on the Castles of the Conquest

On the nomination of the President, the following were appointed Auditors of the Society's Accounts for the year 1901:

Lionel Henry Cust, Esq., M.A.
Arthur Henry Lyell, Esq., M.A.
Edward William Brabrook, Esq., C.B.
Mill Stephenson, Esq., B.A.

Viscount DILLON, President, read an account of some familiar letters of Charles II. and James duke of York, addressed to their daughter and niece, the Countess of Litchfield, and exhibited the originals in his possession.

The President's paper will be printed in *Archaeologia*.

The PRESIDENT also exhibited the original Summons to the Coronation of William and Mary, and letters of dispensation from attending the same, addressed to the Earl and Countess of Litchfield, on which he read the following notes

"The two sign manuals exhibited may have an interest for some this year, when we are looking forward to the pomp and circumstance of a coronation. It will be seen that things have changed since 1689. Now those generally supposed to have a right to be present at the ceremony have been directed to apply to the authorities for authorisation to appear. Then the summons was, as will be seen by the first of these letters, peremptory.* The first document runs as follows:

WILLIAM R.

Right Trusty and Right Welbeloved Cousin We Greet you well. Whereas y⁰ 11ᵗʰ day of Aprill next is appointed for yᵉ

* According to similar letters printed in *The Genealogist*, N S. xviii. 65, summons in 1714 and 1727 were couched in the same style as in 1689.

Royall Solemnity of our and yᵉ Queens Coronacon, these are to Will and com̃and you and yʳᵉ Counteſs your Wife—(all Excuses Sett apart) To make your Personall Attendance on Us at yᵉ time abovemencõned furnished and Appointed as to Your Rank and Quallity appertaineth There to Do and Perform such Services as shall be required and Belong unto You respectively Whereof You and She are not to Faile And so Wee bid you very heartily Farewell Given at our Court at Whitehall yᵉ 21ˢᵗ day of March 168⅞ In yᵉ First Year of our Reign.

By his Majⁱʳˢ com̃and,

NORFOLKE & MARSHALL.

To yᵉ Earl and Countess of Litchfield.

For Our Right Trusty and Right
   Welbeloved Cousin Edward Henry
   Lee Earle of Litchfield.

The seal is that of the Duke of Norfolk as Earl Marshal.

This was Henry Howard, Duke of Norfolk, born 1655, died April, 1701.

The second document is as follows :

WILLIAM R.

Right trusty and right welbeloved Cousin We greet you well. It having been represented unto Us that neither you nor the Counteſse your wife can without great prejudice attend at the Solemnity of Our and Our Royall Consort the Queen's Coronation on the 11ᵗʰ instant. We have therefore thought fit and accordingly do hereby Dispense with your and her attendance upon that occasion. And so We bid you heartily Farewell. Given at Our Court at Whitehall the 9ᵗʰ day of Aprill 1689 in the first yeare of Our Reigne.

By his Majˠ command,

NOTTINGHAM.

Earle and Countesse of Litchfield's Dispensation.

This was Daniel Finch, Earl of Nottingham, born 1647. He was appointed Secretary of State three days before the date of this letter. He died 1st January, 1730.

The parties to whom these mandates were directed were Edward Henry, Earl of Litchfield, and his Countess, the Lady Charlotte Fitzroy. The Earl of elder son of Sir Francis

Henry Lee, fourth Baronet, by Elizabeth, daughter and heiress of Thomas Pope, Earl of Downe. Born in 1656, he succeeded his father as fifth Baronet in 1667, and was created Earl of Litchfield, Viscount Quarrendon, Baron Spelsbury, June 5, 1674 On 11 August, 1674, they were contracted. On 30 February, 167$\frac{3}{4}$, the marriage took place, the bridegroom and bride being respectively 12 and 10 years of age

It is clear that when the first summons to the coronation of her cousins by blood, William and Mary, was issued, it was forgotten that the Countess was also niece of the king who had abandoned the throne of England, and it was hardly to be expected that she and her husband would view with much satisfaction the succession of the cold-blooded William to the position formerly held by her uncle, who on all occasions had exhibited a more than friendly feeling for her and her husband.

The unsuitableness of the attendance of the Earl and Countess does not seem to have struck the authorities at the time, for the dispensation was dated only two days before the coronation, and we do not know whether it was in answer to a protest or spontaneous

Lord Litchfield is described by Macky * as 'a man of honour, never could take the oaths to King William, hath good sense, is not yet come to Queen Anne's Court, fifty years old.'

The seal on this 'dispensation' is the privy seal of William and Mary. It is circular, $1\frac{7}{16}$ inch in diameter, with a crowned shield of the royal arms within the Garter, circumscribed :

GVIL . III. ᴇᴛ MARIA II. D. G: ANG FRA III: REX ᴇᴛ REG: FID: DEF. &c.

The shield is · 1 & 4, France Modern and England Quarterly ; 2 & 3, Ireland , with Nassau in pretence ; as on the great seal of William and Mary."

W. H. Sᴛ. Joʜɴ Hoᴘᴇ, Esq., M.A., Assistant Secretary, exhibited a number of lantern slides of selected examples of English armorial medieval seals.

Thanks were ordered to be returned for these exhibitions and communications.

* John Macky, *Characters of the Court of Great Britain*, 1732

Thursday, 13th February. 1902.

Viscount DILLON, President, in the Chair.

The following gifts were announced, and thanks for the same ordeied to be returned to the donors:

From the Author —On Saxon Churches of the St. Pancras Type. By C R. Peers, M.A., F.S.A. 8vo. London, 1902

From the Author :—The Penmanship of a Book-keeper, *temp* Henry VIII By W L. Rutton, F S A 8vo. London, 1902

From the Author .—Did St. Augustine meet the British Bishops at Aust? By Rev C. S Taylor, M.A , F S A. 8vo Bristol, 1901

From the Editor .—The Muses Gardin* for Delights, or the fift Booke of Ayres Composed by Robert Jones, edited by W. Barclay Squire, F S.A. 12mo. Oxford, 1901.

From Charles H. Read, Esq., Secretary —A Description of the ancient monument of Henry Howard, Earl of Northampton, K G , the Founder of Trinity Hospital, East Greenwich. By C H Tatham. 8vo. Greenwich, 1838

From Rev. J C. Cox LL D , F S A —A History of the Church of All Saints, Northampton. By Rev R M Serjeantson 8vo Northampton, 1901.

PHILIP NORMAN, Esq., Treasurer, read a paper on the destroyed Church of St. Michael, Wood Street, in the City of London, with some Notes on the Church of St. Michael Bassishaw.

Mr. Norman's paper will be printed in *Archaeologia*.

C. J. PRÆTORIUS, Esq , F S A., read the following Report as Local Secretary for North Wales:

"The communication I have the honour to make to the Society, although in itself of no great importance, may be of use if placed on record, especially as it relates to a somewhat neglected part of the county of Anglesey.

In the month of September, 1901, by the courtesy and assistance of Lady Reade of Carreglwyd, a small excavation was made in a field belonging to a farm named Hên Shop, situated at Llanfaethlu, in Anglesey.

The name Hên Shop means "Old Shop," and gives no indication of this spot having been used for a burial ground or as the site of a church.

Llanfaethlu church is some five furlongs distant.

There are three farms within five miles, each having a number of graves near the house; many of these have been partially destroyed, and the covering stones used for building.

The late Mr Lloyd Griffith examined several graves, which were accidentally laid bare during the building of a wall at Hên Shop, in the year 1894. An account of his examination is printed in *Archæologia Cambrensis*[*]

It was with the hope of finding evidence as to the period of these burials that a further examination was made.

The field is said to contain about an acre of graves; judging by the number of gravestones used in the building of a boundary wall, it is evident that a number of the graves have already been distui bed by the plough.

Some 20 feet from the place where Mr. Lloyd Griffith made his examination, a trial trench some 2 feet deep was dug; the covering stones of a grave were soon found, the soil was then removed and the complete grave laid bare.

Four flat roughly-hewn slabs formed the covering; these rested horizontally on the top edges of other stones, which were set vertically, forming the sides or lining of the grave.

The cover stones were removed, and the grave was found to be 6 feet 2 inches in length, 15 inches wide where the shoulders rested, the inside measurement at the head and foot stone was about 10 inches.

When the cover stones were taken off, this grave was found to be full of fine, loose, brown soil, quite free from stones, the earth was taken out and examined, not a vestige of bone, pottery, or wood was discovered, the solitary object found being a lozenge-shaped piece of slate, in which there are two drilled holes, the sides look as though the object had been made by rubbing

The stones, of irregular shape, which formed the lining and sides of the grave were some 18 inches in depth; there were six on either side, with a head and foot stones. These lining stones were well fitted together, and rested on a hard mixed soil, which formed the bottom of the grave. This bottom earth was quite different from the loose soil with which the grave was filled, it was of a cement-like colour and hardness, intermixed with fragments of slaty rock and small stones, and was most difficult to dig (or rather pick out).

It was suggested that the burial might have been at a greater depth, and underneath this hard soil. Accordingly one grave was excavated to a depth of 5 feet, but the results were entirely negative.

[*] 5th *S.* vii

The absence of remains makes it difficult to assign to them
a date, all the graves were parallel and ran east and west,
the feet being laid to the east.

I also exhibit three purses and a ring, which are good
examples of their kind   The largest purse was found in the
ruins of an old house named Plas Berw, in Anglesey. The
wing in which it was found was destroyed by fire some years
ago, and is said to have been a building of the fifteenth
century.

In a hole where a joist formerly rested this purse was discovered, it contained gold coins, since lost, but which showed
it was hidden during the Civil Wars.

The two other purses are said to have been found in the
same house, and are probably of the seventeenth century.

The bronze finger ring, in which is set a carnelian intaglio
gem of late Roman period, has engraved on it a man's head,
wearing a helmet, underneath the head is a small bird. The
setting is of bronze, and suggests Italian workmanship of
mediæval times   this ring was dug up in Carnarvonshire.

In the prehistoric room of the British Museum is to be seen
a sepulchral urn, which was found in a grave on the banks of
the river Alaw, Anglesey.

It is said that Bronwen the Fair, daughter of Llyr
Llediaith, and aunt to Caractacus, was buried here about
50 A.D.

When this grave was opened in 1834, two beads are
known to have been found, one of pale blue, the second, of
similar size, and almost black.

I also exhibit lantern slide of a stone lamp and spindle-
whorl both found at Llanfaethlu; the lamp has a notch in the
top edge in which the wick rested.

An interesting account is printed in *Archæologia Cam-
brensis* * of the exploration of Moel Trigarn by the Rev. S.
Baring Gould, M A., Mr. Robert Burnard, F.S A, and the
Rev Irvine K. Anderson.

In the excavation of these hut sites three stone lamps similar
to the one shown were found, together with beads, spindle,
whorls, and cup-like stones were found by Sir Francis Tress
Barry in the Brochs at Keiss Bay, Caithness, and were
associated with spindle-whorls, rubbers, and querns of stone,
together with objects of iron."

Thanks were ordered to be returned for these communications.

* 5th S. xvii. (1900).

Thursday, 20th February, 1902.

J. T. MICKLETHWAITE, Esq., Vice-President, in the Chair.

The following gifts were announced, and thanks for the same ordered to be returned to the donors

From Lionel H. Cust, Esq , M A , F S A.

1. Memoirs of James Lackington 8vo   London, 1794
2. Treatise on the Ecclesiastical Architecture of England.   By John Milner. 8vo   London, 1811.
3. Letters on Gothic Architecture. By Rev. John Haggitt 8vo   Cambridge, 1813.
4. Essays on Gothic Architecture. By Rev. T. Warton, etc.   3rd Edition. 8vo. London, 1808.
5. Ecclesiastical Antiquities of France. By Rev. G D Whittington 8vo London, 1811
6. Annales of England   By Francis Godwin, Bishop of Hereford   Folio. London, 1630
7. Osservazioni sopra alcuni frammenti di vasi antichi di vetro ornati di figure trovati ne cimiteri di Roma. By Filippo Buonarruoti. Folio. Florence, 1716.
8. Notes relative to the manor of Myton. By J Travis-Cook. 8vo. Hull, 1890.

From C. J Prætorius, Esq , F.S A. .—Three Lantern Slides of stone-lined Graves at Llanfaethlu, Anglesey

A special vote of thanks was accorded to Mr. Cust for his gift to the Library.

Walter Jonathan Andrew, Esq., was admitted Fellow.

Notice was given of a Ballot for the election of Fellows on Thursday, 6th March, and a list of candidates to be balloted for was read.

C. E. KEYSER, Esq., M A., F.S.A., read the following notes on some wall-paintings lately discovered at Rothamstead Manor, Herts .

"Rothamsted Manor House is situate in the parish of Harpenden, the gates opening on to the high road from London to Bedford It was formerly within the important parish of Wheathamstead, and in early times was known as Wrackhamstead. Some account of its early owners is given by the various historians for Hertfordshire, whence we learn that in the middle of the fifteenth century it was in the posses-

sion of the Cressys, in the following century it was in the hands
of William Cressy, who died in 1558, from whom it came to
his son Edward Cressy, who left issue an only daughter
Elizabeth, who married Edmund Bardolf, and conveyed the
manor to him.   About the year 1640 it passed by sale to
John Wittewronge, who was created a baronet in 1662, and
from him is descended Sir Charles Bennet Lawes, Baronet,
the present owner

The house itself is of considerable interest.   It is alleged to
have been built about 1470, and to have been materially
altered by Sir John Wittewronge about 170 years later, but
there can be no doubt that there was a substantial reconstruction in the middle of the sixteenth century, and that a
good deal of that work still remains in the hall, dining-room,
fine stacks of chimneys, etc.   The whole house, which is built
of brick, has been carefully restored by its present owner, and
presents a pleasing and old-fashioned appearance.   There is a
large amount of antique furniture, and a curious relic is preserved here, viz. a doll's house of early seventeenth century
date, with the massive mantelpieces and other characteristics
of the mansions of that period

During the restoration which has been recently progressing,
some remains of painting have been found, in addition to that
portion which is the special subject of this paper   On the
staircase and in the passage on the first floor is an imitation
bannister rail with angle posts and ball terminations, probably
of the seventeenth century period.   In the hall, on the face of
the partition dividing it from the dining-room, were apparently
a series of large figures of renaissance character, which were
very faint.   One of these had his arms stretched out, and a
curious sort of brooch or pendant hanging from each.   There
is also a merman with two tails, which he holds in either
hand, and part of an archer.   These paintings could not be
preserved, but careful tracings have been taken by Mr. Victor
T. Hodgson, and were exhibited during the reading of this
paper.

The dining-room has been panelled and perhaps enlarged
in the early part of the seventeenth century.   On one of the
panels has been scratched a date, 1632.   On the plaster wall
above one of the fireplaces can be made out an upper cornice
with fruit, apples, and grapes, and part of a glass vase.

The principal painting is on the opposite side, on the partition wall dividing this room from the hall.   It was found
during some repairs to the panelling, and will still be protected by the panelling, which has been fixed on a hinge, so
that it can be swung out from the wall for the exhibition of

WALL-PAINTING AT ROTHAMSTEAD MANOR, HERTS.

the picture. It occupies one compartment between the door
and the window, and it is probable that the subject was
continued right up to the window, and possible that there
may be or have been more paintings on the other side of the
door, and perhaps also on the other walls of the room. The
width of the compartment is about 7 feet 5 inches, and the
subject has been delineated on a fine surface of plaster laid
over a considerable thickness of hard mortar, and the solid
oak upright which form the main support of the wall.

On the lower portion, coloured in various shades of brown,
is some imitation panelling with three, and parts of two
more, semicircular arched divisions These have a bold shell
pattern in the head, and rest on small engaged shafts attached
to imitation Corinthian columns with rich capitals, which
support the cornice or entablature above. These columns
stand on pedestals, on each of which is depicted a lion's head.
Within each panel is a large animal, namely on the half panel
nearest the window part of a panther, on the next a bear,
on the next a hound with long ears sitting up on its
haunches, on the next a cat lying down, and on the furthest
part of an animal with a long tail. On the lower part of the
shell canopy of the panel above the cat is represented a
brooch or pendant similar to those on the arms of the monster
already mentioned. The height of this part of the work is
4 feet 9 inches, and of the cornice or entablature, which
forms a border to the main picture, about 7 inches more.

This is about 2 feet 8 inches in height, and is carried up to
the ceiling. The ground work is white. In the foreground
is a large bare hill. On either side at the back is a green hill
with hedgerows and part of a town, and on the summit of the
higher one a beacon or windmill. On the slope of the main
hill is shown a large square formation of a yellowish colour,
which at first sight would appear to be a stockade, but on
comparison with a print of an early picture of this date of a
somewhat similar scene, illustrated in Vertue's *Historical
Prints*, No. 8, and representing the 'Battle Array of Carberry
Hill, 1567,' there is no doubt that here are portrayed the
pikes of a battalion of infantry advancing from behind the
hill. In the foreground on the side towards the window are
five cannons. Four have just been fired, and are pouring
forth dense clouds of smoke; the gunners, a basket of shot,
four powder kegs, etc, being introduced. Behind them, and
painted on the upright oak beam, is a knight on horseback,
holding a halbert, with open vizor, armour on his body, but
not protecting his legs. His horse is brown, of rather a heavy
type, and with black trappings. Behind him is a procession

of twelve horsemen, all carrying lances and pennons (22 lances and pennons are shown), and all in armour similar to that of their leader, and with the same black trappings to their horses, which are coloured white, grey, and brown, and all are of the same character as that of their general. Behind them, and on a lower level, is another knight galloping up to join the others. The back only of his helmet is seen, and seems to differ from and to be a later type than the others. All the horsemen are delineated in black and white, and the lances are of the tilting kind with projection on the handle to protect the hand, probably intended to denote their knightly rank. The lower part of this portion of the picture is painted a pale red, the hedges being in green. The horses and their riders are about 9 inches in length and height. The date of the painting appears to be early in the second half of the sixteenth century.

It is presumed that the picture is intended to portray some real battle scene, in which the owner of the house took a prominent part. A suggestion has been tendered that it may represent the battle of Flodden Field, at which one of the Cressys is supposed to have been present, but of this it is feared there is no corroborative evidence. The treatment is in many respects similar to that of the picture of the Battle Array of Carberry Hill, to which reference has already been made, and it is a good example of the paintings of the time of Elizabeth and James I., which are from time to time being brought to light in our domestic buildings. A few have been noted in this neighbourhood, viz. at the Manor House, Little Gaddesden, where on a panel was a representation of the arrest of the Princess Elizabeth in 1554, illustrated in Cussans's *History of Hertfordshire*.* A great deal of decoration also remains on the walls of the hall of the same house. In the dressing-room attached to the tennis-court at Hatfield House, being part of the earlier buildings, is a large subject all round the walls, probably representing a lion hunt with various gentlemen on horseback, etc., of about this same period. At Monken Hadley, near Barnet, in an old house called 'Cockfosters,' is a hunting scene, with perhaps a portrait of James I., and therefore of later date. These and many other examples which could be adduced from other parts of England tend to demonstrate the common practice of decorating the walls, before the system of panelling was generally adopted, in the principal apartments of our more important domestic buildings.

* Vol. iii. 138.

Proc. 2nd S. Vol. XIX.

FEAD MANOR, HERTS.

As has been already suggested, the picture at Rothamsted was probably executed early in the reign of Queen Elizabeth, and may be regarded as an interesting example of wall painting of that somewhat unartistic period."

W. J. KAYE, jun., Esq., F S A., read the following notes on an inscription in Scandinavian runes found near Harrogate:

"In July, 1901, in the construction of their new reservoirs at Scargill, near Beckwithshaw, situate some six miles south-west of Harrogate, the Harrogate Corporation found it necessary to remove two tumuli formerly reputed to be British barrows, and known locally as 'Pippin Castle'; the smaller one being conical in shape, the larger one long and oval. The former measured about 15 feet in diameter at the base and about 15 feet in height; the latter about 90 feet in length (east to west) and 50 feet in breadth, and varied in height from about 15 feet to 20 feet, sloping upwards towards the eastern end.

Lying on the north-west side of the small mound I found the stone, with the inscription uppermost, of which a photograph is appended.

The photograph has been sent to the Rev. Canon Fowler, D.C.L., F.S.A., of Durham, and to Mr. P. M. C. Kermode, of Ramsay, I.O.M, who has recently made many discoveries of Runic inscriptions in that neighbourhood. They read it:

ᛁᚢᚾᚷ

SUNA (? gen. pl of SUNR), showing it to be a fragmentary inscription in Scandinavian runes of the eleventh or twelfth century.

Mr. Kermode writes · ' Clearly they are Scandinavian runes of the eleventh or twelfth century, similar to those we have in the Isle of Man. I do not remember to have seen the U formed as in this instance. Usually the left stroke (as you look at it) is the straight stem-line, the other having a bow-form.' He goes on to suggest that if there be no indication of the first stroke being prolonged downwards below the level of the \ (s), it might be a ᛏ (T), which does not appear improbable. In that case he thinks it may be a contraction such as are often met with in the Isle of Man and elsewhere, e g., SUR=SUNR, KRS=KRUS, THNA=THENA, THSAR=THESSAR. If the second character were read as a T, such a phrase is suggested as ST(E)NA BRU=stone bridges, or it might be part of a name in STEIN as THORSTEIN. No other stone could be found near bearing any runes.

Beside a quantity of glazed pottery, in fragments, of a later date, and numerous marks of fire, several beams of oak were found in the mounds, together with some objects of iron (which latter objects Sir J Evans thinks may be coeval with the inscription)   These things include an axe-head (8¼ in in height, 4 in across the top, 5¾ in across the lower part of the blade, and 2¾ in in the narrowest part), two small horse-shoes, and the blade of a large saw about four feet in length, and in shape resembling the modern Swedish ones.   In addition three small flints and the *humerus* of a small ox were discovered "

The following Report on the present state of the Roman station of *Clausentum* at Bitterne, near Southampton, was read :

' 14th May, 1901.

The site of the Roman station in question is on a peninsula formed by two bends of the river Itchen about two miles above the junction of that river with the Southampton Water. Across this peninsula at its broadest part, which is towards the east, runs a wide fosse from bend to bend of the river, cutting off a triangular area roughly 27½ acres in extent, the point of which is to the west, the base being to the east.   In a somewhat parallel direction to this trench, but 800 feet west of it, another trench crosses the area parting off the end of the triangle, and forming with the river on the other two sides a second enclosure   It is this smaller enclosure which is the station proper, and its triangular area may be roughly estimated at 6½ acres.   Towards the river it is margined by a wide foreshore, and was apparently fortified on all three sides by a wall, the trench last mentioned running in front of the landward wall   Of the walls there appear to be now no visible remains, but such remains, and also those of bastions, probably one at each angle, are mentioned by Sir Henry Englefield in his work entitled *A Walk round Southampton*, published at the beginning of the nineteenth century.

It seems that this second enclosure, which contains Bitterne Manor House and grounds, will not be touched for another two years, but that the space between the eastern line of the Roman station and the fosse across the base of the peninsula will be taken in hand first   Trial holes have been dug in it at different places.   None of these which had been dug in the ground south of the modern road which traverses the site from west to east showed, as far as I and Mr Hope, who accompanied me, could see, any signs of Roman material.   The vegetable soil was shallow, and beneath it lay river shingle ;

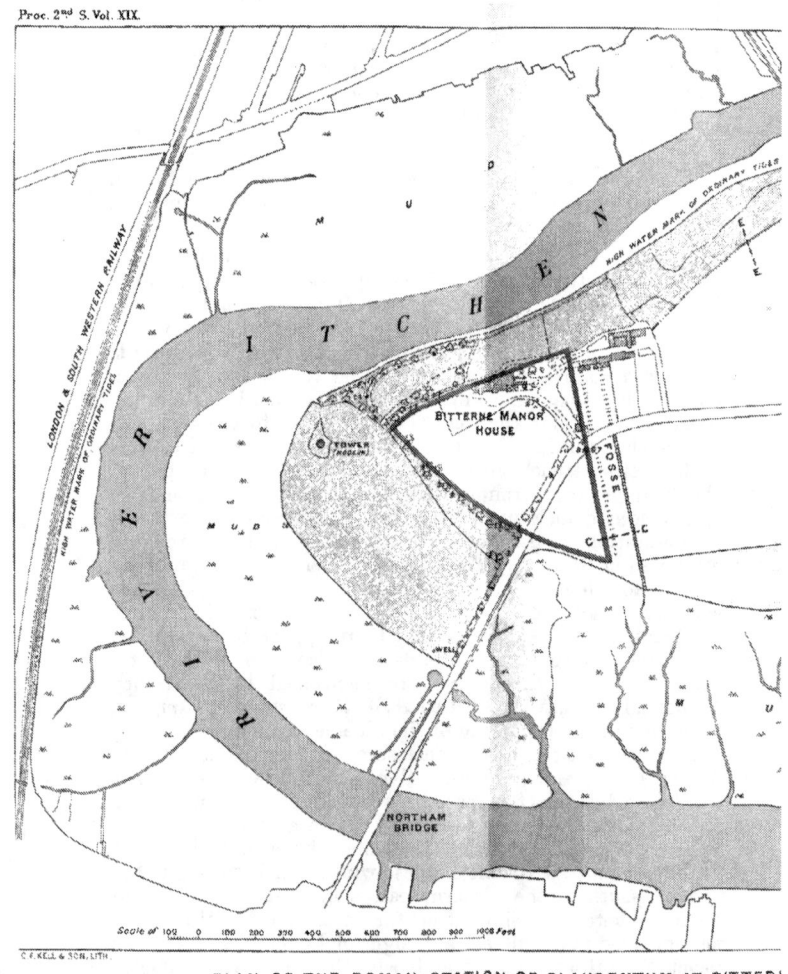

PLAN OF THE ROMAN STATION OF <u>CLAUSENTUM</u> AT BITTERI

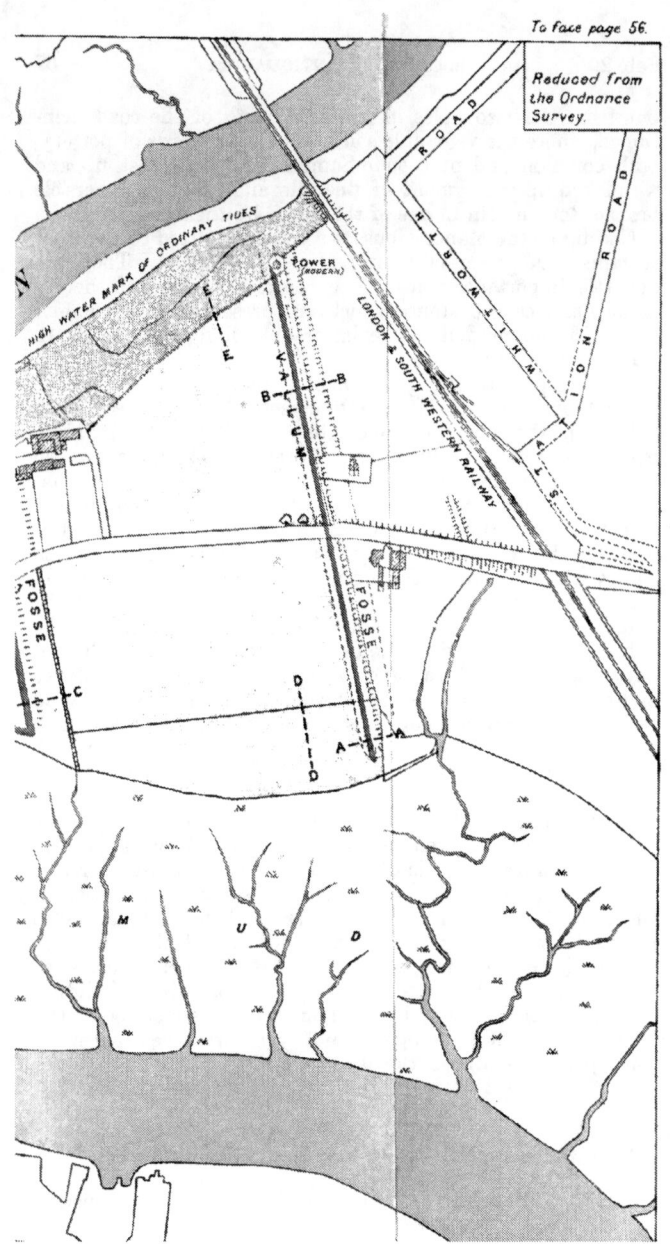

To face page 56.

Reduced from
the Ordnance
Survey.

but from the two holes in the area north of the road mentioned, where the vegetable soil was deeper, shards of pottery,
both common and of pseudo-Samian, had been cast up, and
we picked up a fragment of flue tile and an undecipherable
bronze Roman coin in one of the heaps by them.

Calling at the Manor House, we were permitted to see what
remains were preserved there and in the grounds. These are
of little importance with the exception of some of the inscribed and carved stones which are preserved in a summer
house in the garden. The latter are all figured in Sir H.
Englefield's work.

With respect to the question of excavation on the site, it
seemed both to Mr. Hope and myself that there are some
points in the portion immediately threatened by building
operations which would repay exploration. These are marked
A, B, C, D, E on the accompanying plan. I would submit that
it would be advisable by sections at the spots so marked to
ascertain the nature of the outer defence, and also to find if
possible the remains of the south-east corner of the station
wall, perhaps at where there might have been a bastion.

As the new streets and houses will completely efface the
outer fosse at some not distant period, the examination of the
points marked should be the first to be undertaken. Whether
any trenching of the area between the outer line of defence
and the station wall west of it would repay the trouble and
expense incurred in doing it, is a matter of some doubt, but at
least it might be recommended that someone should watch
the building operations on the site when they are fairly
undertaken.

As to the area of the station proper, when the time came
for it, it might be well worth excavation. Only the portion
of the site more immediately threatened is dealt with here.

In the appended plan the red lines show the direction of
the outer defence and the lines of the walls of the station, so
far as they can be conjectured. The pink tint marks the
width of the foreshore on the two sides of the enclosure next
the river, and the dotted area is that on which building
operations have already been commenced. As mentioned, the
area of the station proper is not yet threatened, except a
small portion at the south-east corner.

GEORGE E. FOX."

W. DALE, Esq., F.S.A., also read the following Report·

"On the 14th of last May the site of Clausentum was visited

by Mr. W. H. St. John Hope and Mr. George E. Fox, and a
report made of its condition.

The recommendations made in this Report were intended
for any committee who should decide to explore the ground
before it was built over, but I am not aware that anything
was done in the direction of forming one until the autumn,
when the Treasurer of our Society wrote me on the subject,
and said that the work could only be done by a local committee, which he asked me, if possible, to get together, and
added that £20 had been voted by the Society, provided it
could be laid out to advantage.

But this time the new roads had nearly been made, and I
had for some time been watching the progress of the work on
my own account. It seemed to me that the cutting of the
roads, in many places as much as 3 feet deep, had sampled
the ground as well as any trial trenches could have done, and
the results were so small that it would not be worth while at
present to form a committee or expend any money. This
opinion was shared by the Rev. G. W. Minns, F.S A , and
Mr. W. E Darwin, whom I consulted.

Except near the inner fosse the soil is thin and the roads
go down into the subsoil of river gravel. Occasionally a
lump or two of Bembridge limestone was turned out and a
few shards of pottery. While the roads were being made
the remains of the vallum within the outer fosse were
removed and carted away to metal the roads. This vallum
was partly destroyed in 1863 by the owner of Bitterne
Manor House Nothing whatever was found in these heaps.

In laying out the roads several of the points where trial
digging were recommended to be made were nearly touched.
I have roughly indicated these roads on the plan prepared by
Mr. Fox (my own copy, that is). The road between the railway and outer defences passes through the fosse near to the
modern tower at the north-east corner some 100 yards north
of B B. There was no trace of any wall although the road
was here cut unusually deep The road then skirts the
northern foreshore coming very close to the point E C Two
parallel roads running north and south join this road at the
foreshore. At the end of the road nearest the Manor House
considerable quantities of Bembridge limestone were found,
and two blocks remain *in situ* about 5 feet apart. This is
the only approach to masonry that I have seen, and may be
the remains of a wall. The points A A and D D remains
untouched. There are two curved roads made in the area
south of the modern highway which cross the inner fosse, and

a causeway has been made over it in two places. The most southern of these comes very near the point c c in plan, but does not quite reach the south-east corner of the triangular area where a bastion was to be looked for. In digging this road a small pot was found of black ware covered with a lid. It contained nothing but earth.

A row of houses has already been built facing the highway, in the area between the outer and inner fosse on the south side   The soil here was black and deep, and in digging the foundations of these houses most of the things shown were found, including nearly all the small bronze objects and most of the coins   There were also portions of fine tile of brick and limestone, but nowhere have I seen any traces of the foundations of buildings. Pottery occurred very frequently, mostly of a common character.   There was, however, an abundance of Aretine or pseudo-Samian ware. Sir Henry Englefield, it will be remembered, mentions how plentifully this ware is found, and he gives a list of potters' names stamped upon the pieces. Several of the fragments on the table have names upon them, but not any of those given by Englefield.

A number of scattered coins have been found, amongst them a denarius of Caligula and Augustus, which I am told is not a common coin. Nearly all are badly preserved and a lot undecipherable. I have purchased all the coins found in the hope of getting more of those of Carausius and Allectus. It is, I believe, thought that a mint of these emperors existed at Clausentum, although it is doubtful if the C found on their coins may not refer to Camulodunum. I showed the coins of Allectus found lately at Clausentum to Sir John Evans at Winchester, in September, and in his Lecture on Coins at the Alfred Millenary he said he was inclined to give Clausentum the benefit of the doubt, but hoped more coins might be found there of this emperor.

The non-Roman objects found were a penny of Henry III. (made in London, moneyer's name Renaud), a portion of a neolithic implement, and in digging a deep hole for gravel a paleolithic implement was turned out. In the area between the outer and inner fosse was an interment of the Bronze Age, marked by a small cinerary urn (broken *in situ*) surrounded by big stones.

In conclusion, I am of opinion that it is not worth while at present to do anything more than watch the ground. By-and-by, when the area around the Manor House is touched, it may be desirable to take more united action."

SIR HENRY H. HOWORTH, K.C.I.E., D.C.L., F.R S, F.S.A., exhibited two small panel paintings of equestrian portraits of the Emperor Charles V. and King Henry III. of France, said to be by Janet.

Another of the series, a portrait of Fiancis I., is illustrated in vol. ii of Shaw's *Dresses and Decorations of the Middle Ages.*

Thanks were ordered to be returned for these communications and exhibitions.

Thursday, 27th February, 1902.

Viscount DILLON, President, in the Chair.

Notice was again given of a Ballot for the election of Fellows on Thursday, 6th March, and a list of candidates to be balloted for was read.

CHARLES H. READ, Esq., Secretary, read a paper on a Saracenic glass vessel of the fourteenth century, which he also exhibited.

Mr. Read's paper will be printed in *Archaeologia.*

Mr. READ also exhibited a number of armorial pendants, etc., chiefly foreign, of medieval date.

W. H. ST. JOHN HOPE, Esq., M.A., Assistant Secretary, read the following notes on a third Great Seal of King Stephen:

"Of all antiquarian discoveries, one of the most unlikely at this time of day would seem to be the finding of an unknown great seal of one of our kings

The documents to which the great seals are appended are both numerous and widely distributed, and the seals themselves have been fully dealt with by Sandford, Willis, Birch, Wyon, and other writers.

I have nevertheless the honour of exhibiting and presenting to the Society this evening casts of a great seal of King Stephen of which no other impression seems to have been noticed.

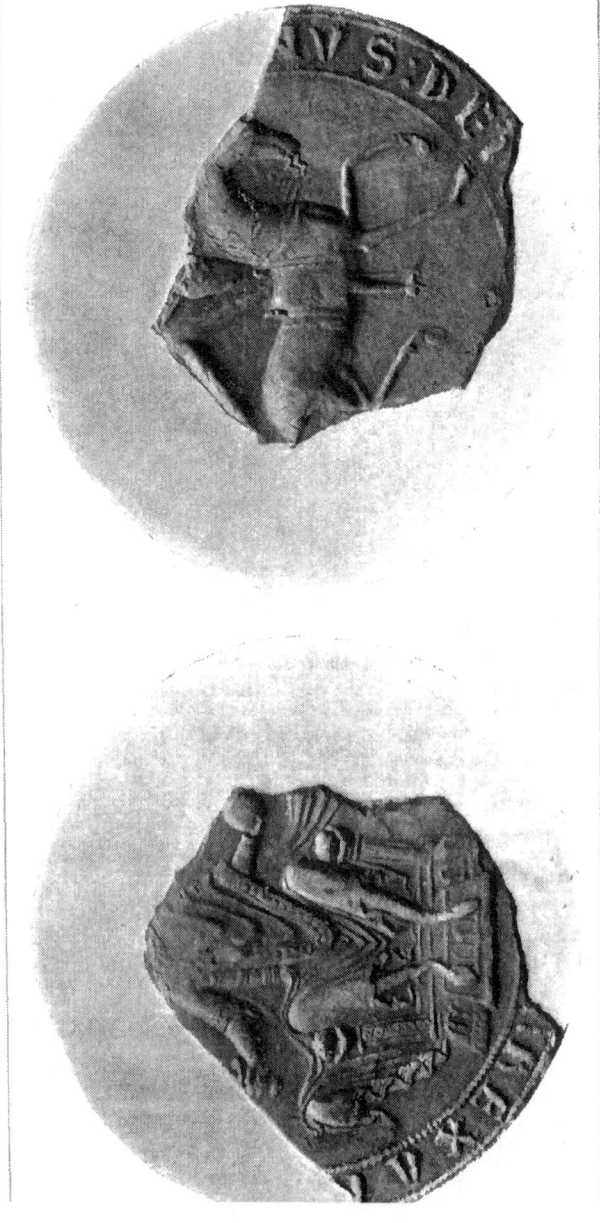

THIRD GREAT SEAL OF KING STEPHEN.

Some years ago, while living at Rochester, I found among the documents of the Benedictine Priory which have descended to the Dean and Chapter, a charter of King Stephen to which was appended a large fragment of the great seal. I was so struck by the unusual sharpness of what was left that I made casts of the seal for my own collection. It was not until some time after that, on comparing the condition of these casts with those of Stephen's seals in the Society's collection, I was astonished to find mine represented an entirely different seal.

In Messrs. Wyon's work on the Great Seals of England, published in 1887, which is the latest written on the subject, two seals of Stephen are described: the first as being in use from probably 1135 to 1141, the second, probably from 1143 to 1154; the king's imprisonment and other troubles intervening. These seals are similar in design, the obverse having a seated figure of the king, crowned, and holding the sword and globe with the cross and dove; the reverse, the king armed and on horseback, holding in the one seal a sword, in the other a lance and pennon, in addition to his shield. The legends are also the same; on the obverses:

✠ STEPHANVS DEI GRATIA REX ANGLORVM ;

on the reverses:

✠ STEPHANVS DEI GRATIA DVX NORMANNORVM

The seals vary, however, somewhat in size, the earlier being $3\frac{1}{4}$ inches and the later $3\frac{1}{8}$ inches in diameter. The Rochester impression is too broken to give its exact diameter, but it seems to have been as nearly as possible $3\frac{1}{2}$ inches. The obverse bears the remains of the seated figure of the king, holding as before the sword and globe, and the legend was evidently when complete:

[+ STEPHANVS DEI GRATIA]: REX ANGLORVM]

The reverse has the equestrian figure of the king, who clearly held a sword, but of the legend there remains only the letters

· · · · NVS : DEI · · · ·

The design of the seal is so similar to that of the others that at first sight no particular difference is observable, but a more careful comparison soon makes it evident that this is a third seal, apparently by the same engraver as the others.

The next question that arises is, when and why was this seal used ?

The document to which it is appended is what the late Mr Henry Bradshaw, F.S.A., would have called an official duplicate, and I well remember his pointing out to me that such were always written on parchment, with the seal in white or yellow wax appended by a parchment tag or semi-detached strip, while the actual charter was always on vellum, and had the great seal in green wax appended by silken cords

The document is a charter of confirmation to the church of St Andrew at Rochester of all manors, lands, churches, etc. which it hitherto had possessed. It unfortunately does not state whence it was issued or on what date, but concludes :

'Et hanc confirmationem meam pro anima patris mei et matris mee et pro anima mea et uxoris mee et omnium parentum meorum stabilio et stabilitate signi sancte crucis domini nostri jhesu propria manu mea et sigillo meo consigno.'

Below this writing the document is divided into three strips. The central one has "*Signum stephani regis*," written above a cross, and at the bottom the impression of the great seal, in yellowish or natural-coloured wax. The dexter strip has

> *Signum henrici Wintoniensis episcopi*
> *Signum algari episcopi de sancto laudo*
> *Signum adelulfi episcopi de carleolo*
> *Signum Rogeri de fiscano*

and the sinister

> *Signum matildis regine*
> *Signum Waleranni comitis de mellent*
> *Signum hugonis bigot*

in each case accompanied by the sign of the cross

The dates of the signatories unfortunately do not give us a closer limit than fifteen years, but there are other reasons for dating the document pretty exactly.

It will be noticed in the first place that Hugh Bigot is simply so described Now shortly before February, 1140-1, the earldom of Norfolk had been conferred upon him. We should therefore have expected to find him described as such, just as Waleran is called Count of Meulan, were the charter after that date. *Prima facie* then, it is earlier. I think it may be also assumed that a mere charter of confirmation, such as this is, is more likely to have been issued early than later in the reign.

In the next place, Mr. J. H. Round has printed in his *Calendar of Documents preserved in France, illustrative of the History of Great Britain and Ireland,* of which vol. i., covering the years 918-1206, was published in 1899, over a dozen charters of King Stephen   Among them are several that were granted in 1137, the one year of his reign when Stephen was absent in Normandy.   Three issued at Evreux are witnessed by the Bishop of Carlisle and Waleran count of Meulan *   Another dated at Pont Audemer is witnessed by Waleran and Hugh Bigot.†   One issued from Rouen includes among the witnesses Queen Matilda, Henry bishop of Winchester, Waleran count of Meulan, and Roger of Fécamp, or four out of the seven in the Rochester charter ; ‡ and lastly a charter issued from Lyons-sur-Font is witnessed among others by Queen Matilda, Bishop Adelolf of Carlisle, and Waleran count of Meulan.§

As this conjunction of names is not found in any of the charters issued in England which are given by Mr. Round, and only in those granted while the king was in Normandy, it seems reasonable to infer that the Rochester charter was issued in ·1137.   Further, since all the known charters of Stephen issued in this country have appended to them Seals I. and II., this Seal III. would seem to have been made for use in Normandy.

The question of the dates of Seals I. and II., and the examples of them known, have been fully dealt with by Mr. Walter de Gray Birch in a paper printed in the *Transactions of the Royal Society of Literature"* ‖

Mr. HOPE also read the following note on the first Great Seal of King Henry III. :

"It is well known that for the first three years of his reign the boy King Henry III. was under the guardianship of William Marshall, earl of Pembroke.   We also know from the Patent and Close Rolls that during this period there was no great seal in use, but the patents conclude :

' Because we have no seal we have caused these letters patent to be sealed with the seal of our faithful William Marshall, earl of Pembroke.'

* *Op. cit.* 99, 100
† *Op. cit.* 198.
‡ *Op. cit* 373
§ *Op cit.* 518
‖ N S xi.

Why there was no seal is somewhat of a puzzle
Richard II., who succeeded his father when he was only
11 years old, was using his seal, with the simple alteration of
the name *Edwardus* into *Ricardus*, within six weeks of his
accession. Why then should not a boy of nine have done
the same ? It had occurred to me that the reason was that
John's great seal had been lost when his baggage train was
overwhelmed and destroyed when crossing the Wellstream
estuary on the 12th or 13th of October, 1216, but there are
charters entered on both the Patent and Close Rolls, dated the
15th, 16th, 17th, and 18th of that month, or up to the day of
his death on the 19th, and none of these documents mentions
the loss of the great seal.

When Henry III.'s great seal first came into use is fixed by
an entry in the Close Roll for the third year of his reign,
between documents dated 2nd November and 5th November,
1218 :

Hic incepit sigillum domini Regis currere.

This fact is of course perfectly well known, but what, so
far as I am aware, seems to have been overlooked, is that on
the same roll are entries giving the cost of the making of the
new seal, and what is of equal interest, the name of the maker.

The first of the entries is dated 7th November, 1218, and
directs the payment to Walter the goldsmith, *qui fecit
sigillum nostrum*, 'of 5 marks for the silver of our seal
weighing 5 marks, and for the work let him so return his
account as he ought rightly to be content.' *

A month later, on 2nd December, occurs a second entry,
directing the payment ' from our treasury to Walter de Ripa
the goldsmith of 40s in payment of the work of our seal
which he has made.' †

As the annual pay of a royal chaplain at this time was
30s. 5d., or a penny a day, a sum now represented by a curate's
salary of from £120 to £150, the 40s. paid for the workmanship of the seal would represent from £160 to £200 at the
present day.

Of impressions of Walter de Ripa's beautiful seal there are
many examples known, and it is interesting to note its artistic
superiority both to John's seal, which preceded it, and Henry's
second seal, which succeeded it in 1259.

The names of the engravers of medieval seals are so little
known, that I have thought it worth while to put on record, if

* Close Roll, 3 Henry III., pt. ii. m. 4.
† Close Roll, 3 Henry III , pt. ii. m 13.

no one has been befoie me, the name of an engraver whose work can certainly be identified."

Thanks weie ordered to be returned for these communications and exhibitions.

Thursday, 6th March, 1902.

Viscount DILLON, President, in the Chair.

The following gifts were announced, and thanks for the same ordered to be returned to the donors :

From Rev. F St John Thackeray, M A , F S A :—The Bodley Head Anthologies. Florilegium Latinum. Translations into Latin verse. Victorian Poets. Vol. II. 8vo London. n.d.

From the Author —The Ancient Crosses of Lancashire. 2 Parts By Henry Taylor F.S.A. 8vo. Manchester, 1899-1901.

From the Historical and Antiquarian Society of Basle ·—Basler Zeitschrift fur Geschichte und Altertumskunde 1 Band, 1 Heft. 8vo Basel, 1901

From the Author ·—The Abbey of St. Mary in Furness, Lancashire. By W. H St John Hope. M A. Large paper copy, with additional illustrations. 4to. Kendal, 1902.

From W. H. Richardson, Esq , M A , F S A :—A Letter to the Right Hon. the Earl of Aberdeen, K T , President of the Society of Antiquaries, on the expediency of attaching a Museum of Antiquities to that Institution. 8vo. London, 1828

This being an evening appointed for the election of Fellows no papers were read.

A. HIGGINS, Esq , F S A., exhibited (i.) a series of Italian plaquettes, chiefly of the fifteenth century, from the collection of the late Mr. Henry Vaughan, F.S.A. ; and (ii.) an illuminated copy of the Koran written at Medinah in the year 964 (=1555 A.D.).

L. B. PHILLIPS, Esq., F.S.A, exhibited two Tickets of Admission to (a) Westminster Abbey and (b) to the Banquet in Westminster Hall, on the occasion of the Coronation of George IV. in 1821.

PHILIP NORMAN, Esq., Treasurer, exhibited a wood carving of a sleeping infant.

W. BRUCE BANNERMAN, Esq., F.S.A., exhibited and presented an original impression of the Great Seal of George III. for Scotland.

Thanks were ordered to be returned for these exhibitions and to Mr. Bannerman for his gift to the Society's Collection of Seals.

The Ballot opened at 8.45 p.m. and closed at 9.30 p.m., when the following were declared duly elected Fellows of the Society:—

> Alfred Cart de Lafontaine, Esq.
> Paul Bevan, Esq., M.A.
> Robert Holmes Edleston, Esq.
> George Crafter Croft, Esq.
> Sir Benjamin Vincent Sellon Brodie, bt., M.A.
> Rev. William Kyle Westwood Chafy, D.D.
> Wilson Crewdson, Esq., M.A.
> Herbert George Radford, Esq.
> Charles Steele Murchison Bompas, Esq.
> Prince Frederick Duleep Singh, M.A.
> Lawrence Weaver, Esq.
> Hamon le Strange, Esq., M.A.

Thursday, 13th March, 1902.

Viscount DILLON, President, in the Chair.

The following gifts were announced, and thanks for the same ordered to be returned to the donors:

From the Author :—A Note on the Arms of Colchester and Nottingham. By W. H. St. John Hope, M.A. 8vo. London, 1902.

From R D. Darbishire, Esq., F S.A

1. Blackie. J. S   The Scottish Highlanders and their Land Laws. 8vo.
   London, 1885.

2. Report on the Exploration of Brixham Cave.   4to.   London, 1872

3. Brown, P. H.   Early Travellers in Scotland   8vo.   Edinburgh, 1891

4. Bush, G. On the Ancient or Quaternary Fauna of Gibraltar. 4to.
   London, 1876

5. Chambers, R   Domestic Annals of Scotland   2 vols 8vo. Edinburgh,
   1858.

6. Cunningham, Alexander   The Stûpa of Bharut. 4to   London, 1877.

7. Dalman, F.   Mapa topográfico de Granada, 1796.

8 Dennistoun, James. Memoirs of Sir Robert Strange   2 vols. London,
   1855.

9. Ferguson, Sir Samuel.   Ogham Inscriptions in Ireland. Wales, and
   Scotland   8vo. Edinburgh, 1887

10 Ferry, H de   Le Maconnais prehistorique   4to.   Paris, 1870

11. Graham, H. G.   The Social Life of Scotland.   2 vols.   8vo.   London,
    1899.

12 Healy, J. Ireland's Ancient Schools and Scholars.   8vo.   Dublin,
   1890.

13 Innes, Thomas   A Critical Essay on the Ancient Inhabitants of the
   Northern parts of Britain or Scotland.   8vo. Edinburgh, 1885.

14. Llwyd, R. The History of Wales. 8vo. Shrewsbury, 1832.

15. Macculloch, J   The Highlands and Western Islands of Scotland
    4 vols. 8vo   London, 1821.

16. M'Lauchlan, Thomas.   The Dean of Lismore's Book   8vo.   Edin-
    burgh, 1862.

17. Madsen, A P.   Afbildninger af Danske Oldsager og Mindesmærker.
    Broncealderen. 4to. Copenhagen, 1872

18. Madsen, A. P   Afbildninger af Danske Oldsager og Mindesmærker.
    Broncealderen II. 4to. Copenhagen, 1876.

19 Madsen, A. P. Afbildninger af Danske Oldsager og Mindesmærker.
   Steenalderen. 4to. Copenhagen, 1868.

20 O'Conor, W. A   History of the Irish People. 8vo. London, 1886-7.

21. O'Curry, Eugene   Lectures on the Manuscript Materials of Ancient
    Irish History. 8vo. Dublin, 1861.

22 O'Curry, Eugene   On the Manners and Customs of the Ancient Irish
   3 vols. 8vo   London, 1873.

23. O'Rourke, T   The History of Sligo. 2 vols. 8vo. Dublin. n.d.

24. Ossian   The Poems of Ossian   2 vols. 8vo. Edinburgh, 1870

25. Ouvaroff, Count. Étude sur les peuples primitifs de la Russie. 4to. St Petersburg, 1875.

26. Catalogue de l'exposition archéologique du Département de la Savoie. (Paris Exhibition, 1878). 4to Paris, 1878.

27. Perrin, A. Étude préhistorique sur la Savoie. 4to. Chambery, 1869.

28. Perrin, A. Étude préhistorique sur la Savoie 8vo Paris, 1870.

29. Probert, W. The ancient laws of Cambria. 8vo. London, 1823.

30. Rhys, J. Lectures on the Origin and Growth of Religion as illustrated by Celtic Heathendom (The Hibbert Lectures, 1886). 8vo. London, 1888.

31. Rhys, J., and Brynmor Jones, D. The Welsh People. 8vo. London, 1900.

32. Rivière, E. Découverte d'un squelette humain de l'époque paléolithique dans les cavernes des Barussé-Roussé. 4to. Paris, 1873

33. Sehested, N. F B. Archæologiske undersogelser, 1878-81. 4to. Copenhagen, 1884.

34. Stokes, G. T. Ireland and the Celtic Church 8vo. London, 1886.

35. Stokes, G T. Ireland and the Anglo-Norman Church 2nd Edition. 8vo London, 1892.

36. Stokes, Whitley. Three Middle-Irish Homilies on the Lives of Saints Patrick, Brigit, and Columba. Privately printed. 8vo. Calcutta, 1877.

37. Trier. Archaologische Funde in Trier. 4to. Treves. 1873.

38. Turner, D. Account of a Tour in Normandy. 2 vols. 8vo. London, 1820.

39. Walter, F. Das alte Wales. 8vo. Bonn, 1859

40 Zumpft, H. Das Romische Denkmal in Igel. 4to. Coblenz, 1829.

A special vote of thanks was accorded to Mr. R. D. Darbishire for his gift to the Library of this further instalment of books.

The following gentlemen were admitted Fellows:

> Wilson Crewdson, Esq., M A.
> William Brown, Esq., B A.
> George Crafter Croft, Esq.
> Herbert George Radford, Esq.

T. F. KIRBY, Esq., M.A., F.S A , Local Secretary for Hants, read a paper on the Charters of the Manor of Ropley.

Mr. Kirby's paper, which will be printed in *Archaeologia*, was illustrated by an interesting series of the documents referred to, in many cases with fine impressions of the seals appendant.

C. A. MARKHAM, Esq., F.S.A., read the following Report as Local Secretary for Northamptonshire on the Queen's Cross and St. Peter's church, Northampton :

"In making my Report as Local Secretary I wish to deal first with the Queen Eleanor's Cross at Northampton, and in saying a few words on this subject, I do not wish to go back to ancient history, or detail the various restorations of the cross, but simply to record the manner in which it has been recently dealt with.

The question of protecting this beautiful building has frequently been considered by the Justices in Quarter Sessions, by the Architectural Society, and by others in this county   Until recently, however, it has not definitely been known to whom the structure belonged.

Soon after the Ancient Monuments Protection Act 1882 was passed, an attempt was made to obtain an Order in Council declaring that the cross should be deemed an ancient monument.   As, however, it is not of the same character as the other monuments scheduled, the attempt failed.

There were three possible claimants :

1. Her Majesty the Queen, as the direct descendant of the builder of the cross.

2. The Lord of the Manor, as the owner of the waste by the side of the road on which it is built.

3. The County Council, as the guardians of the present main road, and as representing the public who have the right to use the same.

Neither the Crown, nor the Lord of the Manor, nor the Highway Authority has ever exercised any rights over the cross; and, with the exception of the grant made by Quarter Sessions towards the first recorded restoration, no contribution has been made out of public moneys for the protection or maintenance of the cross, the various restorations having been entirely carried out by private subscriptions

The Northamptonshire County Council at their meeting on the 29th April, 1897, appointed a special committee to inquire what steps (if any) could be taken to protect the crosses erected to the memory of Queen Eleanor in the parishes of Hardingston and Geddington, in this county, from further injury.

On the 20th January, 1898, the special committee reported to the County Council that they did not consider it necessary that steps should be taken for the preservation of Geddington Cross, because it stands in the centre of the village, and was repaired as far as was considered necessary by the late Duke of Buccleuch.

The committee considered that the case is different with regard to the Northampton Cross, which stands remote from buildings; they considered that the County Council should acquire the ownership of the same.

The chairman of the committee (Mr. E. P. Monckton, M.P.) therefore communicated with the First Commissioner of Public Works and Buildings; and the Right Hon. A. Akers-Douglas wrote on the 26th July, 1897, that 'Neither the Crown nor the Office of Works has any rights over Queen Eleanor's Cross at Northamption.'

Application was secondly made to the trustees of the Bouverie Estate, on behalf of the Lord of the Manor. The trustees agreed to relinquish all claim to the cross, and by an indenture dated the 29th March, 1900, they gratuitously conveyed to the Northamptonshire County Council all their estate and interest (if any) in the cross, and the ground on which it stands, subject to the County Council undertaking to keep the structure in repair.

The cross is now vested absolutely in the County Council; and by the Ancient Monuments Protection Act 1900 the County Council have full powers to maintain and manage this structure.

The committee appointed by the County Council to take charge of ancient monuments have recently had a scaffold erected round the cross, and it has been carefully examined by Mr. J. A. Gotch, F.S.A., and others of the committee.

The stonework was found in a good state of preservation, and there was no necessity for much to be done beyond the clearing away of the dirt, stones, and vegetable growth which had accumulated from various causes, and the unblocking of the lead pipes which drain the stage on which the statues stand.

The figure of the Queen on the north side was broken many years ago, and fastened together by two vertical cramps The large iron cramp which holds the figure in position at the back was found to be giving way, and the figure is now leaning slightly forward. It has not been thought advisable to move the statue at all, but strong copper cramps have been fixed on each side into the shoulders of the figure, connecting it with the main building, and thus making it safe.

The committee have caused notices in the following terms to be placed near the cross :

'NOTICE.

THE PUBLIC ARE REQUESTED BY THE

NORTHAMPTONSHIRE COUNTY COUNCIL

TO ASSIST IN THE PRESERVATION OF

QUEEN ELEANOR'S CROSS

Erected 1291-4

Any Person found Injuring the Cross will be Prosecuted

By Order '

The committee took the opportunity of the scaffold being erected to have authentic drawings made of the cross, and asked Mr. W. A. Forsyth, A R I.B A., to make these drawings, which include careful elevations of two sides of the erection, together with measured drawings of the whole of the details.

Mr. Forsyth, in the course of six days' measuring and sketching, had much opportunity of studying the detail and construction ; and he also read a good deal of literature of the last century upon the subject, but his views do not agree with the theories of the writers to whom he referred.

By the courtesy of Mr. Forsyth I am enabled to give the results of his observations as an architect. He does not, however, contend that all the difficulties presented to the archæologist have been or are capable of being cleared up, but he considers that much error has crept into the writings on this subject

'The first impression gained of this "Eleanor Cross" is, that it is an orthodox example of a beautiful fourteenth-century design, and that the greater part of what now exists appears to be original work. A closer examination, however, leaves one in considerable doubt not only as to the date assigned to it but also as to the Gothic spirit of the detail, and to the extent of the actual work of the "Decorated" period which remains.

There is practically little doubt that the whole structure above the octagonal ground storey (and probably below) has been taken down and rebuilt, in the course of which it is reasonable to infer that the crestings, which have such a cast-iron feeling in design, were added to the lower and to the two upper stages. The rebuilding has been done with considerable care, but much restoration, sadly lacking the spirit of old work, has been resorted to.

During this latter process a most remarkable system of "piecing" old stonework with new in the decayed parts has been carried out over the whole of the upper stages, and in the gables and tracery of the panels of the octagonal base. I am of opinion that this could not have been undertaken *in situ*, but from the fineness of the joints I can only imagine that most of it was worked on the mason's banker This "piecing" resembles joiner's work more than that of a mason, and has been set in a bright yellowy-brown mortar, and as most of the ordinary jointing is bedded in the same material the theory of rebuilding is somewhat strengthened.

Further, I am strongly of opinion that comparatively little original carved work remains, and it chiefly occurs where this piecing is absent, and bears a true stamp of mediæval craftsmanship. Most of the other carvings are very coarse and lack the spirit and charm of the old work, in addition to having much foreign detail.

Generally speaking the restored mouldings are good, but the lines of the arches and tracery do not possess the subtlety or charm to be found in English "Decorated" work.

A large variety of stones is to be seen throughout the fabric, being oolites of different beds and quarries which have weathered rapidly in the exposed position, many stones in the restored work have been "face-bedded" and have decayed.

The surface water which collects on the top of the octagon stage is drained by means of lead pipes discharging through the centre flowers of carved bosses in the cornice below, there is small doubt to my mind that this is a device of later times, for I do not remember to have seen specimens of fourteenth-century $\frac{3}{4}$-inch or $\frac{1}{2}$-inch heavy lead piping, and moreover the design of the bosses through which the pipes protrude is of an unusual character for this period of stone carving.

The date attributed to the erection of this cross, 1291-4, seems to me open to question, and I understand that much research has disclosed very little that is decisive.

The four sculptured figures of the Queen are exquisite examples of such work, beautiful in execution and composition, and in a fair state of preservation. They have suffered much from wilful damage, hands have been cut off, and the faces injured by stone-throwing, the figure facing the road being more defaced than the others I am again inclined to think that these figures are of later date than 1294, having regard to the character of contemporary examples, the delicate manner of the carving, and the floriated details of the crowns.'

Mr. Beeby Thompson, F.G.S., has also kindly given me his opinion as to the material of which the cross is built, after a careful examination made from the scaffold in January last.

'The cross looks fairly homogeneous in lithological character as seen from the road, but when more minutely examined it becomes evident that much patching and replacing has been done at various times.

It appears pretty certain that the whole structure, with the exception of the figures of Queen Eleanor, was originally built of an oolitic rock known as the "Lincolnshire Oolite," a Lincolnshire limestone, which may have come from Weldon, or Ketton, or Stanion.

At least two varieties of stone were used, though these might have and probably did come from the same quarry.

The finer ornamental portions, which have withstood atmospheric weathering best of all, are of pure, fine-grained oolite; a perfect freestone without traces of bedding. This stone was probably selected by the carver himself.

Other portions of the structure, some of the simpler ornamentation and the panels, consist of a less pure oolitic rock, which may be described as a fine-grained ragstone, being a rock similar to the "Barnack Rag." The oolitic concretions in this are interspersed with water-worn fossils and fragments of fossil shells, and the stone in places weathers in layers inclined at various angles, owing to its having been "false bedded" or "current bedded."

Considerable portions of this ragstone are of a yellowish colour, and this yellowish stone is very inferior in quality, and a source of weakness to the whole structure. The yellow colour is sufficiently pronounced to admit of detection in various parts when standing some distance away, because it weathers too easily for lichens to get a permanent habitation on it.

At some period the cross as a whole was pointed up and generally repaired with a red mortar (by courtesy a cement? decidedly soft, however). Not only the faults in, and joints of, the stones, but numbers of the older names, crosses, or other devices scratched on the monument by reverend (?) hands, are filled up with this red mortar, the figures even are repaired with it. The large panels behind the figures have

been completely covered with this same mortar, where, as I
believe, the badly wearing qualities of the yellow stone
suggested this means of preservation. Why a red mortar
should have been used it is difficult to surmise.

As to the figures of the queen. These consist of a limestone
that I do not know; it is neither oolitic nor shelly, and has
no representative in Northamptonshire. I sent up two small
portions to Jermyn Street Museum, the headquarters of the
Geological Survey, in the hope of getting the stone identified;
but Mr. Horace B. Woodward, F.R.S., wrote that he "cannot
say anything definite about the tiny chips of rock."'

On examining the cross carefully from the scaffold, two
things particularly struck me. First, the perfect drainage of
the structure, each portion being so arranged that no ledge or
cavity is left where water could rest. The stage on which
the figures stand is drained by eight lead pipes, which pass
right through the stone work. Secondly, the delicacy and
beauty of the details of the cross when seen near. The little
grotesque heads of men and animals which are carved below
the crockets of each of the little spires or pinnacles are of
extreme beauty, being instinct with life and motion. The
finials, too, are all different, and are very unequal in execution,
the greater part being excellent, though some are clearly
inferior restorations.

Now as to the discoveries which have recently been made
at the fine old church of St. Peter in Northampton.

This church has been the subject of much speculation to
archæologists; especially as to whether the tower has been
rebuilt, and, if so, at what period this rebuilding took place.

St. Peter's was erected between 1140 and 1160 by Simon
de St. Liz, and consists of a nave and chancel both with
aisles, and a tower, much of the Norman work being late in
style. It was restored in 1850 by Mr., afterward Sir, George
Gilbert Scott.

The tower is certainly the most curious part of the church;
and architects have differed as to the period at which it was
built. Some have thought that the present church was built
as the chancel for a larger church, which was never completed, the tower being erected at the west in a somewhat
disjointed manner, when it was found impossible to do more.
Others have thought that the tower at first stood more to the
west, and that it was rebuilt in the present position at
some period which is unknown, but probably during the
sixteenth century. Certainly foundations of building have

been found to the west of the present church, and it is
probable that these formed the foundations of the first
Norman tower.

This was the opinion of the late Sir Henry Dryden, a most
competent guide in all questions relating to architecture, who
ever maintained that the tower had been rebuilt.

As it at present stands, the tower presents some extraordinary features.

First, there is the very rich Norman arch on the outside of
the west of the tower. This consists of three orders, which
have, however, been all brought level with the face of the
wall, clearly showing that this arch is not in its original
position. Indeed Sir Henry Dryden used to say that he had
never seen such a prank played with a Norman arch in any
other place in the world

Secondly, the three circular buttresses at each corner of
the tower seem to have been built at a time far later than the
eleventh century, the curves at the base having quite lost all
Gothic feeling.

Thirdly, the beautifully carved tower arch of three orders
inside the church does not accurately fit on to the nave
arcade, it is also much too wide for the present tower; in short
it shows every appearance of having been rebuilt.

Last autumn the western face of the tower was repaired
under the direction of Mr. M. H. Holding, A.R.I.B A. The
stones which had perished were taken out carefully one by
one, and replaced by new.

During this process the theory of the rebuilding of the
tower has received signal confirmation. Many of the stones,
at least fifteen, were found to have been elaborately
wrought, the moulded portions being turned inwards, and the
backs of the stones dressed to form the outer face of walling
stones in the rebuilding.

These moulded stones are almost all of the Early English
period, and probably formed parts of arches and other
features. Only four pieces are of the Norman period, a small
octagonal shaft, two pieces of arch moulding, and a small
capital of unusual design. These stones are local, and some
of them show traces of whitewash on the carved portions.
The whole of the Early English fragments apparently came
from some other ecclesiastical building, we know not what.

The fine, large, and bold sections of these recovered stones
point, without doubt, to their having formed part of a building
of large scale and treatment.

The question therefore arises as to which of our fine local
monasteries formed the quarry whence these stones were

procured. St. Andrew's and St. James were near, and both were large and important foundations. There were also two or three small churches near, which were dismantled about the same time, and the chapel in the castle, which was probably a small Norman building, but the stones could hardly have come from any of these.

If we assume that the moulded stones came from one of these monasteries, we can fix the rebuilding of the upper part of the tower at a period soon after the dissolution of the monasteries. Indeed there is reason for saying very soon after that event, for the details of the belfry window have no debased appearance about them, always supposing that they are contemporaneous with the work of the upper stages.

It is to be remembered that while the building of the tower was proceeding with these Early English stones, a quantity of Norman stones were also used, which were identical with the details of the Norman stones already used in the lower stages of the tower.

That there was a plentiful supply of these stones is clear, from the fact that in building the upper stage the masons used three or four small octagonal Norman shafts laid side by side to form the inside stone lintel of one the smaller windows."

Sir J. CHARLES ROBINSON, F.S.A., exhibited a gold and enamelled jewel, in form of a book with silver leaves, on which he communicated the following note:

"I send for exhibition a little gold enamelled jewel in the form of a miniature prayer book with silver leaves, which I have recently acquired. As you will see, it was evidently made for suspension to a lady's girdle, and it is one of a class of art objects of which there are several other examples. This little book, however, is, so far as I am aware, unique in several respects, being in the first place, I think, the earliest known specimen of its kind.

My impression is that its date is not later than about the year 1300 or perhaps some 20 years earlier.

It is to my mind a specimen of the purest 'Gothic' as displayed in the goldsmith's art, and of French origin (although it has been suggested that it may be English).

I think no other 'Gothic' book of this kind is known, the earliest specimens hitherto being the little English enamelled book at the British Museum of the period of Henry VIII. and the similar one in the possession of Lord Romney, followed by the Spanish gold enamelled book containing the private prayers of the Emperor Charles V. in my own collection, now lent to the South Kensington Museum."

Mr. Read said he found a difficulty in reconciling the appearance of the outside with that of the leaves within, as it seemed to him that there was a difference of style of about two centuries between the binding and the leaves, and further that the leaves themselves appeared to be of two different dates. In the British Museum there is also Queen Elizabeth's prayer book in an enamelled gold cover, given by Sir A. Wollaston Franks, and the two enamelled covers of a second similar book.

Mr. Micklethwaite, V.P., called attention to the form of the prayer inside, which was not popularly in use in England before the sixteenth century and not officially before the middle of the century.

Sir E Maunde Thompson, K.C.B., V.P., expressed an opinion with regard to the lettering that it was not in accordance with the style of the thirteenth or any succeeding century.

Thanks were ordered to be returned for this communication and exhibition.

Thursday, 20th March, 1902

Viscount DILLON, President, in the Chair.

The following gifts were announced, and thanks for the same ordered to be returned to the donors :

From the Author .—Early Hull Tobacco Pipes and their Makers. By Thomas Sheppard, F.G.S 8vo. Hull, 1902.

From Sir Francis Tress Barry, bart , M P , F.S A. —Notices of nine Brochs along the Caithness Coast from Keiss Bay to Skirza Head. By Joseph Anderson, LL D. 8vo. n d 1902

From W H. Richardson. Esq., M A , F.S.A. .—A Letter (from J. H Markland) to the Earl of Aberdeen, K T , President of the Society of Antiquaries, on the expediency of attaching a Museum of Antiquities to that Institution. 8vo. London, 1828.

O. M. DALTON, Esq., M.A., F.S.A., read a paper on the Origin of Encrusted Jewellery.

Mr. Dalton's paper will be printed in *Archaeologia*.

F. G. HILTON PRICE, Esq., Director, exhibited a number of examples of inlaid Egyptian jewellery

Sir GEORGE SITWELL, bart., F.S.A., exhibited an early edition of Clenard's *Institutiones in Græcam Linguam*, on which he read the following note :

"This is the earliest example known of a binding stamped with the arms of Cambridge University, but my chief reason for exhibiting the book is that it illustrates the system of education within a few years of the time when Shakespeare was at school. The book itself is the *Institutiones in Græcam Linguam* of Clenard, the 'prolix Greek Grammar of Cleonard,' which Aubrey in his *Brief Lives* tells us was used until 1597, when Camden's Grammar first appeared. The particular edition, of which this is a copy, appears to be unknown to bibliographers ; the preface is dated 21st August, 1587, and the book was apparently published in that year, but Brunet and Ebert knew of no edition in octavo between 1586 and 1650. The history of the book, as shown by the autographs it contains, appears to have been as follows. It was bought, I suppose, early in 1588, by my ancestor George Sittwell, of Eckington, who reached the age of 18 years on the 18th September, 1587. From him it passed, probably in 1593, 1597, and 1599 to George, Godfrey, and Henry Wigfall, the sons of Henry Wigfall, of Carter Hall, in Eckington. Godfrey was baptised on the 13th March, 1579-80, and buried on the 24th January, 1600-1, and Henry was baptised on the 20th January, 1581-2. It appears by the University registers that George Wigfall, of Caius College, matriculated in 1593 and took his degree in 1596, and that Godfrey Wigfall, of St. John's, matriculated in 1598. The four young men whose autographs are written in the book probably used it when they entered Cambridge University at the age of 17 or 18. All four were able to write an Italian as well as an old English hand, and must have learnt something more than the rudiments of Greek at a Grammar School, and we may fairly deduce from these facts that provincial education was better than Sidney Lee in his *Life of Shakespeare* is willing to admit. George Sittwell's uncle, Robert Sitwell, of Staveley Netherthorpe, founded and endowed a Grammar School at that place, which is three miles from Eckington, in or before the year 1586, in conjunction with Judge Rhodes and Mr. Frecheville, of Staveley, and the successive owners of this Greek Grammar may have been educated there or at the more famous Grammar School of Derby."

Thanks were ordered to be returned for these communications and exhibitions.

Thursday, 10th April, 1902.

PHILIP NORMAN, Esq, Treasurer, and afterwards
J. T. MICKLETHWAITE, Esq, Vice-President, in the Chair.

The following gifts were announced, and thanks for the
same ordered to be returned to the donors ·

> From Sir Thomas Brooke, bart, F.S A .—The Metz Pontifical. Edited by
> E S. Dewick, M A , F.S.A (Roxburghe Club). fol. London, 1902

> From the Author ·—The Prehistoric Rock Engravings in the Italian
> Maritime Alps. By C Bicknell 8vo Bordighera, 1902.

> From H. Yates Thompson, Esq , B A , F.S A .—A Descriptive Catalogue
> of the Second Series of Fifty Manuscripts in the Collection of Henry
> Yates Thompson. The notices contributed by various hands 8vo
> Cambridge, 1902.

> From the Author ·—King Arthur and the Round Table at Winchester. By
> T. W. Shore, F.G S. 8vo. n.p. 1900.

Special thanks were accorded to Sir Thomas Brooke for his
gift to the Library.

The following gentlemen were admitted Fellows ·

> Charles Steele Murchison Bompas, Esq.
> Paul Bevan, Esq., M A.
> Lawrence Weaver, Esq.

Notice was given that the Annual Election of the President, Council, and Officers of the Society would be held at the
Anniversary Meeting on St George's Day, Wednesday, 23rd
April, at 2 p.m., and that no Fellow in arrear of his annual
subscription would be entitled to vote on that occasion.

The Report of the Auditors was read, and thanks were
voted to the Auditors for their trouble and to the Treasurer
for his good and faithful services

We, the AUDITORS appointed to audit the ACCOUNTS of the SOCIETY to the 31st day of December, 1901, having examined the find the same to be accurate.

CASH ACCOUNT FOR THE YEAR

RECEIPTS.		£	s.	d.	£	s.	d.
1901.							
Balance in hand, 31st December, 1900					674	1	1
Annual Subscriptions :							
8 at £3 3s., arrears due 1900		25	4	0			
7 at £2 2s., ditto		14	14	0			
1 at £1 1s., completion ditto		1	1	0			
471 at £3 3s., due 1st January, 1901		1483	13	0			
120 at £2 2s., ditto		252	0	0			
1 at £1 11s. 6d.		1	11	6			
2 at £3 3s. 0d., paid in advance for 1902		6	6	0			
1 at £2 2s. 0d., ditto		2	2	0			
					1786	11	6
Compositions :							
2 Fellows at £55					110	0	0
Admissions :							
33 Fellows at £8 8s.					277	4	0
Dividend on £10583 19s. 7d. Metropolitan 3 per cent. Stock					299	13	3
Works sold					130	19	0
Stevenson Bequest :							
Dividend on Bank Stock and other Investments					639	11	11
Owen Fund :							
Dividend on £300 2½ per cent. Annuities					7	2	0
Sundry Receipts					226	6	10

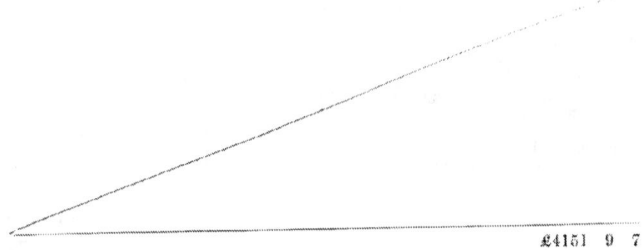

£4151 9 7

OF ANTIQUARIES OF LONDON, from the 1st day of January, 1901,
underwritten ACCOUNTS, with the Vouchers relating thereto, do

ENDING 31st DECEMBER, 1901.

EXPENDITURE. 1901.	£	s.	d.	£	s	d.
Publications of the Society:						
Printers' and Artists' Charges and Binding .				856	9	7
Library:						
Binding .	53	14	11			
Books purchased	387	11	4			
Subscriptions to Books and Societies .	38	7	0			
				479	13	3
Grant to Research Fund				600	0	0
House Expenditure:						
Insurance	29	13	9			
Lighting	117	5	11			
Fuel	42	2	0			
Repairs .	309	4	3			
Tea at Meetings	16	13	7			
Cleaning and Sundries	51	17	1			
				566	16	7
Income Tax and Inland Revenue License				49	13	9
Legacy Duty and Costs: Stevenson Bequest .				13	14	8
Pensions:						
C. K. Watson, deceased, half-quarter's allowance	43	15	0			
E. C. Ireland .	160	0	0			
				203	15	0
Salaries:						
Assistant Secretary	350	0	0			
Clerk .	160	0	0			
				510	0	0
Wages:						
Porter, and Wife as Housemaid, and Hall Boy				104	1	6
Official Expenditure:						
Stationery and Printing	140	10	6			
Postages	37	4	8			
Ditto and Carriage on Publications	13	6	5			
Sundry Expenses	71	4	7			
				262	6	2
Cash in hand:						
Coutts & Co., Deposit Account	300	0	0			
Ditto Current Account	202	1	11			
Petty cash	2	17	2			
				504	19	1
				£4151	9	7

RESEARCH FUND ACCOUNT for

RECEIPTS.

		£	s.	d.
Balance in hand, 1st January, 1901	. . .	23	4	7
Dividends :				
12 months' Dividend on £1805 13s. 4d. India 3½ per cent. Stock .	58 18 8			
12 Months' Dividend on £500 J. Dickinson & Company, Limited, 5 per cent. Preference Stock	23 14 0			
		82	12	8
Grant from General Account		600	0	0
Donation, Viscount Dillon		10	0	0
		£715	17	3

STOCKS AND INVESTMENTS.

	Amount of Stock.	Value on 31st December, 1900.
	£ s. d.	£ s. d.
Metropolitan 3 per cent. Stock . . .	10583 19 7	10689 16 4
Bank Stock	2128 9 6	7077 3 7
Great Northern Railway Consolidated 4 per cent. Perpetual Preference Stock . . .	2725 0 0	3365 7 6
London and North Western Railway Consolidated 4 per cent. Guaranteed Stock . . .	2757 0 0	3625 9 1
North Eastern Railway Guaranteed 4 per cent. Stock	2761 0 0	3603 2 1
Midland Railway 2½ per cent. Consolidated Perpetual Guaranteed Preferential Stock .	592 5 10	473 16 8
	£21547 14 11	£28834 15 3

OWEN FUND.

½ per cent. Annuities . . .	300 0 0	280 10 0

RESEARCH FUND.

India 3½ per cent. Stock . . .	1805 13 4	1950 2 4
J. Dickinson & Co., Limited, 5 per cent. Preference Stock	500 0 0	582 10 0
Victorian Government 3 per cent. Consolidated Inscribed Stock, 1929-49 . . .	527 13 0	506 10 10
	£2833 6 4	£3039 3 2

THE YEAR ENDING 31st DECEMBER, 1901

EXPENDITURE.

				£	s.	d.
Waverley Abbey Excavation Fund	.	.	.	10	0	0
Caerwent Exploration Fund	.	.	.	10	0	0
Silchester Excavation Fund	.	.	.	100	0	0
Verulamium Excavation Fund	.	.	.	15	0	0
Excavations at St. Augustine's, Canterbury	.	.	.	10	0	0
Purchase of £527 13s. Victoria 3 per cent. Stock .	.	.		500	0	0
Balance in hand, 31st December, 1901	.	.	.	70	17	3

£715 17 3

31ST DECEMBER, 1901.

	Amount of Stock.		
	£	s.	d.

In the High Court of Justice, Chancery Division.
In the suit of Thornton v. Stevenson.
The Stocks remaining in Court to the credit of this cause are as follows:

	£	s.	d.
Great Western Railway 5 per cent. Guaranteed Stock .	8894	0	0
Midland Railway 2½ per cent. Preferential Stock .	15145	12	7

£24039 12 7

After payment of the Annuities, now amounting to £400 per annum, the Society is entitled to one-fourth share of the residue of the Income on the above Funds. This is payable after the 10th April and 10th October in every year.

Witness our hands this 12th day of March, 1902.

LIONEL CUST,
ARTHUR H. LYELL,
E. W. BRABROOK,
MILL STEPHENSON.

INCOME AND EXPENDITURE ACCOUNT for the Year ending 31st DECEMBER, 1901.

INCOME.

	£ s. d.	£ s. d.
Subscriptions received	1758 4 6	
,, unpaid, 30th December, 1901	57 15 0	
	1815 19 6	
Less 1900 Subscriptions unpaid	3 3 0	
		1812 16 6
Compositions		110 0 0
Admissions		277 4 0
Dividend on £10,583 19s. 3d. Metropolitan 3 per cent. Stock		299 13 3
Works sold		130 19 0
Stevenson Bequest :		
Dividend on Bank Stock and other Investments		639 11 11
Sundry Receipts		76 6 10
Balance carried to Balance Sheet		173 6 10
		£3519 18 4

EXPENDITURE.

	£ s. d.	£ s. d.	£ s. d.
Publications of the Society :			
Printers' and Artists' Charges and Binding			830 9 7
Library :			
Binding	53 14 11		
Books purchased	386 18 10		
Subscriptions to Books and Societies	38 7 0		479 0 9
Grant to Research Fund			600 0 0
House Expenditure :			
Insurance	29 13 9		
Lighting	207 15 4		
Fuel	33 0 0		
Repairs	139 13 7		
Tea at Meetings	17 19 11		
Cleaning and Sundries	47 14 4		466 16 11
Income Tax and Inland Revenue License			49 13 9
Legacy Duty and Costs			13 14 8
Pensions :			
C. K. Watson (deceased), half quarter's allowance	43 15 0		
E. C. Ireland	160 0 0		203 15 0
Salaries :			
Assistant Secretary	350 0 0		
Clerk	160 0 0		510 0 0
Wages :			
Porter, and Wife as Housemaid, and Hall Boy			104 1 6
Official Expenditure :			
Stationery and Printing	140 10 6		
Postages	37 4 8		
,, Publications	13 6 5		
Sundry Expenses	71 4 7		262 6 2
			£3519 18 4

BALANCE SHEET, 31st DECEMBER, 1901.

Dr.

	£ s. d.	£ s. d.
To Sundry Creditors		193 2 7
" Unexpended balances:		
Owen Fund	10 8 1	
Research Fund	70 17 3	81 5 4
" Balance, 31st December, 1900	30446 9 8	
Less Balance, Income and Expenditure Account, being excess of Expenditure over Income	173 6 10	30273 2 10
		£30547 10 9

Cr.

	£ s. d.	£ s. d.
By Investments:		
£10583 19s. 7d. Metropolitan 3 per cent. Stock	11060 5 2	
£2128 9s. 6d. Bank Stock	7162 6 4	
£2725 Great Northern Railway Consolidated 4 per cent. Perpetual Preference Stock	3692 7 6	
£2757 London and North Western Railway Consolidated 4 per cent. Guaranteed Stock	3763 6 1	
£2761 North Eastern Railway Guaranteed 4 per cent. Stock	3741 3 1	
£2592 6s. 10d. Midland Railway 2½ per cent Consolidated Perpetual Preference Stock	491 11 3	29913 19 5
" Sundry Debtors:		
Subscriptions unpaid		57 15 0
" Cash:		
At Bankers, Messrs. Coutts & Co.	572 19 2	
In hand	2 17 2	575 16 4
		£30547 10 9

We have prepared the above Balance Sheet and Income and Expenditure Account from the Books and Statements provided by the Treasurer of the Society, and certify to the accuracy of the same. The Investments, which have been taken at Stock Exchange List prices, on the 30th December, 1899, do not include those belonging to the Research and Owen Funds. No account has been taken of the Books, Furniture, Antiquities or other Assets of the Society.

36 Walbrock, London, E.C.
12th *March*, 1902.

C. F. KEMP, SONS, & Co.

WILLIAM PAGE, Esq., F.S.A., Local Secretary for Herts, read a Report on further excavations on the site of *Verulamium*.

Mr. Page also read a Paper on the St. Albans School of Painting, mural and miniature. Part I. Mural Painting. This will be printed in *Archaeologia*.

The Rev. C. H. EVELYN WHITE, F.S.A., exhibited a piece of linen damask 37½ inches long and 27½ inches broad, woven with heraldic insignia.

At the top are two crowned shields: (1) England quartering France modern ; and (2) France modern ; and between them four rows of crowned roses and fleurs-de-lis disposed alternately.

Below are the words :

ANNO ✠ 1603   INDE · 4 · DEMAENT

In the middle is a large shield crowned and within the Garter, with lion and dragon supporters, with the motto SEMPER EADEM below. The shield contains an extraordinary collection of quarterings :

1. Grand quarter : England and France quarterly.

2. Grand quarter : (i.) a cross paty and four martlets, (?) for St. Edward the Confessor ; (ii.) three crowns, for St. Edmund or St. Oswyn ; (iii.) a cross formy ; (iv.) a cross paty and four crowns, for St. Edward the Martyr ; with the arms of Norway in pretence.

3. Grand quarter : the arms of Rome, the letters S.P.Q.R. between double cotises.

4. Grand quarter : (i.) a lion ; (ii.) three crowns bendwise ; (iii.) three crowns in pale, perhaps for King Arthur ; (iv.) a plain cross for St. George.

In base is the harp of Ireland, and in pretence N. Wales and S. Wales quarterly.

Below the shield are two crowned shields of St. George and of Scotland respectively, with a row of two roses and as many fleurs-de-lis all crowned and alternating.

The whole is within a double border of chain and dice pattern.

Thanks were ordered to be returned for these communications and exhibitions.

Thursday, 17th April, 1902.

Viscount DILLON, President, in the Chair.

The following gifts were announced, and thanks for the same ordered to be returned to the donors:

From the Author
1 A History of Nottingham Castle. By Emanuel Green, F.S.A 8vo. London, 1902

2. Bibliotheca Somersetensis : A Catalogue of Books, Pamphlets, Single Sheets, and Broadsides in some way connected with the County of Somerset. By Emanuel Green, F S A. 3 vols 8vo   Taunton, 1902.

From the Author —The value of mineral condition in determining the relative age of Stone Implements.   By S. H Warren, F.G.S.   8vo. London, 1902.

From N. H J Westlake, Esq., F S.A. —Notice sur la Collection de Tableaux Anciens, faisant partie de la Galerie de Mr J P Weyer   Par W H J Weale. 8vo. Bruges, 1863.

From the Author :—The Giant and the Maypole of Cerne. By H C March, M.D., F.S A   8vo   Dorchester, 1902

From the Trustees of the British Museum ·—A Guide to the Department of Greek and Roman Antiquities in the British Museum. 2nd Edition. 8vo London, 1902.

The following gentlemen were admitted Fellows.

Frederick William Cock, Esq., M.D.
Rev. William Kyle Westwood Chafy, D.D.
Thomas Hesketh Hodgson, Esq.

Notice was again given that the Annual Meeting for the election of the President, Council, and Officers of the Society would be held on Wednesday, 23rd April, being St. George's Day, at 2 p m., and that no Fellow in arrear of his subscription would be entitled to vote on that occasion.

Lists were also read of those who on that day were to be submitted for ballot to fill the offices of Council, President, Treasurer, Director, and Secretary respectively.

J. ROMILLY ALLEN, Esq , F.S A., read the following paper

on an inscribed and sculptured Norman tympanum in Hawksworth Church, Nottinghamshire :

The village of Hawksworth is situated 8 miles south-west of Newark-upon-Trent and three miles north of Aslacton railway station on the line from Grantham to Nottingham, in the comparatively level stretch of country lying between the rivers Trent and Witham. The Roman Foss-way passes $2\frac{1}{4}$ miles to the westward, and the Great Northern main line is about the same distance off on the east.

The tympanum which forms the subject of the present paper is now built into the south wall of the western tower of Hawksworth Church, but its original position before 1851 was over the entrance to the north porch.

My attention was first called to the existence of this interesting specimen of Norman sculpture in 1894 by the late Precentor Venables, of Lincoln. In 1897 Dr. W. Stevenson of Hull, was good enough to visit Hawksworth at my request, and he afterwards sent me a careful description of the sculpture with an accurate reading of the inscription. I went to see the tympanum myself on 10th July, 1900, in order to procure a rubbing of the inscription, and I now have the honour of laying before the Society the results of my investigation.

Perhaps I ought to mention that the inscription is not newly brought to light, as a reading of it is given by the Rev. S. Pegge in his "Sylloge of the remaining Authentic Inscriptions relative to the Erection of our English Churches," published in 1787 in the sixth volume of the *Bibliotheca Topographica Britannica*. There is, however, nothing in Mr. Pegge's account to suggest that the inscription was on a tympanum, so that the sculpture and inscription as a whole are now illustrated for the first time. To show how completely Mr. Pegge's description had been forgotten, I may observe that Mr. C. E. Keyser, F.S.A., who has made Norman doorways his life-long study, was not aware of the existence of the example at Hawksworth until I called his attention to it quite recently.

The tympanum at Hawksworth presents a unique combination of a dedicatory inscription with a cross, figure sculpture and elaborate geometrical ornament. A Saxon cross-shaft, which formed the lintel beneath the tympanum when it was in its original position, was removed at the same time as the tympanum, and the architect for the restoration has thoughtfully placed the shaft in an angle of one of the buttresses of the tower instead of destroying it altogether. The cross-shaft is 5 feet

6 inches long by 1 foot 2 inches wide at the bottom, and 1 foot
wide at the top by 1 foot 3 inches thick at the bottom by 1 foot
1 inch at the top. On one face there is a cross with transverse arms at each end on a background of three-cord plait-
work. I may observe in passing that the ivy with which the
tower is clothed is rapidly pushing out its branches over the
surface of the tympanum, so that in a year or two it will
effectually disappear from view.

The tympanum is 3 feet 6½ inches wide by 2 feet 2 inches
high, made of one solid slab of sandstone. Round it is a
semicircular arch composed of twelve voussoirs, and ornamented with a pattern composed of six-pointed stars. Three
of the arch stones have a double star upon them and the
remainder only single stars, making fifteen stars altogether
The arch terminates at each side in the projecting head of a
beast.

The tympanum has an ornamental border of seven circular
eight-leaved rosettes alternating with six eight-spoked wheels,
making thirteen altogether. In the centre of the tympanum
is a cross of somewhat unusual form,* having expanded ends
to the arms with pairs of small knobs or projections at the
points where the expansions commence. On each side of the
upper arm is a small circular medallion, that on the left containing the Agnus Dei and that on the right an angel with
outspread wings. On each side of the shaft is a standing
figure, that on the left being an angel with outspread wings,
and that on the right a man clothed in a tunic, with outstretched arms. The background is decorated with stars,
rosettes, and triangles of the usual Norman type.

The inscription begins close to the end of the left arm of
the cross, and is continued in six short horizontal lines, until
it reaches the level of the bottom of the cross, concluding
with three longer horizontal lines extending across more than
half the width of the tympanum. The inscription, which is
in Latin, and in Roman capitals of the twelfth century, is as
follows:

GAVTERVS ET VXOR EIVS CECELINA FECERVNT FACERE
ECLESIAM ISTAM IN ONORE DNI NRI ET SCE
MARIÆ VIRGINIS ET OMNIVM SCORVM DEI SIMVL

The only palæographical peculiarities of the inscription are
the ligature between the A and the V in the first line and the

---

* Not unlike the cross of King Canute represented in the Register of Hyde
Abbey (illustrated in J C. Wall's *Alfred the Great*, 25)

contractions DÑI, ÑRI, SĈE, and SĈORVM [for *Domini, nostri, sanctæ,* and *sanctorum* respectively]. The only letter of the rounded shape used is the α, so that the inscription as a whole belongs to the period before the introduction of the Lombardic capitals of the thirteenth century   Two mistakes in spelling are to be noticed, namely, the omission of the aspirate in the word ONORE and of the C in ECCLESIAM.

With regard to the identification of the persons whose names are given in the inscription as the benefactor and benefactress who caused Hawksworth Church to be built, the Rev. S. Pegge has suggested that they were Walter de Aslacton and his wife. The rector of Hawksworth informs me that there is a tradition in the parish that Walter was of Blankney, Lincolnshire.

The decorative and symbolic sculpture which accompany the inscription have next to be considered. All that need be said about the purely decorative portion of the design is that the incised triangles and the star, rosette, and wheel patterns forming the background, are of a type common throughout Norman architecture from about 1125 to 1175. The symbolism, however, deserves fuller examination

I think it may safely be said that the figure subject sculptured in the middle of the tympanum is not intended for the Crucifixion, as in place of the personifications of Sol and Luna in the circular medallions (on each side of the top arm of the cross) we have the Agnus Dei on the left and an angel on the right, and in place of St Mary and St. John or the soldiers with the spear and sponge (on each side of the shaft of the cross) we have an angel on the left and a figure with outstretched arms on the right. The crucified Savour is also absent. The accessories are therefore not those which usually accompany the conventional representations of the Crucifixion, nor are the figures surrounding the cross those of the symbols of the Four Evangelists, as is often the case.

The only suggestion I am able to make is that the sculpture is meant to typify in some way the Adoration of the Cross. At the same time I am fully aware that this explanation is not altogether satisfactory, and I shall therefore gladly welcome any further light that may be thrown on this somewhat obscure representation   I should like to direct particular attention to the figure with extended arms on the right of the shaft of the cross, which taken by itself is not unlike a Crucifixion. Can this be intended for the Saviour, or for one of the thieves who suffered at the same time ?   It is very puzzling in any case. If it be the Saviour why is He not on the large cross in the middle of the tympanum ? and

again, if it be one of the thieves, why is there not a similar
figure to correspond on the other side of the cross (as on the
Norman font at Lenton, near Nottingham) ?

Having described the chief peculiarities of the symbolic
sculpture on the Hawksworth tympanum we are now in a
position to compare it with other examples which present
similar features.

Tympana with crosses may be divided into three varieties,
namely:

(1) Those with one or more crosses on a plain background.

(2) Those with one or more crosses on an ornamented
background.

(3) Those with one or more crosses in combination with
figure subjects.

As examples of the first kind we may take the tympana at
Tottenhill, Norfolk, and Rame, Cornwall. In the former there
is one cross in the centre of the tympanum, and in the latter
a central cross with smaller ones on either side of it.

As an example of the second kind we have the tympanum
at Wold Newton, Yorkshire

The tympanum at Hawksworth belongs to the third kind,
and may be compared with other examples at Beckford,
Gloucestershire; Little Paxton, Huntingdonshire, Salford,
Oxfordshire, Egleton, Rutland; South Ferriby, Lincolnshire,
and Tissington and Findern, Derbyshire. These have been
fully described in Mr. C. E. Keyser's paper on the "Sculptured
Tympanum of a Dormer Doorway in the Church of South
Ferriby," in *Archaeologia*.*

The Christian practice of placing crosses over doorways
was probably derived from the preceding Pagan custom of
placing some object above the lintel to act as a charm against
the Evil Eye, or to keep away devils, ghosts, lightning, etc
The lucky horseshoe, so often seen nailed up over doorways
in this country, is a curious instance of the survival of this
heathen superstition. E W Lane, in his *Modern Egyptians*,†
refers to the use of inscriptions for a similar purpose in the
following passage:

"Besides the inscriptions over shops, we often see, in Cairo,
the invocation 'O God!' sculptured over the door of a private
house; and the words, 'He is the Creator, the Everlasting,'
or 'He is the Great Creator, the Everlasting,' painted in

* Vol. xlvii. 166.
† Vol. i. 320.

large characters upon the door, both as a charm and to remind the master of the house whenever he enters it of his own immortality."

After the introduction of Christianity the Chi-Rho monogram of Christ took the place of the Pagan charm for frightening away evil spirits and preventing them entering the house over the doorway of which it was sculptured. Numerous illustrations of lintels of doorways inscribed with the Chi-Rho monogram are given in C. J. M. de Vogué's *Syrie Centrale.* At a later period again the Chi-Rho monogram was succeeded by the equal-armed cross, more frequently within a circle than not. The earliest instance of a cross over a doorway in Great Britain occurs in one of the dry-built stone bee-hive cells on Skellig Michael,[*] co. Kerry, which may be as old as the sixth or seventh century. Other pre-Norman examples of crosses over doorways may be seen in the Irish round tower at and in churches at Fore, co. Westmeath; Clonamery, co. Kilkenny; Inishmurray, co. Sligo; Glendalough, co. Wicklow; Killiney, co. Dublin;[†] and Stanton Lacy, Shropshire. [‡]

Now although crosses are so frequently found over the doorways of Celtic, Saxon, and Norman ecclesiastical buildings the Crucifixion very rarely occurs in the same position, the only instances I am acquainted with being at Maghera,[§] co. Londonderry; Donaghmore,[||] co. Meath; Teghadoe, co. Kildare; Brechin,[**] Forfarshire; Bolsover[††] and Normanton,[‡‡] Derbyshire.

The reason why the cross is so often sculptured over doorways of churches and the Crucifixion so seldom may be because the equal-armed cross, being directly descended from the Chi-Rho monogram, was intended to symbolise the name of Christ rather than His Passion. It must also be remembered that the most appropriate positions for representations of the Crucifixion were considered to be either on an erect cross of sculptured stone in the churchyard or on the screen between the nave and the chancel.

---

[*] Miss M. Stokes' *Early Christian Art in Ireland,* 161. There is a similar cross over the doorway of the oratory on Senach's Island illustrated in the same work, p. 156.
[†] See books on Irish Architecture by Petrie and Lord Dunraven.
[‡] Rickman's *Gothic Architecture* (6th edition, London, 1862), 91.
[§] Miss M. Stokes' *Early Christian Art in Ireland,* 165.
[||] G. Wilkinson's *Ancient Architecture of Ireland,* 72.
[**] Dr. J. Stuart's *Sculptured Stones of Scotland,* ii. 1.
[††] *Reliquary,* xxii. 119.
[‡‡] *Reliquary,* ii. 4.

The Norman tympana with crosses, and figure subjects combined, form rather an interesting series. On those at Beckford, Salford, and Egleton the cross is in the centre, and on each side is a beast or fabulous creature acting as a " supporter," using the term in its heraldic sense. The scene represented on the tympanum at Little Paxton shows an ecclesiastic with a crozier and a beast on the left side of the central cross and two other beasts on the right apparently adoring the cross. On the tympana at Tissington and Findern, Derbyshire, the background of the cross consists of a chequer-work pattern, and there are little human figures at each of the two lower corners.

On the tympanum at South Ferriby, Lincolnshire, a bishop is represented standing in the centre giving the benediction with his right hand and holding a crozier in his left. On each side is a circular cross. The subject is probably St. Nicholas dedicating the church.

The only remaining point to be noticed in connection with the Hawksworth tympanum is its use as a dedication stone. Although the inscription on the tympanum is obviously a dedicatory one it seems doubtful whether the cross which accompanies it is a consecration cross.

The following list shows the dedication stones still existing in England arranged in chronological order with the positions they now occupy :

SAXON PERIOD.

685	St. Paul, Jarrow, co. Durham	Built into west wall of central tower, facing nave, above arch.
11th century	St. Mary Castlegate, York	Fixed against chancel pier of north aisle.
11th century	St. Mary le Wigford, Lincoln	Built into west wall of tower.
11th century	Aldborough, Yorkshire	Built into south wall of nave.
11th century	Weaverthorpe, Yorkshire	Over south doorway.
1055-1064	Kirkdale, Yorkshire	Over south doorway of nave.

SAXON PERIOD—*continued.*

	St. Nicholas, Ipswich	On tympanum built into north wall of nave, inside.
1053	Deerhurst No. 1, Gloucestershire	Dug up on site of destroyed chancel in 1675, and now preserved amongst Arundel Marbles at Oxford.
	Deerhurst No. 2, Gloucestershire	Found built into the chimney stack of a Tudor house adjoining Saxon chapel. Now placed inside chapel.

NORMAN PERIOD.

1125	Castor, Northamptonshire	On tympanum of south doorway of chancel.
	Hawksworth, Notts.	Formerly on tympanum of outer doorway of north porch, now built into south wall of western tower.
1185	Temple Church, London	On tympanum over little door next cloister.
1192	Clee, Lincolnshire	On slab built into central pillar of south arcade of nave.

THIRTEENTH CENTURY.

1241	Ashbourne, Derbyshire	On brass plate.
	Postling, Kent	On brass plate under window in north wall of chancel, inside.

FOURTEENTH CENTURY.

	Great Bookham, Surrey	On slab built into east wall of chancel, inside, on south side of altar.
	Egham, Surrey	On slab built into east wall of south aisle of nave, inside, of modern church built in 1817.

Unfortunately many of the stones given in the above list have been removed from the positions which they originally occupied, but judging from those still in place it would appear that the most usual position for a dedication stone was over the south doorway.

In Saxon times the dedication stone was generally combined with a sundial in the wall above the doorway, and in Norman times it formed the tympanum of the doorway. After the twelfth century the dedicatory inscription was sometimes engraved on a brass plate instead of being carved on a slab of stone.

The language of the inscriptions is generally Latin, the only exceptions being the examples at Aldborough, Kirkdale, and St. Mary Castlegate, York, in Yorkshire, and St Mary le Wigford, Lincoln, all of which are in the vernacular

The formulæ of the inscriptions vary, but they are usually to the effect that so-and-so caused the church to be built or repaired, and dedicated in honour of a particular saint at a particular date. The longest inscription in Latin is the one from Deerhurst, now at Oxford, and the longest in the vernacular the one at Kirkdale, Yorkshire. The inscription at Aldborough, Yorkshire, omits the name of the saint, but states that the benefactors caused the church to be built for the sake of their souls, a formula which occurs more frequently on the sepulchral monuments of the Anglo-Saxon period."

W. G. COLLINGWOOD, Esq., M.A., read the following Report as Local Secretary for Cumberland :

"I have the honour to report upon some finds and explorations in Cumberland during 1901.

Crucifix mould from Portinscale.—The stone which the Trustees of the Fitz Park Museum, Keswick, through Mr. R. D. Marshall of Castlerigg Manor, have kindly lent for exhibition, was found by Mr. Charles Birkett of Keswick, while making a road to the new house called Moss Garth on the north-west side of Derwentwater, shortly before the discovery of greenstone celts in the grounds of the same house. The stone measures 3½ inches by 2⅛ inches and is over ⅜ inch thick On one side it has incised a cross 2 inches by 1 inch, with a ring at the top, and a rudely drawn emaciated figure crucified, from which a leaden crucifix might be cast. On the other side it has five small wheel crosses arranged in the form of a cross, also incised, and two moulds for nails, perhaps the implements of the Passion, with other figures, defaced.

H 2

The photographs of the stone have been lent by Canon Rawnsley, who suggests, what is very probable, that this mould was connected with pilgrimages to St. Herbert's Island. The worship of St. Herbert (who died 687) was instituted or revived in 1374, when a chapel was built upon the island, and annual services established. An ancient road called Finkle Street runs from the north of the lake, past the spot where the stone was found, to Nichol end landing, the most convenient place for taking boat to St. Herbert's Island.

Mr. H. S. Cowper, F.S.A., has lent for comparison his unpublished drawings of a stone mould, 3¼ inches by 2 inches and a little more than ⅓ inch thick, found at Butterilket, Eskdale, Cumberland, on the Roman and mediæval road from the old port of Ravenglass to Ambleside and Kendal. This stone seems to have been prepared on both sides for making buttons.

The Portinscale Celts.—Mr. Tindall Harris, of Moss Garth, Portinscale, has sent me for exhibition a photograph of the celts (reduced scale) already mentioned, including the fifth, a partly polished stone, formed by himself in the boulder-clay dug out of the pond. The first four were found on the surface of the boulder-clay under 18 inches of peat; this last was in a mass of the clay which had been excavated by his workmen, but the exact depth at which it had been lying is unknown.

Gosforth Holy-well.—In March, 1901, we uncovered the foundations of a chapel known to have existed in a field called Chapel-brow, on the hill above the church famous for its pre-Norman cross and other early remains. Some had entertained the idea that it was the ruin of a chapel earlier than the Norman church. We found a small rectangular building, 33 feet by 19 feet, external measurement; the corners and parts of the facing were of cut red-sandstone, and the rest of cobbles with a rubble core. The doorway was to the south, in one of the longer sides; some of the flooring slabs appeared to remain *in situ*, and there were fragments of roofing flags of red-sandstone, like those found at Gosforth church and Calder abbey. An arm of a cross was found at the east end, perhaps part of the finial of the gable, and not pre-Norman. In the middle of the building was the main source of the spring, of very pure water. A local tradition collected by Miss Senhouse, of Gosforth, says that at certain feasts (date not known) wine used to be poured into the well, and the villagers caught it at the outflow below to drink. This appears to have been a mediæval well-chapel, the only one of its kind known to me in Cumberland. The well has now been cleared and covered, and the foundations turfed for their preservation by the owner, Mr. J. S. Ainsworth, of Harecroft.

Excavations at Foldsteads ' Camp.'—Near Kirkbampton is an earthwork, on a hillside, traditionally said to be a pele-garth, or retreat for cattle during Scottish raids ; but rather more than half a century ago a Roman stone, 6 inches by 4 inches, with the inscription DEAE LATI LVCIVS VES (as read by the late Dr. J. Collingwood Bruce), was found in the field called Foldsteads, adjoining the ' camp,' and it was supposed that the place was Roman.

In the summer of 1901 the Rev. James Wilson and Mr. E. W. Stead, of Dalston, made some excavations, which showed that the ramparts are not cespititious, and that they contain neither stones nor masonry. No relics were found. Only one corner of the original structure remains intact, but from this it is seen that there were two ramparts and two ditches, and that the corner was very distinctly rounded, somewhat resembling Caermote, which used to be thought Roman, but soon, I hope, will be explored for the local society by Mr. Haverfield. There are many of these minor earth-works, put down by former antiquaries as pre-historic or Roman, which seem to deserve attention, even if the results are comparatively small. In some cases they may be the tungarths of early settlers, and in some they may be the pelegarths, as this appears to be, of the mediæval or even sixteenth century villagers during the period of the Scottish raids.

Threlkeld ' British Settlement.'—The photograph, by Mr. W. L. Fletcher, of Stoneleigh, Workington, shows a quern and a fragment of the upper stone, found in the 'British Settlement' on Wanthwaite Fell, south of Threlkeld, which was explored in the spring of 1901 by Mr. C. W. Dymond, F.S.A., and Mr. T. H. Hodgson, F.S.A. Their report is given in the *Transactions* of the Cumberland and Westmorland Antiquarian and Archæological Society,* giving full particu-lars of the remains and excavations, with a detailed plan by Mr. Dymond. In two of the cairns a little charcoal was found, but no definite interments ; these, however, seem to have been previously disturbed. In the hut circles which were opened no relics were seen, except fragments of charcoal and bone. At the north-west corner of the inclosures, or 'homesteads,' the quern of local granite had been already found by quarrymen making a trial hole, and near the same place Messrs. Hodgson and Dymond found the red granite fragment which appears to fit the larger piece.

* N. S. ii. 38.

Megalithic circle of Sunkenkirk, Swinside.—In March, 1901, through the kindness of the owner, Mr. W. Lewthwaite, of Broadgate, Mr. C. W. Dymond, F.S.A., and myself were able to make a searching exploration of this, the third greatest circle in Cumberland The full report will be found in the *Transactions* of the Cumberland and Westmorland Antiquarian and Archæological Society,* but perhaps I may be allowed to summarise the results by saying that they were entirely negative. No traces of interments or ancient fires were found, there had been no tumulus within the circle, as the evenly distributed subsoil plainly showed. The one slight disturbance of the ground was owing to an attempt at excavation made some years ago, and a few scraps of charcoal can be explained by top-dressing and a picnic fire in the ' gateway ' of the circle. No finds were made except a Lancaster halfpenny token of about 1791.

Chinese Tombstone from Cargo.—This stone was dug up in August, 1901, in a field west of the road between Cargo and Rockcliffe. It is 12½ inches long, 4 inches wide, and ⅜ inch thick, with a neatly carved inscription, read by the professor of Chinese at Owens' College, Manchester, as follows · ' The dutiful sons Wên-shou and Wên-mao weep blood ; the grandsons Wu-t'an, Wu-hwang, Wu-ch'êng, and Wu-tsêng offer sacrifice.' I am told by the Rev. James Wilson (editor of the *Victoria History of Cumberland*) that ' in the olden days, it is said, ships used to come up the Eden as far as Rockcliffe.' He suggests that a Chinese officer might have died there, and that this stone might have been sent out to mark his grave, or that the stone might have been brought from China as a curiosity. Mr. Thomas Robinson has kindly lent it for exhibition."

With reference to the Chinese inscription reported by Mr. Collingwood, the following note has been kindly communicated by Mr. Robert K. Douglas, of the British Museum

' The inscription is such as is commonly found on ancestral tablets, and I quite agree that it, judging from the transcript, shows no sign of age.

There is nothing to identify it with a locality.'

ARTHUR F. LEACH, Esq., M.A., F.S.A., by permission of the Master of Sidney Sussex College, Cambridge, exhibited the original copy of the Statutes of Jesus College, Rotherham, 1498.

The front page has an illuminated border, with a picture in

* N S. ii. 53

mass vestments of the founder, Thomas Scott alias Rotherham, archbishop of York, 1480-1500, in the initial letter,
over which is his 'reason,' *Da te deo*. In the border are
two shields. That at the top has the arms of the arch-
bishopric of York, *azure the archiepiscopal gold cross surmounted by the pall*, impaling Scott, *vert three white harts
trippant*. The other shield, in the middle of the side border,
has the arms of Scott alone. Each shield is accompanied by
a scroll lettered *Da te deo*.

The LONDON COUNTY COUNCIL exhibited a number of terra-
cotta architectural fragments of the early part of the sixteenth
century, found together with fragments of Roman and
mediæval pottery in the churchyard of St. George the Martyr,
Southwark.

PHILIP NORMAN, Esq., Treasurer, made the following
remarks with regard to the topographical aspects of the
find :

"There is nothing remarkable in the discovery here of
Roman and mediæval remains, because ancient Southwark
extended as far south as this spot. But to what building could
these important specimens of terra-cotta, dating apparently
from the earlier part of the sixteenth century, have belonged ?
They were certainly not ecclesiastical, and though found near
old foundation arches, appear to have had no connection
with them, but were huddled together without order as if
they had been thrown promiscuously into a pit.
They had, I believe, formed part of a great dwelling house,
which is clearly shown in the view of London by Van den
Wyngaerde, lately reproduced for the London Topographical
Society. Here the tower of St. George's church is in the
immediate foreground, and across the road to the left is the
splendid mansion of Charles Brandon, Duke of Suffolk, who
married Mary, sister of Henry VIII., and widow of Louis XII.
of France. He built this mansion about 1516, or a little
after. Its style and the details of Van den Wyngaerde's
drawing warrant the belief that it was decorated with
terra-cotta. Here in 1522, when Charles V. visited England,
he received both the king and emperor, and they dined and
hunted with him. Here too, in all probability, Cardinal
Campeggio was lodged when dealing with the subject of the
King's divorce from Catherine of Arragon.
On an old print, somewhat resembling that executed by
Vertue for the Society of Antiquaries, but said to be from

'the original in the possession of Samuel Egerton Brydges, of Denton, in Kent,' the duke and his wife, the dowager queen, appear hand in hand, and beneath are the lines:

> 'Cloth of gold do not thou dispys
> Though thou be mached with cloth of fries.
> Cloth of friez be not thou to bould
> Though thou be mached with cloth of gold.'

After the duke's death in 1545, if not before, Suffolk House and the ground attached to it passed into the possession of the king and became a mint for coins. Part, however, may have been still kept as a dwelling-house, for Edward VI. dined here in the second year of his reign. Queen Mary gave the property to Nicholas Heath, archbishop of York, who, as Stow tells us, sold it 'to a merchant or to merchants that pulled it down, sold the lead, stone, iron, &c., and in place thereof built many small cottages of great rents to the increasing of beggars in that borough.'

It was then, perhaps, that the fragments of terra-cotta found their way into St. George's churchyard.

Under the name of the Mint the site of the duke's palace became a sanctuary for insolvent debtors, and a place of refuge for lawless persons of all descriptions, not effectually suppressed until the reign of George I. There are many allusions to it in eighteenth century literature."

Thanks were ordered to be returned for these communications and exhibitions.

ANNIVERSARY,

ST. GEORGE'S DAY,

WEDNESDAY, 23rd APRIL, 1902.

PHILIP NORMAN, Esq., Treasurer, and afterwards, HAROLD ARTHUR, Viscount DILLON, Hon. M.A. Oxon, President, in the Chair.

CHARLES EDWARD KEYSER, Esq. M.A., and EDWARD TOWRY WHYTE, Esq. M.A, were nominated Scrutators of the Ballot.

At 2.30 p.m. the PRESIDENT proceeded to deliver the following Address·

GENTLEMEN,

When I last had the honour of addressing you on the Society's Anniversary we had to lament the death of our Queen and Patron. I now will preface my remarks by informing you that His Most Sacred Majesty King Edward VII. has been graciously pleased to inform us that he is willing to continue the protection and favour which this Society so long and so fully enjoyed at the hands of Her late Majesty Queen Victoria.

His Majesty, I may remind you, has been a Royal Fellow of the Society since 16th April, 1863, a date to which only 30 of the present 768 Fellows can claim priority of election. I am not aware for how many years Her late Majesty was our Patron, but probably His Majesty Edward VII. will in a few years be the Father as well as the Patron of the Society.

In the last year I reported the election of 1 Honorary Fellow and 28 Fellows. Now I have the pleasure of stating that we have added 3 Honorary Fellows and 31 Fellows. What is still better is that against 36 losses by resignation and death in the previous year, we have since last Anniversary to regret from the same causes but 21 of our numbers at that date.

In other respects also the Society is, thanks to the care of our Treasurer and the Finance Committee, in a very healthy state, while the publications are, I venture to think, in no way inferior in interest, and certainly not in fulness of illustration to those of previous years. The study of antiquarian subjects has no doubt increased of late years, and if we have to deplore the gradual but certain loss of those giants of the antiquarian world who adorned the late century, we may congratulate ourselves on the springing up of an under-wood in which may be found future forest trees of a size worthy of our country.

Since the last Anniversary the following have been elected :

As Honorary Fellows :

> M. Henri Hymans.
> M. Léon Morel.
> Dr. Woldemar von Seidlitz.

As Ordinary Fellows :

> Walter Jonathan Andrew, Esq.
> William Bruce Bannerman, Esq.
> Rev. Henry Barber, M.D.
> Paul Bevan, Esq. M.A.
> Sir Benjamin Vincent Sutton Brodie, bt. M.A.
> Sir Thomas David Gibson Carmichael, bt. M.A. M.P.
> Rev. William Kyle Westwood Chafy, D.D.
> Rev. William Gilchrist Clark-Maxwell, M.A.
> Frederick William Cock, Esq. M.D.
> Wilson Crewdson, Esq. M.A.
> George Crafter Croft, Esq.
> Robert Holmes Edleston, Esq.
> Lieut.-Col. Henry Leslie Ellis.
> Rev. George Herbert Engleheart, M.A.
> Francis Frederick Fox, Esq.
> Richard Oliver Heslop, Esq.
> Thomas Hesketh Hodgson, Esq.
> Alfred Cart de Lafontaine, Esq.
> Robert Alexander Stewart Macalister, Esq. M.A
> Rev. Morgan Thomas Pearman, M.A.
> Herbert George Radford, Esq.
> Gordon McNeile Rushforth, Esq. M.A.

Rev. Charles William Shickle, M A.
Prince Frederick Duleep Singh, M.A.
Hamon le Strange, Esq. M A.
Rev. Charles Samuel Taylor, M A.
Godfrey Charles, Baron Tredegar.
Lawrence Weaver, Esq.

The following have resigned ·

Sir Edward Henry Sieveking, knt M.D.
Samuel Timmins, Esq J P.
Warwick Wroth, Esq.

The following Fellows have died since the last Anniversary :

James Lewis André, Esq.   9 August, 1901.
Lieutenant-Colonel Alten Augustus William Beamish, R.E   21 March, 1902.
Sir Walter Besant, knt. M A. 9 June, 1901.
* Cecil Brent, Esq.   20 March, 1902.
Daniel Charles Addington Cave, Esq   23 July, 1901.
Richard Cox, Esq. M D.   8 October, 1901.
* John Lewis Fytche, Esq.   14 February, 1902.
* Augustus William Gadesden, Esq   15 August, 1901
Joseph Jackson Howard, Esq. LL.D Maltravers Herald Extraordinary.   18 April, 1902.
* George Lambert, Esq.   12 September, 1901.
Hugh Leonard, Esq.   15 December, 1901.
Stanley Leighton, Esq. M.A., M.P.   4 May, 1901.
Sir John Braddick Monckton, knt.   3 February, 1902
Benjamin Nattali, Esq.   6 December, 1901.
Edmund Oldfield, Esq. M.A.   11 April, 1902.
Sir Cuthbert Edgar Peek, bt. M.A , F.R.G.S.   6 July 1901.
Thomas Preston, Esq.   10 December, 1901.
Benjamin Franklin Stevens, Esq.   5 March, 1902.
Joseph John Tylor, Esq.   5 April, 1902.
* Denotes Compounder.

Of these Fellows :

Mr. JAMES LEWIS ANDRÉ, who died 9th August, 1901, was elected a Fellow 8th June, 1891. Mr. André was a frequent contributor to the publications of the Royal Archæological Institute, St. Paul's Ecclesiological Society, and the Surrey Archæological Society.

Lieutenant-Colonel ALTEN AUGUSTUS WILLIAM BEAMISH, R.E., was elected a Fellow 8th June, 1893. At the time of his death he held the office of Inspector-General of His Majesty's Prisons. He died 21st March this year somewhat suddenly.

In Sir WALTER BESANT, M.A. Camb., who died 9th June, 1901, the world has lost a favourite writer and the popular side of antiquarian study an active student. Born in 1836, he was educated at King's College, London, and Christ's College, Cambridge. Originally intended for the Church he changed his career and was appointed Senior Professor of the Royal College of Mauritius. Ill health compelled him to return to England, when he devoted himself to literature, and in collaboration with Mr. James Rice he produced several successful novels. For many years he was secretary to the Palestine Exploration Fund, and he took an active part in the proceedings for the protection of authors' rights. In 1886 he founded the Society of Authors, of which he was president until 1890. Of later years he devoted himself to the study of the History of the Metropolis, and in 1893 published a History of London.

Mr. CECIL BRENT, who died 20th March this year, was elected a Fellow 30th May, 1867. He contributed many papers to local and other societies, but beyond exhibiting various objects here I do not find that our publications contain any contributions from him.

Mr. DANIEL CHARLES ADDINGTON CAVE, who died 23rd July, 1901, aged 41, was elected a Fellow 13th June, 1898. He was an active member of the Council of Clifton College, and materially assisted the fortunes of the Fine Art Academy, of which he was President.

Dr. RICHARD COX was elected a Fellow 1st March, 1888, and died 8th October, 1901.

The late Mr. JOHN LEWIS FITCHE, of Freshwater, Isle of Wight, who died 14th February last, at the ripe age of 85, was elected a Fellow in June, 1852.

Mr. AUGUSTUS WILLIAM GADESDEN, who was elected a Fellow 7th May, 1840, died 15th August, 1901.

On the 18th of this month died Dr. JOSEPH JACKSON HOWARD, Maltravers Herald Extraordinary. He was elected a Fellow of this Society as long ago as 2nd February, 1854, and his name was very familiar to many of us, especially to genealogists.   He contributed papers to the *Archaeologia*, especially one in 1873 on the Will of Edward Grimston, and his name occurs often in past years in the *Proceedings* of the Society.

In collaboration with Colonel Chester, Mr. Howard edited the *Visitation of London*, 1633-4, for the Harleian Society, of which he was Hon. Treasurer and an active Member of Council.

Mr GEORGE LAMBERT, who died 12th September, 1901, in his 78th year, was elected a Fellow 28th May, 1870, and was for many years a constant attendant at our meetings, where his great knowledge and experience in matters of silver plate often proved of interest and value.   Mr Lambert was a no less active member of the Royal Archæological Institute, whose annual meetings he often attended.   He was a very ardent and one of the earliest volunteers, and though his health of late prevented his coming to our meetings as often as he wished, his face will be missed by many of the older Fellows. Major Lambert, as he liked to be styled, was an active member of many of the City charitable institutions, a liveryman of several City Companies, and held in 1887 the office of Prime Warden of the Goldsmiths' Company.

Mr. HUGH LEONARD, who died 15th December, 1901, was elected a Fellow 10th January, 1901.

Mr BENJAMIN NATTALI, who died 6th December, 1901, was elected a Fellow 12th June, 1894.

Mr. STANLEY LEIGHTON, M.A , M.P , who died 4th May, 1901, was born in 1837, and educated at Harrow and Balliol, after which he practised for some time at the bar.   He travelled much and was interested in colonial questions.   He was one of the founders of the Central Council of Diocesan Conferences, and concerned himself with many Church questions. He took an active interest in the proposals for the proper preservation and transcription of parish registers.   He represented his county of Shropshire in four Parliaments, having also unsuccessfully contested Bewdley in 1874.   He

was elected a Fellow of the Society on 8th January, 1880.
Mr. Leighton was a member of the Council of this Society
in 1888.

Sir JOHN BRADDICK MONCKTON, knt., who died 3rd February
this year, was elected a Fellow 18th February, 1875, but though
his surname by itself was for many years a familiar one on
notices concerning the City, I cannot find that the late
Town Clerk of the City of London ever contributed to our
publications. Born in 1832 and educated at Rugby, he
practised as a solicitor for many years. In 1873 he was
elected Town Clerk of the City of London, to which office he
was annually re-elected until his death

Mr. EDMUND OLDFIELD, M A , and in the last year of his life
elected an Honorary Fellow of his old college, Worcester,
joined our Society May 1st, 1856. He was an acknowledged
authority on architecture and classical archæology, and was
for many years the Honorary Librarian and only Lay Fellow
of his college. Later he became Assistant-Keeper of Antiquities at the British Museum, and was with the late Sir Charles
Newton for many years associated with the organisation and
development of that department. He was the author of many
papers in the *Archaeologia*, and as late as June, 1893, contributed an important one on the Mausoleum of Halicarnassus.
As a member of the committee for the decoration of St. Paul's
Cathedral he found himself in strong opposition to the views
of the late Mr. Burges, F.S.A., who in his scheme of decoration
for Mr. Oldfield's college had already aroused his strong
criticism.

In many ways Mr. Oldfield was recognised as an authority
on artistic taste, and in matters of historical fact his opinion
commanded the fullest respect. Papers on Roman bronze
vessels found at Castle Howard and on mosaics in the Bassian
Basilica, Rome, are printed in vols xli. and xlv. of *Archaeologia*.

Mr Oldfield was on many occasions a Member of Council
(as late as 1897) of our Society, in whose work he took an
active interest and part.

Mr Oldfield died at his residence, Rushmore, Torquay, on
the 11th inst. at the advanced age of 85

Sir CUTHBERT PEEK, bart., M.A., F.R.G S., was elected a
Fellow 6th March, 1890. Born in 1855, he was educated at

Eton and Cambridge. Though an F.S.A., his chief pursuit
was astronomy and its kindred sciences.   A great traveller,
he was a member of the Council of the Royal Geographical
Society, which body he has endowed with a medal for the
advancement of geographical knowledge.   He was also honorary secretary of the Anthropological Institute. Sir Cuthbert
died 6th July, 1901.

Mr. THOMAS PRESTON, who died 10th December, 1901, was
elected a Fellow 4th March, 1897.   He was for twenty-five years
Record Clerk in the Judicial Department of Privy Council.
He had served as secretary to Earl Cairns, Lord Westbury,
and Lord Romilly, and had published several works, chiefly
on legal procedure, etc., but including a History of the
Yeomen of the Guard.   Mr Preston, who died at the age of
67, was in his younger days an officer in the 19th Middle-
sex R.V.

Mr. BENJAMIN FRANKLIN STEVENS, who died 5th March this
year, was elected a Fellow 3rd March, 1898.   He acted, I
believe, as agent in this country for many of the American
Genealogical Societies.

On the eve of our last Anniversary Meeting the country
lost one of the most eminent historians of the latter part of
last century. The Right Reverend WILLIAM STUBBS, D D.,
Bishop of Oxford, was born in 1825, and educated at Ripon
Grammar School and Christ Church, Oxon, where he took a
first class in Classics. Ordained in 1848, he became vicar of
Haverstock, Essex.   Ten years later a sketch of the episcopal
succession in England in his *Registrum Sacrum Anglicanum*
established his repute as an investigator of mediæval history.
In 1862, being appointed librarian to the archiepiscopal
library at Lambeth, he began his great series of editions of
Mediæval Chronicles for the Rolls Series His work in this
line is too well known to need more than a passing mention.
In 1866, appointed Regius Professor of Modern History at
Oxford, he began, in collaboration with the Rev. A. W. Haddan,
the publication of a collection of *Councils and Ecclesiastical
Documents relating to Great Britain and Ireland based on
the Concilia.*   In 1870 he published *Select Charters and
other Illustrations of English Constitutional History from
the Earliest Period to the Reign of Edward I.* This was

followed by the great and well-known work, *The Constitutional History of England in its Original Development.*

Dr. Stubbs was consecrated Bishop of Chester in 1884 and translated to Oxford 1888. He became F.S.A. January 8th, 1880.

Mr. JOSEPH JOHN TYLOR died suddenly at his villa at Cap d'Ail, near Monaco, on 5th April. Mr. Tylor was fifty-one years of age, and was the eldest son of the late Mr. Alfred Tylor, of Carshalton. A correspondent writes: "Though by profession an engineer, Mr. Tylor had a well-merited reputation among specialists in Egyptian archæology. His purpose in wintering in Egypt was to regain lost health, but he soon employed himself in excavation, and experience made him sensible of the extent to which published hieroglyphic inscriptions, even in costly and monumental works, are untrustworthy. Especially wall-painting inscriptions, fast perishing and only to be replaced by copies, have suffered from the imaginative methods of the artist restorer. Mr. Tylor adopted the method of completing by hand enlarged photographs, by filling in the minutest details, such as the texture of the material represented, and, lastly, comparing on the spot every line with the original. His series of the 'Wall Drawings and Monuments of El Kab' (1895-1900) thus presents a near approach to absolute reproduction of these important documents of ancient history."

Dr. F. G. LEE, who died on 23rd January, though he left the Society a few years ago, had for many years been a Fellow, and at one time was a regular attendant at our meetings. An exceedingly prolific writer, he associated himself with ecclesiastical subjects, and his last contribution to the publications of the Society was a paper on *Episcopal Staves*, printed in *Archaeologia*, vol. li. Dr. Lee became a Fellow in 1857. He left the Society in 1893.

Though not a Fellow, in the late Dr. SAMUEL RAWSON GARDNER the world has sustained a heavy loss, as the late Professor unfortunately did not live to complete the history of the period which he had so thoroughly made his own. Born in 1829 and educated at Winchester and Christ Church, Oxon, where he took a first class in 1881, he was for many years Professor of History at King's College, which office he resigned in 1885. In 1882 he had granted to him a pension of £150 from the Civil List in recognition of his historical labours.

In 1884 he was elected a Fellow of All Souls, and then began
his *magnum opus*, the history of the Civil War. The period
from the accession of James I. he had already fully and fairly
treated in other large works. Amongst his many writings
may be mentioned two of the small Epochs of Modern
History series and the *Student's History of England*, a work
in which greater attention to illustrations from contemporary
authorities was given than had hitherto been the custom.
For the Camden Society, of which I believe he was a
Secretary, he edited the *Fortescue Papers*, the *Hamilton
Papers*, and the *Parliamentary Debates in* 1610 *and* 1625.
Great as our loss is in his death, the country is fortunate in
having as his successor in the unfinished work the experience
and full acquaintance with his subject of Mr. Firth, whose
recently published *Army of Cromwell* will be a necessary
handbook for all students of the seventeenth century, and for
military students especially. It may be well to mention also
that the late Professor was more than once mentioned as a
great constructive historian by the late Bishop of Oxford, to
whose appreciation of his ability his later connection with
the University was probably due. A writer in the *Guardian*
has drawn attention to Dr. Gardner's work as destroying
the fiction that a new English Church was created under
Henry VIII. or Elizabeth when he says: "In theory and in
sentiment the Church of England was still a branch of the
Catholic Church, one in doctrine and in discipline with the
Continental Churches."

Probably the most important antiquarian work of the year
has been the restoration to its normal upright position of one
of the large stones of Stonehenge, probably the largest native
monolith in England. The work was performed at the expense and with the favourable consent of the owner of
Stonehenge, Sir Edmund Antrobus, bart. Messrs. Detmar
Blow and Carruthers actually took charge of the work, and
the whole was successfully accomplished with the assistance
of several gentlemen who devoted much time and care to
this national work. Our Fellow, Mr. Gowland, with his
great experience of such work in the far East, took a most
active part in the operations, and generously devoted much
time to the undertaking, further contributing to the successful issue by the preparation of a valuable memoir on the
work and its results, which will I hope soon be in the hands
of all our Fellows in part 1 of vol. lviii. of *Archaeologia*.

The value of the work done can be hardly over estimated,
particularly when it is remembered that the age of Stonehenge

as calculated by the astronomers has been confirmed by the results of the digging during the work, a common goal having been thus reached by distinctly separate inquiries.

It is to be hoped that the success of these first operations may induce the owner to undertake, or perhaps allow to be undertaken, further work on this important site. I hope I may not be thought indiscreet if I suggest that, while fully recognising the rights of the owner, it might be arranged that the cost, which may amount to a considerable sum if all that is wished for be accomplished, should not fall on an individual.

While on this subject I may mention that the appointment of an Inspector of Ancient Monuments as a successor to our late Fellow, General Pitt-Rivers, is considered very desirable by many persons, and though the working of the Act has not been as fruitful of results as one might wish or as many hoped, yet the office should not, I think, be allowed to lapse.

Another interesting archæological event of the year has been the municipalisation, if I may so call it, of one of the beautiful Eleanor Crosses. This one at Northampton has now been handed over to the County Council, who will, we have every reason to believe, prove an excellent protective body for this historical monument. So far as the matter has gone in this instance it is an excellent example and a happy omen for similar action to be taken in other parts of our country. The placing under the protection of the local authorities of antiquarian and historical objects of this class seems a very proper and effective way of preserving for future times what has survived the dark and unintelligent periods of history.

At our last meeting we have had another instance of the thoughtful action of the London County Council in the exhibition of various portions of terra-cotta ornaments recently found in Southwark, and assigned by our Treasurer to the magnificent house of Charles Brandon, Duke of Suffolk, of which Wyngaerde's map gives us a sketch.

The question of the Irish gold ornaments having been again raised, a resolution was passed in the following terms:

"That the Fellows of the Society of Antiquaries of London in special meeting assembled, desire most earnestly to protest against the action of the Lords Commissioners of the Treasury in raising claims on behalf of the Crown which would deprive the British Museum of valuable antiquities in the national collection, under allegation that they were treasure trove."

A copy of this resolution was ordered to be sent to the Commissioners of the Treasury and laid before His Majesty. This was done, and a gracious notice of acknowledgment was made by His Majesty.

London, as we knew it some years ago, is passing away so quickly before the housebreakers of the London County Council, that our younger brother, the London Topographical Society, will have plenty to do, and not too much time to do it in, to record the rapid changes now taking place. However, its work is progressing well, and its publications are and will be of very great value when we, or our successors, have time given us to pause and think of how much of really old London has vanished in the last twenty years or so.

During the past year the advice of the Society was asked for on various matters, notably on the reconstruction or merely preservation of one of the rooms in Carisbrook Castle. The Council advised the roofing without disturbance of the room.

With regard to the examination of the site of *Uriconium*, it was decided that until Silchester has been fully explored it would be unwise to commence work of the same nature elsewhere, and at a considerably greater distance from London.

At the suggestion of Sir Norman Lockyer, it was decided to apply for a grant of £300 for the object of obtaining a census of archæological monuments to determine certain astronomical conditions, and for this purpose a sub-committee, consisting of Sir Norman Lockyer, Mr. Gowland, and General Sir T. H. Holdich, K.C.I.E., C.B., was nominated.

The great work of excavating systematically the site of the Romano-British town at Silchester was continued in 1901 for the twelfth year in succession, a fact upon which the Society has good reason to congratulate itself, since probably no excavation on such a scale has hitherto been carried out in this country for so long a time. The results last season, if not quite up to the level of some more fruitful years, were quite enough to justify the labour expended. A further addition has been made to the plan of the town, and the buildings uncovered have furnished several new facts, not the least important being interesting proof of the half-timbered construction of many of the houses. The finds of pottery, etc., have been also up to the average.

The season's work was directed almost throughout by Mr. Mill Stephenson, to whom antiquaries cannot be too grateful for so large a labour of love. As in past years, the Council has been able to materially assist the work by grants from the Research Fund, and the Fellows at large have continued to show their interest by their liberal subscriptions.

The end of the work of exploration is now within sight, and in five or six years the Committee in charge hope to complete this great undertaking.

With regard to the approaching building over of the site of *Clausentum* at Bitterne, Hants, our Fellow, Mr. G. E. Fox, visited the site and reported on the state of things. In consequence the Council requested him to obtain local assistance with a view to the ground being examined before building operations should prevent perhaps for ever such examination, and it is hoped that any discoveries to be made will not be prejudiced by neglect on the part of the local authorities. The Council further made a small grant in aid of any explorations which may be deemed necessary. Mr. Nevill was also associated with Mr. Fox to watch the matter.

Grants in aid of diggings have also been made to the Surrey Archæological Society, who are examining the site of Waverley Abbey, and to Mr. Page, whose explorations at St. Albans have from time to time been reported at our meetings. To the investigations now going on at St. Augustine's, Canterbury, the Society has also contributed.

The question of the preservation of the handsome market cross at Chichester having become urgent, our Fellows, Messrs. G. Rice, Peers, and Towry Whyte, acting as a committee, made such recommendations as were necessary, and it will it is hoped be possible to satisfactorily strengthen this ornament of the town without the proposed re-edification.

The operations of the Cretan Exploration Fund Committee have this year, owing to the limited subscriptions, been confined to Knossos, where Mr. Arthur Evans has for a third season continued the excavation of the prehistoric palace. Heavy rains hindered the work, but already a new hall has been uncovered south of the hall of the double axe, with an unique system of stylobates, a small bath room with remains of a painted frieze, and a small staircase, two flights of which, apparently leading to the Thalamoi, still remain, and there is evidence that the stairs led to a third storey. Some interesting remains of fresco painting have also been found, and a kind of lararium with a small painted terra-cotta figure of a goddess and another of a male votary, each with doves, and between them an ex-voto double axe of steatite A series of late Kamari pots with naturalistic painted designs have also been found, and tablets referring to the armoury, etc also were unearthed.   Large stone walls are also beginning to appear.   The work at Knossos will occupy the excavators for the rest of the season, and it should be remembered that below the Mycenean level there are remains as at Tiryns and Phylakapi of yet earlier settlements.

At Santa Maura Dr Dörpfeld is continuing his explorations for the German Archæological Institute at Athens, based on the hypothesis that in Santa Maura and not in the modern Ithaca, we have the ancient Ithaca, which conforms but slightly to the Homeric description. The resolution of the Greek Archæological Society to reconstruct the loose fragments of the Erectheum has caused some doubt as to its advisability, considering the very doubtful success which attended the re-erection of fallen columns of the Parthenon, owing to the strong contrast of the old with the new marble, of which there was a good deal, and which it will require many years to harmonise with old.

In Rome we have within the last few days heard of the important excavations by Cavaliere Giacomo Boni in the Forum Our distinguished Honorary Fellow appears to be on the way to make discoveries concerning the very early history of that city which will be of the very greatest interest to all antiquaries.

Sir John Evans and the Earl of Crawford were appointed to represent the Society at the Ninth Jubilee of the University of Glasgow in June next.   The Society has also been requested to send a representative to the tercentenary of the Bodleian Library at Oxford.

The usual permissions have been given for various societies to use our meeting room for special occasions Amongst these were the Ruskin Union, the Henry Bradshaw Society, and others.

The Hellenic Society have also been allowed to hold their councils in our rooms some four times a year.

A loan of certain of our royal portraits was made to the New Gallery for the exhibition of the Sovereigns of England held there.

The meetings of the Museen-Verband, who held their session in London this year, were held in our rooms, and the favour was much appreciated by the representatives of many European museums.

The ever-recurring question of how to find room for the numerous additions to our library has received special emphasis this year from the increase due to the selections from the library of the Royal Archæological Institute, which that body generously placed at our service. The immediate need for more shelf room suggested the erection of a large bookcase in the hall near the staircase, and an addition to our shelving in the council room in the shape of a large group of bookcases. The valuable MS. collection of the Society has now been placed under glass all together close to the Assistant Secretary's office.

During the past year among the more important additions to our library, we must mention the gift of some 350 volumes from the Royal Archæological Institute. These we were allowed to select from their library before its dispersal, and we have thus filled up some gaps in our own. Professor Rahn has also presented a number of important pamphlets on painted glass and other subjects; Mr. R. D. Radcliffe has also added to our collection several pamphlets on prehistoric, Roman, and Irish subjects.

A fine series of drawings illustrative of the topography of Lincolnshire by the late Mr. E. J. Willson, F.S.A., has been purchased, and will be of value to many of our Fellows.

The assistance of a boy in the library has been obtained so as to enable the necessary work of Mr. Clinch to be carried on with less interruption.

With a view to obtaining still more room for our books and store room for our stock of publications, arrangements have been made for the boarding out of the porter and his family. This has, of course, entailed an increase in our expenses, but we shall have more space available for the above storage.

The suggestion made a year ago, as to the collection of and cataloguing of a collection of lantern slides available for the illustration of papers has been acted on, and the Society is indebted to several of the Fellows for a good number of slides, which will be of great use and convenience to all.

I again have to thank the officers of the Society for the cordial co-operation they have at all times given in the maintenance of the dignity and aims of our Society. Our clerk, Mr. Clinch, has also been very helpful on all occasions."

At the conclusion of the President's Address the following Resolution was moved by EDWARD WILLIAM BRABROOK, Esq., C.B., seconded by WILLIAM GOWLAND, Esq., and carried unanimously:

"That the best thanks of the meeting be given to the President for his Address, and that he be requested to allow it to be printed."

The PRESIDENT signified his assent.

The Scrutators having reported that the Members of the Council in List I. and the Officers of the Society in List II. had been duly elected, the following List was read from the Chair of those who had been duly elected as Council and Officers for the ensuing year:

Eleven Members from the Old Council.

Harold Arthur, Viscount Dillon, Hon. M.A. Oxon, *President.*
Philip Norman, Esq., *Treasurer.*
Frederick George Hilton Price, Esq , *Director.*
Charles Hercules Read, Esq., *Secretary.*
William Paley Baildon, Esq
Arthur John Evans, Esq., M.A., Litt.D., F.R.S.
Sir John Evans, K C B., D C L , LL.D., Sc.D., F.R.S.
Arthur Henry Lyell, Esq., M.A.
Walter Llewellyn Nash, Esq.
Robert Garraway Rice, Esq.
Sir Edward Maunde Thompson, K.C.B., LL D., D.C.L.

Ten Members of the New Council.

David Lindsay, Lord Balcarres, M.P.
Edward William Brabrook, Esq., C.B.
The Rt. Rev. George Forrest, Bishop of Bristol, D.D. D C.L.
John Willis Clark, Esq., M.A.

William Gowland, Esq.
Charles Trice Martin, Esq., B.A.
John Linton Myres, Esq., M.A.
William Page, Esq.
Mill Stephenson, Esq., B.A.
John William Willis-Bund, Esq., M.A., LL.B.

Thanks were returned to the Scrutators for their trouble.

The following Resolution was proposed from the Chair, seconded by the Treasurer, and carried unanimously :

" The President, Council, and Fellows of the Society of Antiquaries of London desire to express and to place on record their gratitude to the President, Council, and Members of the Royal Archæological Institute for the gift from their library of such books as were required in the Library of the Society of Antiquaries. The gift is appreciated not only for its utility but for the evidence it affords of the goodwill of the Institute towards the Society."

The Treasurer made a short statement as to the financial condition of the Society, showing that it was in every way quite satisfactory.

Pursuant to the Statutes, ch. iii. § 3, the names of the following, who had failed to pay all moneys due from them to the Society, and for such default had ceased to be Fellows of the Society, were read from the Chair, and the President made an entry of their amoval against each of their names in the Register of the Society :

Paul Henry Foley, Esq., M.A.
Alfred Gilbert, Esq., M.V.O., R.A.
John Horsfall, Esq., M.A., F.R.C.S.
William Jones, Esq.

The following Resolution was proposed by Sir ERNEST CLARKE, seconded by Mr. H. B. WHEATLEY, and carried by 15 votes for to 13 votes against :

" That the new Council be respectfully requested to take into consideration the desirability of changing the hour of the Ordinary Meetings from the evening to the afternoon, at 4·30 p.m. or 5 p.m., and to ascertain the views of the Society at large by the issue of a circular on the subject."

Thursday, 1st May, 1902.

Viscount DILLON, President, in the Chair.

The following gifts were announced, and thanks for the same ordered to be returned to the donors:

From the Author:—Worlebury, an ancient stronghold in the county of Somerset, New edition, revised and partly re-written, with additions.   By C. W. Dymond, F.S.A. 4to. Bristol, 1902.

From the Author:—Denton, near Gravesend, its Manor, its Court House, and Chapel of St. Mary. By G. M. Arnold, F.S.A. 8vo. Gravesend, 1902.

From the Author:—The Dundee Market Crosses and Tolbooths. By William Kidd. 8vo. Dundee, 1902.

The President announced that he had appointed William Gowland, Esq., to be a Vice-President of the Society.

SOMERS CLARKE, Esq., F.S.A., submitted the following report as Local Secretary for Egypt:

"I beg leave to lay before the Fellows of the Society of Antiquaries a few notes on subjects connected with Archæology in Egypt.

It becomes more difficult than of old to communicate as much as could be wished on the subject of investigation and discovery,

Since M. Maspéro has been at the head of the Department of Antiquities the more important and best known sites up and down the country are more carefully guarded than heretofore. Assisted by the inspectors Mr. J. E. Quibell and Mr. Howard Carter, the hopeless neglect of past times is at an end.

The result is that the antiquity dealers who stand at the back of the plunderers find it more difficult than heretofore to get objects to sell to the tourist. Not only so, the plunderers become more bold. Their reward is greater, whilst the chance of punishment they run is hardly worth considering.

During the summer time, when the archæologist is not at work, raids are made on the very sites where the work of investigation is yet unfinished, or on any site which the archæologist may have inadvertently mentioned as one of promise for future examination.

Sites, references to which may have appeared in a newspaper in England, have been promptly pounced upon by the dealers and plunderers.

All visitors who wish to see the antiquities are required to purchase a ticket at the price of one pound Egyptian (£1 0s. 6d.). The money thus collected, amounting to several thousand pounds per annum, is used to pay for the guardianship of the monuments and sites, for setting up protective walls and gates to tombs and temples, etc., etc.

It is obvious that such guardians are of no use unless the law adequately supports the authority delegated to them. This it does not do.

The most ludicrously inadequate fines are imposed. The most absurdly ridiculous excuses are accepted. The thieves and plunderers practically escape free.

Fortunately the very centre of authority in Upper Egypt has been attacked.

One of the Tombs of the Kings at Thebes, that of Amenophis II., recently cleared by M. Loret, has been broken into. This was the only tomb in which the mummy of the king rested in the sarcophagus covered with the withered wreaths of flowers laid upon it at the time of burial.

The mummy was taken out of the sarcophagus, cut open and searched, the wreaths were scattered and taken away, whilst from another part of the tomb two large models of funereal barques were taken.

Whether the ordinary fine of about five piastres = one shilling, will be imposed I am not able to say. The case was not decided when I left Thebes.

It is perhaps needless to say that the penalty to be imposed rests, not with the Director of Antiquities, M. Maspèro, but with those who administer the law. Four years since Mr. J. E. Quibell, acting for the Egypt Research Account, excavated the site at Hierakonpolis. Some of the greatest treasures in the Gizeh Museum were then found, and the site was not exhausted. Last summer this place was ravaged by the plunderers, such a spectacle of yawning graves, skulls, bones, and broken pottery, such devastation I have never seen. Some men were apprehended, but the penalties imposed were ridiculous.

There are undoubtedly considerable difficulties in dealing with these cases. The troubles we have at home with poachers give us some sort of parallel.

At Abydos, Professor Petrie has again been busily engaged for his third year. He is working for the Egypt Exploration Fund. His season's work will shortly be published, but as to his hopes or prospects for the future it is best to keep silence.

On the west side of the river at Assuan some tombs have been opened by Lord and Lady William Cecil   Lady William has personally assisted at the work, making some excellent drawings.   Several good tombs and fine sarcophagi have been found.

At Naga ed Deir, opposite Girga, one of the best pieces of scientific investigation now going on in Egypt is being carried on.

Here a vast number of tombs, sundry untouched ones, have received most careful examination by Mr. George Reisner, acting for Mrs. Hearst, an American lady.   The finds, after passing through Gizeh Museum, go to the museum at San Fiancisco.   The tombs are chiefly of the III. and IV. Dynasties.

It is not easy to speak too highly of the cautious way in which the investigations are made.   Photographs are taken at every stage of the proceedings, with a multitude of notes, drawings, and measurements.

Mr. Reisner is fortunate above his fellow investigators. Those who work for societies are, alas, always hampered by lack of funds, and, what is worse, are expected every year to produce some results for subscribers to see, and a book for them to finger, not perhaps always to read.

An investigation conducted as it should be on purely scientific lines cannot every year lead to such results.   I venture to say that in few instances have sites, on which one season only has been spent, been even half worked out or examined as they should be, and none are more conscious of this fact than those who do the work.   Unfortunately for them, there hangs over their heads the inevitable book and exhibition.

Mr. Reisner is directed to do his best, he is not cramped for funds nor hurried for time or results, and consequently he is able to do his work in a way that makes others justly envious.

At Thebes the ruins of the Palace of Amenophis III. are being investigated in the same painstaking and deliberate manner.

Mr. Percy Newberry is superintending the work, assisted by Mr. Titus, an American gentleman, who provides the funds. The building, as far as it has been uncovered, is entirely of crude brick, the surfaces of the walls, floors, and ceilings being plastered and painted.   The colours are in many places still quite brilliant. Some ceilings are ornamented with flights of birds painted with great freedom and dexterity. Some of the floors are painted, as at Tell el Amarna, with reeds and fishes drawn with remarkable skill, the touch swift, sure, and exactly suited to the purely decorative character of the work.

Here, again, there is not a terrible book to be produced each season to amuse subscribers, but when the time is ripe the work will be thoroughly and adequately illustrated and described.

Mr. Theodore Davis, also an American gentleman, who has previously contributed towards investigation, has provided funds for further researches in the Valley of the Tombs of the Kings.

Under the direction of Mr. Howard Carter, Chief Inspector of Antiquities for Upper Egypt, six of the Tombs of the Kings have now been provided with electric light, namely the tombs of Amenophis II., Seti I., and Rameses I., III., VII., and IX.

The conjunction of electric light and the Tombs of the Kings may, to some, appear a little astonishing. When, however, the damage done by candles, torches, and magnesium wire is appreciated, it will be seen how much we owe to M. Maspèro for introducing electricity. The reckless and wilful damage done by tourists is beyond belief. One of the above-named tombs had not been uncovered two days when it was found that some one had, with a candle, smoked initials 12 inches high on the hitherto absolutely clean ceiling.

At Karnak, the work of making a solid floor on which the fallen columns of the Hypostyle Hall can be reinstated is rapidly moving forward.

Some remarkably fine lintels and square columns of the XII. Dynasty have been uncovered at a level of some two meters below the door sill of the Pylon of Thothmes III. and immediately north of it.

The remains are in limestone, and although the stones are in many cases broken, the preservation of the sculptures is only equalled by the beauty of their style.

At Philae the work of underpinning the temples and colonnades, so that the security of their foundations may be assured, has been going on rapidly.

The picturesque little streets of brick ruins have, alas, been of necessity cleared away. To leave this crude brickwork, impregnated as it is with salt, which under the action of the rising water would quickly act on the stonework, would lead to its rapid destruction. The result of the removal has been that half the picturesque charm of the place is lost ; but the government is doing its best under the circumstances and following the only course that seemed open to it.

An unfortunate incident has happened at Assuan.   An example of Saracenic art which, apart from its intrinsic value, played nearly as prominent a part in the general landscape as does the mosque of Mahomet Ali at Cairo, has been overthrown.

I quote from a letter sent to the *Egyptian Gazette* on the subject, and which appeared on January 10th last

'A most unnecessary act of vandalism in the destruction of a picturesque and interesting object in the immediate neighbourhood of Assuan has just taken place. It is very desirable that public notice should be called to such an act with the hope that, for the future, a more intelligent care may be taken by those officials who have so much in their power to preserve or destroy.   Immediately south of Assuan lies a large cemetery, a place of high antiquity, dotted over with a multitude of picturesque domed tombs.

On the salient points of the granite ridge are seen tombs of a more ambitious character, and these contribute a marked individuality to the prospect.   The northernmost of the large tombs, known as the tomb of the Saba wa Sabeen Wâli, was —alas, I must say was—a building of no small importance.

Ruined and neglected as it was, yet it had interest even as a piece of Arab architecture.   In addition it was still held in veneration by many.   On two occasions in every year a large number of pilgrims resorted to the spot.   Why was this place destroyed ?

A very laudable enterprise has just been undertaken at Assuan, the supply of the town with water.

An engineer, some understrapper as it seems from the Public Works, with characteristic disregard for everything but engineering, induced the Mudir' (the equivalent to the Mayor)' to approve the site of the picturesque tomb above referred to as the most suitable for the high level tanks.   The tomb was promptly overthrown and a square box-like structure is now being set up in its place.'

The letter goes on to show that whilst Lord Kitchener was Sirdar, and Assuan, being as it then was in the frontier province, was under military rule, great care was taken by him that the picturesque charms of the place should not be defaced.   Now the province is under civil administration, and the firm hand being removed the vandalism is perpetrated.

At the same time that I wrote this letter I also wrote informing the Comité de Conservation des Monuments de l'Art arabe of what had happened.

In England we may venture to criticise the actions of a department. Not so in Egypt.

Although my letter to the Comité was of the mildest description I was requested to withdraw it, as it was stated that it gave pain to some of the officials. This I have naturally declined to do, as I merely stated facts ; to my last communication I have not yet received a reply.

FIG. I. TOMB AT ASSUAN.   THE TOMB DESTROYED WAS VERY SIMILAR IN CHARACTER.

One must not disturb the heights of official serenity. The position is the more amusing as I am an honorary member of the Comité de Conservation des Monuments de l'Art arabe. I was as I believed doing my duty towards that body in calling attention to the vandalism, and was also I hope doing my duty as correspondent in Egypt to the Society of Antiquaries.

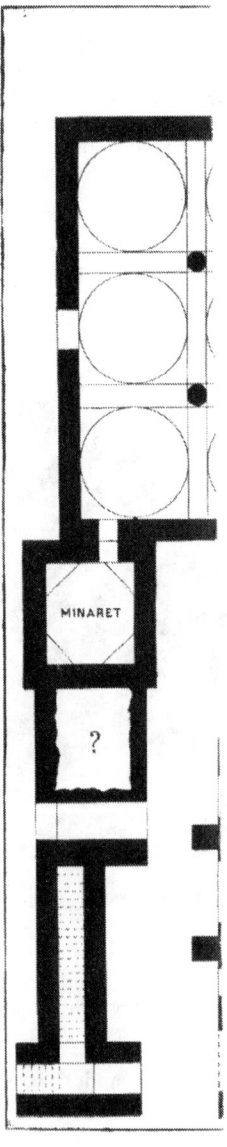

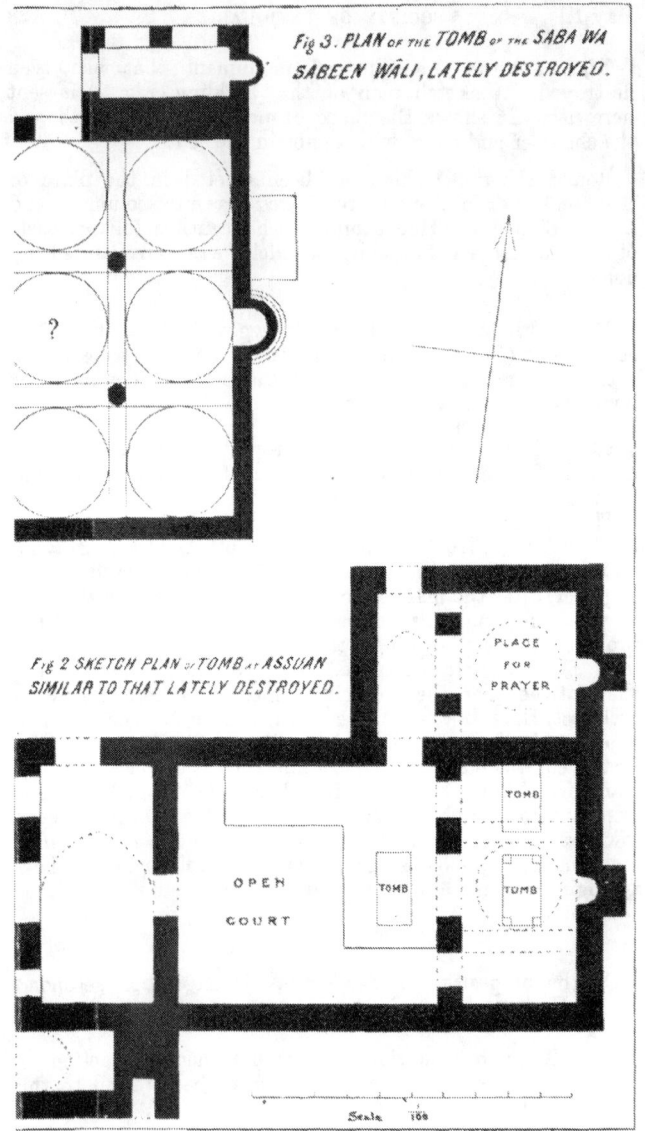

Fig 3. PLAN OF THE TOMB OF THE SABA WA SABEEN WÂLI, LATELY DESTROYED.

?

PLACE FOR PRAYER

Fig 2 SKETCH PLAN OF TOMB AT ASSUAN SIMILAR TO THAT LATELY DESTROYED.

TOMB

OPEN COURT

TOMB

TOMB

Scale

Fig. 1 shows the type of monument that has been destroyed. A sketch plan of this building (Fig. 2) is sent herewith. It shows the place of prayer to the north and the chamber and court with tombs in the south.

Round the tank which has been erected in the place of the tomb lie four overthrown red granite columns, and a piece of a Byzantine capital, with acanthus foliage, parts of the destroyed monument, which was surmounted by domes.

By the kindness of Professor Strgygowski I am enabled to send a plan (Fig. 3) of the monument so needlessly destroyed.

To this a minaret was attached, the building having more importance as a mosque than as a tomb.

P.S.—Since writing the above report I have heard of a proposal for the wanton destruction of an interesting and picturesque tower at Alexandria.

The municipality of Alexandria desired to make a wide road on the sea front towards the east of the town. Having no appreciation of the tower or care for its antiquity, their engineer, after the manner of engineers, proposed to throw it down The Comité de Conservation fortunately heard of the project, but were informed that their remonstrance was too late. The tower was destroyed. However, not quite believing the statement of the municipal officers, the Comité sent its architect, Herz Bey, with a camera, and he returned with a photograph of the tower, which, although it was stated to be destroyed was standing, a substantial mass of masonry very many feet high. It had, in fact, hardly been touched. The Department of Public Works intervened, and not only is the tower saved, but it will make an object of interest in the new road, and be in nobody's way. It is remarkable to observe how an engineer seems almost to delight in an act of gratuitous vandalism."

On the proposition of Sir HENRY H. HOWORTH, seconded by Mr. HIGGINS, it was resolved :

> " That the question of the continued destruction of ancient monuments in Egypt be referred to the Council for consideration."

W. H. St. JOHN HOPE, Esq., M.A., Assistant-Secretary, read

a paper on the London Charterhouse, its ancient water-supply and arrangements.

Mr. Hope's paper will be printed in *Archaeologia*.

The Rev. W. HAIG BROWN, Master of the Charterhouse, exhibited a vellum roll of the fifteenth century showing the course of the Charterhouse water-supply.

Thanks were ordered to be returned for these communications and exhibitions.

———

Thursday, 15th May, 1902.

WILLIAM GOWLAND, Esq., Vice-President, in the Chair.

The following gifts were announced, and thanks for the same ordered to be returned to the donors:

From the Trustees of the British Museum —The Waddesdon Bequest. Catalogue of the Works of Art bequeathed to the British Museum by Baron Ferdinand Rothschild, M P., 1898. By C. H Read 4to London, 1902.

From Sir John Evans, K C.B , V P.S A. ·

1. Catalogue Raisonné des Objets Archéologiques contenus dans le Musée d'Oran. 8vo. Oran, 1895.

2. Catalogue Illustré du Musée National des Antiquités Algériennes. 8vo. Alger, 1899.

From W. E. Foster, Esq., F.S.A. .—South Lincolnshire Families. Sanders of Weston 8vo. Peterborough, 1902

From W. S. Appleton, Esq :—Family Letters from the Bodleian Library. 8vo. Cambridge, U.S.A., 1902.

From W. H. Aymer Vallance, Esq., M.A , F.S.A. :—Certain plates and pages of letterpress to help to complete the copy of "Churches of Yorkshire," in the Society's Library.

From the Author ·—Some notes on the Lowthers who held judicial office in Ireland in the 17th century. By Sir E. T. Bewley, LL.D. 8vo. Kendal, 1902

Notice was given of a Ballot for the election of Fellows on Thursday, 5th June, and a list of candidates to be balloted for was read.

W. DALE, Esq., F.S.A., read the following notes on the discovery of an Anglo-Saxon cemetery at Droxford, Hants:

"The discovery I have to record was made during the construction of the new railway between Fareham and Alton. This railway passes up the Meon Valley, but does not follow the low ground in all its course. At the village of Droxford it cuts through the top of the hill overlooking the valley on the eastern side, and it is at this point, immediately above Droxford Church and close to the place marked Brockbridge on the map, that the discovery was made.

During the summer of 1900 I was informed that human bones had been found here, in some cases covered with big flints, associated with spearheads and pieces of much corroded ironwork. I went to the spot and obtained some spearheads and battered fragments of iron, which I brought here. The spearheads were pronounced by Mr. Read to be Anglo-Saxon, and the fragments part of the umbo and bracers of a Saxon shield. Going again a few days later I got some smaller objects, which I had no difficulty in identifying by means of the fine series of Anglo-Saxon antiquities in the British Museum, and especially those of the Gibbs bequest. I thought the discovery was one of interest, and more especially as just at the time I had read Mr. Reginald Smith's excellent article in the *Victoria County History of Hampshire* on the Anglo-Saxon remains of our county.

After quoting Bede as to the district appropriated by the Jutes in Hampshire, Mr. Smith says: 'The stages of the Jutish progress are marked by a succession of townships along the Meon Valley from mouth to source. Meon, Titchfield, Wickham, Soberton, Droxford, Meon Stoke, Corhampton, Warnford, and Meon East and West were all existing in the eleventh century, and in all likelihood had then been founded nearly 600 years * * * Bede's statement is, however, precise enough to justify the expectation of finding characteristic Jutish remains in the Island and its neighbourhood, and a general resemblance was long ago noticed between the objects found in the pagan graves of Kent and the Isle of Wight. As both districts are definitely recorded as the seats of Jutish immigrations, there is every reason for assigning their name to this particular type of relics. The parallel, however, is not complete, for up to the present time no discoveries on the coast opposite the Island have revealed any trace of Jutish occupation.' Here a footnote is added. 'With possibly one exception, noticed in *Hants Notes and Queries*, where a newspaper paragraph is quoted. "Brooches of a peculiar form which have been found in Kent and the Isle of Wight have been discovered in the Meon country. They occur nowhere else in England. They do occur in certain of the Danish mosses, and the natural conclusion is that the design and peculiar decoration were Jutish." These objects have not been traced.'

Mr. Smith continues: 'It is possible, though hardly to be expected, that similar finds will some day be made in the Meon district, or on the edges of the New Forest; but it seems clear that at least no such conspicuous grave-mounds exist in these regions as have yielded so much to exploration on the Island Downs. Perhaps the true explanation is that the lower ground on both sides of the water was inhabited by a poorer population, whose graves would have no mounds or deposits of ornaments and utensils.'

Very little progress was made with the railway in 1900, owing to the scarcity of labour, and the cutting, after going about halfway through the field where the interments were, stopped until last autumn, when the work was again resumed and fresh discoveries made. The place is 20 miles from my home and 5 from any railway station, but I managed to go once or twice every week and was present on several occasions when burials were struck. I was also fortunate in enlisting the help of a couple of navvies who were more intelligent than is usual with their class, and who had a keen eye for business, so that I have been able to obtain almost everything of any importance. The work was, however, somewhat disappointing. The burials were very close to the surface and in a tenacious clayey earth (the clay with flints of the geologist which here caps the chalk), out of which it was very difficult to extract anything of any size whole. The ironwork was oxidised almost to destruction. Only the larger bones of the skeletons were preserved. Skulls could not be got out except in fragments, although the teeth were perfect and well-preserved. Moreover, the employment this winter of a steam navvy did not help matters, and probably some few objects were lost.

The surface of the ground gave no indication of burials If there had ever been anything in the form of tumuli, all traces of them had been removed by cultivation. Some bodies were buried east and west, but I saw two femurs lying due north and south, and I think there was no rule in the matter. The area of the cemetery was confined to the top of the hill, and the railway cut through about 100 yards of it north to south. It no doubt extended further east and west in the ground not touched by the railway. The interments were numerous and close together. Big flints were put over some, but not all. With many no articles at all were buried. In reading of the discoveries at other Anglo-Saxon cemeteries it strikes me that this one was not by any means so rich in objects as usual, which bears out the suggestion of Mr. Reginald Smith that this part was inhabited· by a poorer population than the Downs of the Isle of Wight. Several swords were found; but shield bosses and spearheads were more frequent. With some only a single knife, or a knife and spear, had been laid. With one of the swords, however, two unusually large spears had been put. The beads, of which there was considerable variety, were only found one or two at a time, never associated in such a number as to have formed a necklace. I conclude that the fibulæ, chatelaine holders, tweezers, spindle whorls of Kimmeridge shale, and a few other things of feminine use indicate that it was not a place of sepulture for warriors only. Vessels are represented by a small rudely-made cup of black earthenware, fragments of two other pots of black ware, and part of a brown glass tumbler, as well as the remains of two small wooden vessels made tub-fashion and hooped with bands ·of bronze. Roman coins occurred twice only; two are pierced. They have been identified for me as of Marcus Aurelius, Faustina, Crispus, Maximinus and Constantine II. Amongst a quantity of much corroded iron-work are probably some horse trappings and several shoes, one quite perfect. I could not discover that any horse-bones were found. A large nodule of pyrites was laid by one of the swords, either as a weapon or a strike-a-light, and there was a small piece of whetstone by one of the spears."

Mr. Read added some remarks on the more significant objects in the collection, and agreed that the cemetery showed signs of comparative poverty, though swords, of which six specimens were recovered, are generally considered to have indicated high rank. It is interesting to notice some striking similarities to the Isle of Wight finds that are assigned, with those of Kent, to the Jutes. The button-like concave brooches (figs. 1 and 2) and the small square-headed variety (fig. 3) are sufficient to classify the interments, which have no admixture of cinerary urns. A semicircular pendant of gilt bronze (fig. 4) resembles Kentish work, and the familiar cross-bow brooch (fig. 5) is a survival from the Romano-British period. The number of male burials may be estimated from the discovery of thirty-two spearheads, of which one or two are of unusual length; eight shield-bosses were found, and with

them are three complete shield handles (fig. 6) with extensions
to the circumference, the like of which has not perhaps been
hitherto found in this country. The whole collection has
since been presented by Mr. Dale to the British Museum.

Figs. 1 and 2.   BUTTON-LIKE
BROOCHES   FOUND   AT
DROXFORD, HANTS. ($\frac{1}{1}$)

Fig. 3.   SQUARE-HEADED
BROOCH   FOUND   AT
DROXFORD, HANTS. ($\frac{1}{1}$)

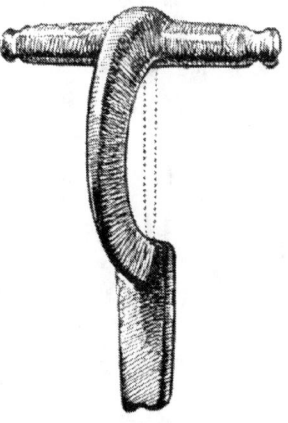

Fig. 4.   GILT BRONZE PENDANT
FOUND AT DROXFORD, HANTS.
($\frac{1}{1}$)

Fig. 5.   CROSS-BOW BROOCH
FOUND AT DROXFORD, HANTS.
($\frac{1}{1}$)

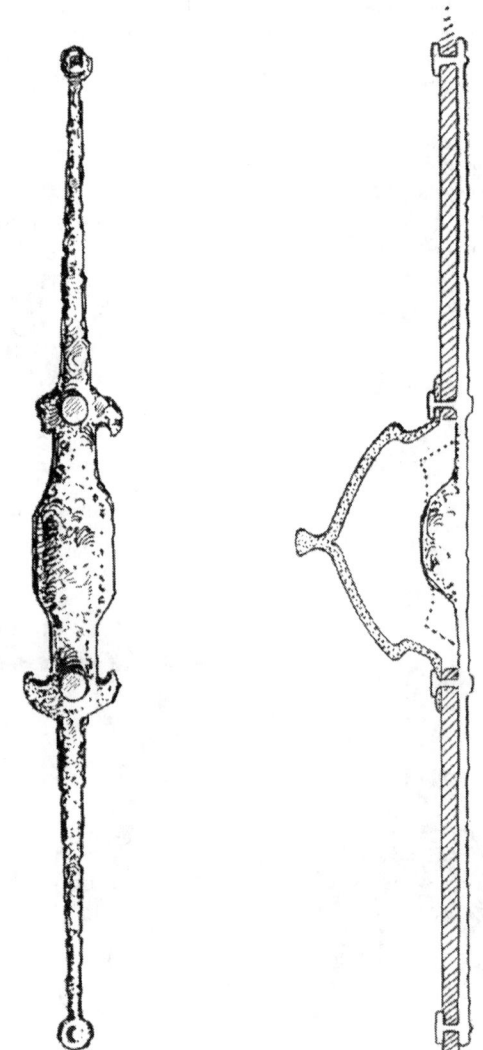

Fig. 6.   SHIELD-HANDLE (AND SECTION WITH ADDED BOSS) FOUND
AT DROXFORD, HANTS.

T. CATO WORSFOLD, Esq., exhibited two large oil jars found in Fetter Lane, London.

H. SWAINSON COWPER, Esq., F.S.A., Local Secretary for Westmorland, exhibited a number of Roman and other antiquities found at Brough-under-Stanmore, Westmorland. One of them, a small circular brooch of Late-Celtic character, is shown in the accompanying illustration.

LATE-CELTIC BROOCH FOUND AT BROUGH-UNDER-STANMORE, WESTMORLAND. (½.)

These objects have since been given to the British Museum.

Thanks were ordered to be returned for these communications and exhibitions.

Thursday, 29th May, 1902.

WILLIAM GOWLAND, Esq., Vice-President, in the Chair.

The following gifts were announced, and thanks for the same ordered to be returned to the donors :

From the Author :—Greek Coins and their Parent Cities. By John Ward (of Belfast), F.S.A. 4to. London, 1902.

From the Society of Antiquaries of Scotland :—Catalogue of the Scottish Coins in the National Museum of Antiquities, Edinburgh. By A. B. Richardson. 4to. Edinburgh, 1901.

From the Trustees of the British Museum :—Catalogue of the Coronation Exhibition, 1902. 8vo. London, 1902.

From the Author :—Report of the Cumberland Excavation Committee for 1900 and 1901. By F. Haverfield, M.A., F.S.A. 8vo. Kendal, 1901-1902.

Notice was again given of a Ballot for the election of Fellows on Thursday, 5th June, and a list of Candidates to be balloted for was read.

A letter from the Town Clerk of Chichester was read conveying an unanimous vote of thanks of the Town Council

to the Society for the trouble and interest taken by the
Society (through the Council) in the repair and preservation
of the Chichester Cross.

Professor A. H. CHURCH, M A., D.Sc , F.R.S , F.S.A , read
the following notes on the material of certain Cypriote
cylinder-seals:

"It was in August, 1899, that my attention was first drawn
by Dr A S. Murray, of the British Museum, to a seal-cylinder
from Cyprus, which presented certain curious features. At
first sight it appeared to be an engraved hæmatite, but on
further examination the seemingly incuse designs which cover
it revealed the characteristics of a casting from a mould in
relief, while the material itself proved to be too soft and too
brittle for hæmatite. · Still the surface possessed the sub-
metallic lustre of that substance, though rather violet in hue.
The specific gravity of the cylinder was ascertained to be 5·36
—a figure near to but rather higher than that of the compact
black hæmatite usually employed for Babylonian and Egyptian
objects of this class. A clue to the composition of this cylinder
was furnished by the presence of a pale greenish deposit which
filled up a part of the hollow axis. This was found to contain
much calcium carbonate, along with distinct traces of calcium
sulphate and of a compound of copper. The calcium carbonate
being obviously extraneous it was possible that the cylinder
itself might have been the source of the sulphur and of the
copper which had been detected, might in fact consist of or
contain a sulphide of copper. This was proved to be the case
by an examination of a few scrapings which responded to
the tests, physical as well as chemical, for cuprous sulphide
($Cu_2 S$), a compound which occurs in nature as the mineral
copper-glance or chalcocite. Some comparative experiments
with scrapings of copper-glance, and scrapings of this Cypriote
cylinder showed that these two materials were virtually, if
not actually, identical. They could not be distinguished
under the microscope; they were alike in degree of fusibilty
and in hardness (about 3^0). The specific gravity of the
mineral ranges between 5·52 and 5·81, while the Cypriote
cylinder under discussion was, it will be remembered, no
higher than 5 36. But one expects to find a casting to be of
lower density than the same material in a crystallised condition by reason of cavities and impurities in the former. And
here I must refer to three other Cypriote cylinders of the
same Mycenaean style, and obviously consisting of the same
substance as the British Museum specimen. They are in

the Ashmolean Museum at Oxford, and possess the specific
gravities here recorded :

> Cylinder A (the largest)   5·504.
> Cylinder B (the next in size) 5 531.
> Cylinder C (the smallest)   5·313.

These determinations, kindly made by Professor H. A.
Miers, are in close accord with the figure I obtained from the
British Museum example.   I may add that I examined a few
filings from Cylinder B, and found in them nothing save
copper, sulphur, and traces of iron ; indeed in chemical as well
as physical character they corresponded with cuprous sulphide.   In this connection a fifth specimen should be cited.
It is described in the ' Catalogue of the Cyprus Museum ' by
J. L. Myres and Dr. M. Ohnefalsch-Richter as a cylindrical
seal of the Bronze Age and of Mycenaean design.   It is
further stated that the design is 'engraved on a black
artificial paste resembling hæmatite,' and that the material
had been analysed by Dr Weeren, of the Technological High
School at Charlottenberg.   I wrote to Dr. Weeren on the 19th
of December, 1899, for details of his analysis, but have
received no reply to my letter of inquiry.

The question now suggests itself, ' Whence did the
Mycenaean craftsman obtain his supply of cuprous sulphide ?'
At first I imagined that he might have had access to the
mineral copper-glance, and have made a casting in a clay
mould from this material after crushing and fusing it.   But a
more probable origin for this imitation of hæmatite was
suggested to me by Mr. W. Gowland during my examination
of a copper ingot, found in the year 1896 at Enkomi in Cyprus.
This ingot (No. 113 in the British Museum Catalogue of
Bronzes), which measures 2 feet 3½ inches in length, 16 inches
in breadth, and 2 inches in thickness, and weighs 81 pounds
10 ounces, bears upon its lower face the Cypriote
character.   On analysing the unaltered central portion ⚏
of this ingot the following figures* were obtained :

	per cent.		per cent.
Copper	98·05	Silver	trace
Tin	nil	Zinc	0 05
Lead	0·31	Iron	trace
Bismuth	trace	Sulphur	0 22

* The amount available for analysis was 6 grams only   The two determinations of copper which were made differed by 0 10 per cent., the mean is inserted
in the table of results   I am indebted to Mr F. W Harbord for all the results,
save the percentage of sulphur , this is probably over-stated

Now the side-light thrown upon the special inquiry in hand comes from the recognition of sulphur in this ingot, and from the detection of particles of a very impure cuprous sulphide amongst the drillings of metal handed to me for analysis. Clearly the ore from which this ancient ingot of copper had been reduced must have contained a fair quantity of un-oxidised sulphides. Mr. Gowland thinks the metal was produced 'by smelting *surface* ores consisting of carbonates and oxides mixed with some sulphide.' He further remarks, 'whenever a certain amount of undecomposed sulphides was present, the products of direct smelting would be copper similar to the Cypriote ingot, and varying amounts of regulus resembling or identical with the material of the cylinders.' Now this regulus, consisting mainly of cuprous sulphide but with some FeS, probably represented a product of the furnace intermediate between the 'blue metal' and the 'white metal' of the modern metallurgist. This then was, in all probability, the substance which, seen in its fused state, the Mycenaean artisan recognised as offering a superficial resemblance to polished hæmatite. It did more than present such resemblance, for it possessed almost the same density as the much harder ore of iron. Here, then, was the very material wanted for casting, by an easy process, these 'shoddy' cylinders, as I may venture to call them. They were cheap and quickly-made imitations of laborious engraved work, executed upon comparatively hard hæmatite. I ought, perhaps, to add here that the bluish-black regulus, obtained as above mentioned, though essentially cuprous sulphide, is by no means of constant composition and density. It is therefore not to be expected that this group of Mycenaean cylinder-seals should present an absolute uniformity in chemical and physical properties.

A striking confirmation of the suggested origin of the material of these Cypriote cylinders is afforded by the occurrence on the largest of the Ashmolean examples of a very good representation of an ingot like the specimen from Enkomi which I have described in the present note."

W. H. St. John Hope, Esq., M.A, Assistant Secretary, sub-mitted a Report on the Excavations on the site of the Romano-British city at Silchester, Hants, in 1901.

Mr. Hope's Report, which was illustrated by a large number of antiquities found during the excavations, will be printed in *Archaeologia*.

Thanks were ordered to be returned for these communica-tions.

Thursday, 5th June, 1902.

Viscount DILLON, President, in the Chair.

The following gifts were announced, and thanks for the same ordered to be returned to the donors:

From Professor J R. Rahn, Hon. F.S.A. :—A Collection of 110 Pamphlets on various Archæological Subjects, written or edited by the donor.

From the Author, W. A. Carrington, Esq. :

1 Papers relating to Derbyshire Musters, temp Queen Elizabeth, comprising the Muster Roll for the whole county made in 1587, in expectation of the Spanish Invasion , from the original documents preserved at Belvoir. 8vo. n.p 1895.

2 The Early Lords of Belvoir. 8vo. n p. n d

3 Haddon : the Hall, the Manor, and its Lords. 8vo n p. 1900.

4 Selections from the Steward's Accounts preserved at Haddon Hall, from 1549 to 1671. 8vo. London,

From the Author —Saint Pancras Open Spaces and Disused Burial Grounds. including a List of Interments of Eminent Persons, and a Brief Sketch of Old St. Pancras Church. By W. E Brown. 4to Lonion 1902.

Also the following Lantern Slides from R. Garraway Rice, Esq., F S.A. :—Four views of the Silchester Excavations in 1901, and one view of Iron Gates at Hall Place, Bexley, Kent

A special vote of thanks was accorded to Professor RAHN, Hon. F.S.A , for his gift to the Library.

This being an evening appointed for the election of Fellows, no papers were read.

W. G. THORPE, Esq., F.S.A , exhibited an original charter of inspeximus of Edward II. to the Borough of Portsmouth, dated 12th February, 1312-13.

Thanks were ordered to be returned for this exhibition.

The Ballot opened at 8.45 p.m and closed at 9 30 p.m., when the following were declared duly elected Fellows of the Society :

George Blundell Longstaff, Esq. M.A., M.D.
Sir John Stirling Maxwell, bt. M.P
Emery Walker, Esq.
Marion Harry Spielmann, Esq.
Reginald Stanley Faber, Esq. M.A.

Ernest Law, Esq. B.A.
Hon. and Very Rev. James Wentworth Leigh, D.D.
   Dean of Hereford.
Captain William Hawley.
James Kendrick Pyne, Esq. Mus. Doc.
Edwin Hadlow Wise Dunkin, Esq.

In accordance with the Statutes, ch. xix. § 1, the following draft of a proposed alteration in the Statutes was laid before the Meeting, and read by way of notice only :

> We, the undersigned Fellows of the Society of Antiquaries of London, do hereby request that a Special Meeting of the Fellows be called under chapter xix. section i. of the Statutes, for the purpose of considering the following Amendment to the Statutes to provide for the holding of the Ordinary Meetings of the Society in the afternoon instead of in the evening as at present.
>
> Chapter iv. section i. line 4 : " To strike out the words " half-past eight o'clock in the evening," and substitute therefor ' five o'clock in the afternoon."

> ERNEST CLARKE.
> HENRY B. WHEATLEY.
> ISIDORE SPIELMANN.

Thursday, June 12th, 1902.

Viscount DILLON, President, in the Chair.

The following gifts were announced, and thanks for the same ordered to be returned to the donors :

From Somers Clarke, Esq., F.S.A. :—Wall Drawings and Monuments of El Kab : the Tomb of Sebeknekht, the Temple of Amenhetep III., and the Tomb of Renni. By J. J. Tylor and Somers Clarke. 3 vols. Folio. London, 1896-1900.

From Emanuel Green, Esq., F.S.A. :—
  (1) An Engraved Plan of Nottingham Castle taken in 1617. Published in 1806.

  (2) A Letter stating the True Site of the Ancient Colony of Camulodunum. By Sir R. C. Hoare. 8vo. Shaftesbury, 1827,

From W. II. Richardson, Esq . M A , F.S.A., :—The History, Antiquities, and
  Present Restoration of Macclesfield Parish Church. By S. A. Boyd, B.C.L.
  8vo. Manchester, 1901

From R. Phené Spiers, Esq., F.S.A. :—Three Pencil Drawings of Rochester
  Castle and old Chapter House, Rochester.

From the Author :—The Place of the Bishop of Bath and Wells at the Coronation. By C. M Church, F.S A 8vo. n.p. 1902.

The following gentlemen were admitted Fellows :

> Emery Walker, Esq.
> James Kendrick Pyne, Esq Mus. Doc.
> Marion Harry Spielmann, Esq.
> Alfred Cart de Lafontaine, Esq.

Lord BALCARRES, M.P , F.S.A., exhibited a double painted
triptych of the sixteenth century, on which he read the
following notes :

"This triptych is a curious example of the interaction of
Eastern and Western pictorial art. As you see, it is a double
triptych revolving on a pivot, each side having two leaves or
shutters painted on either side with four scenes.* Thus
beside the two central panels, the Crucifixion and the Last
Judgment respectively, there are 32 pictures all illustrating
incidents in the life of Christ or His Mother. The painting
is miniature in character, there being some 950 figures and
faces depicted in all.

Mr. O. M. Dalton, of the British Museum, has written me
the following note on the relations of some of the late Greek
artists with the West:

' There is good evidence to show that from the time of the
Renaissance onwards, the old connection of Greek and Italian
art was maintained, though the parts played by East and
West were henceforward completely changed. Whereas in
the earlier centuries of the Middle Ages, and especially in
South Italy, Byzantine painters were teachers, they now
appear as learners, and there are various works in existence
to prove the extent of their debt to Western art. The
examples which have attracted most attention are to be seen
in the churches of the convents on Mount Athos, which have

---

* The extreme height of the triptych is 23 inches, and the extreme breadth
14 inches. The painted panels are 9 inches high and 7½ inches broad, extreme
measurements

been less exposed than other similar buildings to destructive influences   Dr. J. P. Richter has drawn attention to many of these works* and further information on the relations between Greek and Western art from the time of the Renaissance onward will be found in the article by Unger in Ersch and Gruber's *Allgemeine Encyklopädie der Wissenschaften und Künste*, vol. 85 (Leipsic, 1867), pp. 32-3 ; Bayet, in his *L'Art Byzantin*, has also a few remarks on the subject. From these sources the following short notes have been extracted.

The Massacre of the Innocents, in the apse of the right transept of the church of St. Athanasius, in the monastery of Lavra, signed by Theophanos of Cyprus in the year 1537, is copied from an engraving by Marc Antonio after a picture by Raphael, while Dr. Richter traces the influence of Ghirlandaio in the fresco representing the Last Supper in the refectory of the same monastery ; the same subject on the walls of the refectory of the monastery of Pantelimon is a copy of the Last Supper by Lionardo. In a Deposition in the monastery of Zographu the artist has derived his inspiration from the great picture by Rubens in the cathedral at Antwerp ; while the Procession to Calvary in the same place is after a Raphael in Madrid. Some frescoes representing scenes from the Apocalypse, in the Narthex of the monastery of Iverôn, painted in 1795, show distinct Italian influence, which may be explained from the fact that the artist Nicephorus is said to have visited Venice. In the library of Lavra are numerous Italian printed books on theology, and it is quite probable that prints of the same date, representing sacred scenes, were introduced at the same time, thus influencing Byzantine art on Mount Athos much as Flemish and German prints influenced Russian art in the sixteenth and seventeenth centuries.

But the effect produced by contact with the Western schools of painting was not confined to Mount Athos. Many Greek artists made a living in the West after the fall of Constantinople, and almost entirely abandoned the Byzantine style. Some of them painted miniatures for manuscripts. Demetrius Sguropoulos, who in 1544 wrote a copy of Aristotle's *Ethics*, now in the Laurentian Library in Florence, probably also executed the decorative initials, which are purely Italian in style, as are those painted by one Anastasius for a manuscript in the library of Rheims, and those of the Cynegetica of Oppian, which were executed by a daughter of Angelos Bergikios of Crete in 1554 for King Henry II., and are now

* *Zeitschrift für bildende Kunst*, 1878, pp 205 ff.

in the Bibliothèque Nationale. Another Greek, Dominicus
Theotokopoulos, commonly known as il Greco, is often said to
have studied in the school of Titian, and settled in Toledo
in 1577, where he died in 1625 ; one of his portraits is in the
Louvre. Yet another, Panagiotis Doxaras, born in the
Morea in 1662, joined the Venetians in their wars with the
Turks. He was an enthusiastic admirer of Western art,
and translated Lionardo's *Trattato della Pittura* into Greek.
On the other hand, Italian artists visited the Turkish
Empire; Gentile Bellini was summoned to Constantinople
by Mohammed II., and other Italian painters probably visited
Greece. The banner taken at Lepanto in 1572, and now in
the church at Gaeta, is said to betray Greek influence. The
above examples are perhaps sufficient to show that late Greek
painters were fully alive to the superiority of Western art,
and that many of them did their best to assimilate its
methods.

With reference to the purely Greek arrangement of some
of the scenes on the triptych, it may be added that a rapid
view of Byzantine iconography may be obtained from the
Painter's Manual of Mt. Athos, probably written in the
sixteenth-seventeenth century ;* and of the points in which it
differs from that of the Renaissance from the second volume
of the *Geschichte der Christlichen Kunst*, of F. X. Kraus.'

This solves many problems suggested by the triptych. Let
me point out a few interesting features.

To begin with, the whole panel seems to be painted on a
gold ground. The colours used are rich and varied, two of
the most noticeable being a deep maroon in the dress of the
Virgin, a colour which is essentially Byzantine. There is
also a grey olive green which was much used by Greek artists,
and the faces are generally painted over a soft green foundation, much as was the custom of the Trecentisti and the
Abyssinian illuminators.

Conventionalism is strong, though it did not dominate the
painter. Contact with Italy—Venice, I believe—had emanci-
pated him. But Greek tradition can be traced in nearly
every picture   The artist was archaic, yet there is great
vivacity and imagination and a clear sense of motion. Italian
richness and brilliance have been introduced, and where we get
a Greek version treated with the Italian feeling, in the
Annunciation for instance, the result is striking.

I am sorry to say that the Last Judgment is quite the

* *See* Didron, *Manuel d'iconographie chretienne*, and Schalfer, *Das Maler-
buch vom Berge Athos.*

most unfavourable example of the painter, but it happened to be the panel most easily reproduced. The treatment is gradual or spiral in character, based upon the familiar tradition embodied in the twelfth canto of the *Paradiso*, and the Throne of the Supreme Judge represents that of Ezekiel's vision. One notices at once that there are no Western saints, at least that there is no attribute, symbol, hat, or monastic habit. There are numerous crowned heads, and the figures in the central tier on the right are dressed like Venetian magnates. Moreover, no halos are used In fact it is most rarely employed in the triptych, even with the disciples. though oddly enough St. Peter, in the scene outside the Prætorium, appears four times with an aureole, at the only inglorious moment of his career. An Italian touch will be observed in the grouping of the evangelistic emblems, and in the little winged cherubs beside the throne. The chequered vestments are remarkable, similar to those found in Armenian manuscripts and on Charlemagne's dalmatic in the Vatican, dating from the tenth century.

Were we to judge from isolated fragments of this triptych one could give it any date one chose We find purely classical architecture and costume; and the River God, emblematic of the Jordan, is of course a Pagan survival.

The purple cupola repeated above several of the buildings reminds one of the Eusebian Canons which precede the gospels from the fifth century onwards. Similar cupolas can be recorded frequently. As an example I would quote the mosaic in the circular church of St. George at Thessalonica, dating from the time of Justinian.

Early Gothic features will be found in the pictures of the Annunciation and the Purification.

Renaissance types are universal. We find this in the charming architecture of the Prætorium, which resembles a beautiful Lombard church of the fifteenth century. We likewise see the Renaissance in the curtains and flowered brocades, in the helmets, armour, and horsetrappings, in the furniture, such as the chairs at the Last Supper.

But we can bring the date of the painting still closer to our own times. The rocky landscape backgrounds, wholly alien by the way to traditional Greek art, seem inspired by Guardi and his school. The Woman of Samaria, and Claudia the wife of Pilate, are in pose, features and costume, typical Venetian ladies, such as we find in Tiepolo's pictures.

Lastly, the frame. This at least is pure Venetian We are justified in assuming it to have been fitted to the paintings. Should the frame and pictures be coeval, the triptych cannot be much anterior to the seventeenth century. At the same time, though I believe it to be comparatively modern, I think it reproduces a version dating back to early times, and where primitive originals are lost or mutilated, be they in architecture, painting, or texts, recent copies or versions derived from some vanished prototype are often of great critical value."

Sir FRANCIS T. BARRY, bt., M.P., F.S.A., exhibited a number of plans and lantern slides illustrating the exploration of a Broch at Hillhead, Caithness, in 1901, on which he also contributed some descriptive notes.

The Rev the Hon GILBERT H F. VANE, M A, F S A., Local Secretary for Shropshire, communicated the following note on the discovery of a supposed lake-dwelling at Pike's End, in the parish of Lyneal-cum-Colemere.

"At Pike's End in the parish of Lyneal-cum-Colemere, about four miles from Wem and five and a half from Elles- mere, in the county of Salop, and near the road which leads from Loppington to Ellesmere, a tenant of Earl Brownlow named Jones, when levelling a low-lying meadow, recently observed that the inequalities consisted in great measure of small mounds of clay, though the soil is peat.   Mr. Jones further observed that these small mounds displayed an approach to symmetry of arrangement, 16 of them being disposed in two rows at the foot of a slope, and a third row of only six lying between these two.   The diameter of the mounds also varied little, being in the first and second rows just about 12 feet, in the third a trifle less.   Lastly, the mounds were for the most part about 10 yards apart and a foot in height.

Being interested by these observations Mr. Jones gave notice of his discovery, and on March 5th the mounds, or their sites, for much of the clay had been removed, were visited by myself and several other persons.   Labourers also were in readiness, and the spade was soon at work.   A trench 3 feet wide was dug east and west to a length of 19 feet across the site of one of the mounds.   This revealed a layer of bark a foot below the surface.   Another foot or rather more of digging brought the labourers to water ; for the land was only drained some thirty-five years ago, up to that time was covered with rushes, and is still very boggy.   The bark appeared to be of fir.   So did also a good sized root which was dug up near, and showed unmistakable marks of fire.

Ashes were found too beneath another mound. And in each of the four which were opened on the day named small trunks of fir were dug out. One log of black oak was also found. This log measured 8 feet 10 inches, and tapered, being 1 foot 5 inches in girth in the middle and 2 feet at its thicker end. Marks of an axe appeared to be traceable on this log. Unfortunately no bones, and no implements of stone or metal were turned up, though beneath one mound portions of the rotted stumps of four upright piles were found in very wet soil. There are no means for approximating to the date of the settlement at present available, nor is it certain that the remains are those of lake dwellings, notwithstanding that at Whettall Moss, only half a mile distant as the crow flies, there was found in 1872 an ancient canoe, which is now preserved at Ellesmere.

The excavations were followed up a few days later by a trench cut right across the meadow to a depth of about 2 feet 6 inches, that is, to the water line, but no further discoveries were made.

Subsequently (30th May), further excavations were made at Pike's End in presence of a number of gentlemen interested in British antiquities, including Dr. Munro of Edinburgh, well-known for his works on Lake Dwelling Researches On that occasion the consensus of opinion was that the moss-buried wood and bark indicated a succession of forest growths; birch, hazel, alder, and other trees being clearly indicated by their bark, which remained after much of the wood itself had entirely decomposed. At the bottom of the natural basin there was a deposit of a white sandy gravel, which, near the margin, could be reached at a depth of about a couple of feet, but, towards the centre, the depth of peaty deposits, leaf mould, and decayed wood amounted to 6 or 8 feet, or even more. The circularly disposed layers of clay, with some gravel and charcoal, which constituted the mounds, were on the surface, and so far no decided evidence of any relationship between them and the submerged wood was detected Dr. Munro, who was chairman of the British Association Committee for the excavation of the Glastonbury Lake-village, was able to point out a material difference between the mounds at Pike's End and those at Glastonbury. While the former consisted of one layer of clay the latter contained several layers, one superimposed on the other, with beds of charcoal, ashes, a hearth, and relics of human industry intercalated. As there could be no doubt that the mounds at Pyke's End were artificially constructed the most probable explanation of their presence in such a locality is that they

were intended to be the sites of habitable huts, but any
further indications as to their purpose would, in the meantime, be pure conjecture.

Thanks were ordered to be returned for these exhibitions
and communications.

Thursday, June 19th, 1902.

Viscount DILLON, President, in the Chair

The following gifts were announced, and thanks for the
same ordered to be returned to the donors:

From W Farrer, Esq —The Lancashire Pipe Rolls of 31 Henry I. and of the
    reigns of Henry II, Richard I, and King John, also early Lancashire
    Charters. 8vo. Liverpool, 1902

From the Author —Joannes Matthens and his Tract *De Rerum Inventoribus*
    By John Ferguson, LL.D., F S.A. 8vo. Glasgow, 1902.

The following gentlemen were admitted Fellows:

> Edwin Hadlow Wise Dunkin, Esq
> Hon. and Very Rev James Wentworth Leigh, D.D.,
>   Dean of Hereford.

ROLAND W. PAUL, Esq , F S.A.. read some notes on further
discoveries at Abbey Dore, Herefordshire.

E. F STRANGE, Esq., read the following notes on the
Rood-screen in Tacolneston church, Norfolk:

"The existence of remains of the rood-screen of Tacolneston
Church was first recorded by Mr. C. E Keyser, F.S.A., in a
paper published by him in the *Archæological Journal* for
1901.* In the spring of the present year I was able to act on
a suggestion of his that I should visit it, and I now have the
honour to lay the results of that visit before you.
The existing fragments of the screen consist only of the

* Vol. lviii.

lower portions of the middle part, those on either side of its entrance to the chancel. They are of carved oak, with tracery attached in the usual way dividing each into panels. The carving of the spandrels is very fine, and its unusual sharpness and freedom from signs of wear and tear may have some significance in connection with the point of greater interest now before us, viz. the paintings. Before passing to these, however, one more small detail is worth attention, the existence of a carpenter's mark, the Roman numeral VIII., on the right edge. It is evidently a guide for the fitter, and the shape of the figures shows them to have been made with a curved chisel.

Only two panels of one portion of the screen, that which would stand on the south of the entrance, appear to have been fully coloured. These are painted in tempera with (1) an Annunciation and (2) a Temptation of St. Anthony. On one at least of the other panels traces of black and red lettering still appear, which might well have been a later makeshift to hide the nakedness of the unfinished work.

The two subjects of the completed panels are executed in a most masterly style, essentially pictorial rather than decorative ; and with the exception of some mutilation of the faces, are relatively well preserved. The "Temptation of St. Anthony" is an exact reproduction of the engraving by Lucas van Leyden (Bartsch, 117), every detail being translated into paint with a skill which, considering the state of the arts of the period, is especially remarkable. The other panel, "The Annunciation," I have not yet been able to identify as a copy. In it the Virgin is represented on her knees, receiving the message of the archangel, who has green wings and is clothed in a richly embroidered cloak with a jewelled clasp. The room is panelled ; it has a red-cushioned bedstead with square canopy ; one casemented window showing a glimpse of distant landscape, and another has Gothic mullions. A book, with book-marker, which the Virgin has been reading is on the left of the composition. In these details and in style the picture belongs to the Flemish School of the second half of the fifteenth century. There appears to be nothing in it which might not have been done by the artist who executed the St. Anthony. But Lucas van Leyden's engraving of the subject is altogether different (B. 100). Several pictures with the same title are attributed to him, but I have not yet been able to obtain a photograph or even a detailed description of any of them to lay before you.

These panels are enclosed in a framework very richly coloured and decorated with both plain gilding and gilt gesso ornament of unusual beauty, as well as lozenges of floral ornament and realistic flowers on a ground of ivory white. The gesso is free-hand and has not been executed with a stamp, and there is no trace of stencilling in the ornament. As far as the painted ornament goes it is well up in artistic value to the high standard of the Ranworth screen and others of the first quality still remaining; while the gesso also is as fine as anything known to me, and is extremely well preserved

As regards the history of the screen there is little authentic information. Blomefield says the church was rebuilt about 1503, and received many benefactions. But he mentions none relating to its decoration. There were two gilds at Tacolneston, one of All Saints, the dedication of the church, and one of St. Nicholas, and we know that such bodies often adopted the charge of a special part of the church. The patronage of the living belonged first to the D'Uvedales, whose heiress married Robert Clere, into whose family it passed She died in 1492, and was buried in the cathedral church of Norwich, leaving many legacies for ecclesiastical purposes, but none (specified by Blomefield) to Tacolneston. The rector was William Isbellys, 1498-1540.

Out of all this some important considerations arise. We have two panel paintings of undoubted Flemish origin, in this case identified, I hope I may claim, beyond possibility of doubt, surrounded by ornamental work of the same character as prevails in many places elsewhere in Norfolk and Suffolk.   These two paintings are entirely pictorial, and differ altogether from the essentially decorative figures of saints and angels which generally accompany the painted ornament and gesso work.   The whole of this work has been by some rather loosely ascribed to Flemish influence.   But I think I am right in saying that examples of it are almost non-existent in the Low Countries; where, if such had been their origin, one would expect to find them in at least as great profusion as in England.   Now in the face of a screen painting demonstrably Flemish, one can easily see how wide is the difference; and I think be content to attribute the great mass of painting and wood carving in the Eastern Counties to craftsmen who were English either by birth or adoption.

In this exceptional case of Tacolneston I venture to put forth the theory that the ornament was painted by an English artist and the panels by a Fleming.   One is tempted to indulge in the speculation that the latter may have been Lucas van Leyden himself; but having no expert knowledge qualifying me to judge of his style of painting, I will only point out the practicability of the idea. The engraving of the St. Anthony is dated 1509, the church was rebuilt ' about 1503." Lucas is now known to have been older than his first biographers thought; and might well have come to England from Liége or Antwerp: an easy journey for him to make, and one that would suggest itself in view of the great traffic between his city and Norfolk, for Tacolneston was a centre of weaving. That is all; apart from the question of style, and a story which I cannot trace the origin of, to show that he really did visit England.

Then there is the question of the other panel That is not, as I have said, a copy of Lucas's engraving. If it can be shown to be a copy of one by another artist, it proves beyond reasonable doubt that both panels were painted by a third person. If, on the other hand, we conclude it to be not a copy of an engraving, but an original treatment of a subject, of which all the details were fairly well recognised by a small school of painters, we must attach some weight to the theory that Lucas himself did the work. His engraved "Annunciation" is ascribed to the year 1514.

Again there is the point that the screen would appear to have been, for some reason, left incomplete, a consideration which might be due to the fact that it was the work not of a craftsman settled in the district, but of a stranger, who for some reason could not be prevailed on to stay long enough to finish it. It was not painted abroad and imported, for no one would have sent over two panels only out of so many.

In considering whether the panels are originals or copies, I would specially draw your attention to the fineness of the drawing of the hands and feet and the heads as far as can be seen. These are the weak points of many copyists who excel in the depicting of drapery and ornament. However it may be, both panels must stand or fall together. Possibly the result of a search more extended than I have yet had time to make will show the source of the "Annunciation." In any case it is curious that this screen should be singled out for exceptional treatment as compared with those of other churches in the county; and also that a composition which stands by itself and does not form one of a series should be selected for the second of a large number of panel-pictures, to the first of which it had no relation

I owe a considerable debt to Mr. Keyser for giving me the opportunity of examining this most interesting piece of work, and to your Society for the opportunity of putting these questions before you. I do so entirely as a student, feeling

well assured that your answers and criticisms will be valuable
to many beside myself who attach some importance to what
still remains of our British art treasures.   In this case
we can now feel sure that, whatever opinions there may be as
to the origin of the screen, its remains will henceforth be well
cared for, and any further mutilation as far as possible prevented   The acknowledgment of the kindness of the rector
in giving us this chance of seeing the screen, and of having it
copied or photographed, lies of course in your hands, but I
should be glad to be associated with it.

I have been permitted by the authorities of the Victoria and
Albert Museum to show several photographs of pictures by
Flemish artists akin in period and method to Lucas van Leyden.
The archangel in the Annunciation by Van der Weyden has
robes like that in the panel.   The others show similar treatment of the furniture, the landscape seen through the window,
etc.   I also show one coloured tracing of a figure from the
Southwold screen, as an example of the kind of painting
generally associated with the best gesso work , and of details
of floral ornament and carving from the screens at Worstead
and other places which are also found therewith.   These,
with the reproductions of Lucas van Leyden's engraved
work, may help you to form your own judgment."

By the kindness of the Rev. J W Corbould-Warren,
Rector of Tacolneston, the portion of the screen described by
Mr. Strange was exhibited.

H. S. HARLAND, Esq , F.S.A., exhibited a late sixteenth
century sword-hilt, found in an old house at Scarborough
about the year 1854.

Thanks were ordered to be returned for these communications and exhibitions.

The Ordinary Meetings of the Society were then adjourned
to Thursday, 27th November.

Thursday, 27th November, 1902.

Viscount DILLON, President, in the Chair.

The following gifts were announced, and thanks for the same ordered to be returned to the donors:

From the Author :—Memorials of the Goldsmiths' Company ; being gleanings from their records between 1335 and 1815. By Sir Walter S Prideaux. 2 vols. 8vo. London, n.d

From the Author ·—Montgomeryshire Screens and Roodlofts By the Ven Archdeacon Thomas, F S.A. 8vo Oswestry, 1902.

From the Author ·—Excavations at St. Austin's Abbey, Canterbury. 1 The Chapel of St Pancras By W H St John Hope, M A. 8vo. London, 1902.

From the Author —The Early Lords of Belvoir Part ii By W A. Carrington 8vo. London, n d.

From the Author, Rev. Samuel Rundle M A ·

  1 Cornish Chairs. 8vo   n.p   n d

  2 Cornubiana   Part iii. 8vo.   n.p.   n d

From the Rev. W K R Bedford

  1 Photograph of armorial embroidered table-cloth.

  2 Photographs of a series of engravings showing the unsuccessful attack of the Turks on Malta in 1565

From the Trustees of the British Museum :

  1. Reproductions of prints in the British Museum. Part xi. Specimens of line engravings by French masters in the eighteenth century fol London 1902

  2 A Guide to the Antiquities of the Stone Age in the Department of British and Mediæval Antiquities, British Museum. 8vo London, 1902.

From the Author —Description and History of the Church of St Mary Magdalene, Munster Square, London. By T. E. Sedgwick. 8vo. London.

From the Author —Harlyn Bay and the Discoveries of its Prehistoric Remains. By R. A Bullen. 8vo London, 1902.

From the Author ·—Christian Frederick Esberger, his Relatives and his Journal. By R W Goulding 8vo Louth, 1902

From the Author —Weston-super-Mare Parish Notes. By E E Baker, F.S A 4to Weston-super-Mare, 1902.

From the Author ·—Genealogical Memoranda relating to the Family of de Vantier, anglais Wanty By Henry Peet, F S A 8vo n p. 1902

From the Author :—John Strype, F S.A., the Leyton Antiquary and Historian
By A P Wise. obl. 8vo. Leyton, 1902.

From the Author :—Aidan, the Apostle of England. By A C Fryer, F S.A
8vo. London, 1902.

From the Author :—A Short History of Colfe's Grammar School, Lewisham.
By Leland L Duncan, F S A 8vo Lewisham. 1902

From Rev. T. S. Frampton, M.A , F S.A. ·

   1. The Chantry of John Denys, in Ickham Church. 8vo London, 1902

   2. St. Mary's Church, Minster, Isle of Thanet. List of Vicars 8vo.
     London, 1902.

From the Author :—Old Pembroke Families in the Ancient County Palatine of
Pembroke. By Henry Owen. D.C L , F S A 4to. London, 1902.

From Arthur F Hill, Esq., F.S.A. —Antonio Stradivari, His Life and Work
(1644-1737). By W. H Hill, A F Hill, and A. E Hill 4to. London,
1902

From the Author —Kharga Oasis . its Topography and Geology By John
Ball, Ph.D., A.R S.M. 8vo Cairo, 1900.

From the Author :—English Travellers and Italian Brigands. A narrative of
capture and captivity By W. J. C. Moens. 2 vols. 8vo. London 1866

From R P Spiers, Esq , F.S A :—Mémoire archéologique sur les découvertes
d'Herbord dites de Sauxay Par le Père Camille de la Croix. 8vo.
Niort, 1883. .

From W. H. St John Hope, Esq., M.A. :

   1. A short guide to the Church of All Saint's, Godshill, Isle of Wight By
     P. R H. Bartlett and H. M. Worsley. 8vo. London, 1898.

   2. Flamstead, its Church and History By I. V. Bullard 4to Luton,
     1902.

   3 Civitas Lincolnia, from its Municipal and other Records [By John
     Ross] 8vo. Lincoln, 1870.

   4. Vestiges of old Newcastle and Gateshead By W. H. Knowles and
     J R. Boyle. 4to. Newcastle, 1890

   5. The English Coronation Service, its History and Teaching. By
     F C Eeles. 8vo Oxford, 1902

   6 The Coronation Service according to the use of the Church of England.
     By Rev. J. H. Pemberton Fourth edition. 8vo London, 1902.

   7. The Form and Order of the Service that is to be performed, and of the
     ceremonies that are to be observed in the Coronation of their Majesties
     King Edward VII. and Queen Alexandra in the Abbey Church of
     S. Peter, Westminster, on Thursday, the 26th day of June, 1902. 4to.
     London, 1902.

   8 The Coronation of the King, its Ecclesiastical Significance. By H.
     Hitchcock 8vo London, n.d.

From Sir John Evans, K C.B , V.P. —La Basilica di Monza ed il suo tesoro fol
Como, 1887.

From R Burnard, Esq , F.S.A. —The Dartmoor Preservation Association,
18th Annual Report, 1901. 8vo. Plymouth, 1902.

From the Author —King Alfred and his Family in Mercia. By Rev C S. Taylor, M A., F.S.A. 8vo. Bristol, 1902

From the London Topographical Society .—Illustrated Topographical Record of London. First series. 4to London, 1898

From the Author :—On the Discovery of a Roman Villa near Rothley, Leicestershire, in 1901. By W T. Tucker, F.G S 8vo Leicester. n d

From the Author ·—Clerks of the Peace and Lieutenancy for the County of Leicester. By W. J. Freer, F S A 8vo. n p n.d.

From the Author —The Bewleys of Cumberland and their Irish and other Descendants. By Sir Edmund T. Bewley, M A., LL D. 8vo. Dublin, 1905.

From the Publishers (Messrs. Seeley and Co., Ltd.) :—Old St. Paul's Cathedral. By William Benham, D.D., F S A 8vo London, 1902.

From F. G. Hilton Price, Esq , Director .—Tallis's Illustrated London ; in commemoration of the Great Exhibition of all Nations in 1851 2 vols. 8vo. London, [1851].

From Sir J Charles Robinson. F S.A :—Proceedings of the Dorset Natural History and Antiquarian Field Club, vols 1, 3, 5, 6, 8, 9 11 12-18, 20, 21, 22 8vo Sherborne, 1877-1901

The following gentlemen were admitted Fellows:

> Reginald Stanley Faber, Esq., M.A.
> Hamon le Strange, Esq., M.A.
> Henry Edward Montgomery Baylis, Esq.
> Robert Holmes Edleston, Esq.
> Ernest Law, Esq., B.A.

At 8.45 p.m. the Meeting was made special for the consideration of the proposed alteration in the Statutes as to the hour of the Ordinary Meetings of the Society.

After the Resolution had been formally moved by Sir Ernest Clarke, it was discussed by Messrs. H. B. Wheatley, who seconded it, E. Almack, W. Rowley, W. A. Lindsay, and C. Welch, who were in favour of the proposal, and by Sir John Evans, Vice-President, Mr. W. Gowland, Vice-President, Messrs. Stuart Moore, Wilfred Cripps, and W. J. C. Moens, Sir Henry H Howorth, Mr. J. W. Willis-Bund, Sir J. C. Robinson, Mr. P. W. P. Carlyon-Britton, the Bishop of Barking, and others, who were opposed to any change.

Finally a Ballot was taken on the proposed alteration of he Statutes, which was rejected by 119 noes to 35 ayes.

Thursday, 4th December, 1902.

Viscount DILLON, President, in the Chair.

The following gifts were announced, and thanks for the same ordered to be returned to the donors:

From Dr. J. Wickham Legg, F S A. :—The Coronation Ceremonial, its True History and Meaning. By Herbert Thurston, S J 8vo London, 1902

From the Publishers, Messrs Cassell and Company Limited :—The Coronation Book of Edward VII. By W. J. Loftie, B.A., F.S.A. 8vo. London, 1902

From the Author :—The Household Goods, etc. of Sir John Gage, of West Firle, County Sussex, K.G , 1556 By R Garraway Rice, F S A 8vo Lewes, 1902

From Sir Lambton Loraine, Bart. —Deed Poll by Sir Lambton Loraine, declaring proper Armorial Bearings Dated 31st October, 1902. 4to. London, 1902

From the Author :—Anglo-Saxon London and its Neighbourhood. Second Paper. By T W Shore, F G S 8vo n p n.d

From the Local Records Committee :—Report and Appendices, 29th October, 1902. fol. London, 1902

From Sir J Charles Robinson. F.S.A. .—Original Drawing by C A. Stothard of Monumental Effigies in King's-Carswell Church, Devon.

From F. G. Hilton Price, Esq., Director .—Tallis's London Street Views. obl 8vo. London. n.d.

Mr. HARPER GAYTHORPE, of Barrow, through H. Swainson Cowper, Esq., F.S A., Local Secretary for Lancashire, submitted the following notes on (1) a Norman tympanum with Runic inscription at Loppergarth, Pennington, and (2) a discovery of bronze implements at Much Urswick :

"I have the honour to report the discovery on 17th March, 1902, of a Norman tympanum at Loppergarth, Pennington, about two miles W.S.W. from Ulverston : and on the 13th June of six socketed bronze celts at Much Urswick, distant about three miles due south from Ulverston.

The tympanum is of local red sandstone, 48¼ inches long by 24½ inches high, and 8 inches thick, and bears the sculptured figure of an angel with a cruciferous nimbus, and a Runic inscription.* It now forms the door head of an outhouse at Beckside Farm.

Mr. T. K. Fell, M.R.C.S.E., of Barrow, made the discovery

* The tympanum is described and fully illustrated in *The Reliquary and Illustrated Archaeologist*, viii 200-201

and photographed the stone. Shortly afterwards I took a squeeze-tracing and made notes of the inscription. The Runic letters are incised, but, owing to the action of time and weather, many have been obliterated.   .   ,

The stone has evidently belonged to the doorway of a ,church or chapel at Pennington. A church is known to have existed there in the twelfth century * and the presence of runes of that date at Pennington is a unique discovery in Furness, and of considerable significance.

At Fell Mount, Pennington, there are several carved twelfth-century sandstones, capitals of pillars, having human heads carved in high relief, which also formed part of the ancient church.

About 100 yards from Beckside Farm is the traditional site of a leper hospital. Little is known of its existence, but there is some record, which the name Loppergaith (leper inclosure) confirms.†

The socketed bronze celts were found in a field on Skelmore Heads called Little Cow Close.

Mr. James Newby, of Scales, made the discovery when quarrying limestone rock. The celts were found lying together in a fissure about 3 to 4 inches wide, between two large blocks of limestone. The root of an ash tree growing in the fissure bears an impression of one of the celts.

They all vary in form, size, and weight; the largest being 5 inches long, and weighs 14 ounces , the smallest 4 inches long, and weighs 10½ ounces. Two are quite plain. One of these is not quite perfect, and weighs 9 ounces. The other four are ornamented with ribs and pellets, one has the ring ornament similar to fig. 166 in Evans's *Ancient Bronze Implements* Another has been cracked across one of the faces, and a hole near the loop is evidently a defect in casting. One has never been used since it came from the mould, the edge being ¼ inch thick All have the sockets wider at the bottom than in the middle. This points to a fox-tail wedge having been used to prevent the handle being withdrawn."‡

---

* *The Coucher Book of Furness Abbey* (Chetham Society, N.S. ix), i. 126-7.
† *The Coucher Book of Furness Abbey* (Chetham Society, N.S. xi.), ii. 411. Will of William de Skelmersherk, 1247 · Item, Leprosis, juxta Ulverston, vid
‡ Implements of the Bronze Age have also been found in Furness and Cartmel it Gleaston Castle (flat celt) 1776 ; Wraysholme Tower (palstave) 1831 ; Long Rigg Field about 250 yards east of the Stone Walls, Urswick (celts and rings) 847 ; Roose (flat celt) 1872 ; Dalton-in-Furness (sword and spear) 1874 ; and iave been described and figured in Volumes 14, 15, and 16 of the *Transactions of the Cumberland and Westmorland Antiquarian and Archaeological Society*.

Mr. W. G. Collingwood has since submitted the following version of the Pennington Runes, as read from the stone :

ᛁᛉᛎᛈᚲᛛ᛬ᛁᛁᛏᛉ᛬ ᛁᛁᚻ᛬ᛈᛁᚱᚲᚺᚾᛒ ᛏᚱᛏ᛬ ᛁᛁᛁᚺᛏ᛬ᛁᚠᚫ᛬ᛈᛉᛁᚥᚫᛏ

The dotted lines are doubtful. This, with help from Mr. Eiríkr Magnússon, he reads :

(KA)MIAL : SETI : ThESA : KIRK : HUBERT : MESUN : VAN : M.....

Gamel (de Pennington) founded this church. Hubert the
                mason wrought . . .

J. H. ROUND, Esq., M.A., exhibited a document bearing the autograph signature of "the Kingmaker" (" R. Warrewyk "),

SEAL OF RICHARD NEVILL, EARL OF WARWICK, 1449-1471.

to which was appendent an impression of his armorial seal, believed to be unique.* The document, of which the date is

---

* It has since been ascertained that a similar impression is appended to a Burford document now in possession of Dr. Cheatle.

To face page 153.

WEST DOORWAY OF THE CHAPEL PORCH OF MAGDALEN COLLEGE, OXFORD, IN 1901.

1st February, 1465 (4 Edward IV.), is in the possession of the Right Hon James Round, M.P.

The marshalling of the Earl's arms on this fine seal was explained and discussed by Mr. Round, who has since then contributed an article on the subject to the *Ancestor* (IV. 143-7), with an illustration of the seal, of which a cast has been presented to the Society for its collection.

OSWALD BARRON, Esq., F.S.A., read a note upon the arms (1) of King Richard I. of England, and (2) of some London citizens under King Edward II.

Thanks were ordered to be returned for these communications.

Thursday, 11th December, 1902.

Viscount DILLON, President, in the Chair.

The following gifts were announced, and thanks for the same ordered to be returned to the donors ·

From the Author —The Church Plate of Surrey   By Rev. T S Cooper, M.A , F.S A. 8vo. London, 1902.

From the Author —A Calendar of Printed Grants of Arms, Grants of Crests, Grants of Augmentations, and Exemplifications of Arms. By J. P Rylands, F.S.A. 8vo. Liverpool, 1901.

From the Author —Roman Africa, an Outline of the History of the Roman Occupation of North Africa. By Alexander Graham, F.S.A.   8vo. London, 1902.

From the Author ·—Dorian and Phrygian reconsidered from a non-harmonic Point of View. By A. J. Hipkins, F S.A. 8vo. London, 1902.

Notice was given of a Ballot for the election of Fellows on Thursday, 8th January, 1903, and a list of candidates to be balloted for was read.

R. T. GÜNTHER, Esq , M.A , read the following contribution to the History of the Chapel Porch of Magdalen College, Oxford.

" It is the purpose of the present communication to record

the state of the fabric of the chapel porch at Magdalen College, Oxford, as it appeared before the most recent reconstruction, and also to bring together some materials for its history.

The west wall is now pierced by a window and a side door. Until 1901 it had never been questioned that the doorway which had been in the middle of the west side at least since 1653 had not been there since the foundation of the College. On the removal, however, of the plaster inside the porch, indications were found that this had not been the original plan, but that antecedent to it, there had been a window and a side doorway: it was also found that a masonry pier between the window and doorway had been removed to the danger of the fabric of the muniment tower, and that a very insufficient arch of soft chalky stone had taken its place; that the ribbed stone ceiling of the passage to the cloisters is not the original one, which was probably low and of wood; and that even the ornate ceiling over the porch itself is very likely a late addition

The plaster was removed from the walls in 1900, because it was found to conceal and thereby to destroy the proper effect of the fluted vaulting shafts in the angles of the porch.

During the progress of the work of stripping the plaster it appeared that the walls of the chapel porch must have been bare and devoid of plaster in their original condition, and were simply whitewashed. That this had been the case for a considerable period is proved by the fact that several distinct layers of whitewash were distinguishable below the deepest layer of plaster. Even now it is possible for anyone to convince himself of this if he will but examine the surface of the masonry on the north side of the entrance gateway, or upon the south splay of the original west window, or on either side of parts of the vaulting shafts in the corners, or on the chamfered edges of the east end of the passage leading to the cloister.

So far as I have been able to judge. the rather wide interstices between the stones were filled up with mortar of a lightish colour to match the stonework, and the entire surface was then whitewashed.

The first result of the removal of the plaster was that the slender vaulting shafts in the angles were revealed in their true beauty and proportion. They are the best of their kind in Oxford. In the porches of New College, St. John's and Lincoln Colleges, there are similar columns with plain round shafts standing out from the walls in three-quarter relief.

At Jesus College the columns are ornamented with two flutings. But it is only at All Souls, the foundation which immediately preceded our own, that we find columns of the same character.

The removal of the plaster from the walls of the passage leading to the cloister has brought to light a face of rough hard Headington stone on the north side, but of fair ashlar upon the south side. The finding of large corner stones at the cloister end, which showed original whitewash laid directly upon them, has convinced many people that the walls of the cloister as well as those of the chapel porch were not plastered in their original condition, but, like those of the cloister at New College, were either bare or whitewashed.

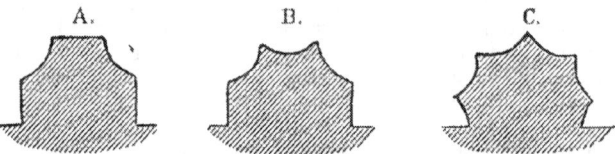

SECTIONS OF VAULTING SHAFTS: A, JESUS COLLEGE; B, ALL SOULS COLLEGE; C, MAGDALEN COLLEGE.

The character of the masonry leaves no doubt that the ground plan of the porch and passage is the original one, but on the other hand there is a suspicion that the ribbed vaulting over the passage is not as old as the walls from which it springs. Perhaps the question may be settled when the plaster is removed from the east end. The reasons for doubting the antiquity of this vaulting, apart from considerations of style, are that at the western end there is an interval of nearly 3 inches between the stones of the vaulting and those of the supporting arch above. This gives the impression that it has been inserted under the supporting arch of the passage after the latter had been built. The rib-motif of the lower vaulted roof may have been suggested by the ribbed arch over the original gateway of the chapel porch, which will be presently described.

Beneath the springings of the ribs of the vaulting are twelve holes, each of which has been carefully plugged with

stone. The plugging was probably done before the wall was
plastered, because the plugs are uncommonly well fitted on
the south side, much better than the then bursars would have
encouraged for under plaster work. The purpose of these
holes may have been to support the ends of the joists of a
wooden ceiling perhaps like that over the cloister walk.
Such a ceiling would have been low, like that of the passage
leading from the little cloister at Christ Church, and to
follow up our speculation, it may have been the very lowness
of this wooden ceiling which led to its replacement by the
stone vaulting at a time when the passage had become the
way to the cloister.

The most important alterations, however, are those which
the west wall has revealed.

Before the removal of the plaster, the middle of this side
presented the appearance of a plaster funnel converging from
the round-topped interior to the pointed arch of the doorway.
When the plaster was stripped it was found that, instead of
being fairly and honestly laid upon good stonework, it hung
from some wooden sticks which were used to conceal a gross
piece of jerry-building. The plaster construction concealed
the unfinished and insecure nature of certain alterations in
the stonework of the gateway. Under this flimsy erection the
chief traffic of the college was conducted for many genera-
tions. History preserves a discreet silence with regard to its
origin, and the very mention of the expense of the alteration
has been so veiled in the college accounts as to elude the
scrutiny of Mr. Macray

The outer masonry of the doorway was not in any way
bonded with the walls within, but had evidently been inserted
into a recess from without, like a picture into a frame. The
angle between the outer doorway and the inner walls was
filled with poor rubble. The internal masonry above the
entrance was insecurely supported by a very flat segmental
arch (d, d) of the feeblest construction, insufficient both in
size and in quality of stone. Indeed it was a wonder that
it held together.

The builder of this arch supported its northern end upon
the ribbed stone (b) which will be referred to later, and for the
better support of the new arch the masons notched the end of
the stone. At the south end the abutment of the arch rested
upon a mass of rubble (g) which was built against the jamb of
an ancient window.

There can be, in my opinion, no doubt but that the gateway of the muniment tower was in its recent position ever

since the alterations of Inigo Jones in 1635, but the evidence is all in favour of this condition having been preceded by a previous one in which there was a window to the south, the doorway being to the north, and of course a pier of masonry in the middle between the window and the door. To this condition we have now returned.

MAGDALEN COLLEGE, OXFORD. WEST WALL OF CHAPEL PORCH AFTER
REMOVAL OF PLASTER IN 1901.

Of the lateral doorway we found the following indications:

1. The inner north angle of the entrance, of well squared masonry with small joints (*a, a*). The surface of the stones was found to be whitewashed after the removal of the rubble and plaster.

2. The northern half of the inner arch (*b*). This is
formed of the single stone already mentioned as one
of the supports of the flat segmental arch. It is
ornamented with two ribs, of which the inner rib is
complete, and is like those over the inner arches
of the west gate of the chapel and of the door to
the great tower. An original coating of whitewash covered this stone, but not the other members
of the segmental arch.

3. The supporting or relieving arch above the ribbed
arch stone (*c, c, c*). Its dimensions indicate that the
original width of the aperture beneath was only
double that of the space covered by the ribbed
arch stone, and that consequently the original
doorway was of the same width as the present
doorway.

We may here mention that the stones of the external doorway could not have been in their original position, because
they projected beyond the face of the wall for about $1\frac{1}{4}$ inch.
They had evidently been inserted into a recess which was too
large for them, and consequently had to be packed in with
small slips of stone.

The window was indicated by the following architectural
features :

1. The inner part of the south jamb with a hollow
chamfer along the inside of the splay (*e, e*). The
chamfer is stopped upon the sill by a broach
stop.
     The hollow chamfer seems to have been ex-
clusively employed in the windows of the college.
We find it in the north window of the chapel
porch, in the cloister windows, and in the
hall windows, although now disguised by the
rope and plaster Gothic fillets of Wyatt which
are shortly to be removed.* It is probable that
it was the sole ornamentation round the inside
of the chapel windows as well. It is the
ornament too which was employed for the
windows of the hall of Winchester College.

2 A small portion of the wall beneath the inner sill (*f*)

* Wyatt's plaster was removed from the hall in July, 1903.

The exposed end of this wall showed marks of having been rudely chiselled through in an oblique direction, evidently to widen the entrance when the doorway was moved to a central position.

3. The oblique jointing of the masonry above some irregular stonework (x). On comparing the masonry on the two sides above the central doorway the inference became irresistible that there must have existed on the south side a supporting arch which had fallen away and had been replaced by rough irregular stonework. Granting this, there was sufficient indication that the supporting arches of both window and doorway occupied symmetrical positions, and that therefore both apertures must have been approximately of equal width.

4. The steps in the low molding outside the building. This molding runs round most of the Gothic buildings of the college, and has been reproduced upon St. Swithun's by Messrs. Bodley and Garner. When this molding arrives at the spot where the chapel porch window is supposed to have been, it is stepped down to get under the window. If there had never been any window in the position indicated the alteration in the level of the molding would be meaningless. The fact that the molding was dropped upon both sides of the late entrance shows, in my opinion, a well intended, though ignorant attempt, to treat this molding symmetrically on both sides of the doorway, which was probably contemporaneous with the moving of the doorway to the central position.

In support of this contention it may be stated that this particular low molding is dropped in the manner described beneath the north window of the chapel porch, and seems to have been similarly disposed beneath the original windows of the senior common room. When the windows of the latter were enlarged, part of the molding was cut away with the original sills of the windows.

The second step down of this molding was meaningless and of late date, because whereas the older stones of the first step were properly

finished by being undercut, so as to prevent
water running down the face of the building,
the newer stones of the second step were not so
undercut Moreover one step only is shown in
the view of 1789, reproduced on p 164.

Such then are some of the facts which were to be
gleaned from an examination of the masonry walls of the
chapel porch. It is a matter for surprise that no record
of these changes should be preserved in the annals of the
college, and it remains for us to endeavour to piece them
together with a few historical data derived from other
sources

Firstly, it is worthy of remark that porches which are
related to chapels of colleges in the same manner as in our
building, viz. at one side, either north or south of the extreme
west end of an ante-chapel, are comparatively rare. Among
all the Oxford and Cambridge Colleges, a ground plan at all
comparable to our own is only to be met with in the closely
related colleges, New College and All Souls. A similar
arrangement is to be found in the two porches of Eton
College Chapel, but in King's College, Cambridge, the two
porches are situated rather further east than in the Oxford
Colleges.

It is moreover significant that these colleges were founded
within the same hundred years and were copied more or less
closely from the designs of William of Wykeham.*

In the case of the Oxford Colleges, New College, All Souls,
and Magdalen, it seems that the purpose of the chapel porch
was to give shelter to the access from a cloister or quadrangle
to the ante-chapel ; a holy water stoup was attached to one
wall at All Souls.

At Eton, according to the founder's original directions, a
larger plan was to be followed. In the document known as
the will of King Henry VI, 1447-8, was prescribed, ' Item
in the south side of the bodie of the church a faire large dore
with a porche over, the same for christenyng of childre and
weddynges.'

We may therefore assume that our chapel porch was built
at the same time as the chapel, an assumption supported by
the fact that similar hard Headington stone is to be found in
the walls of both, and was originally intended to serve the

---

* There is no chapel porch at Winchester College.

purposes of a chapel porch alone and not those of a main thoroughfare of the college.

The plan of the college indicates that the tower which bears our founder's name should mark the main entrance to the cloister, and there is little reason to doubt but that the great gate under it was so used during the first few decades of the existence of the college.

There are, however, indications that at a comparatively early period the great gate under the founder's tower was abandoned as the ordinary entrance to the college cloister and that the smaller doorway in the chapel porch took its place. Then, if we may accept the evidence of a picture, the window was walled up.

The illustration of Magdalen College referred to forms part of the border of Agas's Map of Oxford. It was copied from one of a series of sketches prepared by Bereblocke for Queen Elizabeth in 1566. In spite of the mannerisms of the artist, this picture affords confirmatory evidence that the doorway of the porch was in a lateral position, and indicates that it was the main thoroughfare to the cloisters in 1566, because the porch doorway is shown open, while the founder's great gate is represented closed, as indeed it is in most subsequent views.

At what time or for what reason the great gate was first closed is uncertain. It is possible that members of the college found the route from the High Street through the chapel porch to the hall and to the buildings upon the south side of the cloister shorter than the route through the founder's gate, and it is certain that they would have found it more sheltered in bad weather. And the practice of using the smaller rather than the larger entrance may have grown into a custom which was encouraged by presidents, who considered that the amenities of the lodgings were impaired by the noise of traffic under their windows.

It is possible that the great gate may even have been closed as far back as the time of Thomas Knollys, when additions to the president's lodgings seem to have been made in 1530-31 upon the present site.

By the closure of the great gate and the change of route, the porch of the chapel became the porch of the college, and considerable architectural alterations were thought needful.

One of the first of these changes we believe to have been the introduction of the present vaulted ceilings into the porch and passage, which had the effect of materially raising this

entrance to the college.   The entrance is believed to have
been given still further importance by the substitution of a
central for a side door, and it was this change which led to
the final destruction of the walled-up (?) window.

It is interesting to note that the walls of the chapel were
plastered (?) for the first time in 1564.   The alterations of
the chapel porch doorway were certainly undertaken in a
plastering age, for in no other would their imperfections
have been tolerated   Consequently we are inclined to fix
the date of the alterations after 1564; an opinion which is
in accordance with the date of the illustration of Bereblocke
(1566).

In 1633 Stone erected the gateway of the Physic Garden
on the other side of the High Street from a design by Inigo
Jones.   The pseudo-classical design seems to have so won
over the architectural heart of the college, that in 1635
Inigo Jones was employed to embellish the main entrance
at the east end of the gravel walk with a new gateway.
' It was a ponderous load of masonry, assuming the form of a
Doric porch, with couple pillars at the sides, and in the
semicircular pediment an ample double niche, having
towards the exterior a corpulent sitting figure of the
founder, and on the other side a standing image of St. Mary
Magdalen.'*

We have many drawings of Inigo Jones's gateway, exhibiting it from various points of view and at various times.   The
earliest is by Loggan in 1674.

In order to bring as much of the remainder of the college
buildings into conformity with the style of his fine new gateway, and the slightly older Physic Garden gate, Inigo Jones
proceeded to graft little ' ornaments ' here and there, with
the evident intention of toning down the severity of the
Gothic, and of elevating it into something more in accordance
with his own work.   Among such ' ornamental ' structures in
the Inigo style, I would mention the rounded west end of
the buildings on the south side of St. John's quadrangle,
the balls upon the east end of the election chamber, the
rounded canopy over the door of the president's lodgings,
the sundial over the library in the cloister (Inigo Jones
was fond of sundials), and what is more important for our
present purposes, the canopy over the doorway to the chapel
porch.

All these structures may be seen in the prints of Loggan,
Williams, Fisher, etc.

* Buckler. *Observations on the Architecture of St Mary Magdalen College.*

It has been suggested that the embellishment of the chapel porch doorway by the Inigo canopy was immediately preceded by the alterations of the doorway and window.

I find it difficult to accept this view in its entirety, because the evidence is in favour of the destruction of the window having preceded the introduction of the present vaulting. On the other hand it is possible that the weak segmental arch inside the doorway was a contrivance of Inigo Jones of the same date as the external canopy.   In any case the manner in which the work was finished off does little credit either to the architect or, if we accept our college historian's account, to President Frewen, who ' himself superintended the whole work.'*

Pictures of St. John's quadrangle of the eighteenth century show that the chapel porch was used exclusively as the entrance to the cloister.   *The Oxford Almanack* for 1730 shows that President Butler had caused the northern portion of the quadrangle in front of his lodgings, including the great gateway, to be separated from the rest by a wooden railing, which by 1733 had been replaced by an iron one.† Later still, this presidential front garden was put down under grass, which still remains, and no doubt with the view of securing nature and privacy, was planted with shrubs and trees,‡ which have lasted almost within the memory of our contemporaries

The Oxford Almanack for 1789 shows that Inigo Jones's doric canopy was still in existence, but that a scaffold for building operations had been erected at the base of the muniment tower. President Routh, probably following the advice of Buckler, determined to purge the college of the ll-chosen ornaments of Inigo Jones, and in 1792§ the canopy was removed from the doorway of the chapel porch.   The part of the wall above the doorway, which was disfigured by the removal, was made good by the insertion of new masonry.   This is conspicuous in the drawing by Buckler which was published on 22nd July, 1799.

Since the restoration by Buckler no changes had taken place in the exterior of the doorway, except that the adjacent wall had become almost entirely overgrown with ivy.   The interior of the porch probably received its thick outer coating

* Wilson, *Magdalen College* (1899), 147.
† Williams, *Oxonia Depicta.*
‡ *Oxford Almanack* for 1789, Buckler's mezzotint of 1799, Mackenzie and Le ux's engravings in Ingram's *Memorials of Oxford.*
§ Wilson, *op cit* 149.

of dark plaster at the time when the cloister walls were re-dressed in the same way after the building operations of Parkinson in 1827.

THE CHAPEL PORCH, MAGDALEN COLLEGE, OXFORD.   FROM THE
Oxford Almanack FOR 1789.

At a quite recent date the lower portion of the plaster,

being in bad condition, was removed and replaced with cement, a practice which has unfortunately also been followed in certain places on the cloister walls.

The Fellows of the college, impressed with the trustworthiness of the indications of the original condition of the chapel porch, as well as with the immediate necessity of replacing the almost ruinous arch and rubble sides by a construction which would give sound support to the muniment tower, determined to be guided by these indications and to restore the original plan of the wall. An opinion had been expressed by Mr. W. H. St. John Hope that the carved external doorway was of original fifteenth-century workmanship, and therefore the greatest care was taken to separate the stones without injuring them; and it is a matter for congratulation that they have been put up in their new (original?) position successfully. The southern half of the internal two-ribbed arch has been copied from the surviving northern half; its springer was found in the wall, but too mutilated to be used again. The window has been imitated from, but has been made narrower than, the north window of the porch, and its supporting arch has been introduced beneath the oblique joint in the original masonry over the middle of the pier. Last, but not least, the level of the ground inside and outside the door has been readjusted, so as to do away with an inconvenient step.

The correctness of the plan of reconstruction proposed received a remarkable confirmation when the aperture necessary for the window was being made in the wall to the south of the doorway. There were found some fragments of a molding identical with the jamb molding of the north window of the porch, and one block was in a sufficiently good state of preservation to allow of its being inserted in the lower corner of the new window at the south side, in what we had the strongest reasons for believing must have been its original position. The external moldings of the new window and the slope and width of the external sill have been taken from this corner stone.

It was held by some authorities that the original window could have had but a single light; they argued that there was no room for a two-light window and that the jamb moldings would have overlapped those at the side of the doorway. The successful insertion of a two-light window is a sufficient refutation of the argument: the architectural indications, however, were hardly less convincing. Firstly, the space for the original relieving arch overhead was too wide

for a single-light window, and was of a width suitable for an
aperture filled by a two-light window. Secondly, parts of
the stonework of a window were found in the wall, which
must have belonged to a two-light window like that on the
north side of the porch. Among other stones there were
found two large whitewashed internal
arch stones (*h, h*), like those over the
inner splay of the north window, but
with the hollow chamfer rudely hacked
away, apparently to make room for the
wooden laths which carried the plaster
over the doorway. Another fragment
was part of the seating for the centre
mullion of a window.

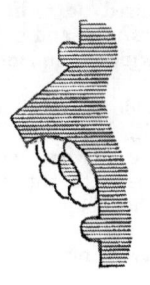

A

Since the hood molding over the door,
which dated from Buckler's restoration,
was poor, it was determined to replace
it by another. A fragment of an old
hood molding was found in the wall,
turned round and used as part of a
course of ashlar. The new molding has
been imitated from this.

B

MAGDALEN COLLEGE,
OXFORD. HOOD-MOLD-
INGS OF (A) CHAPEL
AND (B) CHAPEL PORCH
DOORWAYS.

It is of a rare type, differing from
the other plain hood moldings about the
college in having two bowtells, one above
and the other below the sloping plane,
instead of the usual angular member
alone. below the sloping plane.* The
introduction of an apparently new type
of molding in an old building would
not have been justifiable had we not
noticed that essentially similar moldings
occur over the western entrance to the
chapel and over the founder's great
gate. Only, in harmony with the
greater beauty and dignity of these
entrances, the moldings are larger and
the hollow under the sloping plane is
ornamented with carved lilies in the former, and with Tudor
flowers in the latter case. Thus by the introduction of this
type of hood molding over the doorway to the chapel porch,
the hood moldings over the three ancient western doors of
the college have been brought into complete relation with

* A similar molding may be seen in Christ Church.

one another, and are in proportion to the importance of the entrances they adorn.

Whether or not we have been well advised in continuing this door hood molding over the window is an open question. The face of the pier between the door and window is, however, so narrow that it would have required no ordinary artistic skill to join the two moldings successfully, and so the plan of a continuous one common to both window and doorway was adopted.

The kneeler at the north side of the door is to be a replica of the exquisitely modelled angel with high stretched wings, and holding a lily stem with three flowers, which until last month formed the southern kneeler to the hood molding over the western entrance to the chapel. This beautiful specimen of fifteenth-century carving was unfortunately broken by an artisan who was endeavouring to obtain a cast from it.

Resemblances between certain details in the chapel porches of Magdalen and All Souls have already been pointed out. If the fragment of the hood molding formed part of the original work, the doorways to the porches were also in agreement in this particular, for in All Souls the hood molding over the chapel porch door is the only hood molding over a doorway in the quadrangle which has a bowtell beneath the sloping plane; all the other hood moldings having an angular lower member.

The dimensions and general character of the two doorways and porches are so similar as to indicate that the details of the Magdalen porch may have been suggested by the All Souls porch, and may perhaps have even been executed by the same workmen. This theory receives confirmation by the fact that it is recorded that when the twelve doors and one hundred and two windows for the chambers in the cloister were being contracted for in 1475, by William Orcheyerd it was agreed that the windows were 'to be as good as or better than' those in the corresponding parts of All Souls College. The builders seem to have interpreted the terms of the contract in a liberal spirit, and so far as the chapel porch is concerned, the slender vaulting shafts in the angles within, and, we would add, the hood molding over the doorway without, show an advance in ornamentation upon those parts in All Souls College.

Appendix A.

List of Carved Stone Fragments found in the Wall on the site of the new West Window of the Chapel Porch.

The portion of the wall represented as newly restored in Buckler's drawing of 1799 had to be almost entirely removed because it was found to consist of an insecure veneer of ashlar (some stones were but 1½ inch thick) covering loose rubble which had settled and had caused the wall to bulge.

In this rubble were found the following fragments which we believe to have once formed part of the fabric of the college

I. Fragments of Anglo-classical moldings, probably from the Inigo Jones doorway of 1635 :

1 and 2.   Fragments of moldings from the right and left sides of the capitals of flat pilasters in low relief (of 1¾ inch).

3. Fragment of molding from the base of the same pilaster.

II. Fragments of Gothic moldings, probably from the original west window of 1474 (?) :

4. South lower corner of window, now built in new work.

5, 6, 7. Fragments of outer jamb moldings of window.

8. Fragments of sill, showing base of centre mullion.

9. Fragment of hood molding.

III. Fragments from a building older than the foundation of the college. We conjecture that these once belonged to the building of the ancient hospital of St. John of unknown origin, but stated in the fifteenth century to have been founded by Henry III. in 1233.   It is possible, however, that Henry endowed an already existing body with a site and new buildings. The chapel of the hospital underwent great alterations in 1665, and possibly, too, about 1635, when the present south side of St. John's quadrangle was built; but over a still surviving eastern doorway runs a molding similar to that of Fragment 10 The finding of these fragments indicates that the debris of part of St. John's Hospital were lying about when Inigo Jones's alterations were being made in the doorway.

10 and 11. Two fragments of hood molding of the early English or decorated period. They exhibit a curvature of about ⅔ inch in a foot.

12. A carved fragment, probably of the small arch over a niche.

<h2 style="text-align:center">APPENDIX B.</h2>

The East Window of the Hall.

The existence of the east window of the college hall was discovered and its aperture reopened during the year 1902. It may have been closed as long ago as 1635, when the 'kitchen staircase' building was added to that end of the hall. Externally the window was concealed by the lean-to roof over the western end of the kitchen staircase, internally it was hidden by plaster. But Mr. Wilson has suggested that the closing of the window may have been a result of the fire of 1719,* when the buttery and adjoining parts of the fabric seem to have been much damaged, and he has ascertained that an old MS. list of armorial glass in the college library contains descriptions both of the glass 'In the great East window q F and E, at each side the Colledge arms,' as well as of glass put into Christ Church after 1650. This, though not a proof, is an indication that the window was not closed until long after the building of the kitchen staircase.

When the rubble filling of the aperture had been removed, it was found that the tracery of the window had been taken out, but that the upper ends of the mullions, depending from the arch stones, were sufficiently well preserved to show that

---

* Hearne's *Diary.*

the window was a three-light window, exactly like the side windows of the chapel. The plain window splay is relieved by the simple hollow chamfer, which is so universal in Magdalen College.

The reconstruction of this window will be undertaken in 1903, and the hall will thus be brought once more into closer relation to the halls of All Souls, Christ Church, and Hampton Court Palace, all of which have windows in a similar position. May not this window in Magdalen College Hall, which has been blocked up and forgotten for so many years, have been the one which was well known to and inspired Thomas Wolsey, when he was engaged in the preparation of the plans of Cardinal College and of Hampton Court?

Built into the aperture were several pieces of the mullions and of the transom of the old window, so that there can be no doubt about its original proportions. There was also found a fragment of beautiful foliage carving which may possibly have been the base of one of the niches for statues in the chapel, it showed traces of an original coat of reddish distemper."

The Rev. R. B. GARDINER, M.A., F.S.A., read the following note on the Monument of Thomas White in Milton Church, Hants, of which he also exhibited photographs ·

" Milton Church was entirely rebuilt about 1830 with the exception of the base of the tower. This forms the western porch, and within it on the north side stands the monument of Thomas White of Fiddleford. It was evidently set up in the old church. It contains, within a sort of alcove with curtain drapery, fastened up with cherubs' heads, and surmounted by an atchievement of arms, a three-quarter length figure of Thomas White, just over life size, carved in stone. He is dressed in a coat, and wears a full wig, round his neck is a lace tie falling over a very narrow steel gorget; on his shoulders he has pauldrons and vambraces with ruffles; and on his thighs cuisses of the same pattern as the gorget, i.e. small scales with a knot in the centre. Round his waist is a scarf, the two short ends of which hang down towards the left having gold fringe, the gilding still remaining. In his right hand he carries across his body a short sword, both edges of which are wavy, the hilt was formerly gilt. On the right-hand side of the figure is carved in stone a helmet with the beaver up, showing on its right side eleven breathing holes. The beaver has ten oblong openings gradually diminishing towards the angle.

The inscription states that the monument is in memory of
Thomas White, Esq., son of Ignatius White, of Fiddleford, in
Dorsetshire. ' He served under three
Kings and Queen Anne in ye Guards.
He was much wounded in the wars of
Ireland and Flanders. He had one
son who dyed before him. He departed this life 17th February in the
year 1720. The monument was erected
by his widow Frarncis (*sic*), one of the
daûrs of Sir Charles Wyndham, of
Cranbury, in the City of Southton
(*sic*).'

Above are the arms, with traces of
colour: *azure three cross crosslets in
bend gold*, for White; impaling *azure
a chevron between three lions' heads
erased gold*, for Wyndham.

In the niche in which the figure
stands is an old sword 3 feet 4½ inches
in length, the blade 2 feet 9⅝ inches,
having both edges wavy as represented
in the sculpture. The hilt is of basket
shape, and though somewhat rusted
still retains considerable remains of
the silver wherewith it was inlaid.
The grip is now bare, and has affixed
to it a hook for suspending the sword,
which also bears traces of silver.

On either side of the blade close to
the hilt are sunken grooves about 8
inches long, beyond which is struck
the armourer's mark, a crowned head
couped, facing to the left. On one
side this is thrice repeated; on the
other once, with the Passau wolf mark,
inlaid with copper. On one side (that
with the three stamps) is engraved in
the groove the word ANDREA, and on
the other side FERARA.

SWORD OF THOMAS WHITE,
IN MILTON CHURCH,
HANTS. (⅛ linear.)

The monument is full of anachron-
isms; the sword belongs to the middle
of the seventeenth century, while the helmet is a tilting
helmet of Tudor date.

Of White himself, it is only known that one Thomas White
received his commission in Oxford's Blues (Royal Horse

Guards) in 1690. The Blues were present at the Boyne and up to the Battle of Aghrim, but they do not appear to have served in Flanders, either under William III. or Marlborough; he must therefore have exchanged into some other Guard regiment.

Thomas White's father, Ignatius White, was James II.'s representative at The Hague in 1688 when the 'Old Pretender' was born."

By the kindness of the Rev. J. E. Kelsall, rector of Milton, the sword in question was exhibited.

WALTER MONEY, Esq., F.S.A., Local Secretary for Berks, exhibited, by permission of Mr. G. Withers, of Newbury, the bronze matrix of a pointed oval seal, 2¾ inches long, with rudely-engraved figures of Our Lord and St. Anthony, standing under canopies. The legend is:

. S⁹ : HOSPITALIS : S⁹ : IHESVS : S⁹ : ANTONI : DE · HOLWEI :

So far this hospital has not been identified. The date of the seal is about 1540, and it is perhaps of foreign workmanship.

HAMON LE STRANGE, Esq., M.A., F.S.A., Local Secretary for Norfolk, communicated the following note on a Saxon brooch found at Hunstanton:

"In continuation of the account of the excavation of the Saxon Cemetery at Hunstanton, submitted to the Society on the 18th April, 1901, I beg to report that we had two days' digging in July of the present year. On the first day, 26th July, when I had the advantage of the presence and active co-operation of our President, we were not very fortunate, finding only two skeletons, with two plain circular bronze brooches, a small iron knife, only one amber bead, and no arms. On the morning of the 28th, Lord Dillon was unfortunately obliged to leave us, and he had hardly gone when we came on the skeleton of a tall warrior, who, by the measure of his thighbone must have been over six feet in height, an iron spear-head lay near him, and bits of the broken boss of his shield; in the afternoon we unearthed a really magnificent brooch of cruciform shape, of bronze, covered with an intricate pattern on which were considerable traces of gilding; on the upper corners were lozenge-shaped plates of silver, welded to the bronze, and round plates of the same metal at the extremities of the transverse arms; the shank portion of the cross was probably

GILT BRONZE BROOCH FOUND AT HUNSTANTON, NORFOLK. (⅔.)

broken by us in digging, as the edge shows a recent fracture, but although we carefully sifted the soil in the vicinity, we were unable to discover the broken portion. The most interesting peculiarity of the brooch, which is perhaps almost unique, is an ancient fracture right across the centre, and the ornament was so highly valued by its owner that he had it carefully mended by two bronze rivets, which have made it as strong as ever, and in fact withstood the blow of the spade which broke off the lower end.

The brooch is now submitted for exhibition to the Society, and by reason of its beauty and the ancient rivetted fracture may perhaps be worth figuring."

HENRY OWEN, Esq., D.C.L , F.S.A., submitted the following report as Local Secretary for South Wales :

" It is, I believe, expected of a local secretary that he should report.

The district for which I am secretary is far too large for me to obtain information thereon, but I send you the last two reports of a society which I have started in this county, the Pembrokeshire Association for the Preservation of Ancient Monuments. It has created a good deal of interest in these monuments, farmers and others are getting to understand that these old things are worth money, an admirable reason for their preservation.

The committee consists of men in different parts of the county , any new find or any likely damage is at once reported.

We have stirred up the owners of old buildings, from the County Council down to the Ecclesiastical Commissioners, which last have agreed to hand over one of the most interesting ruins in the county to us.

It should be counted to us for righteousness that we have restored twenty-four stones with Ogam inscriptions from gate posts and other dangerous places to parish churches and churchyards."

Thanks were ordered to be returned for these communications and exhibitions.

Thursday, 18th December, 1902.

Sir JOHN EVANS, K.C.B., D.C.L., LL.D., Sc.D., F.R.S.,
Vice-President, in the Chair.

The following gifts were announced, and thanks for the same ordered to be returned to the donors:

From the Author:—A Lecture on some English Illuminated Manuscripts. By H. Yates Thompson. Privately printed. 8vo. London, 1902.

From the Author:—The Site of Lincoln's Inn. By W. Paley Baildon, F.S.A. 8vo. London, 1902.

From the Author:—The Signs of old Lombard Street. By F. G. Hilton Price, Dir. S.A. 8vo. London, 1902.

From the Author:—The Churchwardens' Accounts of St. Andrew's and St. Michael's, Lewes, from 1522 to 1601. By H. M. Whitley. 8vo. Lewes, 1902.

From Harper Gaythorpe, Esq.:—Photograph of Norman tympanum at Pennington, near Ulverston.

From Rev. R. B. Gardiner, M.A., F.S.A.:—Photographs of (1) Monument to Thomas White in New Milton Church, Hants, and (2) Sword belonging thereto.

From E. M. Beloe, jun. Esq.:—A collection of 165 Lantern Slides of architectural and monumental antiquities principally in Norfolk.

A special vote of thanks was accorded to Mr. Beloe for his valuable contribution to the Society's collection of lantern slides.

Notice was again given of a Ballot for the election of Fellows on Thursday, 8th January, 1903, and a list of candidates to be balloted for was read.

Sir JOHN EVANS, K.C.B., F.R.S., V.P., read the following paper on a silver-mounted jug in his possession, which he also exhibited:

" I venture to call attention to a silver-mounted earthenware jug in my own possession, which is not only interesting in itself but has some interesting details of family history attaching to it.

The jug itself is about 5¼ inches in height with a nearly spherical body about 4 inches in diameter, standing on a moulded base, and it has a quasi-cylindrical neck about 2½ inches in internal diameter. In form, therefore, it much resembles many of the brown-ware jugs of the Elizabethan period The material is, however, of a much finer character and is nearly white on the inner side, while the outer is a pale-grey mottled with blue and a purplish brown. The surface is highly finished and beautifully glazed. There are in the British Museum several jugs of much the same form and material, but for the most part darker in colour. Some of them date back to the middle of the sixteenth century. The place at which they were manufactured is not known with certitude, but it was probably in England and possibly at Lambeth.

At some period my jug has been broken into numerous fragments, which have, however, been most skilfully put together, so that externally it shows little or no traces of its fractured condition. The silver mounting is unfortunately not hall-marked, but it seems to belong to two distinct periods. The older portion consists of a flat band round the base of the neck, the lower edge of which is neatly festooned and engraved. It is secured in its position by a hinged joint just under the handle. This band is connected with another of similar character at the base of the body of the jug, by three hinged bands, with a central rib, the sides being festooned and engraved. There are round perforations at intervals on each side of the rib. The base of the jug is protected by a moulded ring of silver with its upper edge foliated and engraved. The more recent portion of the mounting seems to have been necessitated by the broken condition of the jug. The original handle is wanting, and one of silver has been substituted which is kept in position by the remaining stumps of earthenware. The handle is connected with a cylindrical ring 1½ inch wide which covers the neck of the jug and is turned over inside so as to form a sharp edge round the mouth. To the handle is hinged a cover in form like a soup-plate reversed, with a kind of double spiral projection forming a handle with which to raise it.

On the cover are the arms of the Miller family, *ermine a fesse gules between three wolves' heads erased azure.* The shield is gracefully mantled and is surmounted by an esquire's helmet and the crest, *a wolf's head erased, collared ermine.* Not improbably this cover belongs to the earlier period.

SILVER-MOUNTED JUG

Formerly belonging to the Miller Family, 1618—1658.

(⅔ linear.)

Around the neck of the jug runs the following inscription, engraved in four lines in an Italian hand:

> *Fragile hoc poculum, emptum per me fuit A° Dnj 1618 et mox Proauunculo meo Nicolao Miller Ar datum. Qui diem claudens extremum A° 1621, ætatis suæ, 85, id inter cætera memoriæ tam digna mihi reliquit ut nifi ingratus efsem, non recordare non pofsum Nicol: Miller Milit Junij 12° An° 1658, Ætatis suæ 65.*

Before considering the actual history of the two gentlemen who have at one time or another been owners of this jug, it will be well I think to regard the history from a purely impersonal, though chronological, point of view. It was bought by a man twenty-five. years of age, and offered by him to a relative who had attained the venerable age of 82, from whom he had expectations This relative can hardly have in reality been a 'proavunculus' whom the dictionaries define to be a 'great-grandmother's brother.' As will subsequently be seen he was probably merely a grandfather, and 'proavunculus' may be a term of endearment somewhat of the same kind as the German 'klein Gross-väterchen.' The Latinity of the whole inscription cannot be termed graceful, and the concluding *Mihi* seems to have been written in error for *Miles*. The jug did not long remain in the hands of the old relative, but reverted to the giver in 1621, within three years of the date of the gift, and it brought with it other valuable property, for which profuse gratitude is expressed. It would seem probable that this fragile vessel was by some means broken into small fragments just forty years after it was originally bought, and that it was carefully restored and the second silver mounting added to it as a family relic in 1658, when the owner was 65 years of age.

As to the Miller family, a considerable number of particulars are given in Hasted's *History of Kent*,[*] and in other books relating to the county There can be little doubt that the first person mentioned in the inscription is Nicholas Miller, the elder, of Wrotham, gentleman, who died on February 17th, 1621, and is buried at Wrotham. He is probably the same Nicholas Miller, of Wrotham, yeoman, who bought land in Broomfield and Ulcomb in 1586.[†] In 1606 we find 'Nicolas Myller, the Elder,' buying 23 acres of land in Bromfield [‡]

---

[*] Vol. ii (1782), 240, 261, 349
[†] *Archæologia Cantiana*, xviii. (1889), 251.
[‡] *Op cit* 434.

His son Nicholas Miller, of Horsnell's Crouch, which he bought at the beginning of the reign of James I., of James Peckham, of Yaldham, resided at Crouch, and was Sheriff of Kent in the eighth year of Charles I. (1632-3). He died August 8th, 1640, æt. 74, and is buried at Wrotham. He left four sons and four daughters.

In 1626 Nicholas Miller, the sheriff, purchased the manor of Oxonhoath in West Peckham, Kent * and his eldest surviving son Sir Nicholas Miller, knight, resided there and greatly augmented and beautified the place In 1644 we find him acting as one of the Sequestrators in Kent.† He died February 20th, 1658-9 æt. 66, and was buried at West Peckham Like his father, he left four sons and four daughters surviving, and was succeeded by his eldest son Humphry who was created a Baronet in 1660.

Comparing the date of his death and his age with the last date in the inscription there can be no doubt that this was the Sir Nicholas Miller, the original purchaser of the jug, which reverted to him on the death of his grandfather. What other property accompanied the jug it is difficult to say, but not improbably it was land which rendered him independent of his father. He seems to have been a man of considerable wealth, and the curious diary of James Masters published in the *Archæologia Cantiana* testifies to his hospitality. On at least three or four occasions Masters stayed at Oxonhoath with Sir Nicholas Miller and sometimes disbursed as much as ten shillings among the servants. This diary throws some light on the sources of the income of Sir Nicholas, as in February, 1651,‡ Masters borrowed from him the sum of £1,000, in addition to £300 already borrowed, on which he paid interest at the rate of 7 per cent., afterwards reduced to 6 per cent.

Philipott § mistakenly calls Sir Nicholas the nephew instead of the son of the purchaser of Oxonhoath, but gives him credit for the ' new additions ' to the place ' which are set out with all the circumstances both of art and magnificence ' The restoration of the jug is quite in accordance with its owner, being possessed of the same good taste at the close of his days as that which led him as a young man to purchase it, and he may well have treasured an object which, from the inscription upon it, was so closely connected with his success in life.

* *Archæologia Cantiana*, xvi. (1886), 64.
† *Ibid.* iv (1861), 138, 141.
‡ *Ibid.* xv. (1886), 196-8, 203-6-8-9 ; xviii. (1889), 161-3.
§ *Villare Cantianum* (1659), 269

Though so closely connected with Wrotham the home of the early brown-ware, ornamented with slip, this earthenware jug is of an entirely different character from the Toft ware."

A representation of the jug is given in the accompanying plate.

The Rev. J. T. FOWLER, D.C.L., F.S.A., Local Secretary for Durham, read the following notes on a fireplace lately opened out in the cathedral church of Durham :

" It has long been known that in the west wall of the south transept of Durham Cathedral, near the south-west corner, there existed a fireplace, built up flush with the wall at some period unknown.   In the cloister outside could be seen,

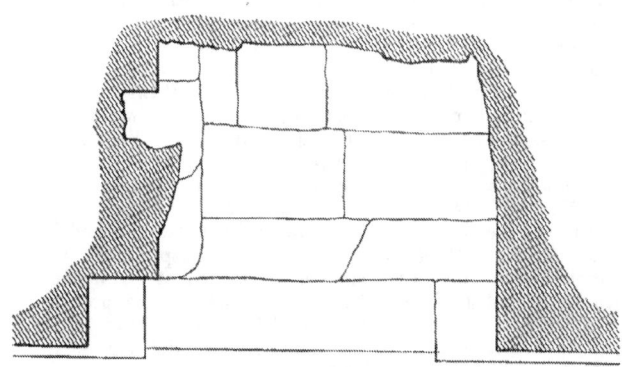

PLAN OF FIREPLACE.   (Scale, ½ inch to a foot.)

walled up probably early in the nineteenth century, the place where the chimney had come out, and, in the wooden ceiling above, an oblong aperture through which it had passed upward and round which the cornice is carried. (See Illustrations.) As the transept wall has been refaced, no further indications of the chimney exist.

In November, 1901, the fireplace was opened out, with the results shown in the accompanying drawings, for which we are indebted to our Fellow, Mr. C. Hodgson Fowler, architect to the Dean and Chapter. (See Illustrations.) I send also a photograph taken before the face was made good ; this, how-ever, is somewhat confused by reason of the wooden props that had to be put in as the work went on. But for these much of the upper part would have fallen, and it was only by taking the utmost care that the stones were kept in their places until they could be secured by new masonry.

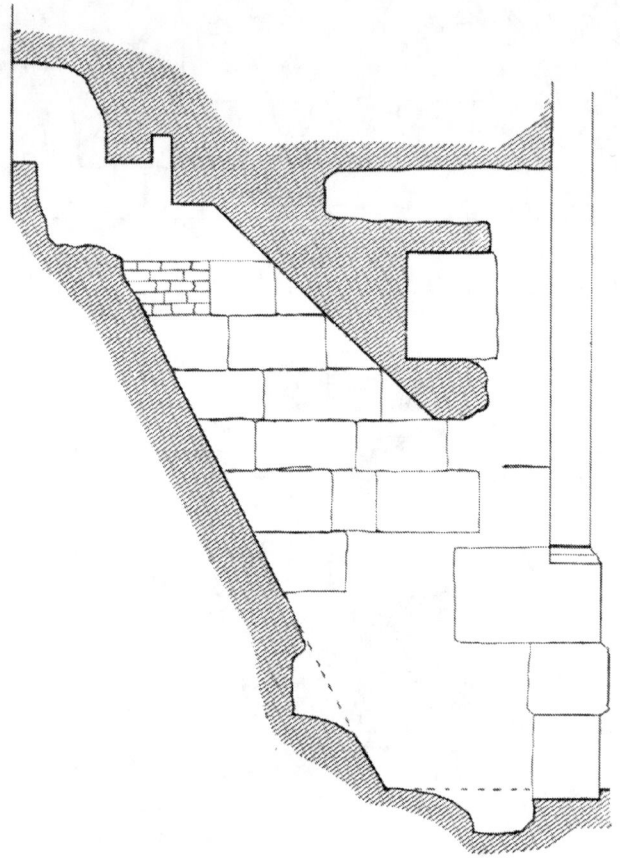

SECTION OF FIREPLACE. (Scale, ½ inch to a foot.)

There is not much to be said about the drawings, which speak for themselves. It will be seen that the fireplace and

To face page 180.

FIREPLACE IN THE SOUTH TRANSEPT OF DURHAM CATHEDRAL CHURCH.

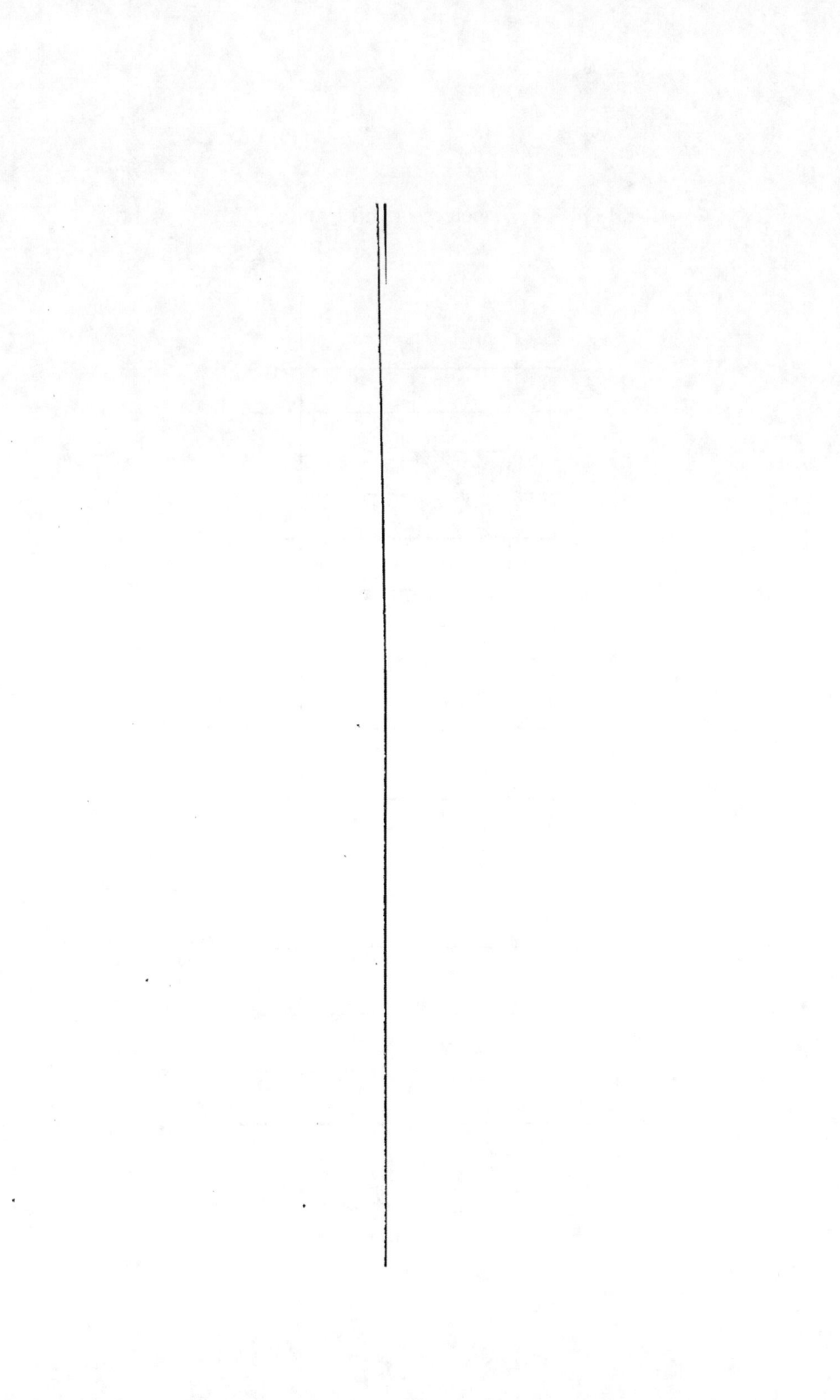

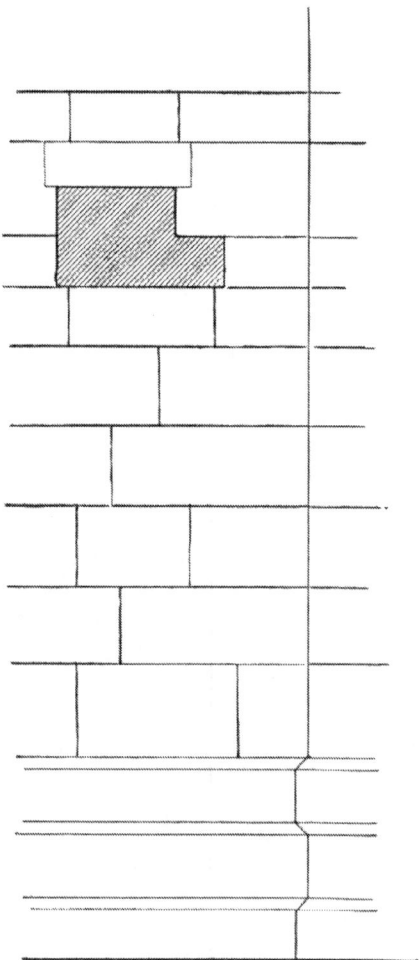

ELEVATION IN CLOISTER, SHOWING OPENING FOR FLUE.
(Scale, ½ inch to a foot.)

chimney have been constructed in the thickness of the Norman wall, and that one twin shaft of the arcade has been removed for this purpose.   There is some appearance of a recess over

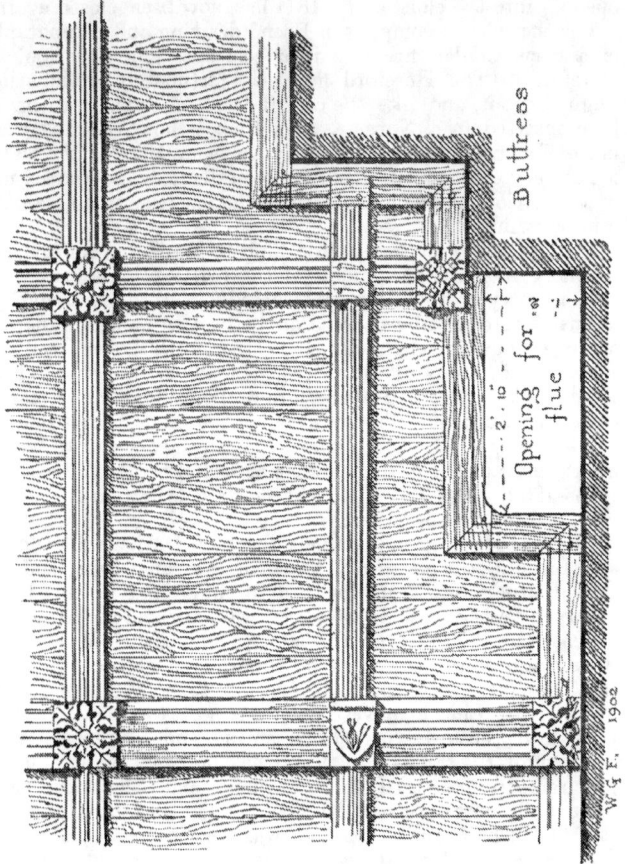

PART OF CEILING OF THE CLOISTER AT DURHAM, SHOWING OPENING FOR FLUE.

the fireplace on the left-hand side, but this may possibly be only a space left after removal of stones.   It has, however, been left open in the new refacing.   The stones at the back of the fireplace are much calcined by the action of the fire. No fuel was found, but there were some animals' bones, and rags, probably thrown down the chimney by workmen. The opening into the cloisters (p 181) has now been closed again.

For the sake of comparison I send drawing and photograph of a very similar fireplace in a corresponding situation at Hereford.* The Hereford fireplace, fortunately, retains its original front, and, like the one at Durham, appears to have been inserted in a Norman wall, though how the flue was made, if it was not constructed at the same time as the wall, is not very evident. It has long been disused, and indeed its upper portion is done away with by the insertion of a fifteenth century window.

In the south-east transept of Lincoln Minster is a fireplace probably of about the middle of the thirteenth century. It is in a vestry of this date, constructed within the transept by means of screen walls, covered on both sides by a rich diaper of large four-leaved flowers By the north screen wall is a long plain stone lavatory trough.† The chimney exists complete, its external features are probably familiar to many from the woodcut of it in Parker's *Domestic Architecture*, vol. ii. facing p. 91. Here again the fireplace seems to be an insertion, crammed into one of the arches of St. Hugh's arcade (1186-1200) If so, the flue has been driven through an earlier wall, as in the other cases.

These three fireplaces, namely those at Durham, Hereford, and Lincoln, are all that I know of the same type, and in similar situations. I am inclined to think that the need for a large vestry with a fireplace was discovered after the Norman period, that at Durham and at Hereford vestries were made in the transepts by running up wainscot screens, that fireplaces were made in the old thick Norman walls, and that at Lincoln a vestry of this sort was made in the thirteenth century with stone screens, and a fireplace and lavatory of the same date. Then, as time went on and ritual requirements increased, large vestries and sacristies were often built outside great churches. Such was certainly the case at Durham, and when this was done there would be no further occasion for internal vestries, and they would be taken away. The walling up of the Durham fireplace did not appear to be of recent date, and very possibly it was done

---

* For these we are indebted to the Dean of Hereford, and to Mr. Robert Clarke, architect to tne Dean and Chapter

† All this is well shown in an illustration in Murray's *Cathedrals*, Lincoln, p 311.

when the new vestry was made, namely in the last years of
the thirteenth century. These fireplaces could have had no
perceptible effect on the temperature of great churches, but
they would be convenient for heating the obley-irons,
providing burning charcoal for the censers, heating water
for various purposes, and keeping the vestments dry.

I have yet to call attention to a supposed fireplace of quite
a different type at Chichester. For the drawings we are
indebted to Mr. Prior, who kindly did them for me at the
request of my old friend, Prebendary Bennett. I understand
from Mr. Bennett that the recess, which has been hollowed
out in the south wall of the choir, had been walled up, but
was opened out by the late Precentor Mackenzie Walcott,
and that charcoal was found in it. Whatever it has been, it
cannot have been a fireplace in the ordinary sense, for it has
no flue. But charcoal would keep alight in such a recess for
some time if there were plenty of it and it were blown or
fanned in any way, and it may have been used for any or
most of the purposes named above.

Since writing this paper I have had my attention directed
by our Assistant Secretary, Mr. W. H. St. John Hope, to two
very interesting vestry fireplaces that have been described by
him.

One is in the east end of the vestry at Hulne Abbey, near
Alnwick To quote Mr. Hope's words, 'It consists of a recess
with a segmental head, 3 feet wide, 5 feet high, and about
18 inches deep, with a stone shelf about 18 inches above the
sill. The central portion of the bottom is cut down to a
depth of $7\frac{1}{2}$ inches, leaving a broad shelf on each side, and
has a circular sinking with sloping bottom and drain to the
outside. Above the shelf, which is unfortunately mutilated,
is a chimney carried up in the wall, which is thickened
externally and carried on a buttress. I think there can be
no doubt that the lower portion of the recess was used in
some way by the sacrist when mixing the flour and water for
the altar breads, and that on the upper shelf was a brazier of
lighted charcoal for heating the irons for pressing the wafers.
The charcoal for the censers could also have been kept
here.' *

The other is in the south wall of the upper vestry at the
church of St. Peter, Mancroft, Norwich. Mr. Hope describes
it as 'a pointed niche, 27 inches above the floor, $3\frac{1}{2}$ feet high,

---

* *Archæological Journal*, xlvii. 116 (plan and plate).

and about 18 inches square in plan, with an ascending flue or chimney in the head.' He goes on to say, 'It was no doubt used for lighting charcoal for the censers and for baking the obleys or wafers used at mass.' " *

The Rev. J. T. FOWLER, D.C.L., F.S.A., also read the following note on a seventeenth-century figure in painted glass in Stoke Poges Church, Bucks :

" In *Notes and Queries* of 26th September, 1896, p. 256, is a short description, under the head 'Evolution of the Bicycle,' of a figure in 'a small stained-glass window bearing date 1642.' This window, which is at Stoke Poges Church, is made up of scraps said to have come from the old manor house, and on one of these, apparently of the same date and character as the figure to be described, may be read, quite distinctly, 'Berghen, 1642,' the B partly cut off. The writer of the note says, ' One of the figures on the glass is a youth clad in a Roman looking garb, and blowing a long trumpet. He is mounted on what resembles very closely a bicycle of the old "boneshaker" type.' On 17th October (p. 318) another correspondent, basing his remarks on a sketch then lying before him of something which must have been altogether different, says that 'the little draped figure is not, strictly speaking, mounted on anything like a bicycle,' and that it is 'holding a partly curved long trumpet as if it was about to play upon, or use, that instrument,' and so on, finally expressing his opinion 'that the figure at Stoke Poges is that of a cherub,' associated with what the glass-painter had meant for a 'symbolic wheel.' Now it is quite clear that the former correspondent described the figure correctly, except that he most unaccountably puts the rider into 'a Roman looking garb,' whereas he is quite naked. The other writer finds a sketch of something else, and on that bases a contradiction of the former account, and thinks 'anything like a bicycle out of the question' in this case. Now, as I am myself a keen bicycler, and something of an antiquary and ecclesiologist, I have felt much interested in this matter, and I contributed to the correspondence later on. More recently the matter excited some interest in America, and early in the present year it was referred to in the *Cyclists' Touring Club Gazette*. The former of the two correspondents of *Notes and Queries*, again comes forward in a somewhat vehemently expressed and not over courteous note, to say, 'The so-called hobby-horse is

* *Norfolk Archæology*, xiv

simply a wheel placed between the feet of an angel, and has nothing whatever to do with a bicycle or a hobby-horse.' * However, on 22nd March, 1902 (p. 231), appeared a detailed description by a writer signing 'Ibagué,' who, instead of sitting down and theorising about the window, had 'just spent some time in carefully examining' it. That description leaves nothing to be desired, and the rider is here 'a naked, childish figure blowing a clarion or post-horn, and seated on a hobby-horse.' I need not quote more, but the hobby-horse is minutely described, and it is amazing that the editor should say in a

SEVENTEENTH-CENTURY FIGURE IN PAINTED GLASS IN STOKE POGES CHURCH, BUCKS. (⅓ linear.)

footnote, 'we do not admit the presence of a hobby-horse, in view of the communications of F. G. S.,' those namely to which I have referred, as denying that there is anything of the kind in the window. The imaginations of the one correspondent are held to be of more value than the careful and accurate description, written on the spot, of another.

I will now refer to the accompanying tracings and photograph.

No. 1 is a tracing that was kindly sent to me last March

* *Notes and Queries*, 28th December, 1901, p. 530.

by Colonel Michael Foster Ward, of Upton Park, Slough. It shows the rider, with parts of subjects in adjoining fragments.

No. 2 is a photograph done for me by a friend who went over from London to Stoke Poges expressly in order to take it. It shows the whole of the group of fragments in which the rider appears.

No. 3 is a tracing done by me last July.

No. 4 is traced from No 3, and coloured from my notes.

It will now be seen that the description by 'Ibagué,' and others in accordance therewith, are perfectly correct, and that the remarks of 'F. G. S.' and of the editor of *Notes and Queries* are altogether beside the mark, being based upon a complete muddle, and showing how desirable it is to be sure there is no misunderstanding, before contradicting others and holding them up to contempt. .

It now remains for me to ask, what is the meaning of the hobby-horse and rider, for such it undoubtedly is. It will be seen that the machine is propelled by the feet on the ground, as were the hobby-horses that were all the fashion in the early part of the nineteenth century. The glass is probably Dutch, and such a machine could easily be driven on the brick roads of Holland, if there were such roads so early, or at any rate on level places such as those around the Vijver at the Hague. The nudity of the figure is probably due to artistic considerations. What there is of the back part of the machine is very puzzling. No rear wheel is shown, nor any provision for steering. If we had the whole of the subject, it would probably be quite intelligible, as it is, it wants elucidation, and I shall be very glad if any light can be thrown upon it. I suppose we may dismiss from serious consideration all suggestions of any connection with 'cherubim,' 'symbolic wheels,' 'tetramorphs,' and the like. The absence of wings alone would be conclusive, to say nothing of any other human characteristics in the representation as a whole. Perhaps the most puzzling thing about it is that the back part of the machine is not like a wheel, and it seems to rest on the ground. Yet there can be no doubt as to the front wheel, nor of its great interest in connection with the 'Evolution of the Bicycle,' however little it may have to do with angelic beings of any description "

Mr. READ pointed out that the painting was of the same character as that commonly found in the engravings of ornament of the time, by Étienne de Laune, D. Mignot, Le Blon, and many others. In all of these none of the main lines have any structural value, the idea of the artist being to cover the surface with agreeable curves, festoons, and the like, with no regard to their fantastic impossibility, and in this case we have simply a terminal portion of such a design.

Dr. FOWLER expressed his great satisfaction with this explanation, but still thought that the idea of the wheel and the rider must have been derived from some actual machine of the nature of a hobby-horse.

The Rev. E. H. GODDARD, M.A., Local Secretary for Wilts., exhibited a number of antiquities found in a Roman house at Great Bedwyn, accompanied by the following note :

"In accordance with a suggestion made to me some time ago by Mr. Read and Mr. W. H. St. John Hope, I am allowed by the Wiltshire Archæological Society to send for exhibition the accompanying gold ring, which was found in a Roman villa at Great Bedwyn, Wilts, in 1853, about half a mile to the east of the Roman road connecting Winchester with Marlborough.

EARTHENWARE STAMP, AND IMPRESSION, FOUND AT GREAT BEDWYN, WILTS. (¼.)

The ring bears an irregular cross, not the fylfot, and, so far as I know, has never been described or figured. I should be grateful for an opinion as to the possibility of it having belonged to a Christian.

I send with it certain other things found on the same occasion, a small bronze figure of a cock, the bowl of a spoon, a bone pin, a bronze armlet, etc. for the sake of a curious triangular earthenware stamp with a pattern of late-Celtic

character which accompanies them. The stamp and the
pattern produced by it are here illustrated."

The Rev. W. K. CHAFY, D.D., F S.A , exhibited a desk-
cloth from Church Lench, Worcestershire.

It measures 7 feet 3 inches in length by 3 feet 6 inches in
breadth, and is made of blue velvet with remains of water-
flowers, which has formed part of an early sixteenth century
cope. The orphrey of the cope has been slit down the middle,
and the pieces used as a border to one end and both sides of
the cloth. By bringing together the pieces it is possible to
recover the design, which consisted of figures of saints on gold
ground, under canopies with twisted shafts, of the usual late
style. The figures were : on one side of the cope (1) a bearded
saint holding a club, (2) a female saint with long golden
hair holding a knife ; (3) a male saint holding a long cross.
On the other side (1) a male saint holding some round object,
of which half is destroyed; (2) a female saint with golden
hair holding a palm branch; (3) St. Peter with a key. The
end strip has portions of two other figures.

Thanks were ordered to be returned for these communications and exhibitions.

Sir HENRY HOWORTH called attention to the decision given a
few days ago by Chancellor Tristram, empowering the vicar
and churchwardens of West Malling, Kent, to sell a stoneware
jug with silver-gilt mountings of the Elizabethan period,
which formed part of the church plate.

This decision had such far-reaching consequences that he
thought some protest should be made on the part of the
Society with regard to the principle involved.

After some discussion it was proposed by Sir HENRY
HOWORTH, seconded by Lord BALCARRES, and carried *nem.
con.*:

"That the matter be referred to the Council for immediate
consideration."

Thursday, 8th January, 1903.

Viscount DILLON, President, in the Chair.

The following gifts were announced, and thanks for the
same ordered to be returned to the donors:

From Alexander Peckover, Esq., LL D., F.S A.:—History of Wisbech and
Neighbourhood during the last Fifty Years, 1848-1898. By F. Gardiner.
8vo. Wisbech, 1898.

From Isidore Spielmann, Esq, F S A :—Exposition des Primitifs Flamands
et d'Art ancien, Bruges. Première Section: tableaux, Catalogue 8vo.
Bruges, 1902.

From Viscount Dillon, President —Heraldik Grundzuge der Wappenkunde
von Dr Eduard Freiherrn von Sacken. 12mo. Leipsic, 1899.

From the Author:—Rambles in Rome. An Archæological and Historical
Guide. By S. R. Forbes 8vo. London, 1903.

From Rev. R. S. Mylne, F S A. ·—Relazione dei lavori compiuti dall'Ufficio
Regionale per la Conservazione dei Monumenti dell'Emilia. Raffaele
Faccioli. 8vo. Bologna, 1901.

Special votes of thanks were recorded to the editors of
The Athenæum, The Builder, and *Notes and Queries,* for the
gift of their publications during the past year.

The following Resolution, which had been drawn up by
the Council at its meeting of 19th December, 1902, in accordance with the desire of the Society, was proposed from
the Chair, seconded by WILLIAM GOWLAND, Esq., V.P., and
carried *nem con* :

"The Society of Antiquaries of London regrets the circumstances that have led to the issue of a faculty for the sale of
an ancient jug from the church of West Malling, and
deprecates the sale of chattels belonging to any church."

The following Resolution was proposed by PHILIP NORMAN,
Esq., Treasurer, seconded by the Rev. R. B. GARDINER, M.A.,
and carried *nem. con.* :

"The Society of Antiquaries of London hears with regret
that there is a proposal on foot to destroy the church of
All Hallows Lombard Street, in the City of London, a building

of interest in itself as being the work of Sir Christopher Wren, and containing much fine woodwork of his time.

The Society ventures to appeal to the parishoners to withhold their assent to any scheme that will involve the destruc- of their church."

In accordance with the Statutes, ch. xii. sec. ii., notice was given from the Chair that at its next meeting the Society would be asked to sanction an expenditure of £197 10s. for fitting up with bookshelves the room in the basement lately vacated by the porter.

This being an evening appointed for the election of Fellows, no papers were read.

The Ballot opened at 8.45 p.m., and closed at 9.30 p.m., when the following were declared duly elected Fellows of the Society :

> Reginald Allender Smith, Esq., B.A.
> Henri Favarger, Esq.
> William Wyndham Portal, Esq., M.A.
> Peter MacIntyre Evans, Esq., M.A.
> Alfred Heneage Cocks, Esq , M.A.
> Joseph Meadows Cowper, Esq.
> Edward Alfred Webb, Esq.
> Henry Taylor, Esq.

Thursday, 15th January, 1903.

WILLIAM GOWLAND, Esq., Vice-President, in the Chair.

The following gifts were announced, and thanks for the same ordered to be returned to the donors :

From the Author :—Ancient Coffers and Cupboards, their History and Description. By Fred. Roe. 4to London, 1902.

From Alexander Peckover, Esq., LL.D , F S.A. —The History of Wisbech and the Fens. By Neil Walker and Thomas Craddock. 8vo. Wisbech, 1849.

From the Author :—For King and Kent (1648), a Romantic History. By Colonel Colomb, F S.A. 3 parts. 8vo. London, 1903.

The following gentlemen were admitted Fellows:

Alfred Heneage Cocks, Esq , M.A.
Reginald Allender Smith, Esq., B.A.

In accordance with the Statutes, ch. xii. sec. ii., a proposal to expend the sum of £197 10s. in fitting up with bookcases the room in the basement lately vacated by the porter, was submitted to the Society, and approved.

REGINALD HAINES, Esq., M.A., submitted the following report as Local Secretary for Rutland:

"As it appears that no reports, at all events for a great number of years, have been sent in from Rutland, perhaps I may be permitted, though only appointed in June, 1901, to say a few words, by way of introduction, concerning archæological matters in this county long prior to that date. The mention of these is almost essential for the proper presentment of the work of excavation lately done, and the discoveries that have resulted therefrom

Small as it is, Rutland contains one or two important and archæologically productive sites, both Roman and Anglo-Saxon. The latter lie in the parish of North Luffenham near Edith Weston. With regard to the former, the locality lying along the borders of the parishes of Market Overton and Thistleton, on the north side of the county, has been known as a Roman site ever since the time of Camden, and it is described by Stukeley, in his *Itinerarium Curiosum* (1733). The extent and limits of the Roman settlement there have been made pretty plain by a series of systematic excavations, and Mr. W. H Wing, of Market Overton, is preparing an accurate plan of the whole, the 'line of which is very well marked as a rule by the pottery visible on the surface of fields and parts of fields.' The Roman camp, within the circuit of which stands the church, is separate, and at some distance from the settlement.

THE ROMAN SETTLEMENT AT MARKET OVERTON AND THISLETON.

The first important discovery of Roman remains at this spot, made upon the pieces of land called 'The Holmes' and 'The Wong,' and in a stone-pit called 'Kirk Hole,' may be referred to the year 1863. The stone-pit contained quantities of skeletons and parts of skeletons, while from the other two places were obtained numbers of objects of various sorts, including about 300 Roman coins dating from Claudius (54 A.D.) to Gratianus (383 A.D.), and two third brasses of Carausius (287 A.D.). Among the smaller coins was one which commemorated the removal of the capital from Rome to Constantinople Besides coins were discovered brooches, rings, pins, steelyards, and many other bronze and bone articles. There was also an abundance of Samian ware, on one piece of which is represented Hercules with the lion's skin, plucking the golden apples from the Garden of the Hesperides (?). A portion of a second vase shows Mercury in one panel and a horse in another. A third fragment bears a wild boar courant. A vine with its tendrils forms the elegant ornament of a fourth. Potters' marks appear, such as QVINTI M and DOV . . . , the remainder being broken off.

In 1866 a very pretty brooch was found here. It is round and of the size of a sixpence, showing a star of inlaid silver, the centre being of green enamel and the spaces within the outer circle of silver with blue enamel. The rim has bronze radiations; the back, on which are the pin and clasp, being also of that metal.*

A Roman silver spoon found on the same site has disappeared since Mr. Bennett's death, together with a remarkable ring with the cryptic letters M. I. S. V. on it.

These finds were for many years in the possession of the late Mr. T. G. Bennett, of Market Overton, at whose death they recently passed into other hands.

During the last two years excavation has been carried on more systematically at these sites, and the previous finds have been greatly supplemented. In November, 1900, were turned up portions of eight vases, complete enough to show their shape, and several objects of bronze and bone. Since then, at various dates, have been found near the eastern boundaries of the parish, fibulæ, knives, hairpins of bronze and bone, an auriscalpium, and fragments of a glass necklace. Also a great deal of pottery, real and imitation Samian being fairly common. One vessel, which is nearly perfect, has the potter's mark 'CARATILLI' on the base inside. The rivets still to be seen in some of the pieces show that this ware had a certain value. The native Durobrivian pottery was made near Wansford, close to the eastern border of Rutland, and some of it is naturally found here. One nearly perfect vase of this kind

* See *The Gentleman's Magazine* for May, 1866.

gives a representation of a red deer, a hare, and a hound. Another vessel in a fragmentary condition, made of rather common ware and light blue in colour, may have been a wine cooler. The chief feature indeed of these finds has been the great variety and amount of the pottery, fragments of which have also been found on the surface in the neighbouring villages of Cottesmore, Barrow, and Edmondthorpe (the last in Leicestershire).

In September, 1901, an interesting bronze coin of Carthage was picked up. Its date appears to be about 200-180 B C It has the head of Persephone on the obverse, and a horse's head on the reverse.

In August, 1901, about twenty Roman coins were unearthed, among them being a fine first brass of Marcus Aurelius, and an ancient forgery of Caracalla.

I exhibit a copy of a sketch by Mr. H F. Traylen of the capital of a column found some time ago in a field at Thisleton, and perhaps of Roman workmanship.

The stone is Clipsham stone, a hard shelly oolite, and Mr. Traylen thinks the serrations represent a fig-leaf ornament, probably acanthus, the leaves on front and sides forming ' a classical knop of foliage at the angles, thus filling up the space under the angles of a square abacus.' The bottom is semi-circular and spreads upwards into a square form. The oblong hole in the centre of the top is for the insertion of a lewis for lifting the stone, and the dovetail holes at the back are for metal dowels to fasten the capital to a wall.

There is no doubt a great deal more beneath the surface at this site awaiting discovery, and as the work is in the hands of an enthusiastic archæologist, the above-mentioned Mr. Wing, we may expect to hear of many further finds in the course of time.

Besides the above, a very perfect brooch with the pin in working order was found by Mr. Wing in a cottage at Barrow in 1901 It had been picked up, it appeared, 30 years previously by a labourer in that parish.

ROMAN PAVEMENT AT KETTON.

Several square yards of tesselated pavement were found in digging the foundations of two new cottages close to the left hand side of Ketton post office, on the left of the road leading to Stamford. This was early in 1902. The remains were hacked up and covered over under the foundations of the cottages. I can find no mention of Roman remains at Ketton previously to this, except that Mr. V. B. Crowther-Beynon, of Edith Weston, has several pieces of similar pavement, which came originally from a sale at the Priory, Ketton.

ANGLO-SAXON GRAVEYARD AT NORTH LUFFENHAM.

Here again a few words of introduction will be necessary by way of preliminary to the recent discoveries. The first important finds on this site occurred in 1863, when many articles were found of bronze, iron, glass, and pottery, such as brooches, tweezers, knives, swords, shield-bosses, buckets, and urns, the latter hand-made of dark brown clay passing into black or dark green. Some of these articles are in the possession of Lord Ancaster, and are kept at the estate works, Normanton.

The above remains were found in two sand-pits between North Luffenham and Edith Weston. The ground called Weston Gate Field stands about 350 feet above the sea, and occupies the brow of one of the hill ridges, which run east and west across Rutland There are no present signs of mounds or tumuli on the spot. Here, after being suspended for some time, digging for the fine Northamptonshire sand began again in the summer of 1901, in one of the above-mentioned pits. A clearing was made 6 feet wide running the whole length of the pit, and the top soil, which is from 3 to 5 feet deep, was gradually removed. Fortunately Mr. V. B. Crowther-Beynon, of Edith Weston, a competent and enthusiastic archæologist, who had previously examined the site, was on the spot to watch the excavation, and it is to him that I am wholly indebted for the following facts. Previous to the re-working of the quarry Mr. Crowther-Beynon had discovered an imperfect skull, and later, a bronze cruciform brooch, and another skull.

The graves were found between 3 and 4 feet below the surface. This is how Mr. Beynon describes the two interments, at the opening of which he was present: 'The body had been buried at full length, with the head pointing nearly due west. Along the left side of the body had lain the warrior's spear, the pointed ferule of which was found near the feet, and the socketed head about level with the skull. Between the spear and the body, or possibly overlying the latter, was an iron sword of typical Anglo-Saxon shape, and over the hilt of the sword lay the iron umbo of a shield. Near the left arm was a large variegated glass bead, while a small pair of brass tweezers was found near the right shoulder.

GILT BRONZE BROOCH FOUND NEAR NORTH LUFFENHAM, RUTLAND.
(Obverse.) ⅔ linear.

GILT BRONZE BROOCH FOUND NEAR NORTH LUFFENHAM, RUTLAND.
(Reverse.) ½ linear.

Slightly beyond the head, and to the south-west of it, I un-earthed a bronze-mounted situla or bucket.'

The second interment was similarly oriented, but 'the spear lay on the right of the body, the sword resting diagonally on the breast, the hilt near the right arm and the point near the left knee. The umbo lay upon the sword, and a small iron knife was near the right hand. On the south side of the head was a bronze-mounted bucket and an urn of elegant make.' *

Both these appear to have been graves of persons of distinction; a third grave, probably that of a woman, appears to have been covered with slabs of stone. With this were found two brooches and three urns more or less perfect. Later were found a very fine bronze gilt cruciform brooch (see illustration), and an annular brooch, which had been tinned or silvered. The former of these had been ornamented with a series of silver plates, of which only one remains. It measures 7 inches long and 4¼ inches across. It has been repaired in ancient times by means of a bronze plate riveted on.

In this and previous excavations at least six swords have been found upon this site, a larger proportion than usual in these interments. The sword found in the former of the two interments described above, was 36½ inches long, the blade being 2⅞ inches wide. The scabbard, and probably the handle, were of wood. The other sword was of similar dimensions The first spearhead was 10¼ inches long, of which 6 inches were the head proper, and the rest the socket. The head was 1¼ inch wide. The spear was of the common Anglo-Saxon type found in England

The bucket found with the first body was almost perfect, though it afterwards warped and came partially to pieces. It was encircled by four flat bronze hoops, and has four straight vertical bands with bronze bicornute ornaments at the top. Both buckets are about 4 inches high, and the same in diameter.

Besides the urns were found broken sherds such as were scattered over the body at burial.

With a view to a more systematic and complete exploration of this interesting site, the noble owner of the land was asked to permit more extensive excavations to be made, but his reply was unfavourable; 'he could not,' he said, 'consent to the desecration of the graves of the dead.'

* For a fuller account of these finds, see Mr. Crowther-Beynon's paper in the *Associated Architectural Societies' Reports and Papers*, xxvi. (1901), Part 1.

PREHISTORIC GRAVES AT WICHELEY WARREN.

In a quarry worked for freestone on Major Brathwaite's land at the above-mentioned place was found in 1900 a skeleton, probably neolithic. The body was in a crouching position, with 'the knees tucked under the chin,' at the depth of about 3 feet. Unfortunately, no one interested in such things was at hand, and the remains were incontinently thrown aside and presently buried under a mass of rubbish from the tunnels which were being worked for stone. Mr. V. B. Crowther-Beynon was only able to recover a few teeth, though he seems to have found a few fragments of animal bones and bits of pottery at or near the spot.

In December, 1901, at a point about 200 yards from the last, where a fresh excavation was being made, a second interment was found. In this case the soil containing the remains came down in one block, and a few broken fragments of bone came to light, with a lower jaw. The jaw is now in Mr. V. B. Crowther-Beynon's possession, who communicated with Lord Avebury on the subject, sending the jaw, and received the following reply: 'to judge from your description (i e. of the interment) it is certainly probable that the interment you mention belonged to the stone (neolithic) age. This, however, in the absence of weapons or implements, cannot be put higher than a probability. I should think that lower jaws very like this might be found among our existing people, though I fear with hardly such good teeth. Their soundness and the way they were worn point strongly to a great antiquity.' Near the second interment occurred little patches of burnt soil of a conspicuously red colour. These may have been the sites of hearths.

The only other relics of the stone age that claim notice here are an arrow-head of flint, picked up in a field near Market Overton in November, 1900, by Mr. Wing.

MEDIÆVAL FINDS AT PILTON.

A discovery in 1881 of six jugs and other pottery first directed attention to this site. The jugs were found in an old well in Pilton brickyard.

These relics probably mark the position of the lost village of Sculthorpe, mentioned in Domesday Book. Since the discovery of the above, and during the last three years, a considerable amount of broken pottery has been found in the same spot.

A little jar (not more than 3 inches high) was turned up in digging near Oakham Station during the last year, and is now in the possession of Mr. Higgs, a builder. Mr. Crowther-Beynon suggests that it may have been one of the *ampullae* worn by medieval pilgrims.

Two querns of late British or Roman date have been discovered. The first of these was found in 1900 near Oakham Station, in a trench made beyond the railway crossing, and is now in the possession of Mr. Crowther-Beynon. The second, which is very similar, was found this year in front of the Manor House, Braunstone. Both were about a foot beneath the surface. The second quern is in Mr. Higgs' possession.

Mr. Wing reports the discovery in 1901 of a lancet window, which he dates approximately at 1220, in the back of a cottage at Barrow. He believes it to have belonged to a grange of Vaudey Abbey (Valle Dei).

There were found in 1899 in a cottage at North Luffenham some stone slabs with the Digby arms; they are now kept at the Normanton Estate Works The chief house of the Digbys in Rutland, was at Stoke Dry, where their monuments are in the church, but a branch of the family lived at North Luffenham, the site of their hall being traceable in a field near the churchyard, and their monuments being in the church. The excellent preservation of these stones is due to the fact that they were turned face downwards to serve as floor slabs.

A stile in the north-west corner of the churchyard at Market Overton has been made from two stones which originally served as mullions in the windows of the adjoining tower before so-called restoration. They have had grooves cut down them to admit of a York stone slab being inserted to form a stile. Probably the supporters have beneath the ground moulded ends, similar to those at the top

Eight separate pieces of painted glass were lately discovered in an old chest at Ayston Hall, the seat of Sir Arthur John Fludyer, bt.

Three of these are ecclesiastical, and the rest heraldic The former represent the visit of the Wise Men and the presentation in the Temple, and a single bearded head, which must have been part of a much larger composition. The colours of the first of these pieces are quite vivid, and the picture in good condition. In the case of the second, the glass has been much rubbed and the figures are blurred. The head is in admirable preservation The glass has the appearance of being of the end of the sixteenth century, or a little later, and was perhaps of foreign (*e.g.* Dutch) manufacture. The pieces are quite small, 18 inches square. The heraldic glass gives various Brudenell coats (the Fludyer ancestry). The largest piece represents a shield with eight quarterings:

1. For Brudenell ; *argent a chevron gules between three morions azure* ;
2. For Bulstrode ; *sable a stag's head or ·a crosslet between the antlers and holding in its mouth an arrow* ;
3. For Entwistle ; *or on a bend engrailed azure three mullets pierced argent* :
4. For Tallyard ; *or and azure a cross flory counter-flory or and azure* ;
5. For Anstey ; *a cross engrailed or between four martlets* ;
6. ? for Warren ; *two four-leaved shamrocks* ;
7. For Reynes , *checky or and gules a canton ermine* ;
8. For Scudamore ; *gules three stirrups argent and a canton.*

The second shield is that of Brudenell alone, with the field *or*, not *argent*.

The third bears *or a chevron gules between three morions azure* with mark of cadency for second son on the chevron, impaling *party or and azure a cross flory or.*

The fourth piece has four quarterings.

1. *Ermine on a chevron gules three escallops.*
2. Brudenell as on the second shield.
3. *Gyrony of eight or and gules.*
4. *Azure a bend cotised gules between three cross crosslets.*

These have now all been set up in a south window of Ayston Church by the vicar.

Some Lyddington men, working in a gravel pit at that village about 1862, found two small jars containing in all some 150 coins, mostly gold. These were claimed by the Crown and the coroner collected as many as he could.

An Uppingham sweep in 1888, riddling the soot from a chimney in an old cottage at Wing, found two small bags of silver coins of the Tudor and Stuart periods. Most of these came into the possession of Mr. Waugh, a hawker and coin collector, whose collection was recently dispersed at his death.

As a small corner of Stamford appears to be in Rutland, I have thought it best to include in this report a mention of one or two quite recent discoveries in that town.

In August, 1902, a number of coins were found,* of which 20 are said to have been Saxon. These are now in the hands of the Treasury. There were also some third brass Roman coins, Caroline silver, and late copper tokens found at the same time

In October, 1902, a silver denarius of Vespasian was dug up; and in September, 1902, a small bronze ring of Roman workmanship

All these were turned up in the course of the works connected with the deep drainage scheme for Stamford."

Colonel COLOMB, R.A., F.S.A., read a paper on a romantic Royalist episode.

Thanks were ordered to be returned for these communications.

Thursday, 22nd January, 1903.

Viscount DILLON, President, in the Chair.

The following gifts were announced, and thanks for the same ordered to be returned to the donors:

From the Author :—A Bird's-eye View of the Minôan Palace of Knossos, Crete By Arthur J. Evans, LL D., F.R S , V.P S A   4to   London, 1902

From the Delegates of the Bodleian Tercentenary .—Pietas Oxoniensis In Memory of Sir Thomas Bodley, Kt., and the Foundation of the Bodleian Library. 4to.   Oxford, 1902.

From the Treasurer and Masters of the Bench of Lincoln's Inn :—The Records of the Honorable Society of Lincoln's Inn. The Black Books. Vol. vi. (1776 to 1845). 8vo. London, 1902

* Near the skeleton of a man, according to a paragraph in the daily paper

From the Author, William Harrison, Esq. :

1. Ancient Forests, Chases, and Deer Parks in Lancashire 8vo. Manchester, 1902

2. Ancient Beacons of Lancashire and Cheshire. 8vo. Manchester, 1898

From H W Fincham, Esq. —Guide to the Remains of the ancient Priory and present Parish Church of St. John, Clerkenwell. 8vo   London, 1903.

From the Author —The History of Ewias Harold, its Castle, Priory, and Church. By Rev. A. T. Bannister. 4to. Hereford, 1902.

Henri Favarger, Esq., was admitted Fellow.

R T GÜNTHER, Esq , M A., read a paper on a submerged Roman foreshore in the Bay of Naples.

Mr. Gunther's paper. will be printed in *Archaeologia.*

Thanks were ordered to be returned for this communication.

<hr>

Thursday, January 29th, 1903.

ARTHUR JOHN EVANS, Esq., M.A., LITT.D., F.R.S.,
Vice-President, in the Chair.

The following gifts were announced, and thanks for the same ordered to be returned to the donors:

From R. Garraway Rice, Esq., F S A. .

1. St. Etheldreda Festival : Summary of Proceedings at Ely in October, 1873. By Charles Merivale, D.D. 8vo. Ely. n d.

2. The Chichester Guide, containing the History and Antiquities of the City. By Richard Dalby. 8vo. Chichester, 1831.

3. Plans, elevation, section, and view of Chichester Cross, with a descriptive account. By T. H. Clarke. 4to. London, 1832

From the Author .—Inventories of the Collegiate Churches of the Holy Cross, Crediton ; and Our Blessed Lady of Ottery. By H Michell Whitley. 8vo. n.p. 1902.

The following gentlemen were admitted Fellows:

William Wyndham Portal, Esq., M.A.
Prince Frederick Duleep Singh.

On the nomination of the President the following were appointed Auditors of the Society's accounts for the past year :

> Edward William Brabrook, Esq., C.B.
> Mill Stephenson, Esq., B A.
> Frederick Andrew Inderwick, Esq., K.C.
> John Challenor Covington Smith, Esq.

The Chairman called the attention of the Society to a proposal to fill with stained glass the west window of the cathedral church of Exeter as a memorial to the late Archbishop Temple.

This proposal, though seemingly harmless in itself, would involve the destruction of the painted glass now in the window, which was executed by William Peckitt, of York, in 1766, the then Dean being Dr. Jeremiah Milles, who was also President of the Society.

The Secretary read the following memorandum on the subject by Mr. C. F. BELL, F.S.A. :

"According to a paragraph amongst the Ecclesiastical Intelligence in *The Times* of last Saturday, a meeting was held at Exeter on Friday last to consider the question of a local memorial to the late Archbishop of Canterbury, and at this meeting it was, upon the proposal of Sir John Kennaway, decided that the memorial should take the form of a new west window in Exeter Cathedral.

It is obvious that, in order to carry out this scheme, the old glass in the west window would have to be taken out. This glass was executed in 1766 by William Peckitt, of York, the last, and in many ways the most eminent, of the long line of glass painters and stainers who kept the art in a flourishing state in England during the sixteenth, seventeenth, and eighteenth centuries, at a time when it was languishing or dead in all the countries of continental Europe

It is by far the largest and most important of those of his works which are still in existence; and, with the exception of the great western window in Westminster Abbey, the only large window of its class remaining in any cathedral or collegiate church

It is, in fact, a monument of unique importance in the history of art Moreover, it was executed under the direct auspices of Jeremiah Milles, Dean of Exeter, one of the most distinguished of the earlier Presidents of the Society of Antiquaries, and is not only a memorial of his taste and zeal, but marks, from its relationship to the revival of mediæval studies, a most interesting moment in the history of British archæology, and for these reasons calls especially for the protection of the Society of Antiquaries.

Whatever modern glass takes its place must be destitute of antiquarian value, and, however opinions as to its artistic qualities may vary, inferior to it in technical merit.

More than once in the past efforts have been made to get this window replaced by modern glass , once when a memorial to the late Earl of Devon was in contemplation, and again, it is believed, when some recent works of restoration upon the west front were in progress.

Upon both occasions these attempts, for lack of funds or other reasons, proved ineffectual, and there is every probability, considering the trend of fashion, that if the removal of the glass can be averted for a few more years its ultimate safety will be assured."

The Secretary also read a letter from the Bishop of Marlborough, Dean of Exeter, in reply to an inquiry from him, stating that he had every reason to believe that the account of the meeting at Exeter about the proposed memorial in *The Times* of the 17th instant "will prove to be accurate, but nothing is at present decided."

After some remarks from the Treasurer and Mr. Micklethwaite, it was proposed from the chair, seconded by the Treasurer, and carried without a dissentient:

> "That the Society of Antiquaries of London having considered a proposal to remove the painted glass now in the west window of the cathedral church of Exeter is of opinion that the glass has an important historical and artistic value and ought by all means to be preserved in place."

It was also resolved :

> "That a copy of this Resolution be telegraphed to the Right Rev. the Bishop of Exeter, with a request that it be read to a meeting announced to be held at Exeter on the 30th instant."

REGINALD A. SMITH, ESQ., B.A., F.S.A., read the following
note on a discovery of Roman interments at Enfield :

"Information of a discovery of Roman remains at Enfield
in October last year was brought to the British Museum by
Mr. Alfred Hodgkinson, coroner for the Duchy of Lancaster,
who has jurisdiction in Enfield Chase. During the excavations for some cottages on the east side
of the Great Eastern Railway, between
Bush Hill Park and Enfield Stations, a
leaden coffin was found about 2 feet
from the surface, and the lid unfortunately damaged by the workmen's picks.
The exact spot was 130 yards north of
Lincoln Road, 40 yards from the railway
fence, and about ⅓ of a mile from the
terminus. The coffin measured 6 feet
7 inches in length, 11 inches in depth,
and had a width of 17 inches, slightly
tapering to the foot; the sides as well
as the lid were imperfect, but the top
portion of the lid has been subsequently
found, and enough remains to justify a
restoration of the design. It lay with
the head to the north-east, and contained
the skeleton of an adult in a deposit of
lime, which had preserved many of the
bones entire, though the skull fell to
pieces on removal.

DIAGRAM OF
COFFIN-LID FROM
ENFIELD, MIDDLE-
SEX, PARTIALLY
RESTORED.

About 18 inches from the foot of the
coffin, 2 or 3 inches lower, were found
two leaden canisters, usually called ossuaries, containing burnt human bones,
and enclosed in a cist or tomb composed
of Roman bricks 12 inches square, while
above and against the sides of the cist
were heaped two or three cartloads of
large flints. The canisters had circular
lids, but the decay of the lead had admitted the clay, which
was evidently introduced by water, and filled the interior.
The coffin was not so filled, and its contents therefore easier
to examine, but nothing seems to have been found besides the
human bones, though a careful search was made by the
coroner, who had the entire find removed to the mortuary
at Enfield, and was good enough to show it to me there. In
the search for coins or other remains he was assisted by the

divisional police surgeon, and I think it is agreed that one of the canisters contained the burnt bones of a child, though in the process of removal the clayey contents were unavoidably displaced and mixed.

The coffin lid had a raised corded band round the edge and two similar bands across the middle. Of the three resulting panels the central one had an asterisk of the same corded pattern, with a scallop shell in low relief at each point, and similar but smaller shells in each angle. The other two panels had each a corded saltire with large and small scallop shells arranged somewhat irregularly; and on each side of the coffin itself were three large shells of the same kind. The eight-rayed star in the central panel may perhaps be compared with the design on the bottom of a cylindrical ossuary found in Warwick Lane, City, 1881. It is figured in *Archaeologia*,* and there said by Mr. Alfred Tylor to be of Mithraic origin, while the same device occurs on the lid of a diminutive leaden coffin of the Roman period, in the British Museum, from Vaison, Vaucluse.

With this possible exception there seems no ground for supposing that the cruciform pattern or the scallop shell ornament had any symbolic significance, and it is to my mind certain that the Enfield interments are all of pagan origin. In the first place cremation was at that time an essentially heathen practice, and the unburnt burial was not orientated in the Christian manner. Instances are recorded of coffins laid with the head westward in this country, as at Croydon, and less exactly at Frilford, Berks, where several lay W.N.W. and E.S.E. But other positions are more frequent: due north and south on two sites in Wiltshire, and the head south at Bexhill, Sittingbourne, while the remarkable sarcophagus now in the British Museum was found in the Minories containing a leaden coffin with the head to the east, and the same position was observed at Caerwent.

The scallop shell was common as a Christian symbol during the middle ages, especially in connection with St James of Compostella, but it has been found on a Roman coffin in the Old Kent Road, London, with two unmistakable figures of Minerva,† and was probably used by the pagan Romans here as an attractive ornament without special significance, its comparative flatness well suiting it for impressing the sand mould in which the lead was cast. It is remarkable, however, that this decorative feature should only occur on coffins from this country, and so far as is known only on examples from

* Vol. xlviii pl. xii   † *Archaeologia*, xvii. 333

Essex and the immediate vicinity of London. Besides the coffin in the sarcophagus and that from the Old Kent Road already mentioned, instances are recorded from Stepney, Battersea, and three each from East Ham and Colchester.* The late Canon Scott Robertson, in an editorial note to a paper † by Mr. George Payne on coffins from Bexhill, gave a useful list of references on the subject, but many are to early accounts of discoveries which are not overburdened with details, and leave us in the dark as to the direction of the graves and other necessary details. Still I have been able to find a very close parallel to the Enfield interments at Colchester. Roach Smith wrote two papers on the subject in the *Collectanea Antiqua*,‡ and quotes from Morant's *History*

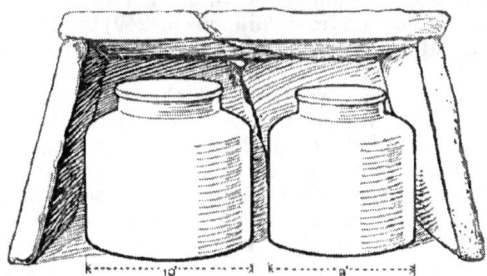

SECTIONAL DIAGRAM OF CIST CONTAINING OSSUARIES
FOUND AT ENFIELD.

and Antiquities of Colchester as follows: 'The 24th of March, 1749-50, in Windmill field, near the west end of the town, was found a leaden coffin, not lying due east and west, but north-east and south-west. . . . . The coffin was cast or wrought all over with lozenges, in each of which was an escallop shell, but no date. Near it was found an urn, holding about a pint, in which were two coins of large brass, one of Antoninus Pius (d. 161) and the other of Alexander Severus (d. 235).'

Both here and in Mansell Street, Whitechapel, cremated interments in pottery urns or leaden ossuaries were found in close proximity to leaden coffins, and a tile-tomb or cist also came to light in the Roman burial ground a short distance

* Several are figured in *Collectanea Antiqua*, iii. pl. xiv.
† *Archaeologia Cantiana*, ix. (1874), 172.
‡ Vol. iii. 45, and vii. 170.

south-west of the Head Gate at Colchester. Two canisters closely resembling the Enfield pair are now in the British Museum, one from Fenchurch Street and the other with no history, but probably also from London. They are both between 8 and 9 inches in height, and one has slight incised lines at intervals round the body. Those recently discovered are of nearly the same diameter, and seem to have been of corresponding height.

Very few of the instances quoted give any clue to the dates of the various interments, and in this connection I should like to draw attention to an opinion expressed by the Abbé Cochet as long ago as 1855 * After examining many cemeteries in northern France he concludes that inhumation begins as early as the second half of the third century, and skeletons are found mingled with urn-burials, but no unburnt Roman burial occurs from Philippus (d 249) back to Augustus, a period during which the rite of burning was alone practised.

I will not venture to decide whether this rule holds good for France as a whole, much less for Britain,† but it is well to keep it in mind, and I think the coins found in coffins generally bear out this view. The following are instances from this country, the latest coin being given in each case as being alone significant : at Colchester, Alexander Severus (d 235); at Stepney, Pupienus and Gordian (238-244) ; at Winchester, Constantine (d. 337), and at Croydon, Magnentius (d. 353). One of the coffins in York Museum contained a coin of Hadrian (d. 138), while a Valens (d. 378) was found near the stone sarcophagus in the Minories.

The date of the Enfield interments is of special interest in connection with the Ermine Street. Its course through Enfield may be ascertained with sufficient accuracy by joining what are evidently two surviving portions of it lying to the north and south ; and it will be found to run about half a mile east of the site of the present discovery. It is well known that the Romans buried their dead for choice by the side of a main road, and it will be granted, I think, as probable that the road was there before these burials Now the Ermine Street south of Lincoln is not mentioned in the Antonine Itineraries, which are generally connected with Caracalla Antoninus (d. 217), though our present version belongs to the early part of the fourth century. The road is by

---

* *Normandie Souterraine*, 2nd edition, esp pp. 29, 165.
† For example, an urn has been found at Winchester containing burnt bones and a coin of Magnentius (d. 353)

some referred to the years between 200 and 250; our choice
is therefore limited in this case to the late third and fourth
centuries, and I think the presence of cremated remains points
to the earlier date.

In conclusion I have pleasure in recording the prompt
action of the coroner, and in acknowledging his services in
the preparation of this paper, in which task I have also been
assisted by Mr. T. W. Scott, clerk to the Urban District
Council, who sent me the map and photographs. The Society
will be gratified to hear that the coffin, at least, will be preserved in the Enfield Public Library, where a local museum is
being formed."

Mr. R. A. SMITH also read the following note on a coin-
brooch found at Canterbury .

" There is sufficient evidence, I understand, to show that
the silver ' coin-brooch ' exhibited by kind permission of the
owner, Mr. W. C. Trimnell, was found in Canterbury some
years ago ; and it gives me great satisfaction to bring this
remarkable relic of the later Saxon period to the notice of
the Society   It is of circular form, with a diameter of
3·1 inches, and consists of a central medal enclosed within a
border of twelve concentric rings, of a pearled and spiral
pattern alternately.   The disc is 1½ inch in diameter, much
larger than a Saxon penny, but seems to have been moulded,
not struck.   The only coined piece that it can be compared
with in size is the so-called ' offering penny ' struck at Bath,
and bearing the name of King Alfred, but there is no other
point of resemblance between them   Both the obverse and
reverse are, however, closely allied to the coinage of Edward
the Elder (d. 925) and Aethelstan (d. 940-1), having a bust
on the obverse (the tunic looped up on the shoulder by
means of a brooch such as the specimen exhibited), and a
small cross in the centre of the reverse, but· the closest
parallel is afforded by coins of Eadgar (d 975), and there
can be little hesitation in referring the Canterbury brooch to
the second half of the tenth century.

The legend on the obverse is :

NOMINE DOMINI

and round the bust are the words :

+ ÞVDEMAN FECID

The name Woodman must have been common enough, and a

moneyer of that name was minting at Shrewsbury under Edward the Confessor ; but there is no clue to the identity of the brooch-maker that I know of. Mr. Grueber, to whom I am indebted for much of the above information as to the medal, points out that the form of the word FECID is altogether unusual for FECIT.

The construction of the border is peculiar. Each ring is formed of moulded wire cut to the required length, the ends being soldered together. The series is then braced together at the back by V-shaped strips of silver, which are in places hammered very thin. The pin is missing, but the hinge and catch are still in position and display rather rude workmanship. Both are formed of broad silver strips doubled over and fastened to the back by hammering out the ends.

Photographs of two smaller brooches will show the exceptional character of the Canterbury specimen. One from Boxmoor, Herts, exhibited to the Society in 1853, measures 1·4 inches in diameter, and is in the collection of Sir John Evans, who was good enough to call my attention to the publication of the second photograph in a recent volume on goldsmith's work in the Netherlands.* The latter is assigned to the sixth century, but though the pattern was no doubt ultimately derived from a late Roman form of coin-pendant,

LEADEN COIN-BROOCH, BOXMOOR, HERTS.

I think there can be little doubt as to the later date of specimens in lead, silver, and bronze found in this country. A certain number were published in 1847,† and there are five that are more or less similar in the British Museum, three being from London, while several found in Cheapside are in the Guildhall Museum. A circular leaden brooch, probably of the same type, was found in the Thames in 1855 with coins of Merovingian kings, and one of Harold,‡ but their association seems to have been purely accidental. Some of the busts and inscriptions are bungled imitations of those on Roman coins of the Lower Empire, and the Boxmoor specimen may be derived from a copy of a coin of Carausius, struck by a Merovingian king in the second half of the seventh century.

---

* *Orfèvrerie antique néerlandaise*, Musée Frison, à Leeuwarde, pl. i.
† *Journal of the British Archaeological Association*, ii. 313.
‡ *Archaeological Journal*, xiv. 177.

The interpretation in most cases is little more than guesswork, and the occurrence in Kent of an example that may be said to tell its own tale is, I think, a matter for congratulation."

J. H. ROUND, ESQ., M.A., read a paper on Garnier de Nablous, Prior of the Hospital in England, and Grand Master of the Order of St. John of Jerusalem.

Mr. Round's paper will be printed in *Archaeologia*.

W. G. COLLINGWOOD, Esq., M.A., Local Secretary for Cumberland, communicated the following note on two bronze armlets from Thirlmere, which were also exhibited:

"The two bronze penannular armlets exhibited were found in December, 1902, at the foot of a rock-precipice called Rough Crag, at the south-west side of Thirlmere. A very ancient road, which the older local antiquaries thought to be Roman, used to run here between the steep hillsides and the lake. When the Manchester Corporation turned the lake into a reservoir a new road was made, cutting through and destroying the ancient road, which is now visible only in parts. At the foot of Rough Crag the new road is a little higher on the hillside than the old, and just above it the crag rises over 'screes,' in which the armlets were found by men digging for road metal. One of the armlets was only a few inches below the fern-roots; the other came down amongst the clay and gravel during the digging. There is no sign of an interment tumulus, nor is such a thing likely on a scree-slope at the foot of a crag; but it is possible that the wearer of the armlets might have fallen from the top of the precipice, since there is no tumulus traceable above.

The armlets are of the frequent penannular type, with expanded ends: one measuring $2\frac{7}{8}$ by $2\frac{1}{4}$ inches in diameter, with simple incised beading, narrow and close-set, not continued for $\frac{1}{4}$ inch on the side of the ring which would come next the wrist; the other measures $2\frac{3}{4}$ by $2\frac{3}{8}$ inches in diameter, and is ornamented with alternate broad and narrow beads, the narrow beads being again broken up by transverse cutting, this armlet also being plain on the side next the wrist.

The armlets are are now in the possession of Mr. R. D. Marshall, of Castlerigg Manor, Keswick, who acquired them

from Mr. W. Hodgson, the road surveyor, by whose men they
were found."

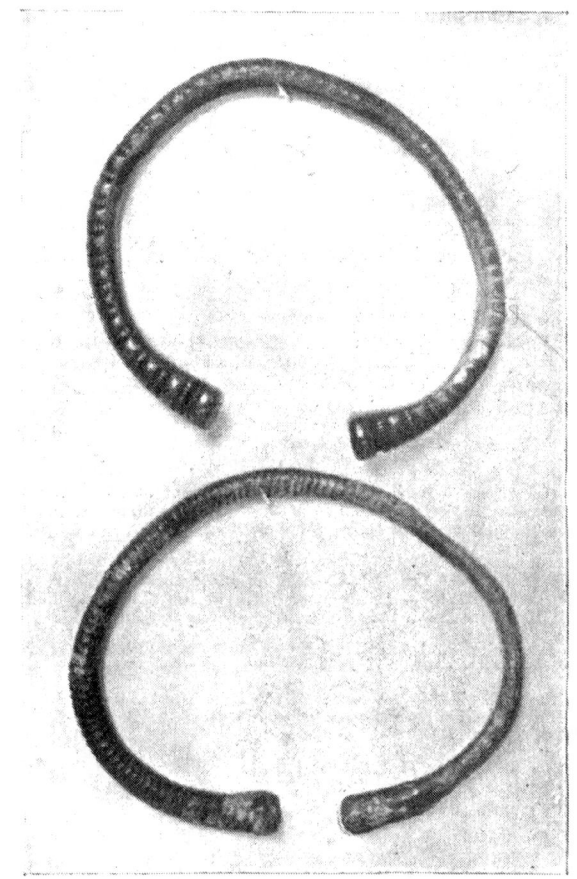

BRONZE ARMLETS FOUND AT THIRLMERE, CUMBERLAND. ($\frac{1}{4}$.)

F. Hodge, Esq., R.N., exhibited (1) a stone axe found in
he Thames near East Molesey, and (2) a stone hammer found

in the Ember, with part of its wooden handle remaining in the socket.

Thanks were ordered to be returned for these communications and exhibitions.

Thursday, February 5th, 1903.

Viscount DILLON, President, in the Chair.

The following gifts were announced, and thanks for the same ordered to be returned to the donors:

From the Trustees of the British Museum :

    1. Subject Index of the Modern Works added to the Library of the British Museum in the Years 1881-1900 Edited by G. K. Fortescue. Vol. I. A-E. 8vo. London, 1902.

    2. Annals of the Kings of Assyria. The cuneiform texts, with translations, transliterations, etc from the original documents in the British Museum. Edited by E. A. W. Budge and L. W. King. Vol. I. 8vo London, 1902.

From the Author ·—Some Account of the Settlement of Refugees (l'Eglise Wallonne) at Southampton, and of the Chapel of St. Julian, attached to the Hospital of God's House (Maison Dieu). By W. W Portal, M.A. 8vo   n p. 1902.

From J. H. Oglander, Esq., F.S.A. —The Oglander Memoirs · Extracts from the MSS of Sir J. Oglander, of Nunwell, Isle of Wight. Edited by W. H. Long. Small 4to. London, Portsmouth, and Newport, 1888.

From Albert Hartshorne, Esq , F S.A. :—Francis Smyth, Rector of Cogenhoe, Northants, 1637-1656. Notes on MS. Sermons. 8vo. Northampton, 1902.

From the Author ·—Ancient Names of the Bays, Creeks, Rocks, etc. on and near the Coast of Guernsey and other Islands of the Bailiwick. By Rev. R. H. Tourtel, B.D. 8vo. Guernsey, 1899.

From the Author, Rev. O J. Reichel, F S.A. ·

    1. Extracts from a Devonshire Lady's Notes of Travel in France in the Eighteenth Century   8vo. n.p. 1902.

    2 Fees of the Bishop of Exeter in " Testa de Nevil," p. 187. 8vo. n.p. 1902.

    3 The Devonshire "Domesday," vi. Some Notes on Part I of "Domesday " Identifications 8vo. n p. 1902

From the Author, T N Brushfield, Esq , M D , F S A. :

    1. John Sixtinus, Archpriest of Haccombe, 16th Century. 8vo. n.p. 1902.

    2 Raleghana, Part IV. Sir Henry de Ralegh, knight, ob. 1301. 8vo. n p. 1902

From the Right Hon. Lord Avebury, F.R S., F.S.A. :
1. Über die culturgeschichtliche Stellung des Kaukasus.   Von Rudolf Virchow.   4to.   Berlin, 1895.
2 Billedkunstens Fremstilling af Menneskeskikkelsen i dens ældste Periode indtil Hojdepunktet af den græske Kunst. Af Julius Lange. 4to. Copenhagen, 1892.

The following gentlemen were admitted Fellows :

Edward Alfred Webb, Esq.
Peter MacIntyre Evans, Esq., M.A.

The SECRETARY read the following letter ·

"The Palace,
Exeter,
Feb 1, 1903.

DEAR SIR,
I am requested by the Bishop of Exeter to acknowledge your telegram of January 30, and to inform you that he communicated its contents to the High Sheriff of the County who presided at the Archbishop Temple Memorial meeting held in the Castle.

Yours faithfully,
GERALD C. FANSHAWE,
Chaplain."

The SECRETARY also stated that since the last meeting of the Society, Mr. Hope had visited Exeter and reported to the Executive Committee that the glass in the west window of the cathedral church was apparently in good order, and that there was no justification whatever for its destruction or removal. The Executive Committee had accordingly drafted the following Resolution to be submitted to the Society for approval :

"The Society of Antiquaries of London having assured itself of the sound condition of Peckitt's glass in the west window of Exeter cathedral church desires to make a strong protest against its removal.

The Society is of opinion that the glass is of such age as to give it historical interest and of such merit that its removal would be an act which a future generation of wider artistic sympathy would condemn."

The Resolution was accordingly put to the meeting, and carried with only one dissentient.

T. F. KIRBY, Esq., M.A., F.S.A., read a paper on Charters of Harmondsworth, Isleworth, Heston, Twickenham, and Hampton-on-Thames, many of which were also exhibited.

Mr. Kirby's paper will be printed in *Archaeologia.*

T. N. BRUSHFIELD, Esq., M D , F.S.A , Local Secretary for Devonshire, exhibited and presented four photographs of military figures in the cathedral church of Exeter, on which he communicated the following note:

"In sending the accompanying four photographs for the acceptance of the Society of Antiquaries, I beg to offer the following remarks.

Three of the number (1-3) are of effigies preserved in Exeter Cathedral, and as their main features are similar to each other, there can be little doubt of all belonging to the same period.

The originals are carved in freestone, and represent recumbent cross-legged figures of knights, armed *cap-a-pie;* the right hand of each rests on the handle of a long sword having slightly depressed guards, while a comparatively small shield, of heater shape, is borne by the left The hood covers the upper part of the surcoat, and has an opening displaying the whole of the features; it has a round top, a fillet over the line of the eyebrows shows a separate coif. In all three the feet rest on animals; in two (Nos. 1 and 2) the heads recline on helmets of conical form, and in the third on a cushion. The surcoat in all is gathered in at the waist, is long behind, but cut away in front, showing a small portion of the hauberk beneath, and in the third example the lower part of a quilted gambeson projects below the latter.

The whole of the figures were originally covered with gesso work, the chain mail worn by all three being depicted by means of a stamp, portions of the impressions overlapping each other, but except in the angles and parts well protected there are not many evidences of it left. The only remains of colour (red) now visible are on the surcoats.

There are no traces of inscription or of any means of identification on any of the figures. It is, however, fairly certain that a coat of arms remained on each shield at the commencement of the seventeenth century, at the time when Sir W. Pole was collecting the materials for his *History of*

Devonshire, as he describes Nos 1 and 2 to have borne respectively the arms of Ralegh of Ralegh and of a member of the Bohun family, and No. 3 of those of Sir W. Stapeldon.

That of No. 2 is corroborated by an epitaph, composed by John Hoker, the city chamberlain, that was painted on the wall above the figure, traces of which yet remain. It recorded the memory of Humphry de Bohun, Earl of Hereford, who was killed at the battle of Burrough Bridge on March 16, 1381. As Sir W. Stapeldon, represented by the third sculpture, died about 1326, the date of No. 1 is to a certain extent indicated. Deeds preserved in the chapter library and amongst the municipal records of Exeter, prove that Sir Henry de Ralegh died in 1301, and was buried in the cathedral; and as there is neither record nor tradition of any other member of that family having been interred there, coupled with the fact of Pole's testimony of the Ralegh arms blazoned on the shield, there is every probability of his being represented by the effigy.

In his description of the last named, Dr. Oliver * has made the erroneous assertion that it had a 'flattened coiffe,' so termed by him in a communication containing an account of the two sculptured figures (1 and 2) made to Sir S Meyrick, and which evidently puzzled the latter, as shown by a part of his reply as it appears in Dr. Oliver's work:

'The recumbent cross-legged effigies are both of the close of the reign of Edward I. or beginning of Edward II. in regard to costume; the flattened coiffe of that which is said to have borne on the shield the arms of Ralegh, would rather bespeak the early part of Edward I., as such was designed for a cylindrical helmet; but both knights (1 and 2) recline their heads on conical ones, for which the rounded coiffe of that of Humphry de Bohun was particularly appropriate'

Now as a matter of fact the coif of No. 1 is not flattened, but higher and more rounded than No 2, and measures vertically from the face line to the crown 4½ inches, whereas the latter is only 3¼ inches. These points are well exhibited in the accompanying photographs.

All three figures represent the knees as protected with plate armour, and the elbows in Nos. 2 and 3, but it is doubtful if No 1 possesses the latter, and seems to point to its being somewhat earlier in date.

The fourth (No. 4) photograph displays the portion of an effigy deposited in the cathedral cloisters, and said to have

* *Lives of the Bishops of Exeter*, 204

been discovered on the site of the Dominican convent in Bedford Circus, Exeter, in 1826.* It exhibits the neck and part of the right shoulder, the latter showing the remains of a plain surcoat over which is a narrow guige. The head and neck are enveloped in a hood of ring mail deeply chiselled; the coif is flattened and contains no appearance of a fillet, or of a line of junction of a separate coif It is of interest for showing the loose overlapping portion of the hood being secured in its place by a strap and buckle. Immediately behind this, and on a level with the ear, is a vertical chase 2 inches long, terminating in rounded extremities"

WALTER MONEY, Esq., F.S.A., communicated the following notes on the Statue of King James II. at Whitehall:

" The extreme interest connected with the statue of James II now lying in a garden at Whitehall, and which seems recently to have been treated with scant consideration, must be my apology, if any be necessary, for submitting a few notes to the Society of Antiquaries on a subject somewhat out of the ordinary range of their transactions

This bronze figure, a work of very great merit, next to that of Charles I at Charing Cross, by Le Sœur, may be deemed the finest royal statue in the metropolis, and is rendered still more valuable because, with the exception of an inferior one at University College, Oxford, it is the only bronze public statue in England representing that ill-fated monarch James II. The likeness is extremely fine, as is the easy attitude of the figure, and the melancholy cast of countenance and gloomy inexorable features, so characteristic of the king, are as legibly inscribed in brass as historian has ever described them on paper. Horace Walpole at one time appears to have entertained some doubts as to the artist, for he says, ' The talent of Gibbons did not reach to human figures, unless the brazen statue of James II., in the Privy Gardens, be, as there is reason to believe it, of his hand' He then mentions that Vertue met with an agreement, signed by Gibbons himself, for a statue of James II., and that the paymaster was Tobias Rustat. Walpole had a correct impression of the truth when he thus wrote, and all doubts which once prevailed as to the artist have long since been cleared up by a passage in the Autobiography of Sir John Bramston, printed by the Camden Society, wherein it is recorded that on New Year's Day, 1686-7, ' a statue in brass was to be seen (placed the day before) in the yard at Whitehall, made by Gibbons, at the

* See *Archæological Journal*, ix 188, where the head is also engraved.

charge of Toby Rustick (*sic*), of the present king, James II.'
'Rustick' being evidently a misreading or misprint for
Rustat.

The statue had not been erected above two or three years
before it was removed from its pedestal, owing to popular
feeling against the late abdicated king. Chamberlayne, in
speaking of James II. at Whitehall, says: 'In one of the
courts stands his brazen statue, which has had better luck
than that of Newcastle-upon-Tyne'

In these remarks, which were written in 1691, Chamberlayne
alludes to the restoration of the figure to its original site;
for William III, on hearing the circumstance, ordered the
statue of his deposed father-in-law to be replaced, whereas
the statue of James II. which stood in front of the Guildhall
at Newcastle-upon-Tyne was pulled down at the Revolution
and never restored.

It is a singular coincidence, as if symbolical of James's loss
of power, that the truncheon originally in the king's right
hand has disappeared since

        'The line of the Stuarts was ended,'

so that the monarch seems now to point with his *finger* to the
ground, which has given rise to all sorts of fanciful conjectures.

In addition to the statue of James II. at Whitehall, Rustat
erected the monument to Charles II. at Chelsea Hospital, also
the work of the inimitable Gibbons, and likewise gave £1,000
towards building and endowing that noble institution

Speaking of this statue of Charles II. at Chelsea, Walpole
writes. 'It is said to be the gift of this Rustat.' There
can, however, be no doubt as to the donor of this and the
statue to James, as in an account of Rustat's public charities
among the Lansdowne MSS. we find the following entry:
'A free gift to their Majesties King Charles ye Second
and King James ye Second, of their Statues in Brass, the
former placed upon a Pedistall in the Royal Hospital of
Chelsea, and ye other in Whitehall, both of them amounting
to ye sum of one thousand pounds, or thereabouts, of which
there is already paid 838^{lbs}, and in Rustat's Will the remainder
is ordered to be paid when ye statue is placed upon a proper
Pedistall.'

The fine equestrian statue of Charles II., spoken of by
Evelyn, in the great quadrangle of Windsor Castle, the work
of Stada, an Italian artist, with a beautiful marble pedestal
by Grinling Gibbons, was also erected at the cost of this
liberal and loyal subject, Rustat, and is thus noticed in the
catalogue of his benefactions:

'A free gift for ye making and setting up of ye statue of His Majestie King Charles ye Second in Brass, in Windsor Castle— ^{lbs}1000 . 0 : 0 ·' to which is added the additional sum of '300^{lbs} more for changing ye same brass figure of his Majestie,' so that its entire cost was £1,300, a large sum when the comparative value of money is taken into account.

The life of Tobias Rustat was an eventful one. He was the second son of Robert Rustat, M.A., vicar of Barrow-on-Soar, co. Leicester, of which advowson he was also the patron, and besides this living he also held that of Skeffington, in the same county. Tobias, whose mother was the daughter of Ralph Snoden, of Mansfield, co. Notts, and sister of Dr. Robert Snoden, bishop of Carlisle, was born at Barrow in 1606. He is said to have been apprenticed to a *barber-chirurgeon* in London, but he seems to have abandoned his profession and entered the service of Basil Feilding, eldest son of the first earl of Denbigh, and in 1633 accompanied that nobleman on an embassy to the Venetian court. After this Rustat was for two or three years in the service of George Villiers, Duke of Buckingham, and making friends at court, bought the reversion of the office of Yeoman of the Robes to the Prince of Wales, afterwards Charles II., which he retained on the Prince's accession to the throne

To tell the story in full of Rustat's adventures after this date, which are so interwoven with those of the unfortunate persons he so long and faithfully served, would be but to narrate that of the country itself from the beginning of the Civil War to the Restoration

As is well known, Tobias Rustat bestowed a considerable part of his fortune upon young students at Oxford and Cambridge, and in the latter university his name is still preserved in the "Rustat Scholarships" which he endowed.

Rustat died a bachelor, 15th March, 1693-4, aged 87 years, and was buried in the chapel of Jesus College, Cambridge, where his name is still annually commemorated. In the chapel is a handsome monument to the memory of Rustat, with an inscription which is printed in Le Neve's *Monumenta Anglicana*, and in Blomefield's *Collectanea Cantabrigiensia.*"

It was resolved:

> "That the President of the Society be requested to confer with His Majesty's First Commissioner of Works with regard to the placing of the statue of King James II., formerly at Whitehall."

J. P. RYLANDS, Esq., F.S.A., exhibited, by permission of W. W. Robinson, Esq, a gold ring of interlaced wires, apparently of the Wiking Period, found about 1890 in a stone coffin in St. Aldate's Street, Oxford, when excavations were being made for a drain opposite the great gateway of Christ Church.

Mr. Rylands also exhibited a small figure of a bronze horse within a ring, probably of the seventeenth century, or even later, found in a garden in Chetwynd Road, Claughton, Birkenhead, about 1892. It almost exactly resembles another example described as a bronze Roman fibula, engraved in *Transactions of the Lancashire and Cheshire Antiquarian Society*, xii. 139.

Thanks were ordered to be returned for these communication and exhibitions.

Thursday, February 12th, 1903.

Viscount DILLON, President, in the Chair.

The following gifts were announced, and thanks for the same ordered to be returned to the donors:

From R. D. Darbishire, Esq , F.S.A..

1. The Story of the Irish before the Conquest. 2nd edition. By Lady Ferguson. 8vo. Dublin, 1890

2. Sir Walter Ralegh in Ireland. By Sir J. P Hennessy. 8vo London, 1883.

3. Ireland in the Seventeenth Century, or the Irish Massacres of 1641-2. By Mary Hickson. 2 vols. 8vo. London, 1884.

4 Old Celtic Romances By P. W Joyce. 8vo. London, 1894.

5. History of Ireland : The Heroic Period. By Standish O'Grady. 2 vols. 8vo. London, 1878.

6. History of Ireland . Critical and Philosophical By Standish O'Grady. Vol. I. 8vo. London, 1881.

7. The Cromwellian Settlement of Ireland. By J. P Prendergast. 8vo. London, 1865.

8. Lectures on the History of Ireland. 2nd Series. By A. G. Richey. 8vo. London, 1870.

9. History of the Land Tenures and Land Classes of Ireland. By George Sigerson. 8vo. London, 1871.

10. Two Centuries of Irish History, 1691-1870. By W K. Sullivan. 8vo. London, 1888.

11. The History of the General Rebellion in Ireland. 7th edition. By Sir John Temple. 8vo. Cork, 1766

12. Fingal and its Churches. By Robert Walsh. 8vo. Dublin, 1888.

From the Author :—Courts cry'd at Chichester Cross. By E. E. Street, F.S.A. 8vo Lewes, 1902.

From the Author —The Disappearing Stone Monuments of Dartmoor. By Robert Burnard, F S.A 8vo n p. 1902

From W. H. J. Weale, Esq —Obituaire du Couvent des Carmes à Bruges. 8vo. n.p. 1901

From the Author Robert Day, Esq , F.S A.

1 The Ancient Manufacture of Gold in Ireland 8vo. n p. n.d.

2. Volunteer Pottery. 8vo n p. n d.

From Miller Christy, Esq. —Some Interesting Essex Brasses. By Miller Christy, W. W. Porteous, and E. Bertram Smith 8vo n.p. 1903.

A special vote of thanks was accorded to Mr. R. D. Darbishire for his gift to the Library.

The PRESIDENT read the following letter :

"H.M Office of Works,
Storey's Gate, Westminster, S W
9th February, 1903.

MY LORD,
I am desired by Lord Windsor to acknowledge the receipt of your Lordship's letter of the 6th instant on behalf of the Society of Antiquaries of London on the subject of the location for the statue of James II.

Lord Windsor directs me to say that your representation shall have his very careful consideration.

I am, my Lord,
Yours faithfully,
H. J. HOPGOOD.

The Viscount Dillon."

The SECRETARY stated that with reference to the Resolution passed by the Society at its last meeting he had addressed a letter to the Dean of Exeter in the following terms :

"7th February, 1903.

VERY REVEREND SIR,
The Society of Antiquaries of London has had under consideration the proposal to replace with modern glass the painted west window of the cathedral church of Exeter, and

at its last meeting unanimously passed the Resolution of
which I enclose a copy.

The Society has assured itself that the glass in the window
is in a sound state, and that its condition cannot furnish any
justification for its removal. A letter in *The Times* of this
morning quotes the late Archbishop as having remarked on
the brilliancy and suitability of the glass. It is therefore
difficult to discover why a large sum should be laid out on
such a work, for which there is no structural need, while as
a memorial to Archbishop Temple the only evidence we have
of his views shows that he would certainly have disapproved
of such an act.

There is only one reason conceivable, viz that Peckitt's
window is held to be in bad taste, but I need scarcely point
out that in such a building as a cathedral this is the most
dangerous of reasons, and, if admitted to be valid, might
eventually lead to the destruction of any or every part of
all our ancient cathedrals, which represent the varying taste
of centuries.

The Society is well aware that its protest, and in fact any
protest from outside, can be ignored by the Chapter, which is
free to treat the fabric under its charge in any way that it
pleases. But the Society would desire to point out that this
very absence of external control makes the responsibility of a
Dean and Chapter the greater. The Society would therefore
ask the Chapter to assure itself of the necessity and propriety
of the serious step now contemplated.

Your faithful servant,
CHARLES H. READ,
Secretary.

The Very Rev. the Dean of Exeter."

To this letter the following reply had been received:

" The Deanery, Exeter,
Feb. 9, 1903.

DEAR SIR,

The Dean and Chapter of Exeter appreciate the motives
of your learned and honorable Society in calling their attention
to the grave responsibility resting on them in connection with
the contemplated work in their cathedral; they are keenly
alive to the responsibility, which they cannot share with others.
They have called in as their adviser one of the most eminent
architects of the day to whose care many of the finest Buildings in England have been successfully entrusted, and who is

moreover specially experienced in the special work which is now contemplated, and they venture to think that having done this, their wisest course will be, not unreservedly, but subject to their collective decision, to follow his advice, and they feel quite confident that, when the work contemplated shall have been completed, the result will give general satisfaction. As to the letter in *The Times* to which you refer, it is misleading and inaccurate. As to the Resolution which you forward, I assure you, without any wish to be discourteous, that it is not in accordance with the facts of the case, and I am at a loss to understand who could have so advised your Society. But my main point is just this, our responsibility is of such a nature that we cannot share with others. We are most anxious in the face of much ignorant and misinformed criticism to do that which is necessary and right, under suitable guidance.

I am, dear Sir, with the fullest appreciation of the motives which have led to this correspondence,

Your obedient servant,
ALFRED MARLBOROUGH,
Dean."

After some remarks from Mr. J. W. Willis-Bund and Mr. Stuart Moore it was resolved:

> "That the Dean of Exeter be asked to state in what respect the Society's Resolution of 5th February is not in accordance with the facts of the case."

The Resolution was carried with only one dissentient.

CHARLES H. READ, ESQ., Secretary, read a paper on a medieval carved ivory Tau-staff head found at Alcester, co. Warwick, exhibited by the Rev. A. H. Williams.

Mr. Read's paper will be printed in *Archaeologia*.

T. CECIL WOOLLEY, ESQ., exhibited the cheek-piece of a Roman helmet in embossed copper, found on the site of the Roman fort of *Crocolana*, near South Collingham, Notts.

The cheek-piece, which bears the figure of a woman standing by a horse, will be illustrated in the Appendix to *Archaeologia*.

W. WEIR, ESQ., exhibited the fragments of a pillar piscina, found in the church of North Stoke, Oxon, as building material built into the north wall of the nave about 3 feet from the floor. (See illustration.)

PILLAR PISCINA FROM NORTH STOKE CHURCH, OXON.

The fragments, when put together, are 21 inches high, and formed part of a circular pillar 5½ inches diameter, with a capital 8 inches square. The whole surface both of the pillar and the capital is covered with interlaced basket work to within an inch of the top, where there is a plain band round, worked into a rude volute at the corners. The top of the capital has a sinking 2 inches deep and $4\frac{1}{2}$ inches square with sloping sides, the bottom being only $2\frac{3}{4}$ inches square. The pillar is possibly of Saxon workmanship.

Thanks were ordered to be returned for these communications and exhibitions.

Thursday, 19th February, 1903.

Sir E. M. THOMPSON, K.C.B., LL.D., D.C.L., Vice-President,
in the Chair.

The following gift was announced, and thanks for the same ordered to be returned to the donor:

From H.M. The King:—Description of the Papyrus of Nas-Khem, Priest of Amen-Ra, discovered in an Excavation made by direction of H.R.H. the Prince of Wales, by the permission of Said Pasha, late Viceroy of Egypt, in a tomb near Gournah, at Thebes. By S. Birch, Esq., LL.D., F.S.A. Privately Printed. 8vo. London. n.p.

JOSEPH MEADOWS COWPER, Esq., was admitted a Fellow.

Notice was given of a Ballot for the election of Fellows on Thursday, 5th March, and a list of candidates to be balloted for was read.

The SECRETARY stated that no reply had been received from the Dean of Exeter in answer to the last Resolution passed by the Society.

Mr. R. GARRAWAY RICE reported that as a result of the appointment of a sub-committee by the Council, on the invitation of the Mayor and Corporation of Chichester, to advise them as to the necessary repairs to the well-known Chichester Cross, it had that day been decided by the Corporation to entrust the repair of the cross professionally to Messrs. E. Towry Whyte and C. R. Peers, two of the members of the sub-committee. The Mayor had already received promise of more than the sum needed for the repairs.

SEBASTIAN EVANS, jun., Esq., read a report on excavations on the site of the church of St. Austin's Abbey, Canterbury.

In illustration of Mr. Evans's paper, which will be printed in *Archaeologia*, a number of interesting objects and carved architectural fragments found during the excavations were exhibited.

Thanks were ordered to be returned for these communications and exhibitions.

Sir HENRY HOWORTH referred in appropriate terms to the loss which the Society had sustained by the death of Mr. F. C. Penrose, and suggested that a letter should be written to his niece by the Secretary on behalf of the Society.

On the motion of the Chairman this was agreed to.

———

Thursday, 26th February, 1903,

Viscount DILLON, President, in the Chair.

The Right Hon. Godfrey Charles, Lord Tredegar, was admitted Fellow.

ALBERT HARTSHORNE, Esq., F S.A., read the following paper on the Cogenhoe family, and Cogenhoe Church, Northants:

"The word Cogenhoe is derived from gucken, to spy, and oe, a hill, signifying the spy or outlook hill, the Spion Kop f modern warfare, the only place so named in England.
The village of Cogenhoe runs in one street on an edge of nd which slopes to the east, with a short spur projecting to ie north into the valley of the Nene. From this point, at ie northern end of the village, on which the church is nspicuously placed, overlooking the shining stream, the ene Valley can be scanned for many miles both up and wn the river. This was, no doubt, as the name implies, an iportant strategical point in remote times, and the common d persistent pronunciation of the name in modern days as

'Cookno' doubtless most closely approaches to the sound
of the ancient Gucken Hoe on the lips of our primæval
ancestors.

A family bearing the name of Cogenhoe was associated
with the place as early as in the reign of Henry II., when
William de Cogenhoe was certified in the *hydarium* of the
county of Northampton to hold here one and a half hides,
and one virgate of land. In the days of King Richard a
certain Henry de Cogenhoe was seized of the manor of
Wellingborough. Then comes a long blank.

It is shown by the Close Rolls that on 13th January, 1273,
Nicholas de Cogenhoe, presumably a grandson of William,
witnessed an agreement at Guildford between Queen Eleanor,
the king's mother, and Sir Humphrey de Bassingburn. He
was so far in favour with the king that on 10th May, 1275,
Giles de Andenard, Constable of the Tower of London, was
ordered to cause Nicholas de Cogenhoe to have three tuns of
the king's wines of the right prise, of the king's gift, to hold
therewith the feast of Nicholas his son at Oxford. A month
later the order was repeated to the Constable that Nicholas,
son of Nicholas de Cogenhoe, and scholar of Oxford, should
have the three tuns of wine to hold the feast of his inception,
unless he had already had them. On 7th May, 1275, on the
acknowledgment of a debt of 200 marks by William de
Montgomery and Stephen de Burgo, Nicholas de Cogenhoe
released, with certain conditions, their rights in the mill and
in a meadow called 'Holm,' and in the advowson of the
church of Ecton, which he and his wife Amice had of the gift
of John de Montgomery. On 24th October of the same year he
was appointed with another, under Pain de Chaworth, to tax
and appraise the fifteenth of all moveable goods. This was
apparently a military levy. On 22nd March, 1276, the sheriff
of Northampton had orders to take with him Nicholas de
Cogenhoe, and other knights, whom he knows to be fit for
this purpose, to inquire as jury into trespass and contempt by
Robert de Boyton at Cranford.

On 12th May, in the following year, the justices appointed
for the custody of the Jews are informed that, at the instance
of Nicholas de Cogenhoe, the late king pardoned Richard, son
of Anselm of Grimscote, the 14½ marks, his debt to three Jews
of Northampton. In 1277, 25th January, the chamberlains of
London were ordered to cause Nicholas to have a tun of wine,
from the royal wines in their custody, of the king's gift, and
on 7th February a further tun of good wine was ordered him
from the king's wine in the custody of the Constable of the
Tower. On the 27th of the same month the steward of the

vast forest between the bridges of Oxford and Stamford was
required to cause Nicholas de Cogenhoe to have five oaks for
timber, and on the same date the keeper of Wichwood Forest
was ordered to supply to Nicholas's daughter Eleanor three
leafless oak trunks for fuel, all of the king's gift. In 1278, in
exercise of his office as steward of the Forest of Brigstock,
'adjoining that of Rockingham, he was carrying out forest
laws.

On 2nd March, 1279, Nicholas de Cogenhoe was appointed
one of the three commissioners in the counties of Northampton
and Rutland to inquire as to the sheriff's proceedings in pur-
suance of the king's precept to all sheriffs to distrain those
who have land to the value of £20 yearly, or one whole
knight's fee worth that amount, and ought to be knighted,
and are not, to take up knight's service at Christmas last
past. At the same time he was associated with another
in a commission of oyer and terminer. On 12th March,
1279, Roger de Clifford, justice of the forest this side of
Trent, was ordered to cause Nicholas de Cogenhoe to have
four oaks in Salcey Forest (five miles off) of the king's gift.
Of these gifts of oak trees none can have been used for the
church of Cogenhoe, and the fact of the keeper of the park
at Northampton having orders in October, 1279, to cause
Nicholas de Cogenhoe to have of the king's gift twelve live
hares to stock therewith a grove of his, seems to point to a
mansion house having been there lately built at Cogenhoe,
with adjacent pleasure or sporting grounds.

Besides his son Nicholas, the Oxford scholar, and his
daughter Eleanor, who had the kindly royal gift of firewood
in the winter of 1277, he had a daughter Amice (named after
his first wife), who married as his second wife Sir John
Chetwode, of the ancient family long seated at Chetwode,
Buckinghamshire.

It is to be noticed that all the royal favour and the
recorded public employments of Nicholas de Cogenhoe are
comprised within the last years of his life, namely between
1273 and 1280, and that of military service nothing is set
down, and that the building of the nave and aisles of his
church must have occupied the attention and formed the
interest of his elder years. There are on the Close Rolls
acknowledgments of debts due to him, between 1275 and
1280, amounting to £236 14s. 8d., and seeming almost to
suggest usurious dealings. He was twice married, first to
Amice, perhaps a daughter of John de Montgomery, who was
living 7th May, 1275, and secondly to Matilda, who survived
him.

R 2

By Inquisition held on the death of Nicholas de Cogenhoe, the writ dated 10th June, 1281, but place and date of inquiry not given, it is shown that he held a moiety of the manor of Cogenhoe of John, son and heir of Henry de Hastings (of the honour of Huntingdon), by the service of half a knight's fee. He held the other moiety of the said manor, and a plough-land in Harndon (now Great Harroden, seven miles off, from whence Lord Vaux takes his title of 'Dominus Nicholas de Haversham') by service of an entire knight's fee. William de Cogenhoe his son is heir, aged 40 years. He was buried in the south aisle, with an effigy to his memory, hard by the altar of St. Nicholas, which was probably set up by himself and in honour of his patron saint.

It must here be stated, for reasons that will be subsequently apparent, that Nicholas de Haversham married Emma, sister of Ernald de Bois (Ernaldus de Bosco), who had held the Cogenhoe fee of the barony of Wardon in the time of Henry III. On the death of Nicholas the fee was divided between his two daughters, Matilda or Maud, and Joan, married to James and William de la Plaunche.

William de Cogenhoe had livery of his lands on the death of his father, as appears from an entry on the Fine Rolls of 1281. All that is recorded of his public or military life is that in 1281 he was witness to a royal confirmation of a charter of Edmund the king's brother to the hospital and fraternity of St. John, Hungerford. In 1286, 26th April, he had protection, with many others, going beyond seas with the king for one year; and again in 1287, 20th December, for himself, having then gone beyond seas until a fortnight after Easter; and again in 1298, with seven others, going beyond seas with Blanche, late the wife of Edmund the king's brother.

As to his more enduring works of piety, he founded and erected within the parish church of Cogenhoe the chantry of Our Lady to maintain one priest to sing for ever for the soul of the said founder, such endowment being estimated in 1548 at 50s. 9d. The north side of the chancel shows the chief part of the work that was then done, and its character gives its approximate date as *circa* 1315, a date first arrived at without any reference to documents.

There is no *Inquisitio post mortem* forthcoming, but we gather from other sources that he was dead in 1313, when he would have reached the age of 72 years, having been born in 1241.

The successor to William de Cogenhoe was his son 'Dominus Egidius.' In 1309 a complaint was made against him in a

commission of oyer and terminer by Alan, son of William
FitzWaryn, that, together with other brawlers, Giles de
Cogenhoe had burnt the houses of his manor of North Ashby,
carried away some of his goods, and burnt others. By an
Inquisition taken on the death of that bright ornament of the
peerage, John de Hastings senior, in 1313, Giles de Cogenhoe
was shown to hold a moiety of the manor of Cogenhoe by the
service of half a knight's fee, together with the advowson.
William his father was therefore dead, and in 1315-16, in the
returns of the names of the lords of townships, etc. for the
purpose of effecting the military levies ordered in the Parliament of Lincoln of 9 Edward II., Giles was signalised as lord
of Cogenhoe. In 1325 a moiety of a fee in Haidingstone and
Coton held by Giles de Cogenhoe was assigned by the king,
with others, in dower of Juliana late the wife of John de
Hastings, and then married to Thomas le Blount, and to be
delivered to them by Matthew Biown, escheator of the
counties of Lincoln, Northampton, and Rutland.

In 1329 Giles had a writ of *quo warranto* exhibited
against him requiring him to show why he had claimed view
of frank pledge, assize of bread and beer, and weyf of his
tenants in Cogenhoe. He did not appear to prosecute his
claim, and these liberties were therefore seized into the
hands of the king. In July of the same year he was
associated in the commission of the peace with William la
Zouche of Harringworth, Northamptonshire, and three others
named, for the said county. In 1346, on collecting aid for
making the king's eldest son a knight, Giles de Cogenhoe was
one of the three collectors for the county, appointed thereto
by letters patent of November 1, 20 Edward III. Three
years later, Nicholas de Cogenhoe, perhaps his uncle the
Oxford man who had the royal gift of wine in 1275, takes
his place in this office

Giles de Cogenhoe presented to the living in 1334 William
de Cogenhoe, apparently his brother; in April, 1343, Nicholas
de Cogenhoe, perhaps his uncle the Oxford scholar favoured
by the king; and eight months later his own son William,
who held the benefice for thirty-six years, and must have
been instrumental in causing the widening of the aisles and
the raising of the clerestories of the church.

By Inquisition held at Cogenhoe on the death of Giles de
Cogenhoe, the writ dated 16th November, 1349, it is shown
that he held the same fees by the same service as his father.
Much minute detail is given as to the land and its value at
different seasons, and under varying conditions, the floods of
the meadows on the banks of the Nene in both lordships

being taken into account, as well as the value of the water mills and dovecotes at Cogenhoe and Harroden, and the rents of assize of bondmen and cotters. Giles de Cogenhoe died on Saint Martin's day, 11th November, 1349 , John de Cogenhoe his son is his heir, aged 30 years and more.

Of this individual nothing whatever is recorded save the two events common to all humanity. namely, his succession to his father and his death. We associate, however, the short period of his twelve years' stay as lord of Cogenhoe with the pious enterprise of raising the clerestories of the nave.

By Inquisition held at Northampton on the death of John de Cogenhoe, the writ dated 12th October, 1361, it is shown that he held the same Hastings and Haversham fees as his ancestors. Again much curious information appears respecting the details of the land tenure and treatment; a curious reaping custom of the bondsmen called *Lovebone* is described, and another in connection with it called *Le Bene*, and ploughing and harrowing usages, and the alternations of sowing, and consequent variations in the value of the arable land. In both this and the preceding Inquisition the Cogenhoe water mill is referred to as worthless on account of its bad condition, probably destroyed again and again by the floods. The systematised arrangements for dealing with the land under somewhat untoward and peculiar conditions seem to imply that the lord was more interested in agriculture than in matters military or political. John de Cogenhoe died on the feast of Saint Denis, 9th October, 1361, aged 42. William de Cogenhoe is his son and heir, aged 25 years and more.

Again very little is recorded in public documents of the new lord of Cogenhoe. During his time the porch of the church was probably built. He married first in 1365 Elizabeth, co-heir of John de Wolverton, and in 1378 he paid £4 for a licence for himself and his wife to enfeoff Sir John Cheyne and others of a moiety of the manor of Wolverton, and for the feoffees, after seizin had, to grant it to the said John Cheyne for life, with remainder to the said William and Elizabeth in tail, and ultimate remainder to her right heirs Thus came into the Cogenhoe family the lands in Buckinghamshire concerning which separate Inquisitions were subsequently held, the connection being further strengthened by a Cheyne marriage later on. As his second wife, William de Cogenhoe took a lady named Margaret, who long survived him. She was living in the time of Henry IV., and it appears from the lay subsidy rolls for Northampton that she had lands to the value of ten marks in Cogenhoe, and further property in other counties, of whose worth the juiors were entirely ignorant, *penitus ignorant.*

By Inquisition held at Northampton on the death of William de Cogenhoe, the writ dated 14th May, 1389, the manor and advowson are held of John, Earl of Pembroke, then under age. Particulars of the manor are again given. Another Inquisition is held at Newport Pagnell concerning the Wolverton lands. William de Cogenhoe died on the Feast of the Annunciation, 25th March, 1389, aged 53. William his son is heir, aged 10 years and more.

Concerning the short span of this youth, it is natural that very little should have been recorded. For his brief spell was almost as the path of a quarrell from a cross-bow through the air, leaving no trace, but there is the inevitable item in the life of a minor who has succeeded, the grant, in 1389, of his marriage, in this case to the king's esquire, Reginald de Braybrok, without payment, and if he die a minor unmarried, the marriage of his heir, and successive heirs, until the persistent match-maker obtain the marriage. The comprehensive terms of the grant were, in a way, prophetic, for the heir died under age in 1399, 'an early trophy of death's conquering power.'

By Inquisition held at Cogenhoe on the death of William de Cogenhoe, the writ dated 26th February, 1399, it is shown that the manor of Cogenhoe, together with the advowson held of Reginald de Grey, Lord Grey of Ruthin, as of the manor of Yardley Hastings, and a wood called Myrydale, in Buckinghamshire, part of the manor of Cogenhoe, and worth nothing because it was cut and wasted in the time of William the father, came into the king's hands by reason of the father's death and the minority of the son. Certain particulars are given of the manor, some of the buildings are frail and ruinous perhaps the result of a minority, as are also the culverhouses or dovecotes. But the water mill is now worth ten shillings, by the year, so it was for the time in order. Again an Inquisition was held at Newport Pagnell concerning the moiety of the manor of Wolverton. William de Cogenhoe the son died 19th February, 1399. Agnes his sister is heir, and of full age, namely 20 years and more.

She was the last of the ancient line of Cogenhoe, and was very soon after married to Sir John Cheyne, who in her right had livery of the lands of her inheritance in Cogenhoe and Harrowden, and accounted for as much under a subsidy of 1427 as in the days of her great-grandfather Giles.

Agnes Cheyne married secondly Edward Molyneux, who survived her, dying in 1484. There are brasses to their

memory in Chenies church. She bequeathed the manor and
advowson of Cogenhoe to her nephew, Sir John Cheyne, of
Chesham Bois, and in this family they continued until
shortly after 1656, when Charles, son of Sir Francis Cheyne,
sold the historic heritage, the first alienation in five centuries, to a person named Bond, who, in 1660, disposed of
the manor to Matthew Linwood, and of the advowson to the
Rev. Peter Whalley, the then incumbent, in whose family it
remained until the middle of the last century.

The church of Cogenhoe forms one of a considerable group
of buildings, often of very limited size, and for the most part
of transitional origin, which cluster in and about the entrance
to the Nene Valley.   Within a circuit of about ten miles from
Northampton these churches are distinguished, with certain
notable exceptions, such as St. Sepulchre's, Spratton, Brixworth, Walgrave, by their towers.   They belong to the
same class of moderate-sized ecclesiastical buildings that may
be met with in plenty in the adjoining parts of the neighbouring counties of Warwick, Oxford, and Bedford.   And
although the ground plans are constantly the same (for the
cross church, as in the isolated examples at Duston, near
Northampton, and St. Giles's in that town, is not indigenous
in the Mid Lands), both in the towered churches of the high
country and in the spired fanes of the lowlands of Northamptonshire towards the Wash, a stranger may well be
surprised, when he enters the Nene Valley proper at
Cogenhoe, at the change in the architectural outline and in
the character of the churches, and their increased size, which
so soon takes place.   Before he arrives at Wellingborough
towers simple or with spires of rudimentary shape are quite
left behind, and the long and matchless processions of towers
and spires, which so rapidly present themselves on either
hand, and all down the river to Peterborough, at once indicate
the transformation that has occurred.   Such was, in the
Middle Ages, the beneficent influence of a faith that never
shrank, and an infinite zeal, acting upon the fortuitous
presence of the quarries at Barnack, Weldon, and Ketton,
and a convenient water carriage, and inducing a wealth of
conception and an architectural skill not surpassed in any
other district of England.

Perhaps the fame of the Nene Valley churches has drawn
the generality of strangers too rapidly into the well-favoured
district, and to the neglect of less conspicuous works.   It may
be taken for granted, however, that the student whose steps
are primarily directed to Cogenhoe at least does not overlook
the tower of Earl's Barton, two miles across the valley, with

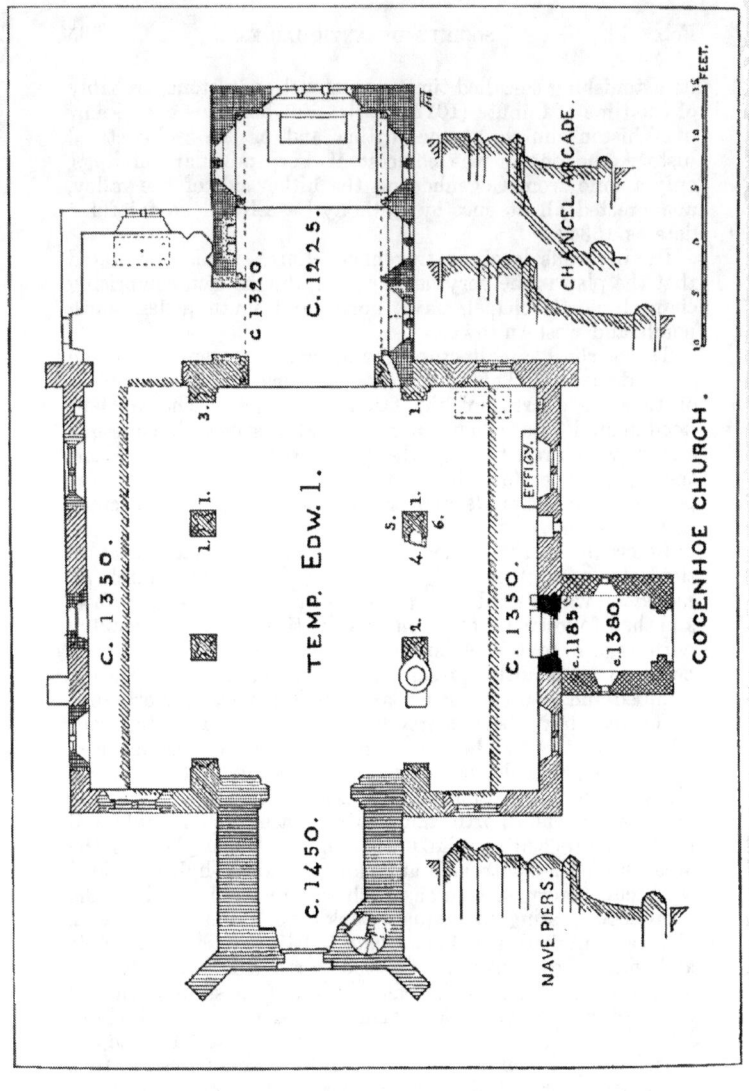

COGENHOE CHURCH.

its astonishing so-called timber construction in stone, probably
of the time of Canute (1017-1035). But how few even know
of Whiston church, at the further end of the architectural
history, and one of the choicest of Perpendicular buildings,
only a mile from Cogenhoe, on the hither side of the valley,
and erected all at once by Anthony Catesby at so fateful a
date as 1534!

Having thus localised Cogenhoe church it may be stated
that the plan is the very usual one of the district, comprising
chancel, north chapel, nave, north and south aisles, south
porch, and western tower.

The earliest architectural evidence is presented by the
south doorway. This is evidently a work about the middle
of the last quarter of the twelfth century. The label or
hood mould and abacus are of that distinct, Romanesque
section which ran through the entire Norman period. Alone
they give no certain date, but the shallowness of the compound cushion capitals, and the form of the arch, sufficiently
bewray them.

Referring to the manorial history, it is probable that in
the latter part of the reign of Henry II. a small church, an
ecclesiola, was erected here, probably by William de Cogenhoe,
and that, following a common practice throughout the country
with regard to the elaborate Norman doorways that have
been so constantly preserved, this modest entrance was
retained and re-used when a larger building was undertaken.

It must have been thirty-five years later, namely about
1225, that the building of a new church was commenced
upon a larger scale, beginning, of course, with the chancel.
Here we have an unusual and beautiful design, consisting
of arcaded walls north and south, resting upon triple and
filleted shafts with capitals with square abaci. Within the
arcades on the south side are pairs of lancet lights, divided
by circular engaged columns with square moulded abaci, the
deep hoods resting upon square nook corbels, similarly treated.
The bases of both arcade and lancet shafts are circular, triple
and single respectively. On the north side are only two
arcade arches, that to the east containing a similar window
to those on the south side. The central bay was originally
left blank, and the third space possibly also left void, or
more likely it contained a door into a small vestry, thus
accounting for the dead wall space. The inner or main
arch of the east window has banded shafts and circular caps
and bases, and is probably quite half a century later than
the north and south chancel arcades. This point will be
returned to.

The chancel having been carried out to this extent there must have been a considerable pause, and when the time came to continue the building of chancel arch, nave, and aisles, a somewhat peculiar work was produced with the remarkable features of shields of arms as well as grotesque heads brought into the capitals, of which the mouldings are but slightly modified from those in the chancel. In the absence of any precise date, which might have been expected from the evidence of this early heraldry, it will be convenient now only to suggest that the nave is of the time of Edward I. That it is the work of a conspicuous and deeply interested member of the locally named family there can be no doubt, and it must therefore be to Nicholas de Cogenhoe who died in 1281, and whose arms are sculptured four times on the capitals of the nave piers, and once on the shield of his effigy, that the main impetus for this building, including very narrow aisles, is to be attributed The five other shields of arms in similar positions will be spoken of later on. Then also was set up the altar of St. Nicholas at the east end of the south aisle.

To continue the dissection of the fabric in chronological order The nave, with its narrow aisles, having been completed, its builder passed away and the church had rest for a while. It must have been during the second decade of the fourteenth century, and in the time of William de Cogenhoe, son of Nicholas, that the chapel on the north side of the chancel was built. This was either then set up entirely new or enlarged from a vestry already suggested. A low archway was formed into it from the chancel with all the width that could be got in the bay of the blank arcade, the outer ring of voussoirs falling with an elbow against a narrow pier fashioned out of the original western respond of the central arch of the north arcade, the inner ring resting upon large corbels. Then also was put in the architectural design within the central arch, comprising an upper trefoiled recess, perhaps a 'sepulchre,' and immediately below it a double aumbry.

About twenty years later, and during the time of Giles de Cogenhoe, a great undertaking was set about which was not unusual in parish churches in the middle of the fourteenth century. This was the widening of the aisles, an alteration brought about by the advancing requirements of the services, and this, in its turn, by setting the windows further from the nave, gave rise in countless cases to the necessity for more light, which the painted windows now so much impeded, and the consequent raising of the nave walls and the forming of clerestories. That such was the procedure at Cogenhoe, both architectural details and the external walling fully substantiate, the window mouldings and the tracery furnishing further unimpeachable witnesses, In no part of England was this change oftener carried out than in the Mid Lands, and in the very district in which Cogenhoe is placed.

From widths of about 6 feet, the north and south aisles were now increased to 10 feet 6 inches, the width of the chapel of Our Lady giving the new dimension. The greater care was expended on the south aisle, where two windows of excellent proportion in flowing Decorated were put in, one at the west end, now filled with modern tracery, and the other immediately over the effigy of the great ancestor Nicholas de Cogenhoe. A smaller window with the same jambs and mullion, and a square oak lintel, was set high up in the east wall, with the sill 10 feet from the floor, making new provision for the altar of which the piscina only remains. All this work must have been completed before the death of Giles de Cogenhoe in 1349. In the north aisle the low doorway is round-headed. It is only plainly chamfered and might be of any date between Romanesque and Renaissance times. As a matter of fact it is part of the work of Nicholas de Cogenhoe. Similarly the jambs of the window adjoining it to the west are of the same date, but spread out in later times to form a two-light window. The other two windows are coeval with the tower.

Continuing the architectural history. Not many years after the completion of the enlargement of the church during the sway of Giles de Cogenhoe, namely in the time of William his grandson, the clerestory was built; it was probably begun about 1360. The six clerestory windows are symmetrically arranged with eight interior corbel heads of white stone and of great excellence, for the support of the main timbers of the roof. The windows, advanced though they are by about thirty years in the Perpendicular style, are very good examples, and their unusual length has the best effect. To a slightly later date than that of the clerestory must be assigned the south porch.

We have seen that Agnes de Cogenhoe became possessed of the manor and advowson on the untimely death of her brother William, under age. in 1399. Her marriage with Sir John Cheyne carrying Cogenhoe, as it eventually did, into another family, it is only natural to believe that she should also have set her enduring mark upon the completion of the building which her ancestors for more than two centuries and a half had delighted to honour. We do not know the date of either of Agnes's marriages, but the

tower is evidently of the middle of the fifteenth century.
It may be permissible to suggest that at this time it
began to arise in its admirable proportions, with its marked
battering lines, and crowned by four pinnacles, in pious
memory of the brother long since dead, and to emphasise
in her old age Agnes de Cheyne's position as the last of an
ancient and God-fearing race.

A search has been made* through the early wills of Cogenhoe persons preserved at Northampton, between the years
1523 and 1547, with interesting results. There are bequests
of barley and money to the high altar, and to the sepulchre
light, the torch light, St. Peter's light, to our Lady's altar,

SHIELD IN COGENHOE CHURCH.

St. Nicholas's altar, to the bells, and to the torches; orders
for masses, bequests of kine for hire for the benefit of the
church, to endure for evermore; the last entry, in July, 1547,
is a bequest of a strike of barley by a conscience-stricken
individual for ' forgotten tythes.'

To touch now upon details and fittings. In the chancel is
a plain stone bench, serving as sedilia, a very rare instance.
There is no stone piscina, nor has there ever been. A
squint is rudely cut through the south jamb of the chancel
arch, but in a curve, so that it gives no command of the high
altar from any point whatever.

* By the Rev. R. M. Serjeantson.

The most remarkable and interesting features in Cogenhoe
church are undoubtedly the armorial shields on the piers of
the nave arcade. With the exception of the shield, *ermine a
chief indented*, on the eastern side of the westernmost pier
of the south arcade, all the remaining eight shields are
sculptured on the eastern responds, and the easternmost piers
north and south.   They are as follows: 1. *A fess between
three mascles*, for Cogenhoe, four times; 2. *Ermine a chief
(or a fillet) indented*; 3. *Barry of ten a bendlet*; 4. *A bendlet
sinister*; 5. *In chief two human hands displayed*; 6. *A bar
and in chief three martlets*. A further shield over the font
is blank.

It is to be noticed that in three of the sculptured
Cogenhoe shields the width of the ordinary or fess is normal,
that on the south pier facing east (1) being quite narrow, of
the early form, as are also (2) the chief or fillet indented
(3) the bars and the bendlet, (4) the bendlet sinister, and
(6) the bar, such being early ordinaries before they were
widened to receive charges.

In the various Rolls of Arms the arms of Cogenhoe (No. 1)
are given as *gules a fess and in chief three mascles argent*, sometimes called three lozenges. It appears that the compilers of
Rolls of Arms copied earlier ones, and thus mistakes were

handed on. The four sculptured shields on the piers and responds of the nave and on the shield of the effigy are certain to be accurate. In the case of the original Camden Roll, of the time of Henry III., the arms assigned to Nicholas de Cogenhoe are unfortunately illegible. It appears from Burke's *Armory*, which may not always be trusted, that a Hastings coat was *argent a fess between three lozenges azure.* The manorial associations of Hastings and Cogenhoe *may* have caused the assumption of this particular bearing of the over-lord by De Cogenhoe.

No. 2. *Ermine a chief or a fillet indented.* This is the

SHIELD IN COGENHOE CHURCH.

coat of Morteyne: *Ermine a chief indented gules,* according to a Roll of Arms of the time of Edward II. for Sir John de Mortein; it is also attributed in the same roll to Sir Walter de Eingrove. Whether it has reference to one of the wives of Sir Nicholas de Cogenhoe, who died in 1281, there is no evidence to show.

No. 3. *Barry of ten a bendlet.* In the Roll of Arms of the time of Edward II. Sir John Pabenham bore *barry of six azure and argent on a bend gules three mullets or ;* Pabenham is some times found without the mullets. 'A certain Sir John Pabenham married the daughter and heir of James de

la Plaunche. This lady's mother, the daughter and heir,
as we have seen, of Nicholas de Haversham, is shown
by the Fine Rolls to have been under age in 1281, and
then in the custody of Queen Eleanor. Her daughter,
therefore, could hardly have been married to De Pabenham much before 1300, so it is manifest that these arms,
though of so early a character, if of De Pabenham, must
have been introduced long after the building of the nave.
But it was not then the custom to leave work in block, as in
modern times (to be carved, or rather, never to be carved,
afterwards), though it became the practice in the fifteenth

SHIELD IN COGENHOE CHURCH.

century; and the coat that one might have expected to find
is that of Haversham, *azure a fess argent between six cross-
crosslets or*, the owner of the knight's fee in Cogenhoe of
the barony of Wardon, at the presumed time of the building
of the nave. The matter is fraught with many difficulties.

No. 4. *A bend or bendlet sinister*. *Gules a bend or* is also
a coat attributed to Hastings, and, if rightly so, its presence
here is properly explained as that of an over-lord. Moreover,
sinister indicates early usage.

No. 5. *Two human hands displayed*. No name can be
assigned to this peculiar bearing. In Banks's *Baronies in Fee*

the arms of Hamont de Bretto, who was slain at the siege of
Calais in 1347, are given as *argent on a chief gules a dexter
and a sinister hand appaumé pileways of the field.* The coat
of this man's father may be intended.

No. 6. *A fess or bar gules in chief three martlets* was the
bearing of Sir —— de Cheny, given in the Roll of Arms of
the time of Edward II. There is no evidence to account for
its presence here, but the propinquity of Buckinghamshire
presupposes an alliance with one of its great families in the

SHIELD IN COGENHOE CHURCH.

middle of the thirteenth century.* Or it may be complimen-
tary to a friend of the family :

'Felix qui potuit rerum cognoscere causas.'

With regard to the blank shield, its being so left is not
considered as greatly affecting the question one way or
another. All the remaining ten spaces are occupied by
grotesque heads, clearly coeval with the date of the piers.

Hard by the head of the effigy is a small recess, with a
loop-hole to without, long walled up. It is possible that the
recess was for an endowed light to be seen from outside.

---

* The writer is indebted to Mr. Thomas Shepard for much help in the
endeavour to unravel the mystery of these shields.

In face of this feature on the west side of the south armorial pier, and forming an integral and original part of it, is a corbelled-out object that has been usually dismissed by casual antiquaries as a holy water stock; and, considered with reference to the second plan of the church, and supposing the south door to have given access, then as now, between the two nave piers, the definition is plausible. But the thing itself is far from convenient for such a purpose. It is 4 feet 1 inch from the floor of the church, which is clearly the ancient level, it is very large for the purpose of a stoup, and is not dished in the invariable way.

SHIELD IN COGENHOE CHURCH.

Eight inches from the east jamb of the south door is a stone bracket 3 feet 10 inches from the floor. It was probably used to support a latten vessel for holy water, being a most awkward place for a light. But it must have proved an unsatisfactory plan, for when the porch was built in the time of the third William de Cogenhoe a new stoup was set up on the right hand of the south doorway. Up to thirty years ago the font contained a pewter tavern punch bowl, considered by many to have been the 'decent bason' of the rubric."

With reference to the restoration of the church in 1870, under the direction of the late Mr. C. Buckeridge, Mr.

Hartshorne showed that the only new structural work consisted in rebuilding on the old foundations the chapel of Our Lady set up by William de Cogenhoe in the first quarter of the fourteenth century, and in devising a triplet, upon the lines of the Early English side windows for the space within the eastern arch of half a century later, an introversion of styles and dates that will form an interesting feature for the bewilderment of antiquaries of the future. The aisles were new-roofed and new tracery placed in their windows, to which no exception can be taken.

Previous to the restoration the north aisle was nearly filled with benches with finialed ends of very peculiar design, and quite distinct from, and earlier than, the square panelled and traceried fifteenth-century seatings of the Midlands. These were taken as the type for the new oak seats throughout the church, with modern modifications. It seems hardly credible, but it is a lamentable fact, that the whole of these rare bench ends, dating perhaps from just after the middle of the fourteenth century, were abolished, and the strictest inquiry at the present day has failed to discover even a trace of them. It is a sad and exasperating passage in the history of the church. It is to be feared that the whole of the surface of the interior ashlar has suffered from modern tooling, and the font of Nicholas de Cogenhoe's time has been shockingly refaced. The walls throughout have been loaded with "restoration" plaster, standing out nearly an inch thick in long hard lines and curves about the windows and arches, and irrespective of the forms of the coigns, to the unscaling and marring of the whole church.

In spite, however, of these errors of thirty years ago, Mr. Hartshorne showed that the church is one that can be studied with less than the usual feelings of anger and shame that "restoration" so constantly excites, and that there was some cause for gratitude that so interesting a building had suffered comparatively so little in the process.

W. J. FREER, Esq., V.D., F.S.A., read the following report as Local Secretary for Leicestershire :

"I have the honour to present a report as Local Secretary for Leicestershire, and take this opportunity of thanking the President, Council, and Fellows for appointing me to that office.

I have four interesting finds of Roman antiquities to report, one in the county, and three in the county borough of Leicester.

The first discovery was made in the latter part of 1900, and I am indebted to the surveyors of the estate, Messrs. Draper and Walters (both members of the Leicestershire Architectural and Archæological Society) for a plan of the remains found.

The field having been ploughed, it is doubtful if much more remains to be discovered, but no further disturbance will take place without due notice being given.

In the course of constructing a new road on the Rothley Temple Building Estate, belonging to F. Merttens, Esq., various fragments of masonry, tiles, pottery, bone, etc., were found, and this led to excavations being made in the hope of disclosing some of the buried secrets of the locality. Work was commenced at a point within fifty yards of Rothley Station (G.C.R.), at the junction of the roads leading to Swithland and Rothley. The excavations have disclosed the foundations and floor of a dwelling-house of considerable extent.

The walls, so far as at present traced, enclose an area of about 45 feet by 30 feet. The floor is composed of concrete still very sound and hard from 4 to 6 inches thick, and lies from 3 feet 6 inches to 4 feet below the present ground surface. The walls are 2 feet 2 inches wide, of large sized granite rammel spaces entirely filled and the whole made solid with mortar. The inside surface has evidently been rendered with mortar.

The top of the walls, as they are at present, seems uniformly level, and is from 1 foot 6 inches to 2 feet above the concrete floor. The field in which the remains are is at present grass, and has been ploughed at one time; this may explain the level surface of the walls.

Standing on the concrete floor are piers about 2 feet apart of red clay tiles bedded in mortar. These piers are of various heights, some mere indications, some 3 inches and some 1 foot 6 inches high. Many of the broken tiles show clay of the sandy nature common to the locality.

They vary in size from 11¼ inches square to 2 inches thick to 8 inches square and 3¾ inches thick.

The inside to the level of the walls was filled with *débris*, containing granite, stones, clay slabs, mortar, and red clay tiles, supposed to be floor and roof tiles, also some small fragments of pottery, bone, horn, etc.

A well was discovered at the north-west corner of the building. It is roughly circular, 3 feet in diameter, and lined for a distance of 3 feet from the top with limestone slabs 3 inches thick; and for the remainder, with granite rammel, no jointing material being used.

The well was filled with *débris* and slabbed completely over to the level of the top of the wall adjoining. It has been excavated, but nothing of particular interest has been found My friend, Mr. W. T. Tucker, submitted a plan to Mr. Haverfield, who says, 'The plan shows a furnace room, hypocaust, and adjacent walling of a Roman villa, but the area uncovered is only a small part of the whole building', and he further adds, 'You may have hit upon the bathing apartments. Anyhow there is much more to be discovered.'

Within the last few days, in the course of excavations for a sand pit, not far from the east side of the site of the portion of the Roman villa, a stone coffin of limestone slabs was found. Unfortunately, the man who was making the excavation broke it considerably before reporting the fact. The stones have been preserved and the bones collected as far as possible. The coffin was found lying two feet below the surface east and west. Mr. Tucker says that it was similar to some found nearer the villa which contained Saxon bronzes. I shall make further inquiries as to this and am arranging for a photograph to be taken.

The road called the Templars Avenue has been carefully made over the remains, which have been disturbed as little as possible, except where it was necessary to lay the drain. At the Annual Meeting of the Leicestershire Architectural and Archæological Society, held at the Old Town Hall, Leicester, on Monday, January 28th, 1901, the following was carried unanimously: ' We desire to convey our sincere thanks to Fk. Merttens, Esq., of Rothley Temple, for the great interest he has shown and the care that has been taken in opening up the ground near the Great Central Railway Station (at Rothley), under which the remains of the hypocaust of a Roman villa have been found, and earnestly hope that he will cause further excavations to be made and that the remains may not be destroyed.' A copy of the above resolution was sent to Mr. Merttens, who replied that on his return from abroad he would try and meet the wishes of the Society.

In *Archaeologia* * it is stated that the late Thos. Babington, of Rothley Temple, found a small piece of pavement about a foot square and some silver and gold coins in making a ditch near the above in 1784-5

I now come to the finding of some pieces of Roman pavement at the corner of High Cross Street and High Street in excavating for cellars under the new Highcross Coffee House

* Vol. x. 370.

in February, 1901, and am indebted to my friend, Mr. Geo E. Mawbey, C.E., the borough surveyor, for a plan of the three pieces of pavement, the second of which is especially fine. Part of a wall of masonry about a foot high was also found. When first discovered the pieces of pavement were under the borough surveyor's charge, and have since been placed in the Leicester Museum.

A large urn (to be subsequently described) was also found on this site.

The site was found strewn over with blocks of granite rubble and pieces of sandstone, some of which showed signs of being worked. The depth was about 10 feet below the crown of the road.

As might be expected, the removal of the old property in the heart of ancient *Ratæ*, for street widening and other purposes, and the subsequent excavations in the made-up ground, have resulted in the discovery of some interesting relics chiefly of the Roman period. Within the last few months excavations have taken place in the cleared ground on the south side of High Street, and midway between Carts Lane and Highcross Street (about sixty yards from the preceding discovery), in the course of which a good number of Roman relics consisting chiefly of bricks, tiles, pipes, bones, and a quantity of pottery, bone hairpins, etc, were brought to light from 7 to 11 feet deep ; with the exception of one piece, all the articles of pottery were more or less damaged before or in getting them out. The principal objects of this find are as follows :

1   A jug of a common red ware uncracked and in a perfect state. It stands $7\frac{1}{2}$ inches high. I am indebted to my friend Mr. Councillor S. Squire for a photograph of the objects now described.

2.   A small plain dish slightly chipped. Upchurch ware.

3.   Two large amphoræ necks.

4   A large Upchurch urn, measuring $22\frac{1}{2}$ inches in circumference and $8\frac{1}{2}$ inches deep.

5.   A small vessel of Upchurch ware, being part of a lamp.

6.   Part of a Caistor ware vase, $4\frac{1}{4}$ inches deep, with two rows of ornamental figuring upon it.

7.   A large mortarium, 11 inches in diameter, 3 inches deep, with a short spout.

8. Greater part of a pretty shaped Samian vase, 4 inches deep, potter's mark MARCELLINI.

9. Part of a large plain Samian ware dish, originally 38 inches in circumference and 3 inches deep.

10. Two fine pieces of embossed Samian ware being parts of different but equally elaborate bowls. One contains figures representing hunting subjects, whilst the other contains nude male and female figures. The characteristic moulding of the latter piece being the festoon and tassel commonly known as the egg and tongue border.

In addition to the pieces above described numerous fragments of broken pottery were met with, from some of which the following potter's names or marks were deciphered ·

IVLLIN
IVSTI · M ·
MARTINI
RICCI ·
RVFIANI · M ·
TITVS · FEC ·
MVXIVII · M ·

A few bone hairpins and a coin (third brass) of Allectus (293-296) in a good state were also found. Fragments of bronze or metal were scarce, although a lady's bronze enamelled scent case or locket was discovered. This is diamond shaped, gilded in centre, and still exhibits traces of the original blue enamel. With the exception of the hinge this ornament is perfect.

On the 2nd October, 1902, on an adjoining site in High Street, several other articles were found of Samian and Caistor ware.

A part of a thirteenth-century holy water stoup was also discovered, but beyond this very few mediæval relics were found. The large urn was found near the recently discovered Roman pavement when rebuilding the High Cross Coffee House. It is of a dark grey coloured earthenware and stands 6¾ inches, 23 inches round, and has a short spout and handle.

During excavations on the north side of St. Nicholas Street for the new Foresters' Institute, a first brass coin of Vespasian and some Roman masonry was discovered, and coins of Antoninus Pius and Aurelianus were found during the improvements made to Applegate Street.

It should be stated that a larger part of the relics above mentioned have found their way into private hands. Most of the pottery and coins were collected by Mr. H. Hartopp, and are now in the possession of Captain Burns-Hartopp of Dalby Hall, Leicestershire. I may also state that about nine months ago a fine first brass of Hadrian was found on the site of the Roman ditch between Market Place and Gallowtree Gate, on the site of the Wheatsheaf Inn, pulled down in January, 1902.

In December last the remains of an ancient wall (Roman) were found in High Street, Leicester, and evidently formed part of the wall discovered in 1861, in St. Martins and Town Hall Lane.*

I regret to conclude my report by having to deplore the loss of 'the Huntingdon Tower,' in High Street, although every pressure was brought to bear upon the Corporation of Leicester, yet as the widening of the street caused the tower to project into the roadway nothing could induce the Corporation to spare it. The brick casing when removed showed the stone tower in a fair state of preservation. Henry Hastings, third earl of Huntingdon, purchased 'Lords Place' in 1569, and built his mansion in High Street shortly after that date, using up some of the material belonging to the old church of St. Peter which stood near." †

Thanks were ordered to be returned for these communications.

Thursday, 5th March, 1902.

Viscount DILLON, President, in the Chair.

The following gifts were announced, and thanks for the same ordered to be returned to the donors :

From the Editor .—Canterbury Marriage Licences : 1st Series, 1568-1618 ; 2nd Series, 1619-1660 ; 3rd Series, 1661-1676 ; and 4th Series, 1677-1700. Edited by J. M. Cowper. 8vo. Canterbury, 1892-98.

From James Curtis, Esq., F.S A. ·—Devonshire Screens and Rood Lofts. By F. B Bond 8vo. n p   1902.

* See *Transactions of the Leicestershire Architectural and Archæological Society*, ii 90, and plan. For a plan of this wall I am indebted to the architect, Mr. A. Wakerley, one of our members.

† Johnson's *Glimpses of Ancient Leicester*, 147-8.

From the Author, H. St. George Gray, Esq. :—

    1 A Guide to the Walter Collection in Taunton Castle Museum. 8vo
       Taunton, 1903

    2. Excavations at the Glastonbury Lake Village in July, 1902. 8vo. n.p.
       1902.

    3. Bronze Sword found in Pitney Moor, Somerset. 8vo. n.p. 1901.

From the Author :—The Churchwardens' Accounts of the Parish of Worfield
    Part I, 1500-1511. By H. B. Walters, F.S A. 8vo n p n d.

From the Author .—The Early and Mediæval History of Lindisfarne, or Holy
    Island. By Rev H. J D. Astley. 8vo London, 1902

This being an evening appointed for the election of Fellows
no papers were read.

WILLIAM W. PORTAL, Esq, M.A., F.S A., exhibited two
horseshoes of ordinary form, and a third with a singular
arched bar arrangement inside, found at Basing, Hants ; also
a small earthenware jar, possibly Roman, found in the bed of
the river Avon of Christchurch, Hants.

Thanks were ordered to be returned for these exhibitions.

The Secretary reported that the certificate of one of the
candidates for election, Mr. Herbert Arthur Doubleday, had
been withdrawn at his own request.

The ballot opened at 8.45 p m. and closed at 9 30 p m. when
the following gentlemen were declared duly elected Fellows of
the Society :

        Rev. Walter Marshall, M.A.
        Rev. Arthur Tompson Michell, M A.
        William Pearce, Esq.
        Edward Stone, Esq
        Thomas Matthews Blagg, Esq.
        William Henry Davison, Esq , M.A.
        The Right Rev. Huysshe Wolcott Yeatman-Biggs,
           D.D., Bishop of Southwark.

Thursday, 12th March, 1903.

Viscount DILLON, President, in the Chair.

The following gifts were announced, and thanks for the same ordered to be returned to the donors :

From J. T. Micklethwaite, Esq , F S A. —Jeypore Portfolio of Architectural Details. By Colonel S. S Jacob 6 parts Fol. London, 1890.

From the Rev G. W. Minns, F.S.A —Choir Stalls and their Carvings. Examples of misericords from English cathedrals and churches. Sketched by Emma Phipson. 4to. London, 1896.

From the Author —The Archæological Remains and Early Historical Associations of Streatham, Tooting, and Balham. By T. W Shore. 8vo   n p. 1903

The following gentlemen were admitted Fellows :

The Right Rev. the Bishop of Southwark, D.D.
Edward Stone. Esq.
William Pearce, Esq

E. TOWRY WHYTE, Esq , M.A., F.S.A., read a paper on Brougham Castle, Westmorland, which will be printed in *Archaeologia*.

The Rev. J K FLOYER, M A , F S A., read a paper on the Medieval Library of the Benedictine Priory of St. Mary, Worcester, which will be printed in *Archaeologia*.

W. B. BANNERMAN, Esq., F.S.A., exhibited a portion of a large hoard of Roman bronze coins found at Croydon, Surrey.

Thanks were ordered to be returned for these communications and exhibitions.

Thursday, 19th March, 1903.

Sir E. M. THOMPSON, K.C.B., LL.D., D.C.L., Vice-President,
in the Chair.

The following gifts were announced, and thanks for the
same ordered to be returned to the donors :

From the Author :—Pedigree of the Families of Newcomen and Hunnings, of
co. Lincoln. By W. E. Foster, F.S.A.   8vo.   Exeter, 1903.

From C. F. Worsley, Esq. :—A Pedigree of the Family of Worsley, of Stan-
worth, Lancashire, and Calais. Privately printed. Single sheet folio. n.p.
1902.

From the Incorporated Church Building Society, through J. T. Micklethwaite,
Esq., F.S.A. :—A Scrap-book of Views of Churches illustrating the early
Gothic revival.

William Henry Davison, Esq., M.A., was admitted Fellow.

WALTER MONEY, Esq., F.S.A., Local Secretary for Berkshire, communicated the following note on St. Bartholomew's
Hospital, Newbury :

" By the courtesy of Mr. F. Quekett Louch, Town Clerk
of Newbury, I have the honour to submit for exhibition the

SEAL OF ST. BARTHOLOMEW'S HOSPITAL, NEWBURY. (⅓.)

common seal of the ancient Hospital of St. Bartholomew in
that town, which was in use down to about a century ago.

The seal, which is of brass, is a circular one, $1\frac{9}{16}$ inch in
diameter, bearing for device two conjoined crosses between
four small stars, with the legend :

✠ DOMUS · ST. BARTHOLOMEI · IN NEWBURY.

A representation of this seal with the legend inscribed in
stone, is inserted in the wall of one of the old buildings of
the hospital, but is of comparatively modern date.

This hospital is said to have been founded by King John,
and on the clock turret of the old almshouses belonging to
this foundation, known from time out of mind as 'King
John's Court,' is this inscription:

HOSPITAL OF ST. BARTHOLOMEW.

FOUNDED BY KING JOHN $\left\{ \begin{array}{l} 1200. \\ 1215. \end{array} \right.$

THIS BUILDING ERECTED   -   1698.

The Charter Rolls from the second to the fifth of King
John are lost, and amongst them, probably, the foundation
charter of this institution.

Gervase of Canterbury bears witness to the early existence
of this hospital in his *Mappa Mundi*, compiled soon after
the year 1200, for he includes in his list of Berkshire hospitals that of 'Sancti Bartholomaei Neuberie.' In 1215, King
John granted to the already existing hospital the right to
hold a two days' fair for its support, as shown by the Close
Rolls (17 John, m 28), and this fair is still held yearly, being
opened by the town clerk or his deputy with all the quaint
formalities of former times; and the profits paid to the alms-
people of King John's Court. There is also collected at the
time of the fair a penny from each licensed house in the
town, the origin of which is not known. The earliest deeds
extant refer to houses or lands in or near Newbury by various
inhabitants of the place, and I send herewith three of these
grants, dated respectively 1256-1261, 1302, and 1302-11,
which singularly enough I purchased in London many years
ago.

From various other documents we learn that the master,
warden, prior, or rector as he is indifferently termed, was
appointed by the commonalty of the town; and that in the
year 1267 the Abbot and Convent of Préaux, in Normandy,
patrons of the parish church, gave to the hospital the right of
free burial in the cemetery of the said hospital. One of the
deeds dated in 1365 was executed 'in the chapel of our
house,' and another, in 1477, is described as *sealed with the
seal of the hospital.*

In 1545 the suppression of the hospital was contemplated
under the Act 37 Hen. VIII. c. 4, by which all colleges,
chantries, and hospitals were to be dissolved and granted
to the Crown, an Act which became inoperative owing to
Henry's death. Edward VI. passed a fresh Act of dissolution

(1 Edw. VI. c. 14), but in this hospitals were not included, and in the returns made under the second Act St. Bartholomew's is not mentioned. It was, however, subsequently seized under the later Act as a chantry, and leased by the Crown to one Thomas Burche, of Kensington, a yeoman of the king's chamber. The commonalty of the town resented such a high-handed action, and resisted the lessee's entry. Hence a lawsuit in the Court of Augmentations, in the records of which are contained many interesting facts about this establishment. The first witness is one of the almsmen of Donnington. He 'sayth that of his owne knowledge he hath knowen this lxxxv. yeres a howse of relygon in Newberye called the Pryorye of St. Bartylmewes,' that it was 'an howse or pryore of chanons,' and that they 'wore whyte apparell after the order of chanons, that is to sey, an onder garment of whyte clothe, and over that a whyte rochett, and above the sam a vyolett gown sleveles.' The chapel, part of which is still standing, is described as 'a proper lyttell churche,' and the chancel 'seated with carolles,' movable stalls used by the brethen for daily private study and meditation. The chapter house and the high altar are also mentioned, and that on the sides of the chancel were two aisles 'made between the bodye of the church, and the said chauncell with altars in them.' According to Deloney, Jack of Newbury was married in this chapel to the widow of his wealthy master.

The result of the case above mentioned does not appear, and a similar action was raised in Elizabeth's time, when the Queen's attorney-general claimed the lands from the lessee, as being chantry or priory lands, and as such escheats to the Crown. From another deposition we gather that the grammar school was engrafted on the hospital foundation in the reign of Edward VI.

Under the Statute of Charitable Uses, and by decree of the Commissioners, dated 1599, the property and management of the hospital were handed over to the Corporation of Newbury, and this settlement remained in force till the passing of the Municipal Corporations Act in 1835.

In consequence of certain irregularities the charity became involved in Chancery proceedings, and from 1836 to 1841 the trustees endeavoured to get the cause out of court, but without success. However, in 1846 this was accomplished, and new grammar school buildings erected on the site of the ancient priory.

The Hospital and Grammar School Foundation are now administered under a scheme of 1883, and new school build-

5

ings have been erected on another site at a cost of some
£10,000, but the old almshouses (King John's Court) have
not been interfered with."

A. T. MARTIN, Esq. submitted a Report on Excavations at
Caerwent in 1902, which will be printed in *Archaeologia*.

Thanks were ordered to be returned for these communications.

Thursday, 26th March, 1903.

Viscount DILLON, President, in the Chair.

The following gifts were announced, and thanks for the
same ordered to be returned to the donors:

From the Author:—A Note on the Church of Cley. By J. T. Micklethwaite,
F.S.A. 8vo. n.p. n.d.

From E. Towry Whyte, Esq., M.A., F.S.A.:—A collection of Seven Lantern
Slides in illustration of a paper on Brougham Castle, Westmorland.

Notice was given that the Annual Election of the President,
Council, and Officers of the Society would be held at the
Anniversary Meeting on St. George's Day, Thursday, 23rd
April, at 2 p.m.; and that no Fellow in arrear of his annual
subscription would be entitled to vote on that occasion.

Professor JOHN RHYS, M.A., F.S.A., Principal of Jesus
College, Oxford, read the following paper on an inscribed
stone found at Llystyn Gwyn, in Carnarvonshire:

"On the first day of July, 1902, I received a letter from
Mr. R. Pritchard Evans, of Felin Llecheiddior, in the Eivion
district of Carnarvonshire, informing me of the discovery of
an old inscribed stone in that neighbourhood, and on the 16th
July I arranged to inspect it in the company of Mr. Evans.
With the kind permission of the Fellows I propose to give
some account of it.

The stone is within a mile of Brynkir station, on the rail-
way between Carnarvon and Afon Wen; it is on a farm called
Llystyn Gwyn, occupied by a tenant of the name of Evan
Jones, and the landlord is Colonel Lloyd Jones Evans, of

Broom Hall, near Pwllheli. The stone may be said to be now a gate post, except that there is no gate there; in fact it forms the end of a hedge where a gate or a hurdle might be set up. The farmer found it at a spot not far off, which he showed us; it lay flat with one of its corners protruding inconveniently near a gap in a hedge So he undertook to remove it, but he was surprised to find it so large and heavy, and when he got it clear he thought it would do for the unsafe position where I saw it, so he had it placed on a sledge and moved thither without any damage, so far as he knows, occurring to it. He calls the material *carreg dân*, 'a fire-stone,' by which he seems to mean a kind of granite which when struck readily yields a spark, but I have had it since on the authority of an expert that it is 'a stone of granitic texture, which is to be found *in situ* in the Bethesda district.' The surface measures parallel to the inscription about 3 feet 6 inches by 3 feet the other way, and in point of thickness it thins out from rather more than a foot to 6 inches at the edge farthest from the lettering. As it then stood, the writing read downwards, near and parallel to the thickest edge of the stone; the opposite edge was both thinner and more irregular, as if the stone had been longer originally in that direction. The following rough sketch will explain what I mean.

The edge *a b* is the thick one and *c d* the thinner and more irregular, which makes me fancy the stone has been shortened by the breaking off of a piece along *c d*. This question of the original shape and dimensions of the stone may have a bearing on that of the age of the writing, and if my guess should prove well founded one would be warranted in saying that the writing is across the face of the stone like Roman inscriptions. For there was besides that a Celtic habit of writing down the face of the stone, and this last is illustrated by many of our post-Roman inscriptions. The late

Dr. Hübner treated those written so, that is to say *more Celtico*, as earlier than those written *more Romano*, which, in my humble opinion, was rather perverse, or at any rate the reverse of the correct order. But be that as it may, you will naturally ask, if this is to be treated as written *more Romano*, why did the inscriber begin so far away from the left-hand edge, and does not the fact of his having done so imply that he continued his first line of letters on a portion of the stone extending beyond the present right-hand edge *b d*? That is partly answered by another question, namely, why in that case did he turn back to finish his POTENTINI and not go

INSCRIBED STONE AT LLYSTYN GWYN, CARNARVONSHIRE.

straight on? There is, however, another answer, namely, that the stone shows no certain sign of having been broken off along *b d*. In fact that edge together with *a b* and *a c* seem to me to show, with the exception of a certain breakage near the top of *b d*, such rounding off that one cannot help concluding that it was so, speaking roughly, when the letters were cut and long before. It would remain then to say, that the fact of the inscriber beginning his writing where he did is to be put down to his inexperience and inability to estimate the space his letters would take upon the stone. Nothing is more common in the case of this class of inscriptions: the

authors of them never seem to have chalked the letters
out or otherwise drawn them beforehand on the stone.
Another possible conjecture may be mentioned, namely, that
the left portion of the face was covered by another stone
when the letters were cut.

Now as to the letters themselves they are on the whole
fairly well cut, and there is nothing peculiar about their form,
excepting that the connecting bar of the first N joins the
perpendiculars at some distance from their nearest ends
respectively ; the result is somewhat of an approach to an H.
And I should have said that the other N is considerably wider
than the first.   There is a difficulty, however, about the
reading of the wider N, for the first part of the letter is not
clear, owing to the stone being uneven at that point and
slightly damaged, probably when it was recently removed to
where it is.   There is one other imperfect letter, namely the
last in the first line.   It is here represented provisionally as
an I, but that is not the reading, as it has a line at right angles
to it suggesting the lower bar of an F, but as the top is gone
it might just as well be the first portion of a P, or even of
an A, excepting that one would hardly expect the first limb
of an A to be perpendicular, which is the case here.   Unfortunately the epitaph supplies no A for one to compare, but
instances undoubtedly occur of the letter A having its first
limb perpendicular or very nearly so.   Whatever the imperfect
letter was, I see no possibility of reading it as an S of any
kind, though that would have completed the word *filius* and
spared us some serious difficulties, among them that of fixing
how many letters followed, if any, and which they were.
At all events I think that the inscriber must have tried to
finish the word following FILI on the edge, so that he cannot have had many letters to write there.   Unfortunately
the rounded edge of the stone near the corner *b* has been
damaged, not lately I think, but some time or other since the
epitaph was cut.   Add to this that though the stone had not
been sunk into the ground, it rested when I saw it on the
edge *b d*,* so that I was not able to examine this part as com-

---

* The stone has since been shifted, as will be seen from the photograph, which
only reached me long after these notes had been written.   My friend Mr. Evans
in the meantime had no less than eight different photographers to look at the
stone, but none of them thought it worth their while to try to photograph it :
they despaired of reproducing the inscription, so he had the letters painted with
blacking, and the present photograph was kindly taken by Mr. T. J. Davies,
Groeslon, Carnarvon.   This was not due to any suggestion of mine, but the
photograph is excellent as a general representation of the stone, nor can I find
any fault with the letters except the B, which, so far as I can remember, is
better than it appears in the photograph ; and I am not sure whether the perpendicular of the P was not rather longer than it is here represented.   For
comparison I submit a rubbing which I took in July.

pletely as I could wish; but on the whole I was persuaded
that there is no more writing to be found there. With these
exceptions the letters are perfectly clear, and yield no decided
proofs of long exposure to the weather; they were found on
the lower face of the stone in its horizontal position in the
ground, and they must have long been protected from injury
in that or some other way.

Now as to the legend as a whole. When Mr. Evans sent
me a facsimile I felt certain that there must have been a line
before the one beginning with ICORI, but the first glance at
the rounded form of the top of the stone and its thickness
showed me how that is utterly impossible. So we have to
deal with the following letters as all that we are likely to get;
at any rate we have the original beginning of the epitaph:

ICORIFILIV . . . .
POTENTI
NI

Now three conjectures suggest themselves to me ·

(1) Read IC ORI FILIVΓ POTENTINI and construe Ori as a
nominative for an earlier Oris (genitive Orias), the whole
would mean Hic iacet Oris filius Potentini The chief objection
to this is that an s even of the improbable gamma form is
inadmissible so far as I was able to judge.

(2) Construe Ori and fili as genitives so as to read

IC ORI FILI V . .. . . . POTENTINI

which would mean Hic est locus Ori fili V . . . Potentini.
In guessing the father's name the choice of suitable vocables
beginning with Up or Uf, especially if the inscription was
that of a Goidel, as I am disposed to think, would be scanty;
and so one would have probably to fall back on UR or
possibly VA. A still greater difficulty would be that of
space, as the name would have to be very short; and I cannot
help adding that a surname or epithet like Potentinus seems
to me to form another considerable difficulty.

(3) Construe Ori as a genitive as in No 2 and read F or F.
as an abbreviation for FILI, it is not usual to have filii as the
genitive case singular in this class of inscriptions. Then we
should have

IC ORI FILIV[S] F(ili) POTENTINI.

It is possible that fili was written in full in a way common
enough in these inscriptions, namely as Fι Lι with one ι hanging from the bar of the F and the other from the foot of the

L, this would only imply additional room for L. But I rather
think that in such case the first ı ought to be still there; not
to mention that as FILIV was not cut in that way, it is hardly
probable that FILI would be; and I fall back on F or F. The
objections to this reading are two, that such abbreviations are
not usual in this kind of inscription, though not quite unknown, and that the whole inscription as now put would
probably make the hair of a Latin epigraphist stand on end.

The former objection need not be regarded as such, but as
only proving that the inscription is a very early one, reproducing an abbreviation which was common in Roman
epigraphy; and the latter objection is not of a serious nature,
if one may treat the legend as a translation into Latin from
another language, namely Goidelic. This is the view which
I am disposed to take; but to make it clear what I mean, I
must enter on a few details. The name *Potentinus* occurs in
one of the Roman inscriptions at Caerleon, and we have
Potenina, which looks like a mistake for *Potentina*, on a
post-Roman stone found at Tregaron, in the neighbourhood of
the Roman site of Llanio, in Cardiganshire. *Potentinus*, as a
derivative from *potens*, 'powerful, strong,' has its parallel in
Irish in the name *Ceithernach*, which comes from medieval
Irish *cethern* or *ceithern*, in Welsh *cadarn*, '*potens*, strong, able-
bodied,' literally 'fit for war,' from *cad*, 'battle,' Irish *cath* of
the same meaning; but the Irish word *cethern* has only come
down in the sense of 'soldiers,' or rather perhaps a 'band of
soldiers,' as it is used in the singular with a plural meaning,[*]
and it has been borrowed into Welsh as such, while in English
it became *kern* and *cateran*. The kern seem to have earned
at an early date a very bad reputation, and *y gethern* is
usually connected in Welsh with hell, and means the rabble of
demons associated with it. To return to the inscription,
Filius Fili Potentini may be treated as the equivalent of
some such a medieval Irish designation as *Mac Meic Ceither-
naich*, or 'Mc Ceithernaigh's son.' In fact it is perhaps needless to look for any other, as *Mac Ceithernaigh* occurs as a
proper name in Irish annals, for instance, in those of Ulster,
A.D. 1382: in the translation of the Four Masters it is
anglicized as 'Mac Keherny,' and it was borne by one of the
chieftains of Connaught.

It is needless to dwell on the omission of the silent *h* of *hic*
or the suppression of the final *s* of *filius*. Some scholars wish
to establish a sharp difference of age between inscriptions

---

[*] See O'Donovan's *Battle of Magh Rath*, page 140, and Stokes's *Saltair na Rann*, line 3538.

which retain the final sibilant and those that do not; but I cannot say that I agree, as there was probably a longish period during which it was uncertain in the writing, though there may have been no corresponding uncertainty in the pronunciation, for which it had become a dead letter. Now as to the name *Ori* I may mention what appears to be a kindred form, namely, *Oria*, on a stone reading ORIA IC IACIT, 'Oria lies here,' at Penmachno, in the same county. I had always treated this *Oria* as the latter portion of some such a feminine as *Avitoria, Censoria,* or the like, but probably without sufficient reason: I should like to see the stone again. In the meantime I cannot do better than quote here the late Professor Westwood's *Lapidarium Walliæ,* p. 175, where he says of *Oria,* that 'there seems to be no reason for thinking any letters at the commencement of the inscription are lost.'

In casting about for the etymology of such a name as *Ori* or *Oria* one comes at once on the old Irish adjective *uar,* 'cold,' Welsh *oer,* but these imply a form *ogro-s,* and as our inscription is an early one it might in that case be expected to have retained the *g.* A proper name *Uar* occurs, however, and it may have had nothing to do with *uar,* 'cold.' Thus in the *Dinnsenchas* or Place-name Stories published by Stokes we have an *Uar Elharchar,* after whom Loch n-*Uair* was called, now better known as Lough Owel, in Westmeath.* This looks a little mythical, but the name occurs elsewhere, namely, in *Acallamh na Senórach* in Stokes and Windisch's *Irische Texte,* series IV part i. p. 35, where we read of the nine sons of a certain Uar mac Idhaist.

Uar, genitive *Uair,* may have been in early Goidelic nominative *Ora-s,* genitive *Ori.* This would fit here, but *Ori* may be rather a shortening of *Orii,* genitive of *Ore,* for an earlier uncontracted nominative *Oria-s,* and this seems to come nearer to the *Oria* already mentioned. In fact one may perhaps suggest that *Ori* is a foreshortened form of some such a name as the genitive *Talori* on one of the stones at Dolau Cothi, in Carmarthenshire. The name *Talori* has parallels in the Welsh names *Tal-haearn,* meaning 'him of the iron brow, or iron forehead,' and *Tal-arian* 'him of the silver forehead:' so *Tal-or-i* should be 'he of the golden forehead.' In that case we may treat it as *Tal-ōr-i,* for *ōr* is the Latin *aurum* borrowed into Goidelic, while it becomes in Welsh *aur,* formerly *eur,* 'gold.' So this name is Goidelic, and so would *Ori* be. Now the compound name is actually to be met with later, namely in the lists of the Pictish kings, who

---

* See the *Revue Celtique,* XVI 80-1

frequently adopted Celtic names. There the nominative is
Talore, which while making a genitive *Talori*, implies early
Goidelic forms *Tal-ōria-s*, genitive *Tal-ōri-i*, that is to say
the declension was not that of *aurum*, 'gold,' but of the
adjective *aureus, aurea, aureum,* 'golden,' which accounts
exactly for the feminine name *Oria* from Latin *aurea,*
'golden' I must here explain that in the Pictish lists *Talore*
is mixed up with other forms such as *Talorc, Talorg, Talargen,
Talorcen, Tolarcan*, and others of the same kind, as one
will find on consulting the index to Skene's *Chronicles of the
Picts and Scots*. The earlier form of the Welsh *Talarian* was
Talargant, made up probably of *Tal(o)-argent-*, but when the *t*
was assimilated the name sounded to a Pict as a genitive, and
he inferred a nominative *Talorg, Tolorg,* or *Tolorc* in the
same way that from a Brythonic *Vepogen-* he inferred a
nominative *Vipoig*. There may have possibly been a certain
amount of confusion in the MSS. between *Talore* and *Talorc*,
but the former occurs too often and too persistently to be
disposed of as entirely due to error; so I make use of it
to explain our genitives *Tal-Ori* and *Ori*; and I assume that
the peoples of Britain borrowed the metal names *argentum*
and *aurum* from the Romans at an early date, witness the
Pict mentioned by Dio Cassius under the name of Argento-
coxos, 'Silver-leg or Silver-foot.'

Returning now to the construction of the epitaph, I may
say that one may treat it as meaning, 'Hic est locus Orii:
filius erat Filii-Potentini,' or 'Here is the burial place of Ore:
he was son of Mac Ceithernaigh.' But the analogy of our
inscription makes it unnecessary to supply the second verb,
since an apposition to a genitive may stand in the nominative:
an instance in point occurs in one of the Ogam inscriptions in
the Royal Irish Academy's Collection, which reads · *Gosocteas
mosac Mapini,* 'The burial place of Gosoctis, servant of
Mapinios.' Here *Gosocteas* is genitive while *mosac* can be
nothing but a nominative.* One might accordingly render
our epitaph into English more simply as follows · 'Here is
the burial place of Ore, son of Mac Ceithernaigh.'

Altogether I regard this inscription as a peculiar one, and
I give my conjectures with great diffidence and in the hope
that others may improve on them. It is very desirable that
the spot where the stone was found should be carefully
searched for burial remains, and this could be all the more
readily done as the landowner takes a keen and enlightened
interest in archæology."

* See the *Journal of the Royal Society of Antiquaries of Ireland*, 1902, p 24 ;
and 1903, pp. 117, 118.

JOHN BILSON, Esq., F.S.A., communicated the following Report as Local Secretary for Yorkshire:

"During the last two years important excavations have been carried out by the Yorkshire Philosophical Society on the site of the eastern part of the abbey church of St. Mary, York. In 1901 the foundations of the northern half of the choir and of the eastern aisle of the north transept were uncovered. In 1902 the foundation of part of the south arcade of the choir was bared. The main arcade of the choir commenced by Abbot Simon of Warwick in 1270 was built upon a continuous foundation wall, with a pilaster projection on each side of the wall beneath each pier. Mr. W. H. Brierley, of York, under whose superintendence the excavations have been carried out, thinks that the greater part of this wall (*i.e.* up to within two bays of the east end) formed the outer wall of an extension of the choir erected after a fire which is recorded to have occurred in the second quarter of the twelfth century. Further evidence on this point will doubtless be revealed when the whole of the south side of the choir has been excavated.

The excavations have also done much to elucidate the plan of the eastern part of the church commenced towards the end of the eleventh century. The plan of the church in *Vetusta Monumenta*,* shows the foundations of two apsidal chapels opening out of the two southernmost bays of the east side of the south transept, the northern of these two apses projecting further to the east than the southern one. The foundations of a corresponding apsidal chapel, opening out of the northernmost bay of the north transept, and part of the apsidal chapel opening out of the second bay, have been uncovered during the recent excavations. In the third bay, next to the north wall of the choir, a chapel has been discovered on the site of the later north choir aisle. This chapel was finished towards the east with an apse internally, and was square-ended externally. It was of much greater length than the adjoining chapel, its eastern face (externally) being about 2 feet to the east of the centre line of the second choir pier east of the crossing. A little further to the east than the outer face of this chapel is a broad sleeper wall across the choir itself, and at the north end of this wall part of the springing of the great apse of the choir still remains. From these data it would appear that the eleventh century church had three apsidal chapels *en échelon* on the east side of each arm of the transept, the inner

* Vol v. pl. 51.

chapel (next the choir) on each side being finished square
externally, and that, including the great choir apse, there
would thus be seven apses in all. It is to be hoped that the
excavations which are to be resumed this year may lead to
the complete recovery of this most interesting plan.

In the course of these excavations three grave covers were
found in the choir. Two of these are ridged with incised
lettering in Lombardic characters cut on one of the top
slopes :

> (1) ħ IACET ALANVS C . . . . , and
> (2) ThOMAS.

The third grave cover, a flat slab, was found a little to the
south of the centre of the choir in the fourth bay from the
east end. It bears an incised effigy of a man in mass vestments
with a mitre, a crosier in the right hand, and a book in the left.
On each side of the head of the effigy is a round doctor's cap.
Of the marginal inscription the greater part of that on the
sinister side remains, and a few letters towards the upper
part of the dexter side. The inscription, so far as it remains,
reads as follows :

> [Ħic iacet Willel]mᵒ ſeforð ſacre p(a)gine p[ro]feſſor
> & quonðā
>
> Abba[s] huiᵒ ɪ[nonaſter]ɪj quᵢ[ɪ obiit ɪɪbᵒ ðie menſis
> maii
>
> Aᵒ ðn̄i M̄ᵒCCCCCᵒ ——— cɪ]ɪi' ar̄e p[ro]pɪɪ[ɪetur
> ðeus Amen]*

William Seford, or Sever, was elected Abbot of St. Mary's,
York, in 1485 ; he was consecrated Bishop of Carlisle, 1495 ;
translated to Durham in 1502 ; and died 14th May, 1505."

By the kindness of Mr. W. H. Brierley a plan of the
excavations was exhibited in illustration of Mr. Bilson's
report.

J. PAUL RYLANDS, ESQ., F.S.A., exhibited (1) a silver ring,
once gilded, of fifteenth century date, in the form of a plain
hoop with two clasped hands, inscribed

> **Jaſper melchezar balthzar**

and (2) a lozenge-shaped pendant of bronze, once gilded,

---

* The parts of the inscription in brackets have been conjecturally restored by
Mr. W. H. St. John Hope.

bearing for device a white bird with red beak and legs, perched on a green twig, with a white flower in front of the bird, all in enamel.

Both objects were found at Norton Conyers, Yorkshire.

JOHN LEIGHTON, Esq., F.S.A., exhibited a knife and fork with chased steel handles, of the eighteenth century, in a shagreen case.*

Thanks were ordered to be returned for these communications and exhibitions.

Thursday, 2nd April, 1903.

Viscount DILLON, President, in the Chair.

The following gifts were announced, and thanks for the same ordered to be returned to the donors:

From the Glasgow University Court :—Prize Lists of the University of Glasgow from session 1777-78 to session 1832-33. Collected by W. Innes Addison. 12o. Glasgow, 1902.

From the Secretary, Rhodesia Museum :—First Annual Report, 1902, and Special Report on the Zimbabwe Ruins. 8vo. Bulawayo, 1902 and 1903.

From Robert Burnard, Esq., F.S.A.:—Eighth Report of the Dartmoor Exploration Committee. 8vo. n.p. 1902.

From the Author :—History of the Vaisyas of Bengal. By Promatha Nath Mullick. 8vo. Calcutta, 1902.

From J. G. Waller, Esq., F.S.A.:—Two volumes of Church Notes by J. G. Waller and L. A. B. Waller 1837-1855.

From George Young Wardle, Esq., through Mrs. Wickham Flower :—A collection of original coloured and other drawings of painted roofs and rood-screens in Norfolk churches.

Special thanks was accorded to Mr. Waller and Mr. Wardle for their gifts to the Society's Collections.

Notice was again given that the Annual Meeting for the election of the President, Council, and Officers of the Society would be held on Thursday, 23rd April, being St. George's

---

*These are engraved in *A Catalogue of the Antiquities and Works of Art exhibited at Ironmongers' Hall, London, in the month of May,* 1861 (London, 1869), p. 325.

Day, at 2 p m., and that no Fellow in arrear of his subscription would be entitled to vote on that occasion.

Lists were also read of those who on that day were to be submitted for ballot to fill the offices of Council, President, Treasurer, Director, and Secretary respectively.

H. St. George Gray, Esq., read a paper on the age of Arbor Low, from recent excavations on behalf of the British Association.

Mr. Gray's paper, which was illustrated by plans and sections, and a carefully executed model of Abor Low, will be printed in *Archaeologia*.

Max Rosenheim, Esq., F.S.A , exhibited (1) a silver watch of unusual form, with pierced filagree case, made by John Schelhorn, of Strasburg, about 1590 (see plate); and (2) a pair of silver parcel-gilt altar cruets made at Frankfort, with the date 1518.

The cruets will be illustrated in the Appendix to *Archaeologia*, vol. lviii.

J. Goulton Constable, Esq., F.S.A., exhibited three cases of Mathematical Instruments of the eighteenth century, consisting of (1) an ivory 2-foot rule, mounted in silver, made by G. Adams, of Fleet Street, London, and bearing the royal crown with the cypher 𝕲 𝕽 (for King George III. and Queen Charlotte), and (2) a silver protractor, engraved with the royal crown and initials C.R. (for *Charlotta Regina*), both in their original green shagreen cases lined with velvet and silver lace; and (3) a set of ordinary instruments of brass, also made by G. Adams, "Inst^r. Maker to the Prince of Wales," in the original case of red shagreen

Concerning the history and ownership of these instruments Mr. Goulton Constable has contributed the following note :

"The mathematical instruments belonged at one time to Leonard Smelt, eldest son of William Smelt, of Kirby Fletham and Leases, in the North Riding of Yorkshire, who was Receiver-General of the revenues of the Island of the Barbadoes, and M P. for Northallerton from 1740 to 1745. He was born in the year 1725, and about the year 1750 married Janet, daughter of Alexander Campbell, of Craigness Castle, in Scotland. He sold leases to one Randolph Marriott,

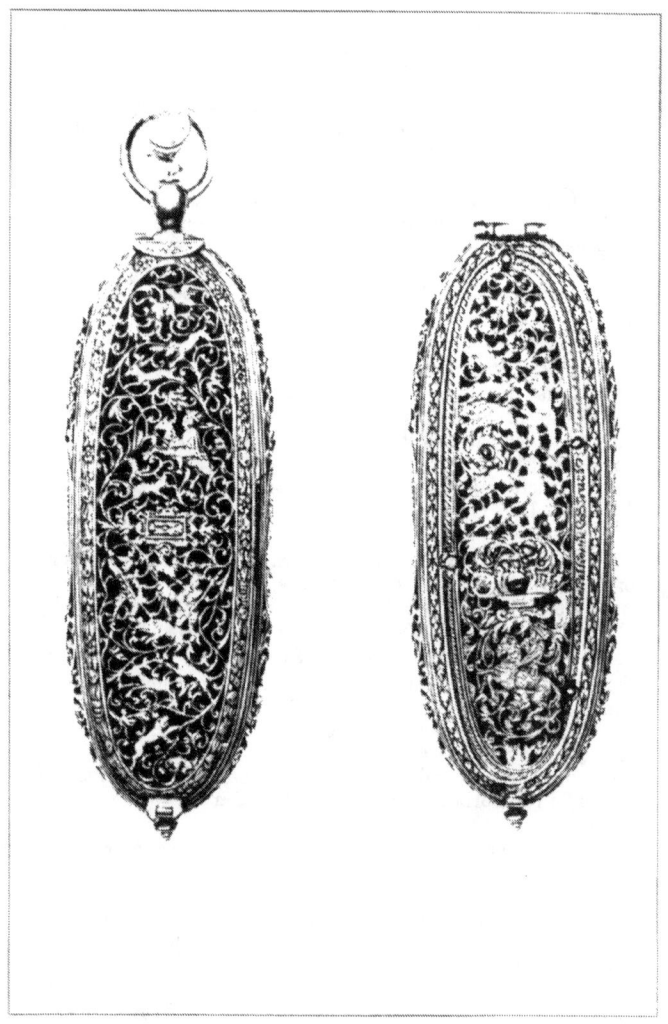

SILVER WATCH WITH FILAGREE CASE, c. 1590.

(Full size.)

SILVER WATCH WITH FILAGREE CASE, c. 1590.

(Full size.)

and went to live at Kew, and was appointed to be tutor or
sub-governor to the then Prince of Wales, afterwards
George IV., which position he seems to have shared with
Lord Holderness. This he held till 1780, when the king gave
him a gold watch, of the possession of which he appears to
have been extremely proud. The silver instruments were
probably given to him by the king and queen while he was
tutor to the prince. He was appointed Deputy-Ranger of
Richmond Park, and a letter written to him by Lord Holderness at the time of this appointment shows in what high
esteem he was held by the king. He was captain in the
Royal Artillery, and in 1797, when he was 72 years old,
accepted a commission in a Yorkshire regiment called
Stapleton's Horse.

His youngest daughter, Dorothy, who was a great friend
of Princess Elizabeth, married, in 1770, Thomas Goulton,
from whom I inherit my Walcot property. They had one
child, who was christened in York Minster by the name of
George Augustus Frederick, and died young. Some beautiful
christening garments worked for this child by Princess
Elizabeth are still in existence.

Leonard Smelt died in 1800, and both he and his wife, who
died 10 years before him, are buried under the chancel of
Alkborough church, in which parish Walcot is situated."

The George Adams who made the instruments was living
at the Tycho Brahé's Head, at No. 60, Fleet Street, in 1767,
and died in 1773.

Thanks were ordered to be returned for these communications and exhibitions.

ANNIVERSARY,

ST. GEORGE'S DAY,

THURSDAY, 23rd APRIL, 1903.

HAROLD ARTHUR, Viscount DILLON, Hon. M.A. Oxon,
President, in the Chair.

HARRY PLOWMAN Esq., and ALFRED RIDLEY BAX, Esq.,
were nominated Scrutators of the Ballot.

The Rev. Walter Marshall, M.A., was admitted Fellow.

At 2.30 p.m. the President proceeded to deliver the following
Address :

"Since our last Anniversary Meeting in 1902, our Society
has had a somewhat quiet year, unmarked by any great
discoveries, but, as our *Proceedings* show, by much good work
on various lines. Our numbers are full, with a goodly list of
gentlemen waiting for admission to our ranks, and I rejoice
to say that our losses by deaths and resignations have been
comparatively few. Of these very few are to be found
among the usual attendants at our meetings, or among those
who, by contributions to our publications, have taken an
active part in the work of the Society. The great event of
last year, the coronation of His Majesty, our Patron, though
retarded by the illness of the chief actor, was happily carried
out with all the heartiness, if not all the brilliance, of the
originally intended pageant, and naturally the public mind
was for some time turned to the consideration of things
ancient. Such a continuity of usage as a British coronation
affords is not to be found in other countries, but our loyalty
forbids us the consideration of any but past ceremonials of
this nature.

Since the last Anniversary the following have been elected :

Thomas Matthews Blagg, Esq.
Alfred Heneage Cocks, Esq., M.A.
Joseph Meadows Cowper, Esq.
William Henry Davison, Esq., M.A.
Edwin Hadlow Wise Dunkin, Esq.
Peter MacIntyre Evans, Esq., M.A.
Reginald Stanley Faber, Esq., M.A.
Henri Favarger, Esq.
Captain William Hawley.
Ernest Law, Esq., B.A.
Hon. and Very Rev. James Wentworth Leigh, D.D.,
    Dean of Hereford.
George Blundell Longstaff, Esq., M.A.
Rev. Walter Marshall, M.A.
Sir John Stirling Maxwell, Bart., M.P.
Rev. Arthur Tompson Michell, M.A.
William Pearce, Esq.
William Wyndham Portal, Esq., M.A.
James Kendrick Pyne, Esq., Mus. Doc.
Reginald Allender Smith, Esq., B.A.
Marion Harry Spielmann, Esq.
Edward Stone, Esq.
Henry Taylor, Esq.
Emery Walker, Esq.
Edward Alfred Webb, Esq.
Right Rev. Huysshe Wolcott Yeatman-Biggs, D.D.,
    Bishop of Southwark.

The following have resigned :

John W. Ogle, Esq., M.D. Oxon, F.R.C.P.
Lewis Edward Upcott, Esq., M.A.
Lieut.-Col. Alfred Cholmeley Welby, M.P.
Alexander Wood, Esq., M.A.

The following Fellows have died since the last Anniversary :

* Major Charles Edward Davis. 10th May, 1902.
* James Fenton, Esq., M.A. 21st September, 1902.
* Rev. Thomas William Prickett, M.A. 26th September,
    1902.
John Major, Lord Henniker. 27th June, 1902.

* Denotes Compounder.

* Thomas Lawrence Kington Oliphant, Esq., M.A. 8th
    July, 1902.
John Linton Palmer, Esq. 5th March, 1903.
William Cotton, Esq 13th November, 1902
. * John Emerich Edward, Lord Acton, G.C.V.O., M.A.
    19th June, 1902.
Col. John Davis, A D.C. 7th July, 1902.
James Joel Cartwright, Esq., M A. 8th January, 1903.
William Henry Cope, Esq. 31st March, 1903.
Joseph Phillips, Esq. 18th October, 1902.
William Dashwood Fanc, Esq. 29th November, 1902.
Rev. Charles Lawford Acland, M.A. 21st February,
    1903.
Thomas Francis Peacock, Esq 11th November, 1902.
Very Rev. William Richard Wood Stephens, D.D.,
    Dean of Winchester, 22nd December, 1902.
Francis Cranmer Penrose, Esq., Litt.D., D.C.L., F.R.S.
    15th February, 1903.

Of these Major CHARLES EDWARD DAVIS was a Fellow
long way the senior, having been elected as far back as
15th June, 1854. He was for some forty years connected
officially with the corporation of Bath, and for many years
was architect to that body. During that period he had much
to do with the uncovering and development of the fine series
of Roman baths there. Major Davis did not at all times find
himself in accord with the expressed views of many of our
Fellows, but certainly the ancient city was much indebted to
him for the long and faithful services which he rendered to
it. It is difficult, we know, to please all. parties in any great
work like that in which he took so prominent a part, and
where antiquarian interests find themselves in opposition to
modern requirements. Nor can we tell how much pressure is
put on a municipal servant when similar work has to be
carried out in a place like Bath, which with an eighteenth-
century reputation strives to combine respect for antiquity
and a nineteenth-century desire for improvement and renova-
tion.

Mr. JAMES FENTON, who died on 21st September last, was
elected in 1868, but as he was never formally admitted we
can only hope he derived pleasure from the perusal of our
publications, in which, if he read them, he must have been
pleased to note the improvement in fulness of matter and
illustration from the days of his first connection with us.

* Denotes Compounder.

The Rev. THOMAS PRICKETT, elected 10th April, 1862, does not appear to have contributed to our publications, nor did Lord HENNIKER, who died Governor of the Isle of Man on the 27th June. Lord Henniker had for some years been Member of Parliament for East Suffolk, and also had held appointments at court.

On 8th July, died Mr. THOMAS LAWRENCE KINGTON OLIPHANT, elected a Fellow in March, 1871 ; on the 5th March this year, Mr. JOHN LINTON PALMER, elected in May, 1873; and on the 19th June, JOHN EMERICH EDWARD, Lord ACTON, who was elected in April, 1876. In the last-mentioned nobleman the world of letters has lost a most distinguished member. Besides many other important offices he held that of Regius Professor of Modern History at Cambridge, but his many occupations and not very good health no doubt prevented him from taking part in our meetings.

Col. JOHN DAVIS, A.D.C. to the King, was elected a Fellow in June, 1878, and died on the 7th July last year. He attended our meetings on many occasions and will be remembered as one of the most industrious of the chroniclers of the oldest constitutional force, the Militia. His history of his own battalion, the Queen's Royal West Surrey Regiment of Militia, and that of the regular battalion of the same regiment, gave an early impetus to this class of records.

In Mr. JAMES JOEL CARTWRIGHT many of the Fellows have lost an amiable and accomplished friend, while the Public Record Office will miss in him an earnest and conscientious worker. He held for many years the post of Secretary of the Public Record Office, and was successively Assistant Secretary and Secretary of the Historical Manuscripts Commission, to which body we owe so many interesting and valuable indications of the whereabouts of those vast stores of material for the history of our country, stores peculiarly plentiful in this land. Mr. Cartwright was member of many learned societies, and amongst other works edited the Wentworth Papers of the memoirs of Sir John Reresby. The rich mine of historical lore in the Hatfield MSS. also received much attention from our late Fellow.

Mr. WILLIAM HENRY COPE, elected in July, 1886, died at a very advanced age on the 31st March last, and was a frequent visitor to our rooms, but like Mr. JOSEPH PHILLIPS, elected in 1888, and who died on 18th October last year, was a silent worker in antiquarian studies. So also were Mr. WILLIAM

DASHWOOD FANE, who was elected in March, 1889, and died
29th November, and the Rev. CHARLES LAWFORD ACLAND,
of Cambridge, elected in January, 1891, and who died on 21st
February last year. Mr. Acland was for some years Head
Master of Colchester Royal Grammar School and Member of
Council of the Cambridge Antiquarian Society.

Mr. THOMAS FRANCIS PEACOCK, elected a Fellow in January, 1893, died on 11th November, 1902, and the Very Rev.
WILLIAM RICHARD WOOD STEPHENS, D.D., Dean of Winchester, elected in June, 1895, died on 22nd December of last
year.

By the death on the 15th February this year of Mr.
FRANCIS CRANMER PENROSE, Litt.D., D.C.L., F.R.S., who was
elected a Fellow in June, 1898, archæological research loses a
valuable worker. Born some 86 years ago the son of Mrs.
Cartwright, better known to many of us as Mrs. Markham of
Markham's *History of England* fame, Mr. Penrose began life
as a student under the well-known architect, the late Mr.
Blore. Combining proficiency in sport with study (for he
rowed for Cambridge three times in the University Boat
Race) he obtained in 1842 the dignity of senior optime in the
mathematical tripos, and later that of travelling bachelor
to his University. In 1851 he brought out for the Dilettanti
Society *The Principles of Athenian Architecture*, and the
next year was appointed Surveyor of the fabric of St. Paul's
Cathedral, an office in which he was succeeded in 1897 by our
Fellow, Mr. Somers Clarke. In 1883 he received the gold
medal of the Royal Institute of British Architects, in 1886
was appointed Director of the British Archæological School at
Athens, and in 1893 he contributed to the *Proceedings* of the
Royal Society a valuable paper on the 'Orientation of Greek
Temples in relation to certain Astronomical Facts.' This was
followed by a supplement in 1897, and the principles involved
in these papers have been successfully applied to the deter-
mination of the age of temples in Egypt as well.
On the death of our late President, Sir Wollaston Franks,
he was elected Honorary Antiquary to the Royal Academy,
a post which, on Mr. Penrose's death, has been conferred on
your humble servant.

Mr. WILLIAM HEATON JACOB, who was a constant
attendant at our meetings, died on 16th April of this year.
He was elected Fellow in February, 1893.

It will be remembered that at our Anniversary Meeting last year a resolution (of which no notice had been given) was carried by 15 votes to 13, that the new Council should consider the question of changing the hour of the ordinary meetings from the evening to the afternoon at 4.30 or 5 p.m., and the Council was asked to ascertain the views of the Society at large by the issue of a circular on the subject. The Council did in consequence seriously consider the question, and came to the conclusion that it was unnecessary to proceed further in the matter. After this the mover of the resolution, Sir Ernest Clarke, and two other Fellows gave notice in accordance with the statutes, ch. xix. sec. 1, that they would propose at a special meeting of the Society to strike out the words 'Half-past eight o'clock in the evening' and substitute therefor 'Five o'clock in the afternoon.' After a correspondence between Sir Ernest Clarke and our Secretary, on 27th November, the day appointed by the Council, the meeting was made special, and the resolution having been moved and seconded was negatived by 119 noes to 35 ayes.

Last year I was able to refer to the satisfactory work, which with the consent of Sir Edmund Antrobus, bart., and under the supervision of our Fellow, Mr. Gowland, and others, had been done in restoring to a vertical position the large monolith at Stonehenge. I am now able to announce that Sir Edmund has by means of timber props temporarily secured the safety of several of the triliths which appear most in need of protection from the action of wind and rain, and we may I believe hope for further action to be taken this year to place beyond the risk of chance other portions of this most interesting monument.

The proposed destruction of the Church of All Hallows Lombard Street was also the subject of a protest from the Society, when the following resolution was passed 'That they hear with regret that there is a proposal on foot to destroy the Church of All Hallows Lombard Street, in the City of London, a building of interest in itself as being the work of Sir Christopher Wren, and containing much fine woodwork of his time. The Society ventures to appeal to the parishioners to withhold their assent to any scheme that will involve the destruction of their church.' As it rests with the parishioners to prevent this loss to the City, it may be hoped that such an event may be averted.

Some of the earliest finds of flint implements in this country have, by permission of the Council, been temporarily deposited in the British Museum, where they will be seen to advantage with the many later collections of similar objects.

On the occasion of the Coronation of His Majesty, our Patron, on 8th August, space was allotted in the abbey church of Westminster for a representative of the Society. Our Vice-President, Sir John Evans, kindly undertook to represent us.

At the Tercentenary celebration of the Bodleian Library your President was deputed to represent the Society and to congratulate that valuable institution.

Attention having been drawn to the destruction of Egyptian temples and other remains, a letter was written to Lord Cromer asking him to continue to exercise that supervision which in the past had been productive of so much good.

An interesting tribute to English work in antiquarian matters was paid on a recent occasion, when the French Archæological Society requested permission for copies to be made of the drawings executed for the Society by the late Rev. W. C. Lukis, F.S A., of the stones at Carnac in Brittany. These ancient monuments had been so subjected to restorers that our drawings were the only trustworthy record of what the stones were some years ago. The permission was granted, and it is pleasing to note that the exactness of British work was so appreciated by our neighbours across the Channel.

The proposal to remove Peckitt's glass from the east window of Exeter Cathedral to make place for a memorial to the late Archbishop of Canterbury aroused much opposition in some quarters, and led to a correspondence in the newspapers. The Society passed a resolution on the subject condemning the proposal There is no doubt that if work which does not please the ideas of to-day is to be removed, there can be no permanence for any work, however much it may have satisfied the ideas of its own day, and the question arises, if a window is erected to Dr. Temple, how long is it to remain. The Society does not question the excellence or otherwise of the glass now *in situ*, but as a record of what evidently did satisfy the public of its day it is valuable, and is a part of the history of the building and glass painting.

By the careful labours of our Fellow, Mr. A. H. Lyell, a large Ordnance Survey Map of the ground occupied by the camps and manœuvring grounds on Salisbury Plain has been marked in such a way as to distinguish by number every tumulus and earthwork. To this has been added a record showing whether the tumuli have been opened, and if so when and with what results. The map it is proposed to reproduce, and so to place within reach of those desiring such a record of work done, or possible damage in the future, materials for the proper noting of this interesting site.

In consequence of the rumoured removal of the statue of James II. formerly placed in rear of the Banqueting Hall, Whitehall, to Windsor, I was directed to convey to the First Commissioner of Works the hope of the Society that the statue might find a resting place in the neighbourhood of its former site, as being closely connected by many associations with the king. Lord Windsor has promised to give favourable consideration to the opinion of the Society.

The Council have made a grant in aid of the St. Austin's Abbey explorations at Canterbury. The results of the investigation so far have been communicated to the Society by Mr. Sebastian Evans, and his report forms a sequel to Mr. W. H. St. John Hope's report on the excavations in connection with the church of St. Pancras on the same site. The exploration of Waverley Abbey, which has also been assisted from the Research Fund, is now approaching completion, and the results have justified the action of this Society.

The recent public sale of the Elizabethan jug belonging to the church of West Malling, Kent, has aroused a strong feeling in many quarters, and the following resolution was passed by the Society on January 8th: "That this Society regrets the circumstances that have led to the issue of a faculty for the sale of an ancient jug from the church of West Malling, and deprecates the sale of chattels belonging to any church."

A grant of money from the Research Fund was also made to the Cretan Exploration Fund. Those who had the advantage of inspecting the plans, photographs, etc. illustrating the results of the explorations at Knossos, which were exhibited at the Royal Academy this last winter, will have seen what an excellent claim these excavations have on the sympathy of antiquaries, and the fact that the direction of these works is under our Vice-President, Mr. Arthur Evans, will further strengthen the action of the Council.

Grants from the Research Fund were also made to the Cardiff Naturalists' Society towards the examination of Gelligaer camp.

The Committee which, under the guidance of our Fellow Mr. A T Martin, is making explorations at Caerwent also received a grant, and a report on the work done was recently read at one of our meetings by Mr. Martin.

The Society was consulted on the subject of the proposal to fill up the moat of York City, and in consequence of a letter written to the municipal authorities it has been suggested to abandon the scheme and to make a garden instead on the site.

The attention of the Society has also been drawn to the destruction of many of the stone monuments on Dartmoor. It is to be hoped that this practice will be discontinued, but it is difficult to successfully cope with all the cases in which these ancient memorials are effaced.

The great work of excavating the site of the Roman town at Silchester has been continued with unabated vigour, for the thirteenth successive year, under the direction of Mr. Mill Stephenson.

Although no large nor important buildings have been brought to light in the particular region explored, the foundations of a number of smaller structures were uncovered, including several of a novel character.

Some additional facts of importance were also obtained as to the way in which the town was laid out after its enclosure by a wall.

The various objects found during the excavations last year were surprisingly few; there being a singular absence of productive rubbish pits within the area of operations.

It is to be hoped that better fortune may attend this year's work.

' The usual exhibition of the results of the year's work at Silchester in 1901 was also held in the meeting room.

As on former occasions, the hospitality of the Society has been extended to the Alcuin Club, the Henry Bradshaw Society, the Society for the Protection of Ancient Buildings, the London Topographical Society, the British School at Athens, and the British Academy.

A wish having been expressed that, for the convenience of many Fellows, the library might be opened in the evening once a week, the Council has decided to give the suggestion a trial from to-morrow until the end of the session, during which period the library will be open on Fridays from 6.30 to 9.30 p.m., or to 9 p.m. should there be no Fellows then present. If it be found that this arrangement is taken advantage of by Fellows, it may be continued during the period that the library is in use.

The Society has during the last year purchased from the Rev. Edmund Farrer, F.S.A., a complete collection of rubbings of Suffolk brasses. They will prove a valuable addition to the already magnificent collection in the possession of the Society.

Our library has been also enriched by the valuable present from Mr. George Wardle of a portfolio of drawings of painted screens and roofs of Norfolk churches.

As we have seen, the past year has been, while a fairly active one for English antiquaries, not marked by any feature so prominent as the Stonehenge discoveries of the previous year, but on the Continent the revival of the question of the authenticity of the so-called Tiara of Saitapharnes, till recently exhibited in the Louvre, has aroused no little stir among European antiquaries, and a large amount of correspondence in the press and in magazines devoted to art has been produced. The question is still undecided, but the parties in the contention are anxiously awaiting the results of the inquiry by the foreign authorities into the statement by Mr. Rachoumowski that he is the author of the Tiara. Our distinguished Fellow, Mr. A. S. Murray, is in the field, and the result of the inquiry will no doubt be of very great importance to the antiquarian world, which has for some time been discussing the increase in the number of clever forgeries offered to museums and to private collectors. This is a question which can and should be dealt with by international action. As time goes on and objects of certain classes which may be considered as limited in number become absorbed into public collections, and so withdrawn from the reappearance from time to time in the market that of course happens with private collections, it becomes more than ever worth the while of clever forgers to introduce their work to the public attention. In fact we may look forward to a time when forgeries properly attributed will possess an interest hardly inferior to authentic objects. The success of these imitators can only be successfully met by the most earnest and careful study of various classes of antiquities by those who not merely collect but also observe, and master the smallest details connected with the objects they select for their attention.

The arrangements proposed last year for an increased space being obtained for our books and publications by the boarding out of the porter have so far worked satisfactorily. But the process of weeding out unsuitable books from our shelves must be kept up, and one hardly sees how we shall be able to house our library some ten years hence at the present rate of increase.

I have, as in former years, to thank all my friends for the cordial manner in which they have assisted me, and I must remind them that my term of office is fast drawing to a close. We must consider the question of a new and more active president, but I am sure no successor of mine will ever have cause to look back to the period of his presidency with more pleasure and gratitude to his Fellows than shall I."

At the conclusion of the President's Address the following resolution was moved by EDWARD WILLIAM BRABROOK, Esq., C.B., seconded by WILLIAM MINET, Esq., M.A., and carried unanimously:

"That the best thanks of the meeting be given to the President for his Address, and that he be requested to allow it to be printed."

The PRESIDENT signified his assent.

The Scrutators having reported that the Members of the Council in Balloting List No I. and the Officers of the Society in Balloting List No. II. had been duly elected, the following List was read from the Chair of those who had been duly elected as Council and Officers for the ensuing year:

Eleven Members from the Old Council.

Harold Arthur, Viscount Dillon, Hon. M A. Oxon, *President.*

Philip Norman, Esq., *Treasurer.*
Frederick George Hilton Price, Esq., *Director.*
Charles Hercules Read, Esq., *Secretary.*
David Lindsay, Lord Balcarres, M.P.
Edward William Brabrook, Esq , C.B
Arthur John Evans, Esq., M.A., Litt.D., F.R.S.
Sir John Evans, K C.B , D.C L, LL.D., Sc.D., F.R.S.
William Gowland, Esq.
Charles Trice Martin, Esq., B.A.
Mill Stephenson, Esq., B.A.

Ten Members of the New Council.

The Right Hon. John, Lord Avebury, F.R.S.
Leland Lewis Duncan, Esq , M.V O.
Edwin Hanson Freshfield, Esq., M.A.
Sir Henry Hoyle Howorth, K.C.I E., D.C.L , F.R S.
Frederick Andrew Inderwick, Esq., K.C.
John Seymour Lucas, Esq , R A.
John Thomas Micklethwaite, Esq.
Sir Owen Roberts, knt., M.A.
John Challenor Covington Smith, Esq.
John Green Waller, Esq.

Thanks were voted to the Scrutators for their trouble.

Mr. W. G. THORPE asked to be allowed to move the following resolution :

"That in the annual official List of Fellows a distinguishing mark be prefixed to the names of those Fellows who have read papers; and that the Geological Society's plan of effecting this be taken as a model."

As the resolution was not seconded the matter was not proceeded with, but Mr Thorpe gave notice of his intention to propose the same resolution at the Anniversary Meeting in 1904.

Mr. C. E. KEYSER inquired why no part of *Vetusta Monumenta* had lately been issued to the Fellows.

The PRESIDENT, in reply, stated that he hoped that a part would be issued during the present year. He also pointed out that owing to the absence of suitable material it was not practicable to issue such a publication yearly.

We, the AUDITORS appointed to audit the ACCOUNTS of the SOCIETY
to the 31st day of December, 1902, having examined the
find the same to be accurate.

CASH ACCOUNT FOR THE YEAR

RECEIPTS.	£	s.	d.	£	s.	d.
1902.						
Balance in hand, 31st December, 1901 . .				504	19	1
Annual Subscriptions :						
10 at £3 3s., arrears due 1901 . .	31	10	0			
7 at £2 2s., ditto .	14	14	0			
2 at £1 1s., completion ditto . .	2	2	0			
490 at £3 3s., due 1st January, 1902 .	1543	10	0			
115 at £2 2s., ditto .	241	10	0			
1 at £3 3s. 0d., paid in advance for 1903 .	3	3	0			
				1836	9	0
Compositions:						
2 Fellows at £55				110	0	0
Admissions :						
30 Fellows at £8 8s. . . .				252	0	0
Dividend on £10583 19s. 7d. Metropolitan 3 per						
cent. Stock				298	0	3
Works sold				113	1	4
Stevenson Bequest :						
Dividend on Bank Stock and other Invest-						
ments				637	13	3
Owen Fund :						
Dividend on £300 2¼ per cent. Annuities .				7	1	0
Sundry Receipts				125	17	7
				£3885	1	6

OF ANTIQUARIES OF LONDON, from the 1st day of January, 1902,
underwritten ACCOUNTS, with the Vouchers relating thereto, do

ENDING 31st DECEMBER, 1902.

EXPENDITURE.						
1902.	£	s.	d.	£	s.	d.
Publications of the Society :						
Printers' and Artists' Charges and Binding .				589	15	2
Library :						
Binding	42	7	10			
Books purchased . . .	221	1	11			
Subscriptions to Books and Societies .	62	0	0			
				325	9	9
Grant to Research Fund . . .				100	0	0
House Expenditure :						
Insurance	40	13	9			
Lighting	190	11	6			
Fuel	23	17	0			
Repairs :						
Bookshelves . . 223 10 0						
General . . 147 0 0						
	370	10	0			
Tea at Meetings . . .	17	10	1			
Cleaning and Sundries . .	24	18	9			
				668	1	1
Income Tax and Inland Revenue License .				27	2	1
Legacy Duty and Costs : Stevenson Bequest .				13	15	4
Pensions :						
E. C. Ireland	160	0	0			
				160	0	0
Salaries :						
Assistant Secretary . . .	350	0	0			
Clerk	170	0	0			
				520	0	0
Wages :						
Porter, and Wife as Housemaid, and Hall Boy				168	9	6
Official Expenditure :						
Stationery and Printing . .	109	4	11			
Postages	20	8	5			
Ditto and Carriage on Publications	37	17	11			
Sundry Expenses . . .	136	6	7			
				303	17	10
Cash in hand :						
Coutts & Co., Deposit Account .	500	0	0			
Ditto Current Account .	497	0	6			
Petty cash . . .	2	17	2			
				1008	10	9
				£3885	1	6

We have examined the above Account and Research Fund Account with the
Books and Vouchers of the Society, and have seen the Stocks and Investments set forth in the annexed List, and certify to the accuracy of the same.

                            C. F. KEMP, SONS, & CO.

36 Walbrook, London, E.C.
    18th March, 1903.

RESEARCH FUND ACCOUNT FOR

RECEIPTS.

	£	s.	d.
Balance in hand, 1st January, 1902	70	17	3
Dividends :			
12 months' Dividend on £1805 13s. 4d. India 3½ per cent. Stock . . 59 7 6			
12 Months' Dividend on £500 J. Dickinson & Company, Limited, 5 per cent. Preference Stock 23 14 0			
12 months' Dividend on £527 1s. 3d. Victorian Government 3 per cent. Stock . . 14 17 6			
	97	15	4
Grant from General Account	100	0	0
	£268	12	7

STOCKS AND INVESTMENTS,

	'Amount of Stock.			Value on 31st December, 1901.		
	£	s.	d.	£	s.	d.
Metropolitan 3 per cent. Stock . . .	10583	19	7	10689	16	4
Bank Stock	2128	9	6	6970	15	1
Great Northern Railway Consolidated 4 per cent. Perpetual Preference Stock . .	2725	0	0	3310	17	6
London and North Western Railway Consolidated 4 per cent. Guaranteed Stock . . .	2757	0	0	3611	13	5
North Eastern Railway Guaranteed 4 per cent. Stock	2761	0	0	3575	9	10
Midland Railway 2½ per cent. Consolidated Perpetual Guaranteed Preferential Stock .	592	5	10	464	19	0
	£21547	14	11	£28623	11	2

OWEN FUND.

2½ per cent. Annuities . . .	300	0	0	282	0	0

RESEARCH FUND.

India 3½ per cent. Stock . . .	1805	13	4	1932	1	3
J. Dickinson & Co., Limited, 5 per cent. Preference Stock	500	0	0	587	10	0
Victorian Government 3 per cent. Consolidated Inscribed Stock, 1929-49 . . .	527	13	0	485	8	9
	£2833	6	4	£3005	0	0

THE YEAR ENDING 31st DECEMBER, 1902.

EXPENDITURE.

	£	s.	d.
Waverley Abbey Excavation Fund	25	0	0
St. Austin's (Canterbury) Excavation Fund	25	0	0
Silchester Excavation Fund	100	0	0
Cardiff Naturalists' Society (Excavations at Gelligaer)	10	0	0
Caerwent Exploration Fund	25	0	0
St. Mary's Abbey (York) Excavation Fund	·5	5	0
Cheque Book	0	4	0
Balance in hand, 31st December, 1902	78	3	7

£268 12 7

31st DECEMBER, 1902.

	Amount of Stock.		
	£	s.	d.

In the High Court of Justice, Chancery Division.
In the suit of Thornton v. Stevenson.
The Stocks remaining in Court to the credit of this cause are as follows: ·

	£	s.	d.
Great Western Railway 5 per cent. Guaranteed Stock	8894	0	0
Midland Railway 2½ per cent. Preferential Stock	15145	12	7

£24039 12 7

After payment of the Annuities, now amounting to £400 per annum, the Society is entitled to one-fourth share of the residue of the Income on the above Funds. This is payable after the 10th April and 10th October in every year.

Witness our hands this 18th day of March, 1903.

E. W. BRABROOK,
MILL STEPHENSON,
J. C. C. SMITH,
F. A. INDERWICK.

INCOME AND EXPENDITURE ACCOUNT FOR THE YEAR ENDING 31ST DECEMBER, 1902.

INCOME.

	£ s. d.	£ s. d.
Subscriptions received	1794 9 0	
„ unpaid, 30th December, 1902	43 1 0	
	1837 10 0	
Less 1901 Subscriptions unpaid	10 10 0	
		1827 0 0
Compositions		110 0 0
Admissions		252 0 0
Dividend on £10683 19s. 3d. Metropolitan 3 per cent. Stock		298 0 3
Works sold		113 1 4
Stevenson Bequest:		
Dividend on Bank Stock and other Investments		637 13 3
Sundry Receipts		125 17 7
		£3363 12 5

EXPENDITURE.

	£ s. d.	£ s. d.	£ s. d.
Publications of the Society:			
Printers' and Artists' Charges and Binding			1066 10 9
Library:			
Binding		42 7 10	
Books purchased		252 11 1	
Subscriptions to Books and Societies		62 0 0	
			356 18 11
Grant to Research Fund			100 0 0
House Expenditure:			
Insurance		40 13 9	
Lighting		97 5 5	
Fuel		23 17 0	
Repairs:			
Bookshelves	223 10 0		
General	147 4 8	370 14 8	
Tea at Meetings		17 12 9	
Cleaning and Sundries		29 0 0	
			579 4 4
Income Tax and Inland Revenue Licenses			27 2 1
Legacy Duty and Costs			13 15 4
Pensions: E. C. Ireland			160 0 0
Salaries:			
Assistant Secretary		350 0 0	
Clerk		170 0 0	
			520 0 0
Wages:			
Porter, and Wife as Housemaid, and Hall Boy			168 9 6
Official Expenditure:			
Stationery and Printing		113 0 8	
Postages		20 8 5	
Publications		37 17 11	
Sundry Expenses		150 10 7	
			321 17 7
Balance carried to Balance Sheet			49 13 11
			£3363 12 5

SOCIETY OF ANTIQUARIES OF LONDON.

BALANCE SHEET, 31st DECEMBER, 1902.

Dr.

	£ s. d.	£ s. d.
To Sundry Creditors . . .		626 2 4
" Unexpended balances:		
Owen Fund . . .	16 12 1	
Research Fund . . .	78 3 7	94 15 8
" Balance, 31st December, 1901 .	30273 2 10	
Add Balance of Income and Expenditure Account .	49 13 11	30822 16 9
		£31043 14 9

Cr.

	£ s. d.	£ s. d.
By Investments:		
£10583 19s. 7d. Metropolitan 3 per cent. Stock .	11060 5 2	
£2128 9s. 6d. Bank Stock .	7162 6 4	
£2725 Great Northern Railway Consolidated 4 per cent. Perpetual Preference Stock .	3692 7 6	
£2757 London and North Western Railway Consolidated 4 per cent. Guaranteed Stock .	3763 6 1	
£2761 North Eastern Railway Guaranteed 4 per cent. Stock .	3741 3 1	
£592 6s. 10d. Midland Railway 2½ per cent. Consolidated Perpetual Preference Stock .	494 11 3	29918 19 5
" Sundry Debtors:		
Subscriptions unpaid .		43 1 0
" Cash:		
At Bankers, Messrs. Coutts & Co. .	1075 4 1	
In hand .	11 10 3	1086 14 4
		£31043 14 9

We have prepared the above Balance Sheet and Income and Expenditure Account from the Books and Statements provided by the Treasurer of the Society, and certify to the accuracy of the same. The Investments, which have been taken at Stock Exchange List prices, on the 30th December, 1899, do not include those belonging to the Research and Owen Funds. No account has been taken of the Books, Furniture, Antiquities or other Assets of the Society.

36 Walbrook, London, E.C.
18th *March*, 1903.

C. F. KEMP, SONS, & Co.

Thursday, 30th April, 1903.

F. G. HILTON PRICE, Esq., Director, in the Chair.

The following gifts were announced, and thanks for the same ordered to be returned to the donors:

From the Trustees of the British Museum —A Guide to the Early Christian and Byzantine Antiquities in the Department of British and Mediæval Antiquities, British Museum. 8vo. London, 1903.

From the Worshipful Company of Pewterers —History of the Worshipful Company of Pewterers of the City of London, based upon their own Records. By Charles Welch, F.S.A 2 vols. 8vo. London, 1902.

From Mill Stephenson, Esq , B A., F.S A :—Historia Rievallensis. containing the History of Kirkby Moorside. By Rev. W. Eastmead. 8vo. London, 1824.

From T. R Way, Esq ·—The Ancient Halls of the City Guilds, drawn in lithography by T R. Way, with some Account of the History of the Companies by Philip Norman, F S.A. 4to. London, 1903

From Sir John Evans, K C.B , V.-P. .—A Magyar Nemzeti Múzeum multja és jelene. Folio. Budapest

From John Leighton, Esq , F.S.A.:—A broadside relating to the Ex-Libris Society. Single sheet folio. London. 1893.

From W. H. Richardson, Esq , M A , F S.A .—Sepia drawing of a fourteenth-century window at Boxley Church, Kent.

From Captain Chamier, F S.A.

    1. Lyobaa ó Mictlan, guía histórico-descriptiva. 8vo   Mexico, 1901.

    2. Explorations of Mount Alban by Leopoldo Batres. 8vo. Mexico, 1902.

    3. Excavations in Escalerillas Street, City of Mexico, by Leopold Batres 8vo. Mexico, 1900.

From the Author —Report of the Cumberland Excavation Committee for 1902. By F. Haverfield, M.A , F S A 8vo. Kendal, 1903.

Freke Guy Rashleigh Duke, Esq., was admitted Fellow.

The Report of the Auditors was read, and thanks were voted to the Auditors for their trouble, and to the Treasurer for his good and faithful services.   (See pages 280-285.)

F. HAVERFIELD, Esq., M.A., F.S.A., read a paper on the Roman Baths at Bath.

Mr. Haverfield's paper will be printed in *Archaeologia*.

Sir THOMAS G. F. HESKETH, bt., through the Director, exhibited a Roman stone head found at Towcester, Northants.

The head, which is that of a woman, is cut out of coarse oolite. It rises abruptly without neck from a block 4½ inches deep, and originally about 14 inches square, which has in

ROMAN STONE HEAD FOUND AT TOWCESTER.

front and on the sinister side a squared dowel hole for a metal attachment. The back and sides of the head have been roughly dressed away as if to fit the head into a recess. The total height is 22¼ inches.

CHARLES H. READ, Esq., Secretary, exhibited a bronze spear-head found in the Thames at Taplow, Berks, upon which he read the following note:

"The bronze spear-head now before the Society is one of unusual character in all respects. As a type of spear-head it is up to the present unique in this country, and even in Ireland

the only example figured by Sir John Evans (fig. 400) makes
no pretentions to the same artistic qualities.   This specimen

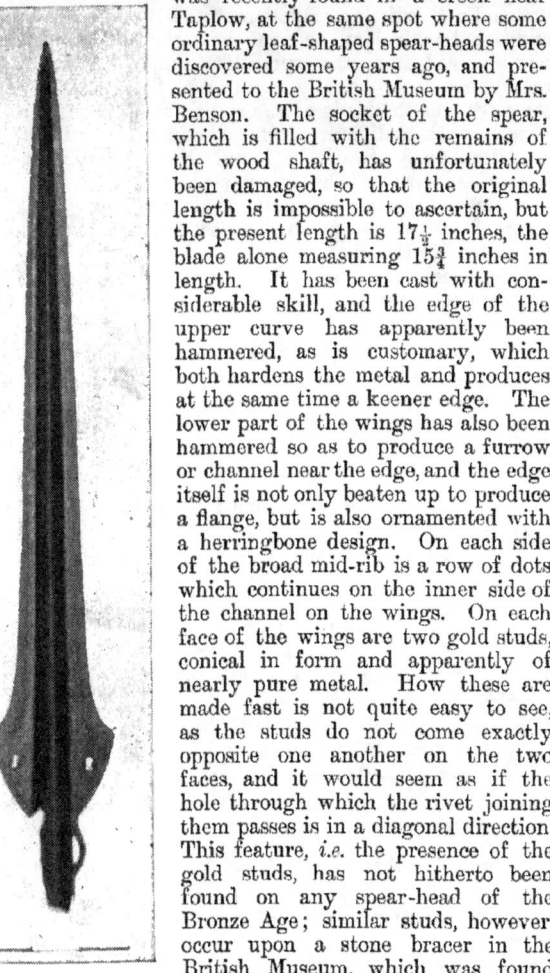

was recently found in a creek near
Taplow, at the same spot where some
ordinary leaf-shaped spear-heads were
discovered some years ago, and presented to the British Museum by Mrs.
Benson.   The socket of the spear,
which is filled with the remains of
the wood shaft, has unfortunately
been damaged, so that the original
length is impossible to ascertain, but
the present length is $17\frac{1}{2}$ inches, the
blade alone measuring $15\frac{3}{4}$ inches in
length.   It has been cast with considerable skill, and the edge of the
upper curve has apparently been
hammered, as is customary, which
both hardens the metal and produces
at the same time a keener edge.   The
lower part of the wings has also been
hammered so as to produce a furrow
or channel near the edge, and the edge
itself is not only beaten up to produce
a flange, but is also ornamented with
a herringbone design.   On each side
of the broad mid-rib is a row of dots
which continues on the inner side of
the channel on the wings.   On each
face of the wings are two gold studs,
conical in form and apparently of
nearly pure metal.   How these are
made fast is not quite easy to see,
as the studs do not come exactly
opposite one another on the two
faces, and it would seem as if the
hole through which the rivet joining
them passes is in a diagonal direction.
This feature, *i.e.* the presence of the
gold studs, has not hitherto been
found on any spear-head of the
Bronze Age; similar studs, however,
occur upon a stone bracer in the
British Museum, which was found

BRONZE SPEAR-HEAD FOUND at Driffield, East Riding, Yorkshire.
IN THE THAMES AT TAPLOW. Below the wings have been originally

two loops of triangular section, only one of which now remains.

Apart from the special interest of this spear-head as an unusual and artistic production of the Bronze Age, it has the additional interest of showing how the socketed spear-head was evolved from the sword-like weapon which has been called, not very happily, a rapier. This weapon has the same form as the blade of the spear-head before us, although usually with a different form of mid-rib, but if the socket be taken away it will be found that in outline it exactly resembles some of the many rapiers figured in Sir John Evans's and other works, and that the two-gold studs on either face are the survival of the rivet-heads which fixed the handle to the weapon.

This specimen will in due course pass into the British Museum collection."

Thanks were ordered to be returned for these communications and exhibitions.

Thursday, 7th May, 1903.

PHILIP NORMAN, Esq , Treasurer, in the Chair.

The following gifts were announced, and thanks for the same ordered to be returned to the donors:

From W E Foster, Esq , F S.A. ·—The South Holland Magazine, vols. 1-3
    8vo. Spalding, 1869-1871

From Rev H J D Astley:
    1 Some Further Notes on the Langbank Crannog. 8vo. n p   1903.
    2 Tree- and Pillar-Worship 8vo. London, 1903

From Charles II Read, Esq., Secretary ·—Catalogue des Fresques de Boscoreale.
    4to. Paris, 1903

Thomas Matthews Blagg, Esq., was admitted Fellow.

The appointment by the President of the Right Hon. John, Lord Avebury, P.C., F.R S., as a Vice-President of the Society was announced from the Chair.

O. M. DALTON, Esq., M.A., F.S.A., read a paper on a carved

ivory pyx of the Carlovingian period, which will be printed in *Archaeologia*.

F. G. HILTON PRICE, Esq., Director, read the following notes on Ancient Egyptian Gold Enamels:

" It has been a matter of surprise to antiquaries, and to Egyptologists in particular, considering the high state of civilization attained by the ancient Egyptians, who practised the goldsmith's art in very early times, and who have left us such admirable examples of inlaid jewellery, dating certainly as early as the twelfth dynasty, that is to say about 2400 B.C., that they should not have understood or practised the art of enamelling on gold and other metals. Some consider they did enamel to a certain extent on pottery and tiles; that is to say, they ran some vitreous substance, whether it was really an enamel or not, into the carvings or incisions made for figures or hieroglyphics, which were afterwards glazed and fired.

There always appears to have been this doubt, for as far back as 1840 Sir Gardner Wilkinson * writes: 'Small gold figures are frequently found with ornamented wings and bodies, whose faces or other coloured parts are composed of a vitrified composition, let into the metal, some again appear to have been really enamelled, and it is probable that the early specimens of *encaustum* were made by tooling the devices to a certain depth on bronze, and pouring a vitrified composition into the hollow space, the metal being properly heated at the same time; and when fixed, the surface was smoothed down and polished.'

Then we are most of us aware that our late President, Sir Wollaston Franks, who was always on the look out for Egyptian enamels, was of opinion that there was no proof that the Egyptians ever practised the art of enamelling on metals, as he had never seen a specimen of it, and I may add that that opinion has been held by most of us to the present time.

A great find of twelfth dynasty jewellery was made by M. de Morgan in 1894, in the tomb of the Princess Nub-hetep, in the Pyramid of Dashur.†

All the specimens of ancient jewellery known to us from this find, and from other sites, are undoubtedly examples of inlaid cloisonné work, that is to say, jewellery ornamented by stones or pastes cut into slices and inlaid in the metal

* *The Ancient Egyptians*, xi. 155   Birch Edition.
† See *Fouilles à Dahchour*, par J. de Morgan.

work, such as may be seen in the little ba-bird or soul in my
collection, which was figured by our Fellow, Mr. Dalton, in
his paper in *Archaeologia*, vol. lviii., 'On some Points in the
History of Inlaid Jewellery.'

I now have the pleasure of exhibiting to the Society two
splendid scarabs, which I have quite recently acquired, and
which may probably upset former opinions, and prove that
after all the ancient Egyptians not only enamelled upon gold
but executed their work in a very masterly manner.

Shortly after becoming the possessor of these scarabs, I
took an early opportunity of getting my opinion corroborated
by showing them to Dr. Wallis Budge, Mr C.-H. Read, and
Mr. Gowland, and they were unanimous in considering that
these specimens are undoubted examples of enamelling.
Upon the larger specimen, towards the tail end of it and at
the sides, the enamel may be seen actually to overlap the
gold layers, a circumstance which may be considered evidence
in favour of its being really true enamel. If this opinion
can be fully substantiated without having recourse to the
drastic measure of extracting a piece of the substance and
submitting it to a chemical analysis (this was suggested by
a friend, but it would certainly spoil the beauty of the
specimen) we have before us the two earliest and probably
only examples of Egyptian enamels known.

I have felt it to be necessary to exercise extreme caution in
pronouncing a verdict upon these scarabs in the face of the
preconceived opinions of Egyptologists, but after careful
examination I have come to the conclusion that they are
really enamelled, and Professor Flinders Petrie, to whom I
showed them, is of the same opinion.

The largest scarab is a very good representation of the
Scarabæus sacer of Linnæus, its head, underparts, and legs
are well and naturally modelled and are of fine gold, and the
elytræ are formed of cloisonné work filled in with a cobalt
blue enamel, which, coming in between the cloisons or gold
partitions, gives it a striped appearance. There is a reeded
loop beneath for purposes of suspension. It dimensions are:
length, 1¼ inch by ⅞ inch.

The second or smaller scarab is of a somewhat different
shape, being flatter and more heart-shaped; the head and
underpart are composed of fine gold. In this specimen the legs
are differently treated, they are not so realistic as in the
former one, but are tooled out and laid in low relief upon the
belly of the beetle, after the manner of those so frequently
found in the tombs, made of various materials. The elytræ
are formed of gold cloisonné work with the interstices filled

in with a cobalt blue enamel, as in the former specimen It has a reeded loop beneath for suspension, and its length is 1⅛ inch by ⅞ inch.

I have been informed that these scarabs were found several years ago by Mariette Bey whilst opening the tomb of a Ptolemy at or near Karnak, Upper Egypt. In the same tomb two very large wooden scarabs were also found, which were deposited in the Museum at Boulag. I am further informed that these two enamelled scarabs were exchanged by Mariette for other objects. They belong to the Ptolemaic Period."

The Director also exhibited examples in carved limestone of builders' or architects' models of Egyptian capitals, on which he read the following notes:

"These limestone models which I have the pleasure of exhibiting to you this evening are both interesting and rare. Unfortunately the locality and circumstances under which they were found is unknown, as the Cairo dealer from whom they were obtained had no particulars concerning them. It is highly probable, however, that they were found in the tomb of a great builder or architect, or, as Professor Petrie suggests, were used as models in a school There are two of the palm leaf order and two of the lotus and papyrus order, all in good state of preservation.

To begin with the palm leaf capitals. The largest specimen here is 6½ inches high and cut out of limestone, it has a square abacus upon which are marked the setting out lines. The second specimen is similar and is 5 inches in height, and the top of the abacus is similarly marked.

This form of column and capital appears to date from the time of the twelfth dynasty. In the Egyptian Gallery of the British Museum are two fine specimens, one of which, presented by the Egypt Exploration Fund in 1891 was found at Heracleopolis, and bears the cartouch of Rameses II. of the nineteenth dynasty (about 1330 B.C.) But these two vary to a certain extent from the models exhibited, inasmuch as in the large columns in the Museum the palm leaves are tied together. In the Victoria and Albert Museum there is one of these model columns, similar to those from Heracleopolis, 8 inches high by 3¾ inches in diameter, with the leaves tied together. The Rev. William MacGregor has seven of these model columns in his collection; six are modifications of the papyrus and one of the palm leaf capitals. In the temple of Seti I., who was father of Rameses II., at Sesebi in the Soudan, there are four gigantic columns of this order, each

EGYPTIAN GOLD AND ENAMELLED SCARABS
OF THE PTOLEMAIC PERIOD
(full size).

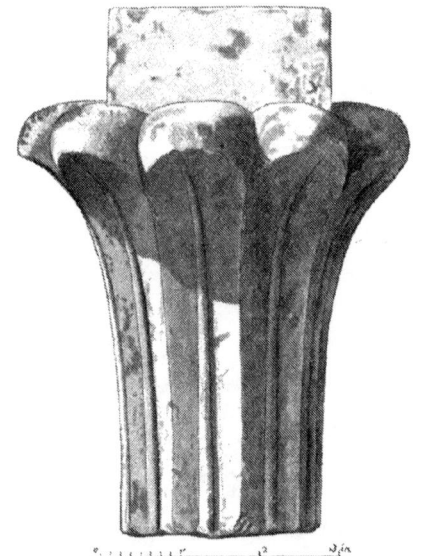

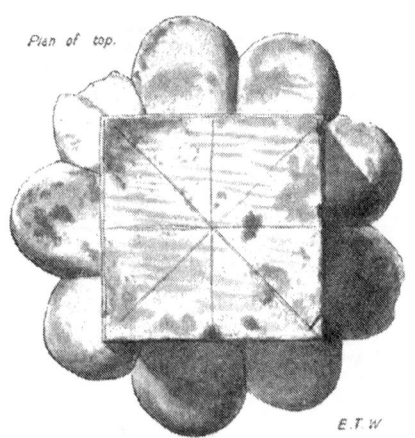

Plan of top.

E.T W

BUILDER'S MODEL OF AN EGYPTIAN CAPITAL.

x 2

capped with the square abacus, quite similar in every way to those now exhibited.*

The palm leaf column was much employed in Ptolemaic

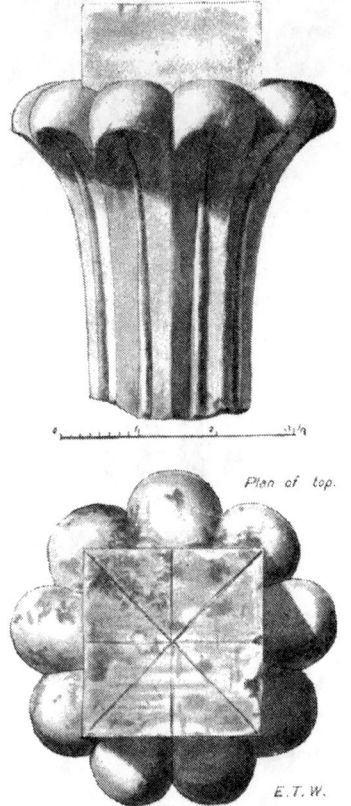

Plan of top.

E.T.W.

BUILDER'S MODEL OF AN EGYPTIAN CAPITAL.

times, but far more conventional and ornate, specimens of which may be seen at Philæ, Edfu, Esneh, and elsewhere.

With regard to the other models exhibited, the two small

* Lepsius, *Denkmaeler*, part I. pl. 119.

columns with lotus flower and papyrus flower capitals. The
larger specimen is of a simple and natural form, more slender

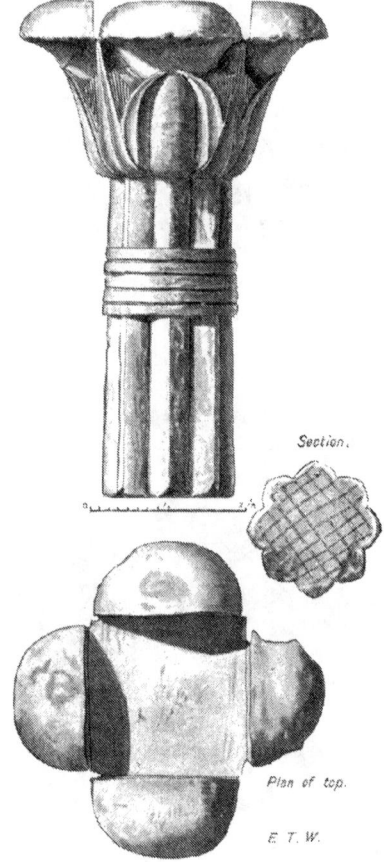

Section.

Plan of top.

E. T. W.

BUILDER'S MODEL OF AN EGYPTIAN CAPITAL.

and graceful than the former, representing a bundle of four
lotus flowers with long stems and four flowers of the papyrus

lashed together with thongs, presenting a sharp edge on the outer side; upon the top of this column is a sunken square for the reception of the abacus; its height is 6 inches. The other is shorter, being only 3¾ inches high and is not so highly finished as the former; it is, however, very interesting as having a square abacus upon the top of the capital.

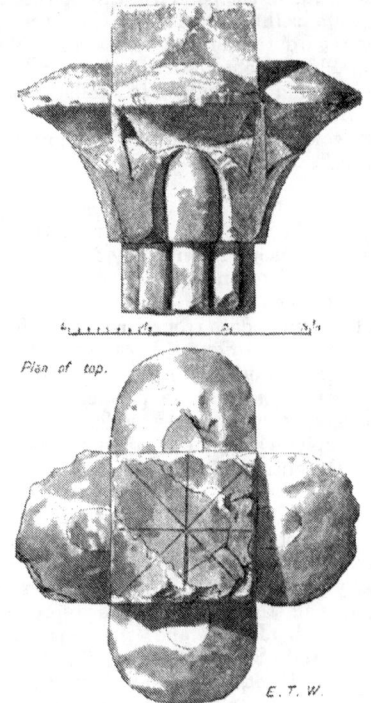

Plan of top.

E. T. W.

BUILDER'S MODEL OF AN EGYPTIAN CAPITAL.

The period of these latter columns is difficult to determine, as, after having searched through all the books at my disposal, I have failed to find one of identical form. There are many to be seen in the Ptolemaic Temples of Philæ, Edfu, Denderah, Esneh, etc. which have the lotus and papyrus capitals, but they are all much more ornate than these, that is to say, the lotus is even more conventionalized than in the instance of these models, by the introduction of several drooping calyx-leaves; and in no cases do the stems of the plants come below the place where they are bound together with the thongs. Notwithstanding this is a simpler form than those capitals seen at Philæ and other temples, from which one would infer it is of earlier date, and as the palm leaf capitals are of decidedly an early form, I am inclined, considering they were found together, and having regard to the fact that these palm leaf capitals are found at Philæ, Kom Ombos and other temple sites, that these models should be assigned to Ptolemaic times

The drawings of the scarabs and these capitals which I also exhibit were kindly made for me by my friend Mr. Towry Whyte, F.S.A."

G ALDERSON-SMITH, Esq., exhibited a strip of medieval embroidery of the fifteenth and sixteenth centuries The strip measures 7½ inches in width by 3 feet 10 inches in length, and is composed of seven panels of orphrey work which have been much cut down.

Four of the panels date from early in the fifteenth century, and contain each two figures of saints, with the remains of cinquefoiled ogee canopies supported by twisted shafts of two colours. The remaining three panels, which alternate with the others, have single figures under the remains of more elaborate canopies carried by panelled pilasters, and are of early sixteenth century work.

All the panels have the same ground of cloth of gold, but the stitchwork differs widely. That of the older panels is identical in character with the famous *opus Anglicanum*, and is pure embroidery. The later panels are more coarsely done, with a totally different stitch, and the figures are applied.

' The figures in the older |panels represent respectively (1) St. Mary Magdalene and ' an Apostle with book; (2) St Paul and St. Margaret; (3) St. Apollonia and St. Philip; and (4) St. Sythe and St. Barnabas.

The later panels represent respectively a female saint with long hair and palm branch, and two figures of prophets.

Nothing is known of the history of the panels.

T. BOYNTON, Esq, F.S A., exhibited an Egyptian arrow-head of flint from Luxor, Egypt.

Thanks were ordered to be returned for these communications and exhibitions.

The following resolution was put from the Chair, and carried *nem con* :

> " That the Society offers its hearty sympathy to
> Mr. Hope in the severe loss he has sustained by
> the death of his wife."

The following resolution was also proposed by the Treasurer, seconded by Sir L. Alma-Tadema, R.A., and duly carried :

> " That it is most desirable that an attempt should be
> made to secure for the Nation the frescoes of
> Boscoreale, to be sold in Paris next month."

Thursday, 14th May, 1903.

PHILIP NORMAN, Esq , Treasurer, in the Chair.

The TREASURER read a letter from Mr. W. H. St. John Hope, Assistant Secretary, asking him to convey to the Fellows his grateful thanks for their kind expression of sympathy with him in his bereavement

Notice was given of a Ballot for the election of Fellows on Thursday, 11th June, and a list of candidates to be balloted for was read.

REGINALD A. SMITH, Esq., B.A., F.S.A , read the following notes on a bronze-gilt brooch found at Canterbury :

" The remarkable brooch on the table is the property of Mr. Parry, and was found at the North Gate, Canterbury, at the end of 1901.

It is through the good offices of our Fellow, Colonel Copeland, who sent it to Mr. Read for examination, that it is exhibited this evening. The pin is now missing, but was no doubt of bronze-gilt like the hoop, and it was only by diligent cleaning that the incrustation of oxide was removed and the original gilding of the face disclosed. A beautiful patina is observable on portions of the edge and back.

It is usual to speak of brooches of this pattern as 'penannular,' and for want of a native word, this must no doubt be retained; but it should be noted that some of the later specimens have the ring entirely closed, and the pin is released for fastening the dress by means of a bolt-like arrangement at the back of its head, or by means of a spring made by bending the pin behind the head. Richly ornamented examples of both kinds are in the British Museum; and the

BRONZE-GILT BROOCH FOUND AT CANTERBURY. (¼.)

famous Tara brooch, of which drawings by the late Miss Margaret Stokes in the possession of the Society are exhibited, may be taken as the extreme form of a toilet article which had its origin in the simple pin of bone or bronze.*　A ring

* Mr. Romilly Allen, F.S.A., has some remarks on the evolution of these brooches in the *Illustrated Archæologist*, i. 162, and illustrates two Irish sculptures of the tenth century, on which brooches of this kind are seen in use.

of wire was first added at one end to prevent the pin slipping
through the material, no doubt a rough loosely-woven frieze;
and in course of time this ring became, by stages that can be
easily traced, the more important member, most of the
ornament being lavished on its flattened faces, while the
pin remained comparatively plain.   It has, however, been
suggested by Mr. T. O'Gorman * that the ring was used as
such from the first to gather the material through which the
pin was passed; and it may be that rings of the neolithic and
bronze periods, whether of stone, jet, or metal, were used to
fasten the dress in this way.   A further stage would then be
marked by such a contrivance as that illustrated in Sir John
Evans's *Ancient Bronze Implements*, fig. 496, in which the pin
passes through transverse holes pierced opposite one another
in the ring itself.

The earlier forms † of the penannular brooch had a ring of
the same breadth all round, merely cut across in one place for
the passage of the pin, the ring being swung round after the
clothing to be fastened had been pierced by the pin.   To
prevent the pin slipping through the opening the ends of the
incomplete hoop were raised by means of studs or ornamental
settings, and gradually widened to afford more space for
surface decoration.   It is by means of their form and decoration that relative dates can be assigned to the comparatively
large number of examples known.   They are mostly found
in Ireland, but several striking examples have been found in
the islands and on the west coast of Scotland, and Dr. Joseph
Anderson claims for them a Scottish origin ‡

The Scots of Ireland may or may not be included in that
definition, but there was probably a close connection between
the spread and popularity of the penannular brooch and the
occupation of the Western Isles of Scotland and the east
coast of Ireland by the Northmen who crossed over from
Norway to Orkney and made their way down St. George's
Channel in the latter half of the eighth century.   These Finn-
gael (white strangers), as they were called, were soon followed
by the Dubhgael, or dark strangers (probably Danes), who
established themselves in what are now the counties of
Waterford, Cork, and Limerick, and had their headquarters,
at Dublin in 856.   The Christian art of Ireland was at its
best between the sixth and ninth centuries, the transition to

---

* *Journal of the Royal Historical and Archæological Association of Ireland*,
3rd series, 1. 164.

† Several are illustrated in a paper by Mr. Fairholt in the Gloncester volume
of the British Archæological Association (1846), p 86, pl v , also in Jewitt's
Reliquary, v. 65.

‡ *Scotland in Early Christian Times* (2nd series), 34

the later decadent style (as shown by the illuminated MSS.) taking place about the year 900; and it is certain that ornamental objects of Irish manufacture were carried away to Norway, and there copied by native artists during those centuries. The Wikings then commanded our seas and were the terror of the maritime districts, but they were not without some appreciation of art and were given to gorgeous decoration of their persons.

Dr. Sophus Müller, the well-known antiquary of Copenhagen, has a good deal to say about the influence exercised abroad by Irish art in the Wiking period, and recognises both original and imitative Irish work in the Scandinavian countries. Not only, he says, have a considerable number of Irish antiquities been found in Norway, the Museum at Christiania possessing about twenty pieces exhibiting the earlier and later Irish styles, but the Scandinavian style of ornament as a whole bears the same foreign stamp, far beyond the district in which actual Irish antiquities are most commonly found. He expresses surprise that a larger number have not been found throughout Scandinavia, in Gothland, Bornholm, and the Danish Islands; but considers it proved that these works of art were imported viâ Norway and diligently copied, or rather adapted, by native workmen, for local peculiarities are apparent in the process of reproduction; and originals can readily be distinguished from products of what Dr. Müller calls *nordisch irisch* art, that is, the mixed style due to Scandinavian imitation of Irish work.[*]

Dr. Hans Hildebrand, the state antiquary of Sweden, says that products of Anglo-Saxon and Irish art found in Scandinavia may be divided into two classes. ornaments used in Scandinavia in the same way as formerly used in the country of their origin; and objects principally ecclesiastical belonging to the churches and monasteries plundered by the Northmen, and in the hands of their new possessors serving other purposes or regarded as valuable curiosities.[†] Examples in point are a penannular brooch of the type before us at Christiania, and a reliquary and part of a crozier at Copenhagen.

Penannular brooches are exceedingly rare in England, but one was found at Bonsall, Derbyshire,[‡] in 1862, and is now in the national collection In this specimen the closing of the ring is almost complete. two rectangular perforations being

* *Die Thier-ornamentik im Norden*, 91, 109, etc.
† *The Industrial Arts of Scandinavia*, 85.
‡ Jewitt, *Grave-mounds and their Contents*, fig 487.

the only traces of the original opening for the passage of the pin. The decoration, too, is, if anything, later than the Canterbury specimen, though the two are very much alike; and it is interesting to find this internal evidence of date and origin confirmed by actual records. The *Anglo-Saxon Chronicle* tells us that in 851 came 350 ships (of the heathen) to the mouth of the Thames, and the crews landed and took Canterbury and London by storm, and put to flight Berthwulf King of the Mercians with his army, and then went south over the Thames into Surrey where they were defeated at Aclea (Ockley) by the West-Saxons. Whence the host came on this occasion is not clear, but it is by no means improbable that so large a fleet was partly drawn from the Northmen's settlements in Ireland; and it is not altogether fanciful to suppose that the brooch before us was lost in an attack on the north gate of Canterbury on that occasion, for this gate lay on the road to Thanet where the army had passed the winter for the first time on English soil. An interval of twenty-five years might account for the difference of form and ornament in the Derbyshire specimen, and a possible date for its introduction into that part of the country is not far to seek. In 877 the Danish army went into Mercia, and some parts of it they apportioned and some they delivered to Ceolwulf. According to Mr. J. R. Green, it was then that the older English North-weorthig became Derby, and the portion that the Danes took for themselves is for the most part marked by the presence in it of their names, and the characteristic termination *by*. Bonsall is about two miles south-west of Matlock.

A penannular brooch of comparatively simple form and certainly of earlier date than the one before us was found at Croy in Inverness-shire, with a coin of Coenwulf, King of Mercia (795-818)* As no trace of the art displayed in the manuscripts appears on this specimen, it is at least probable that the more elaborate specimens are of somewhat later date, and the runes engraved on the back of the Hunterston specimen (similar to the Tara brooch) are declared to be of about the tenth century.

All this bears upon the brooch exhibited and helps to explain elements in its ornamentation that would otherwise be obscure. The accompanying illustration will render any minute description of the ornament unnecessary; but the original must have had in addition a pin about 7 inches long with an angular or oval head decorated in the same style as the gilt ring, and settings of various colours.

* Both are figured by Dr. Anderson, *op cit.* 23, 24

The outer edge is almost a true circle, being 3·6 inches across at the points where the face of the bronze is most worn away by the pin, and the same from the bottom of the opening to the outside of the rosette at the top. The whole of the front has been deeply incised, or cast from an incised original, and gilt, but the upper edges are in most places worn away and the gilding is most conspicuous in the hollows. The broad ends have each a rosette with three crescents attached to the circumference, while the remaining space is filled with what is meant to represent a horse's head seen from above, the nostrils being replaced by a circular setting similar to those in the angles of the extremity and in the centre of the rosette. The narrower parts of the hoop are separated from the expanded ends by a raised border to keep the pin from slipping towards the opening, and the entire thickness is here ⅛th inch. A pattern resembling a bamboo-stem occupies the narrowest parts, and at the top is a slight expansion, flanked by horses' heads of the same type but without the curved lines that enclose the larger pair. The settings are here again empty, but were in all probability filled with blue glass and amber, which actually remain in a brooch of the same character from Snaasen, North Trondhjem * (at a latitude five degrees north of the Orkneys), and also in an example at the British Museum. A penannular brooch of this kind has been found associated with the typical tortoise brooch in a Wiking grave in the island of Westray, Orkney.

The brooch exhibited seems therefore to be a Scandinavian edition of a Keltic original of which the Tara brooch, for instance, was the native development, and this type we may refer to Scotic artists. Most of the specimens, at least in the British Museum, come from Ireland, and it was certainly on Irish soil that the wonderful art displayed in metal-work and illuminated MSS. had developed, and flourished during what is generally called the Wiking period. But a word of caution is here necessary to prevent misunderstanding. In what is known as the 'Late-Keltic' period, Britain seems to have been more prolific than the sister-isle, owing partly to its proximity to the continent; and the excellent enamels of that time are widely distributed. The Roman occupation of Britain, however, stifled native genius, and it was principally, if not solely, in Ireland, where the Roman arms never penetrated, that native industries survived into Christian times. Again, the type of which the finest example known is the Tara brooch is closely connected with the indigenous art of the MSS., and

* O. Rygh, *Norske Oldsager*, fig 697, *a* and *b*

must be clearly distinguished from two other types that are found in various parts of these islands. First may be mentioned the 'thistle' type of penannular brooch, of which some prodigious examples are extant, the pin of one in the national collection measuring 22½ inches, another 15½ inches, and the hoop of a third 5¾ inches in diameter. The length of the pin is supposed by some to have corresponded to the rank of the owner.

These are severe in character, the ornament being confined to the spherical head of the pin and ends of the hoop, which resemble nothing so much as a Scotch thistle. The material is silver without gilding and the hoop has a cylindrical section, being in many cases very ponderous. A period can be assigned to this type from coins associated with them at Cuerdale, Lancashire (about A.D 910), Douglas, Isle of Man (925-975); and Goldsborough, Yorkshire (after 920). And the fact that among these coins occur many Cufic specimens suggests that the 'thistle' type was traded in, if not worn, by the merchants engaged on the trade-route between the Caspian or Black Sea and the Baltic. The absence of living forms in the decoration is compatible with a Mahomedan origin, and the large number of Cufic coins found in Scandinavia and on the trade-route in Russia range between the years 880 and 955, the latest found in Sweden being 1010 The third and last type we can notice here is distinguished by the ribbon-animals so common in the later Irish MSS. and in the Scandinavian metal-work of the same period; and as good a specimen as can be wanted is the Orton Scar brooch * in the possession of the Society. Some authorities are inclined to attribute this degradation of the animal form to contact with Scandinavia; and there at last we find a type that can in a special sense be attributed to the Wikings, even though the majority were no doubt manufactured by settlers in Ireland. Their date would be about 900-1050 A D

The majority of the Cufic coins found in Scandinavia, where they are naturally more common in the eastern provinces of Sweden than in the western and in Norway, were struck by the Samanid dynasty in Persia and the country beyond the Oxus, the modern Turkestan, between 874 and 999 During that period Bokhara and Samarkand became the centre of civilisation, learning, art, and scholarship for a large part of the Mahomedan world, Saman the founder of the dynasty having renounced Zoroastrianism for Islam. It may be noticed in passing that many of the coins found at Golds-

* _Archaeologia_, xxxiv pl xxxviii. p. 446.

borough with the ' thistle' brooch are known to have been struck in Samarkand and Alshash, both included in the Samanid dominions. The silver too, so abundant in the latest iron age of Scandinavia, must have been brought from the East, and with it were doubtless imported the stamped patterns seen on the Cuerdale ornaments and on the pin-heads of the later penannular brooches "

The Assistant Secretary exhibited a number of lantern slides, part of a series now being made for the Society, of the imagery on the west front of the cathedral church of Wells.

Thanks were ordered to be returned for this communication and exhibition.

Thursday, 28th May, 1903.

WILLIAM GOWLAND, Esq., Vice-President, in the Chair.

The following gifts were announced, and thanks for the same ordered to be returned to the donors :

From the Society for the Protection of Ancient Buildings —Notes on the Repair of Ancient Buildings. 8vo. London, 1903

From the Author, W. E. Foster, Esq., F S A..

1. Extracts from Cole's MSS relating to the Parish of Moulton, co. Lincoln, with list of Vicars of Moulton 8vo. Peterborough, 1903.

2. Pedigree of the Families of Newcomen and Hunnings, of co Lincoln. 8vo. Exeter, 1903

From the Author —Battlefield Church, Salop, and the Battle of Shrewsbury. By Rev W. G D Fletcher, F.S.A. 8vo. Shrewsbury, 1903

From the Author —A Guide to Tideswell and its Church By Rev. J. M J Fletcher. 2nd edition 8vo. Tideswell, 1903.

Notice was again given of a Ballot for the election of Fellows on Thursday, 11th June, and a list of candidates to be balloted for was read.

W. H. ST. JOHN HOPE, Esq., M.A., Assistant Secretary, submitted a report on behalf of the Executive Committee of the Silchester Excavation Fund on the excavations carried out on the site of the Romano-British town at Silchester, Hants, in 1902.

Mr. Hope's report will be printed in *Archaeologia.*

Thanks were ordered to be returned for this communication.

Thursday, 11th June, 1903.

Viscount DILLON, President, in the Chair.

The following gifts were announced, and thanks for the same ordered to be returned to the donors:

From the Author, T. M Blagg, Esq , F.S.A. :
1. Newark as a Publishing Town   8vo   Newark, 1898.
2. The Parish Registers of Farndon, in the County of Nottingham, 1695—1718.   8vo.   Worksop, 1899.
3 The Parish Registers of Shelton, co. Nottingham, 1595-1812.   With Appendices.   8vo.   Worksop, 1900
4. Seventeenth Century Parish Registers ; Transcripts belonging to the Peculiar of Southwell.   Edited by T. M. Blagg.   8vo   Newark, 1903.

From the Author : Staple Inn and its Story.   By T. Cato Worsfold   8vo , London, 1903.

From F R. Fairbank, Esq., M.D., F.S.A. .—Catalogue of the Loan Collection at the Brassey Institute, Hastings, 1896. Third Edition   8vo   St. Leonards, 1896 ; and a collection of 11 pamphlets relating to ecclesiological subjects.

From the Author ·—British Family Names, their Origin and Meaning   By Rev. Henry Barber, M.D , F.S.A.   Second Edition.   8vo.   London, 1903.

From Philip Norman, Esq , Treasurer ·—Ground Plans of Allhallows Church Barking, and St. Olave's Church, Hart Street, London.

This being an evening appointed for the election of Fellows, no papers were read.

The Ballot opened at 8.45 p.m. and closed at 9.30 p.m., when the following gentlemen were declared duly elected Fellows of the Society .

Colonel Eustace James Anthony Balfour, A.D.C., M.A.
John Garstang, Esq., B.A.
Rev. Thomas Taylor, M.A.
Rev. Grevile Maivis Livett, B.A.

Thursday, June 18th, 1903.

Viscount DILLON, President, in the Chair.

The following gifts were announced, and thanks for the same ordered to be returned to the donors:

From the Author, Professor J. R. Rahn, Hon. F S.A.:—A collection of eight pamphlets on archæological subjects

From the Author Die Limesanlagen im nordlichen England. Von Emil Kruger 8vo Bonn, 1903.

J. G. WALLER, Esq. F.S.A. presented a copy of an early printed edition, in the original binding, of the *Sermones Discipuli* of John Herolt.

Special thanks were accorded to Mr. Waller for his valuable gift.

The following gentlemen were admitted Fellows:

Henry Taylor, Esq.
Col Eustace James Anthony Balfour, A.D.C. M.A
Rev. Grevile Maivis Livett, B A.

J. A. GOTCH, Esq. F.S A. Local Secretary for Northampton-shire, read the following notes on some Anglo-Saxon antiquities found at Kettering:

" The recent discovery of a considerable number of cinerary urns in the outskirts of the growing town of Kettering, in the county of Northampton, has caused much excitement locally, but will probably be regarded with equanimity by those who are familiar with the subject. Among the latter I can hardly include myself, and I apologise for intruding into strange regions, but as one of the Local Secretaries for the county, it was incumbent on me to bring the matter before this Society, and my official capacity must be my excuse for taking upon myself the description of things which were more closely observed by others, viz. Mr. George, of Northampton, and Mr. Bull, of Kettering.

It was building operations which brought these urns to light. They were found from time to time on three adjoining building plots, situated on the main road leading out of Kettering in an easterly direction to Stamford. The plots were laid out some six years ago, the land being then, and having been for many years, a ploughed field. The road no doubt is an ancient one, but I am not able to account for it any earlier than 1587. There is a survey of Kettering still extant made in that year, which, although it does not go so far afield as the spot in question, yet shows the start of a broad, well-defined road, entitled 'the waye to Wickley,' Weekley being the first village, about a mile and a half off, which the road passes through on its way to Stamford.

There have been many remains, chiefly Roman, found in the neighbourhood of Kettering at various times, thus showing traces of early occupation and other remains of yet earlier occupation were found years ago about half way between the town and the place where the urns were discovered, and not far off the road, in the shape of the bones of a fine ichthyosaurus. But I am not proposing to advance him as a link in the chain of continuous habitation along a great line of traffic.

The urns have been found, as already said, on three building plots, two 36 feet wide, and one 40, and the strong probability is, from such excavations as have been made on either side, that they do not extend beyond these plots, the total length of the ground affected would be, therefore, about 100 feet. The plots are bounded on the south side by the main road, and in laying in a drain from one of the houses to the sewer in the road, one of the urns was found close by the metalled horse-road, and beyond the asphalted footpath. Whether they extend under the road I am unable to say, but in a direction away from it they extended some 110 feet, thus giving a cemetery, if it may be called so, of about 100 feet by 110 feet. The middle plot of the three, and half another, were thoroughly dug over under the auspices of the Northamptonshire Exploration Society; the remainder of the ground has only been searched so far as the foundation trenches and a certain amount of gardening operations gave opportunity.

Altogether some 80 or 90 urns, either whole or in fragments, have been found, and among them six skeletons. The urns varied in shape, in size, and in markings, and no two were exactly alike; in size they ranged from a diameter of 4½ inches, and a height of 4 inches, to a diameter of 11 inches, and a height of 10 inches. The depth at which they lay from the existing surface varied from 18 inches to about 3 feet, and the broken state in which some were found was no doubt owing to the repeated ploughing operations which went on just above them. They were spread fairly evenly but in irregular groups, over the whole area so far as it was thoroughly dug over.

Of the whole number of urns found, some twenty or twenty-five are in good condition. They vary a little in shape, although conforming to one general type, and most of them are ornamented, only four or five being quite plain. The ornament consists, as a rule, of incised straight lines interspersed with punched dots and circles Some of the lines are grouped in bands round the urns, some are vertical, some form zig-zags The ornamentation, on the whole, is rough, but in a few cases is worked in carefully designed patterns. None of it extends more than half-way down the side. A few had projecting knobs among their ornaments, and in one case the knobs were worked up to a point resembling short horns. They are not very hard-burnt, and are rather fragile They were all full of earth when found, and not many articles of interest were discovered in the earth, but there were fragments of partly calcined bone, three or four good bronze tweezers, a broken comb, bits of molten glass, probably beads, and a small knife. One urn also contained twenty-seven round discs of bone about $\frac{3}{8}$ inch in diameter, and very thin. The six skeletons were found for the most part among the urns Of the six one had its feet to the west, and four had theirs to the south-east, the position of the sixth was not noted. Of the four, one had its head on the right side, and three (it is believed) on the left. They are all roughly enclosed by large unshaped stones, some of which appeared to bear marks of fire. The most perfect skeleton was of small size, probably that of a woman ; the others were so much disturbed as to render an opinion difficult. There were no remains of weapons discovered anywhere. The stone enclosures were of little use in keeping out the earth, for the bones were as much embedded in it as were the urns.

Such are the principal facts relating to this find. Further details will no doubt be supplied by Mr. George and Mr. Bull, who were present during most of the time occupied by the excavation. I was only able to pay occasional visits, but I saw a large number of urns brought to light, and also the most perfect of the skeletons."

Mr. Thos. George observed that cremated interments of the Anglo-Saxon period at Kettering had already been noted in the *Victoria History of Northants* ,* but it was only recently that there had been any signs of a mixed cemetery, and it

* Vol. i. p. 244.

might be that the present site formed part of that field near Weekley, where, according to Whellan's *Gazetteer* of the county, two skeletons, a dagger and a spear-head were found in 1846. The excavations, from which the urns exhibited and others were recovered, were mainly due to Mr. F. Bull, of Kettering, whose photographs of the burials in position show that the unburnt skeletons, of which five were found, were interspersed among the cinerary urns and were therefore probably contemporary. Mr. A. Haldinstein, of Norwich, gave permission for the exploration of the site, and over seventy urns were found during March and April last in an area of 84 feet by 34 feet, in addition to the skeletons. The urns were from 6 inches to 2 feet below the surface, but very few could be taken out whole. Of the total, about ten were quite plain, the rest decorated in the usual manner with impressed designs, no two specimens being exactly alike. A plain vessel, not a cinerary urn, was found close to the skull of a skeleton. Among the calcined bones in the urns were found four pairs of bronze tweezers, melted glass beads, portions of three bone combs, and a spindle-whorl of bone.

At the bottom of one urn were nine small round pebbles, and in another twenty-seven bone discs similar to those found at Castle Acre and Pensthorpe in Norfolk, and probably used, like the pebbles, for some game like draughts. They were evidently turned on the lathe, and it should be noted that twenty-eight were found in a barrow at Cold Eaton, Derbyshire. From many of the urns were obtained numbers of a small shell (*Caecilioides acicula*), no doubt the same species as occurred in urns at Long Acre, and with skeletons at Frilford, Berks, and Kempston, Beds. Of the twenty-five localities where Anglo-Saxon interments have been recorded in the county, fifteen have yielded urns, but Kettering has so far proved the most prolific site.

Mr. George also exhibited a series of bronze ornaments from Anglo-Saxon burials at Duston, which has hitherto produced only Roman antiquities. At least six unburnt burials have come to light, the bodies having been laid with the head to the north-west, like some at Kettering. With them were found eight spear-heads, seven knives, four shield-bosses, a small bucket about 4 inches high, and fragments of a bronze bowl, besides a circular brooch of Roman work with rings of coloured enamels. Some iron nails may point to the use of wooden coffins, while the ornaments consist of one large square-headed brooch of bronze (see illustration), one large saucer-brooch with star pattern (see illustration), three openwork

ANGLO-SAXON BROOCH FOUND AT DUSTON, NORTHANTS. (½.)

circular brooches with fylfot design,* four plain circular and
two small square-headed brooches, besides two necklaces, one
of which consisted of seventeen amber beads and the other of
one large green glass bead, two blue glass and eight amber.
The burial place lies about half a mile due west of the
Romano-British site, both being on the property of Lord
Cowper, who has added these to his other exhibits in the
Northampton Museum.

ANGLO-SAXON SAUCER-BROOCH FOUND AT DUSTON, NORTHANTS. (⅓.)

A 'drinking cup' of the early Bronze period was also
exhibited by Mr. George. It is of rare type (see illustration)
with a moulded lip, somewhat resembling one found at Mouse
Low, Staffs.† It was discovered at Loddington, near Kettering, last month, and is the third recorded from the county,
the two others being from Brixworth ‡ and from Norton, the

---

* Similar to an example from Islip, Northants, illustrated in *Proceedings*,
2nd S. ix. 90.
† *Journal of Anthropological Institute*, 1902, pl. xxvi. No. 15.
‡ *Proceedings*, 2nd S. xiii. 301.

latter associated with a finely worked flint dagger, but unfortunately broken by the workman.

Mr. Reginald A. Smith called attention to the marked similarity between the ornaments from Duston and those

DRINKING CUP FOUND AT LODDINGTON, NORTHANTS.

recovered from similar unburnt burials in the south-west angle of the county, and further west in the valley of the Avon. The large square-headed brooch is found in various parts of the country, but chiefly in Warwickshire and Leicestershire, while the open-work fylfots occur in Cambridgeshire and Warwickshire, and the saucer-brooch seem to indicate a West-Saxon origin, as indeed do all the interments of that part of the county west of and bordering on the Watling Street.

East and north of the county town mixed cemeteries occur, and with these Kettering must now be classed; but there are also sites in this area that have as yet yielded only cremated remains, like several large cemeteries outside Northampton. Though the records are defective, the tendency seems to be for the mixed cemeteries of this county to show the Christian orientation of unburnt bodies, the head lying to the west; and it may be that the missionaries persuaded the inhabitants to give up burning their dead and to adopt the east and west position at their conversion about the middle of the seventh century. The east end of the county, the neighbourhood of Peterborough, was more exposed to incursions from the sea, and no uniformity as to interments is apparent.

The Rev. J. T. FOWLER, D.C.L. F.S.A. Local Secretary for Durham, and W. H. ST. JOHN HOPE, Esq. M.A. Assistant Secretary, read respectively a paper on Recent Discoveries in the Cloister of Durham Abbey, which will be printed in *Archaeologia.*

Thanks were ordered to be returned for these communications.

The Ordinary Meetings of the Society were then adjourned to Thursday, 26th November.

INDEX

TO

PROCEEDINGS, SECOND SERIES, VOL. XIX.

CORRIGENDA.

Page 266, line 10,
    For " Abor Low." *read* " Arbor Low."

Page 266, line 39,
    For " leases," *read* " Leases."

Page 287, line 11,
    For " Taplow, Berks.," *read* " Taplow, Bucks."

Printed by J. B. Nichols & Sons, Parliament Mansions, Victoria Street, S.W.